Edwardian Durrington & Salvington

The story of a community between 1901 - 1913

By

Jane Dore

With contributions from the following

Edwardian Durrington Project volunteers:

Wendy Funnell
Sarah Godfrey
Jean Hull
Gordon Latham
Malcolm Linfield
Poppy Little
Sue McMahon
David Nicholls
Sarah Rickwood

Publisher: Verite CM Ltd

2016

Copyright © Jane Dore

The right of Jane Dore to be identified as the author of this work have been asserted by her in accordance with the Copyright, Designs and Patents Act 1988.

ISBN: 978-1-910719-21-3

All rights reserved. No part of this publication may be reproduced or transmitted in any form or by any means, electronic or mechanical. Including photocopying, recording, or any information storage and retrieval system without permission in writing from the author.

Published for Jane Dore by
Verité CM Limited,
Unit 2, Martlets Way, Goring Business Park,
Goring-by-Sea, West Sussex BN12 4HF
+44 (0) 1903 241975

email: enquiries@veritecm.com
Web: www.veritecm.com

British Library Cataloguing Data

A catalogue record of this book is available from The British Library

Printed in England

Front Cover photograph design by Dave Pryce

CONTENTS LIST

Preface	ii
Introduction	iii
Abbreviations and Sources	vi
Chapter 1 - Durrington Lane (South)	1
Chapter 2 - Durrington Lane (North)	28
Chapter 3 - Salvington Road	48
Chapter 4 - Franklin Road	92
Chapter 5 - Greenland Road	98
Chapter 6 - Stone Lane and Selden's Way	110
Chapter 7 - Ashacre Lane	128
Chapter 8 - Half Moon Lane	168
Chapter 9 - Arundel Road	176
Chapter 10 - Coate Street	181
Chapter 11 - High Salvington	194
Chapter 12 – Littlehampton Road	212
Chapter 13 – Offington Lane	229
Appendix	239
Bibliography	241
Index	242

PREFACE

I have great pleasure in welcoming the publication of this book. It is a truly ground-breaking and excellent title, the outcome of a community-based project, ably led by Jane Dore, supported by New Life Church and paid for by the Heritage Lottery Fund.

The book is ground-breaking in three ways. Firstly, a detailed study of Durrington's people, their occupations, homes, buildings, facilities and industries has been revealed for the first time. Indeed this study, focussing on Edwardian times, is the most substantial account of the village's past ever published. Secondly, at its heart is the use of a neglected and underused primary source: the Inland Revenue Valuation, a detailed and invaluable record of people and properties, compiled at the end of the Edwardian period. Thirdly, recent technological advances have been used to enable more comprehensive research. Specifically, all surviving issues from the *Worthing Gazette* from 1901 to 1913 were digitised and the scanned text indexed such that people, properties and events can be easily found. A selection of such articles appears throughout this volume.

Excellence is represented by the breadth and depth of research, the use of a variety of local history sources, including census returns, newspapers, maps, directories and photographs. The standard of the writing and range of illustrations both add to the quality of the finished product.

The project was embraced by the community with many volunteers working on the book, and on other initiatives, undertaking research, writing, photography, scanning and design. Jane Dore has been an inspirational leader of the project, undertaking most of the research and writing, and assembling such a committed team. New Life Church staff and members have supplied a great deal of logistical and practical support too. Finally, without the generous grant from the Heritage Lottery Fund, the scale of this publishing project would have been almost impossible to achieve.

The result is an exceptional account of Durrington's people and properties at the turn of the 20th century, a key period of development, never previously told in such breadth and detail. I commend it to anyone interested in the history of this fascinating ancient parish.

Martin Hayes
County Local Studies Librarian
West Sussex County Council Library Service
March 2016

Introduction

'DURRINGTON is a pleasantly-situated village, about a mile north-west of Salvington, but contains nothing of striking interest to the visitor.'

(From: The Visitors Guide to Worthing & Neighbourhood. 4th Edition. 1869. p.51)

The above small booklet does go on to speak a little more favourably of Salvington but in general this seems to have been the opinion of most visitors and probably many of the inhabitants of the surrounding areas throughout the eighteenth and nineteenth centuries. Both Durrington and Salvington have their origins in the Saxon period, but in terms of written history there is virtually nothing of any depth that has been recorded for either of the hamlets. Salvington was for many years part of the parish of West Tarring and has merited mentions in the history of this village but Durrington has largely been ignored, acknowledged as a place where there was very little, if anything, worth writing about.

Salvington has long been known as the birth place of John Selden, a very talented and brilliant lawyer, writer, politician and historian in seventeenth-century England. Durrington's claim to fame appears to come from the same period when the parish church was abandoned after a political dispute between the villagers and their vicar during the English Civil War. Apart from these events there is little known and recorded about the village.

It was against this back-drop that I began to research the area some years after I moved into the village myself, having been a member of the local New Life Church in Salvington Road for around 30 years. By day I worked as an Information Librarian based at Worthing Reference Library and in this role I spent much of my time helping others with their local history research. I began to discover many hidden stories about the Durrington area and was encouraged by Martin Hayes, the Local Studies Librarian for the County of West Sussex, to 'do the job properly' by applying to the Heritage Lottery Fund for a grant to enable the research to be completed and many people from the village to be included in the journey. The application was successful and this book is the culmination of nearly three years of research and discovery.

The joy of being provided with an HLF grant is that it does enable many people to join in with such a project. I have worked with a wonderful team of local people and schools as together we have begun to unwrap the reality of life in an Edwardian village. We have digitised newspapers and street directories, indexed censuses, newspapers and electoral registers, poured over maps and re-created costumes. We have learned new skills in cooking and hand sewing, walked the village streets with school children and sketched and studied the architecture of buildings still standing. We have visited record offices, some volunteers for the very first time and regularly met together to talk about what we had been learning. The annual Durrington Festival has been a great place to celebrate and share with the village all that we have discovered and many times it has been a rich source of the oral tradition as stories have been shared and added to the archive. The collection of data, family records, and many photographs both old and new has created a small village archive which with the help of the local studies collection at Worthing Library and the County Record Office in Chichester will ensure that the information is available to everyone and will be the basis for many additions in the future.

The people of Durrington and Salvington, in general, lived quiet hard working lives but amongst them were foreign theatrical folk, older people who retired to the village from many interesting occupations and places, women, who were some of the first in the Worthing area, to set up in business, poachers, untimely deaths, mental illness, health and cleanliness issues as well as the grumbles, local disputes and demands of a growing community. The Edwardian period saw the explosion of nurseries into Durrington and Salvington as the land further south was already full of working nurseries and market gardens. The first local council school was opened and the Free Church was established. It was only to be later that Durrington would have its own parish church restored, but during the later years of this period the demand for such a building was clearly gaining momentum.

The book includes information on the people of Durrington and Salvington, who they were, where they lived, a little of their family background and any interesting stories that we have discovered along the way. One thing is very clear; this was not an insignificant village with little happening, it was a thriving and very interesting place to live and work during the years between the turn of the century and the outbreak of the First World War which took many of the young men away to fight and in some cases to die for their country – but that is another story still to be told.

Having no previous written material to base this research on we have used original documentation of the period. The 1901 and 1911 censuses, Inland Revenue Valuation Maps and their corresponding Field Book data taken at the time, electoral registers and street directories as well as other material listed in the sources list. I am sure there is so much more to discover and there are probably mistakes and wrong assumptions within the pages of the book. I accept responsibility for all the errors and hope that people will feel free to contact me with any corrections and further information which will add to the story of this area.

I have listed in the Acknowledgments all the people without whose help this project would not have materialised. I thank them all and hope that they enjoy the end result and can see their hard work reflected in the pages of this book.

Jane Dore (2016)

Contact details: edwardian.durrington@hotmail.com

Acknowledgements

Project Team:

Lyn Tiller for the finance, organizational management, research and most of all the sisterly hand holding when life became difficult due to the passing of our adored father, Eric Tiller, in 2014.
Dave Pryce for the continuous enthusiasm and encouragement plus all the photographs he took especially for the book. The wonderful production of this book is down to his skill and energy.
Jenny Dowling and the amazing costumes she researched, the materials she resourced and the way she created wonderful period re-creations for the project.
Sue & Peter Rowe for the Edwardian scones which became a speciality both in the village and in the schools as the various tea-parties were held.

My colleagues at Worthing Reference Library deserve a special thank you, especially Sarah Godfrey and Sue McMahon who helped research all the queries and questions and Anne Bevis for her work in creating the detailed index.
My thanks also go to all the following for their research, photography, indexing, family photographs and knowledge sharing:

Amos, Philip	Holmes, Margaret	Nicholls, David
Atfield, Owen	Hull, Jean	Norris, Mark (Australia),
Blower, Val	Jeffery, Tony	Pryce, Wendy
Connelly, Linda	Jones, Helen	Rice, Dawn
Dexter, Joan D	Kirk, Jean	Rickwood, Sarah
East Sussex Record Office	Knapp, Isla	Robards, Paul
Elwood, Jennifer	Latham, Gordon	Saunders, Robin
Funnell, Wendy	Linfield, Malcolm	Steel, Mary
Green, John	Little, Poppy	West Sussex Record Office
Hayes, Tony	Manning, Carole	White, Gerald

Special thanks have to go to Martin Hayes, the West Sussex County Local Studies Librarian, for his encouragement to ever begin such a project, and for his mentoring all the way through. The special cache of chocolate held in his desk in Worthing Library, for the difficult moments, will never be forgotten. I trust he is pleased with the outcome.

Lastly I want to thank New Life Church, Salvington Road where the elders and deacons were so supportive throughout. The use of the church buildings and equipment whenever we needed it and the covering of their oversight have been exemplary. They love and seek to serve this community in many ways and I thank them for allowing me to be part of what they seek to do. I am proud to serve as a deacon with such a group of men and women of God. Thank you Reverend Philip Amos and the leadership team at New Life Church.

Abbreviations

b.	Born – [Example - b.1906]
b.c	Born circa- [used where the date of birth has not been verified from GRO indexes]
©	Copyright
d.	Died – [example - d.1911)]
EPRD Min	East Preston Rural District Minutes
ESRO	East Sussex Record Office. The Keep, Brighton
ff.	Folio number when referring to a census
GRO Index	General Register Office Index of Births, Marriages and Deaths
NTS	Not to scale [This refers to the extracts of OS maps which are not to scale]
OS	Ordnance Survey Map
RHS	Royal Horticultural Society
sch	Schedule number when referring to the 1911 census
TNA	The National Archives, Kew, Surrey
Vol.	Volume number. Used in references for the GRO Index to Births, Marriages and Deaths
WSL	Worthing Reference Library. Local Studies Collection
WSRO	West Sussex Record Office, Orchard Street, Chichester

All names are given in **BOLD** usually for the first instance when they are used with birth dates

All house and commercial names are in *italics*

All quotes are in *italics*. This includes excerpts from case studies

Sources

The book is based on original sources; the details of which are listed below.

Census records for England and Wales were, with one exception, recorded every ten years between 1841 and 1911. This book focuses on the records for 1901 and 1911, although other years have been consulted. The original documents are held at the Public Record Office, Kew and are also now widely available on line through Ancestry and Find My Past websites. All entries are referenced with the PRO number (ie RG13 for the 1901 census) and folio (ff.) numbers; except the 1911 census where schedule (Sch) numbers are quoted.

Durrington Council School Admissions Register (Digital copies held at WSL. Original books at Durrington Junior School in 2016)

Durrington Council School Log Book 1908-1928 (Digital copies held at WSL. Original books at Durrington Junior School in 2016)

Durrington and West Tarring Parish registers (Copies held at WSL)

Electoral Registers for Durrington and Salvington 1901-1913. (Held at East Sussex Record Office)

East Preston Rural District Council minute books. Durrington and Salvington were part of the East Preston Rural District during Edwardian times. (The originals of these minute books are held at West Sussex record Office)

General Register Office Index of Births, Marriages and Deaths for England and Wales. These indexes list the civil registration of births, marriages and deaths in England and give the certificate reference number for each entry. The usual format for reference gives the quarter, the volume, the page number and the district where the event was registered. For example: (Sep Q, Vol. 2b, p.543 Lewes).

Inland Revenue Valuation. These are records and maps created between 1910 and 1915 in the course of the national Valuation Office survey. The valuation was initiated by the Finance (1909-1910) Act (10 Edw. VII, c.8 section 26(1)) which provided for the levy and collection of a duty on the increment value of all land in the United Kingdom. There are two main types of records, the first is maps which were based on Ordnance Survey maps and annotated by hand with numbers for each property and the second are the field books, small bound books arranged numerically, which provide varying degrees of information on each property. The records are quoted using the Field Book number plus The National Archive reference (IR58). When the Field Book is quoted, wording in brackets is added to make the meaning clear.

Ordnance Survey Maps. 25":1 mile Sheet LXIV(64): Sections 1, 2, 5, 6, 9 & 10. 3rd Edition 1912
These are not reproduced to scale as the extracts are only added for the purpose of identifying the plots. Some of the map extracts have the Inland Revenue Valuation numbers added, as detailed above, where it was considered helpful.

Street Directories 1900-1913 (Held at WSL)

Tithe Maps for Durrington and West Tarring. The originals are held at West Sussex Record Office. The maps and their respective Apportionment details have been digitised and transcribed. (The digital copies are held on CDRom at WSL)

Worthing Gazette 1901-1913 (Digital copies held at WSL)

Area covered in this book

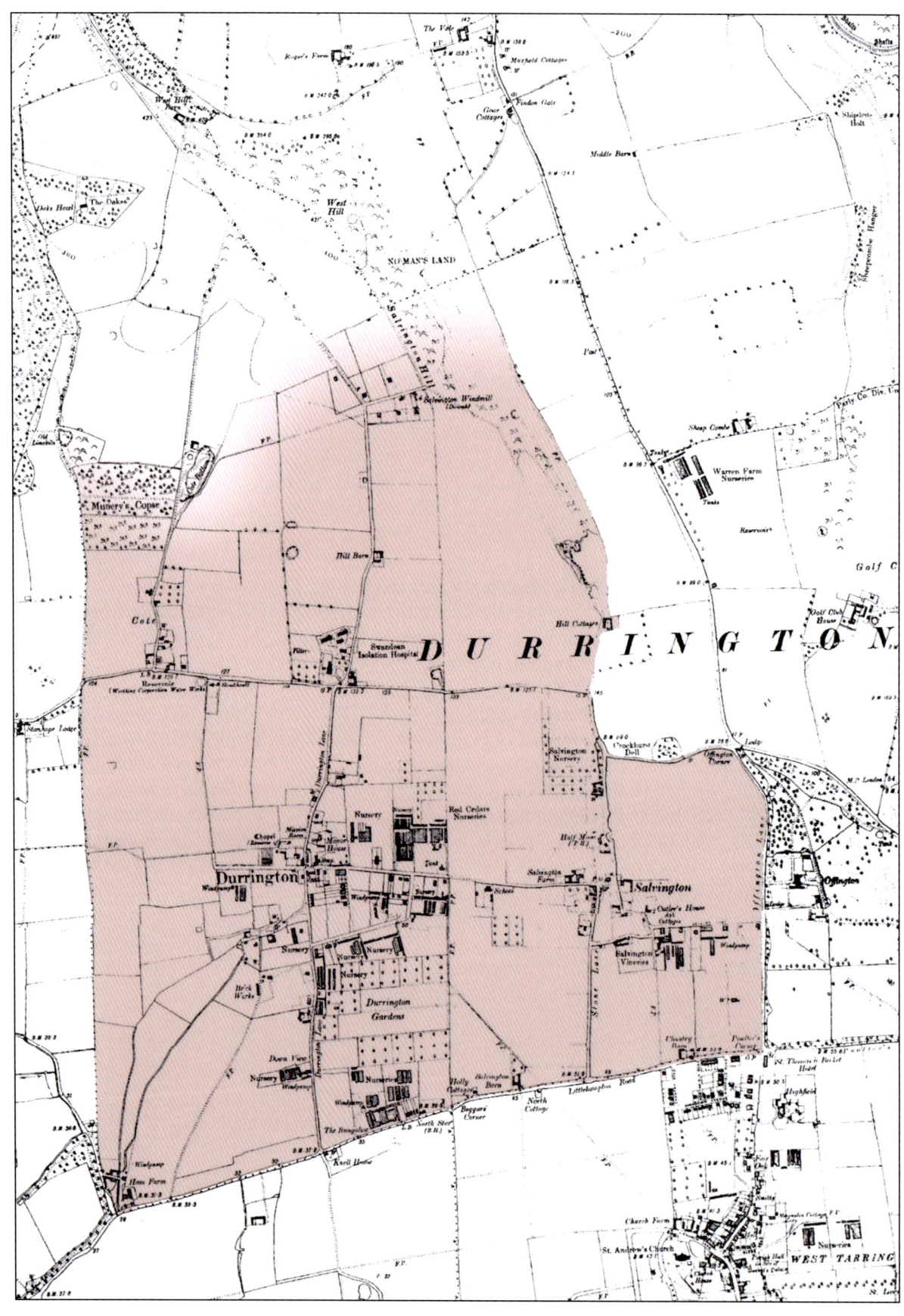

Chapter 1
Durrington Lane

Durrington Lane – Introduction (south to north)
(Inc. Pond Lane & South View Terrace)

This is one of the main roads in Durrington which runs from Littlehampton Road in the south, northwards to the Arundel Road. The Ordnance Survey map names the full length of the road as Durrington Lane but other documents sometimes use Durrington Street while the northern part is also called Durrington Hill.

The Edwardian village consisted of Durrington Lane with Pond Lane leading off on the western side about halfway up the road. Greenland Road was beginning to emerge on the eastern side as well as Salvington Road, which is the main thoroughfare running east to west connecting Durrington and Salvington. All of these roads were notorious for their muddy state in bad weather with constant complaints and efforts to improve things noted in council minutes and local newspapers. East Preston Rural District minutes contain an increasing number of planning applications during the Edwardian period giving permission for properties to be built, and with them came the requests for the laying of water mains along this and other roads in Durrington and Salvington.

The southern part of Durrington Lane around 1900 was lined by fields, a brickworks, a small number of nurseries and some cottages. The northern section of the road, running northwards from the junction with Salvington Road, included the *Manor House*, a small number of dwellings and the plot of land where the ruins of the original *Durrington Church* still stood. The Edwardian period saw many changes in the lane and by the outbreak of the First World War there were terraces of new houses, brick workers cottages, the establishment of Greenland Road and New Road and many more nurseries.

A view up Durrington Lane showing *Down View House* on the left and the entrance to *Star Nursery* on the right
Worthing Library

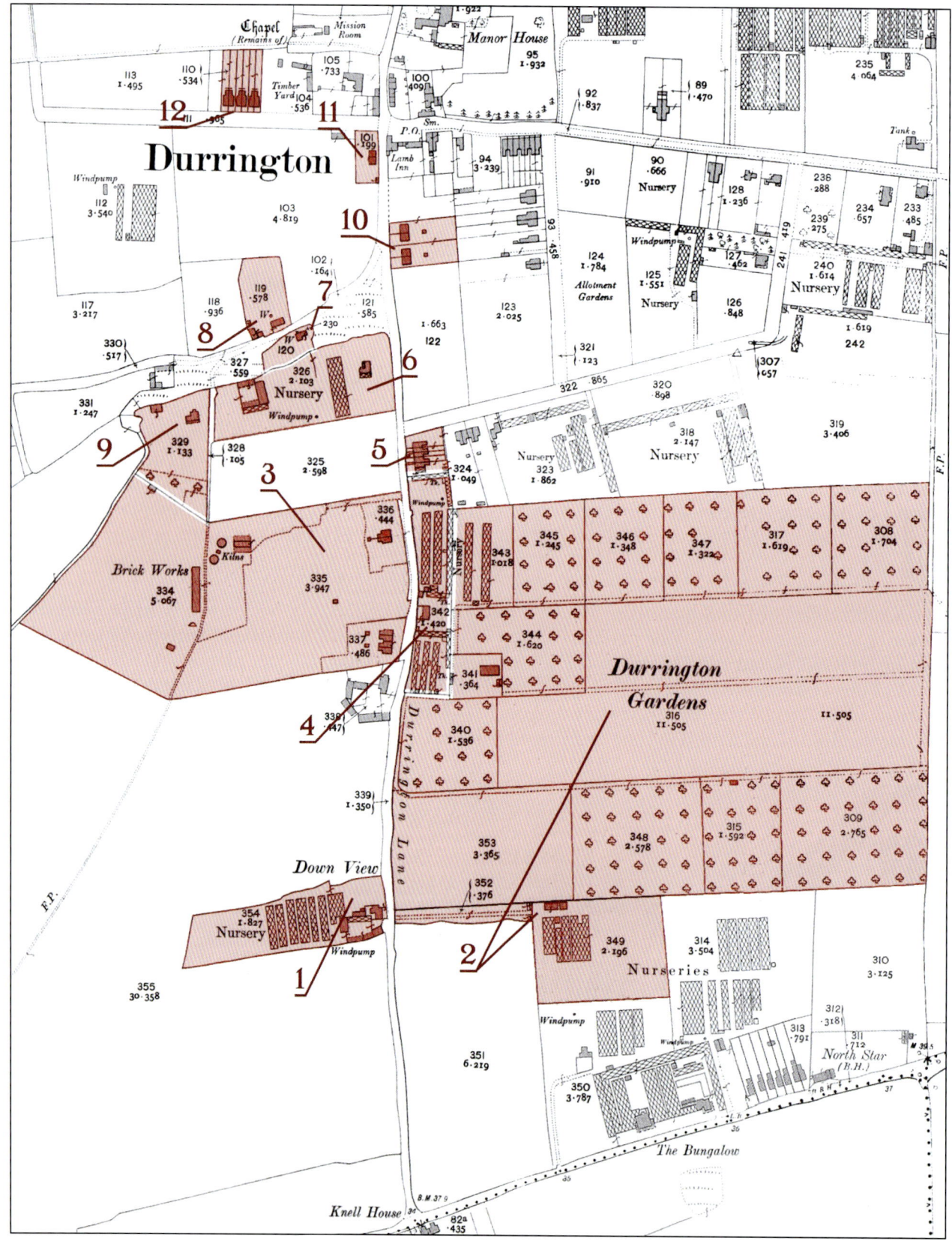

Excerpt taken from OS 25":1 mile Sheet LXIV: 5, 9 3rd Edition 1912 (NTS)

1. Down View House & Nursery, Durrington Lane
(No longer standing)

The sale of the land that was to become *Down View Nursery* appears on the Durrington Estate Sale Catalogue in 1895 as Lot No. 6. This lot included land on the opposite side of the road which eventually became *Star Nursery*. Luke Leggett was the name of the purchaser of the land and house which was firstly recorded in the street directories and electoral registers as *Ham Nurseries* but soon became known as *Down View House and Nursery*.

The 1911 census records **Luke** (b.1863) living and working this nursery with his wife **Susan** (b.1864 nee Older) and their one son, also called **Luke** (b.1905)[1]. This was a very successful business as Malcolm Linfield describes:

> *'One of the nurseries started around the turn of the century and operated by the same family through its entire existence was Down View Nurseries. Luke Leggett had two glasshouses on his market garden at Down View House by 1898, on the western side of Durrington Lane, devoted to fruit. By 1910, he had expanded his glass considerably with 11 glasshouses providing an 1104ft run of protected cropping. Interestingly he also grew mushrooms in an old shed, a risky crop in those days because of its unreliability;[2] a good crop often depended on the quality of the spawn, which he probably sourced locally from piles of old stable manure and grew on in a special bed. It would then be used to inoculate the specially made mushroom beds, which were usually laid out on the floor. However, whether the eventual crop was worth the effort was anybody's guess – but if it was, then a lot of money could be made, so the cultivation of the edible mushroom particularly appealed to the more adventurous growers.*
>
> *It is interesting to speculate why individuals started in the growing business. Luke Leggett, who was born around 1864, was living with his parents in Broadwater in 1891. Their next door neighbour was local nurseryman **Henry Apted**, and since Luke's occupation is recorded as 'gardener', it is quite probable that he was working on Apted's nursery at the time. Not surprisingly, after a few years, Luke felt confident enough to start up on his own, and hence the move to Durrington. Luke passed on the nursery to his son, Luke junior, who was born in 1905 and still running the nurseries in the 1960's.'*[3]

Luke Leggett held many posts around the village. He was one of the men elected to the very first Parish Council in 1902[4], having already been the Chairman of the former Parish Meetings held in the village. He was an active campaigner for the building of the school in Durrington, later becoming the Attendance Officer at the school. His signature is shown in the Log Book opposite. It was some time after the school had been successfully opened, that the village began to campaign for the re-building of the church, originally destroyed during the Civil War. Luke, as the Chairman of the Parish Council, was fully in favour and ready for the campaign. In the report of the meeting in the Worthing Gazette a week later it states:

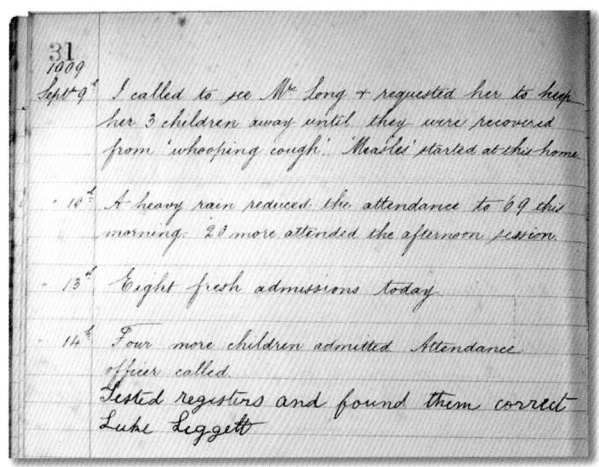

> *'There was no doubt the Parish was greatly on the increase and the present seemed an appropriate time to move in the latter. It had been said that they would never get a church in the village, but the same thing was said concerning the school; and after all, the difficulties ought to be overcome if they were tackled properly.'*[5]

He was correct as the church was indeed re-built some years later. *Down View House* with its nursery is no longer standing, the land now hidden under Colombia Drive.

Photograph showing Luke and Susan Leggett outside of *Down View House*.
Worthing Library

Modern photograph showing the approximate site of where *Down View House* once stood. © Dave Pryce 2016

2. Star Nursery & Durrington Gardens, Durrington Lane
(No longer standing)

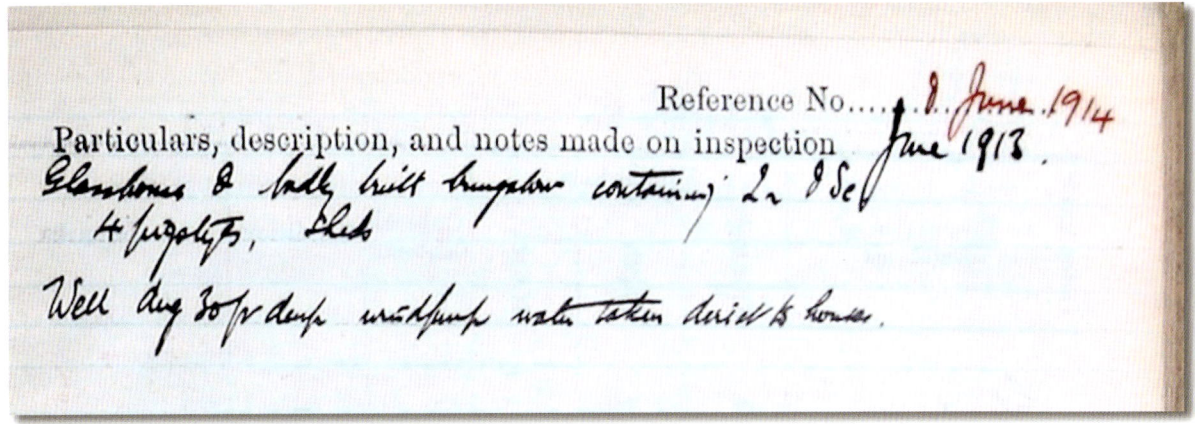

The Inland Revenue Valuation describes this site as *'Lane, Glasshouses, Pipes, Packing Shed"* and adds that it includes a *"badly built bungalow containing 2 R(ooms) & Sc(ullery)."*[6] Malcolm Linfield explains:

> *'Taylor Bros (T.O. and C.A. Taylor) set up the nursery ...... They appear to have rented the site on a 21 year lease from 1905, but by June 1914 they were no longer there. There were 7 glasshouses on 1.3 acres. These two brothers appear to be unrelated to the Taylor Bros of Salvington Nurseries.'*[7]

The Taylor Brothers living at *Star Nurseries* in 1911 were **Thomas Otto Taylor** (b.1878) and his younger brother **Claude Arthur** (b.1883), both fruit growers who had previously worked in Hampshire.[8] Although the bungalow only had two rooms, Claude shared this property with his Worthing born wife **Maud** and their two sons, **Philip** (b.1904) and **William** (b.1909) as well as his brother, so living conditions must have been very cramped.

Directly above the *Star Nurseries* site was the large 34 acre *Durrington Gardens* run by **Alfred Chipper** (b.1842) who was born and lived in West Tarring. It largely consisted of multiple acres of orchard, but there were two glasshouses each 200 foot in length and some arable land included. The land was owned by the Henty family from Henfield and had, in previous years, been worked by **Thomas Bushby.** Alfred had been working a smaller nursery bordering the Littlehampton Road before taking a 6½ year tenancy on *Durrington Gardens* in March 1909, for the annual rent of £210.[9]

3. Durrington Brickfields & Brickfield Cottages, Durrington Lane
(Now No's 61, 63, 65, 67, 85 & 87, Durrington Lane)

The Brickfields and the cottages associated with them has been researched and partly written by Sue McMahon one of the Edwardian Durrington project volunteers.

Although there was a brickyard operating west of Cote Street in High Salvington as early as 1768,[10] the brickworks on the west side of Durrington Lane are first shown on the Ordnance Survey map of 1898. The *Durrington Brick Company* who owned and worked the land was established in 1896.

Land was often acquired for brickfields by property developers close to the land on which they intended to erect houses. Once the supply of brick earth became exhausted, they moved the brickfield to another part of the site. In the case of Durrington, the land was bought by **William Wenban Smith**, a local builder and businessman. There were several other brickfields in the Worthing area which William was developing between 1878 and 1899. He later entered into partnership with **George Mills,** one of the landowner's in Durrington, to establish brickworks alongside the railway at Southwater, south of Horsham, bringing bricks into Worthing by rail.[11]

The original directors of the company were William Wenban Smith and George Mills. After their deaths in 1901 and 1903, **William Edmund Wenban Smith**, son of **William Wenban Smith** and local builders **James Blaker** and **Frank Sandell** joined the board of directors.

Other land and properties in Durrington previously owned by William Wenban Smith were offered for sale after his sudden death in 1901. The story of this sudden and unexpected death was reported in the local paper.[12]

By the time of the Inland Revenue Valuation a decade later, only two shops, two houses, one acre of arable land and a 22 perch building plot are shown as being owned by Mr Wenban Smith.[13]

The Durrington site was a small field, detailed in the assessment of 1911 as land, buildings and royalty on 800,000 bricks worth a gross value of £1,440. It is further described as a three acre brickfield with *'3 kilns not used for 12 years. Burnt in clamps near the timber built shed.'* A clamp was an alternative and traditional method of firing bricks by building them into a pile rather than placing them inside a kiln.[14]

Photograph of *Brickfield Cottages* with *St Mary's Barn* in the background. Worthing Library
(*St Mary's Farmhouse* and barns were unoccupied during this period)

Adjoining the field, fronting Durrington Lane and still standing today are six red brick cottages. Built by the *Durrington Brick Company* for its workers, each cottage consisted of one room plus a kitchen scullery and three bedrooms. The occupiers were mainly employees of the company often with strong family connections.

No 1 was occupied by the Bowers family who originally came from Hampshire. **John Samuel Bowers** (b.1862) was head of the household and both he and his son **Thomas** are recorded working in the brickfields in the 1901 census.[15] His younger son **George** (b.1889) had joined them in later years as he is listed as a bricklayer on the 1911 census.[16]

In 1901,[17] *No 2 Brickfield Cottages* was occupied by **James Stoner** (b.1865), a brickmaker, followed in 1911 by the **Wingfield** family.[18] **Edmund William** (b.1858), head of the household is shown as a general labourer, but son **John** (b.1888) as a brickmaker.
On the 1901 census, **Edwin Alfred Reed** (b.1852), a brickmaker originally from Hampshire, was living at No 3.[19] In 1891, he had been employed at a brickfield in Heene, along with the Bowers family and was married

to **Sarah**, daughter of **George Bowers**.[20] By 1911 the occupiers are **Thomas Hide** (b.c1842) and his wife. His occupation is given as a general labourer.[21] By June 1913 when the Inland Revenue Valuation was completed, the occupier had changed to George Bowers, the son of **John Samuel Bowers** from No 1.[22]

George Bowers, father of John Samuel and foreman of the brickworks, was living at No 4 in 1901.[23] According to earlier censuses, he had been employed as foreman at other brickyards in the Worthing area.[24] By 1911, the occupiers were **Samuel Baynes** (b.1849), a retired policeman from Thaxted, Essex and his wife **Emma** (b.c1841 nee Price) who do not appear to have any connection to the brickfields.

No 5 Brickfield Cottages was the home of **William Terry** (b.1876), a brickmaker and his family who are listed at the address on both censuses[25]. His wife **Helen** (b.1868 nee Bowers) was another daughter of George Bowers.

No 6 was the home of **Fanny Saunders** (nee Lloyd), and her son, **William James** (b.1899). Fanny and William are listed on both censuses. The 1901 census lists her as the wife of a private in the 5th Dragoons, **Gosden William Saunders** (b.1871), who left the army a few years after this census was taken. In 1905 the Worthing Gazette carried a report of a sudden death at the brickfields and named the deceased as Gosden Saunders. He had become a brickmaker after leaving the army and died whilst working in the brickfields.[26] By 1911 Fanny was still living in the house as a widow with her son and there was also a lodger, **Albert Henry J Wingfield** (b.1879), another brickmaker.[27]

Worthing Gazette April 1905 revealing details of the death and inquest of Gosden Saunders in the brickfields

In addition to the employees living in the cottages in 1901 there were other brickworkers recorded in the area. **James Burridge** (b.1871) was living in a caravan next to the *Half Moon Inn*[28] and brothers **Cephas Walter Mills** (b.1880) and **Albert** (b.1883) from Wick near Littlehampton were lodging with **Thomas Saunders** in *Elder Tree Cottage*, indicating perhaps that they were only employed on a temporary basis[29]. The Mills brothers had certainly returned to Wick where they were working as brickmakers in 1911,[30] whilst the number of men listed as brickmakers in Durrington had fallen from ten to six.

The *Durrington Brick Company* eventually ceased trading in 1923[31] probably because the brick earth had been exhausted, and areas such as Southwater, were prospering with more plentiful raw materials and better transport links. It had served its purpose in providing brick stock for the rapid expansion of the village of Durrington during the Edwardian period.

Modern photograph of the Cottages. © David Nicholls

4. Bushby's Cottage & Nursery, Durrington Lane
(No longer standing)

Bushby's Nursery and the small cottage included on the site were situated on the right hand side of Durrington Lane. The land was originally part of the Durrington Estate which had been let to Thomas Bushby from as early as 1879. The cottage on the nursery land was known as *'Bushby's Cottage'*. It had stood there for many years, described on the Inland Revenue Valuation in 1913 as *'very old, half thatched'*.[32]

The Durrington Estate sold much of the land in 1895 and this plot with its cottage was offered for sale at the time. Pencilled in on the copy of the catalogue for the sale in July 1895 was the price of £540, with an added note that it had been withdrawn.[33] No reason was given for this withdrawal, but we do know that by the 1913 Inland Revenue Valuation, Thomas Bushby, is listed as the owner and the occupier of the nursery and cottage having purchased it in 1895 for £400. It is possible that as he was already the occupier he was able to negotiate the purchase for a more favourable rate. He then spent a further £1500 on the site, buying the many glasshouses he erected on the land. Malcolm Linfield reveals more details:

> *'In 1896, Worthing grower Thomas Bushby, who also had a nursery in Heene Road, owned the largest glasshouse nursery with 9 houses, providing a total growing area of 30,000 sq. ft.'* [34]

The nine glasshouses can be clearly seen on the OS map.

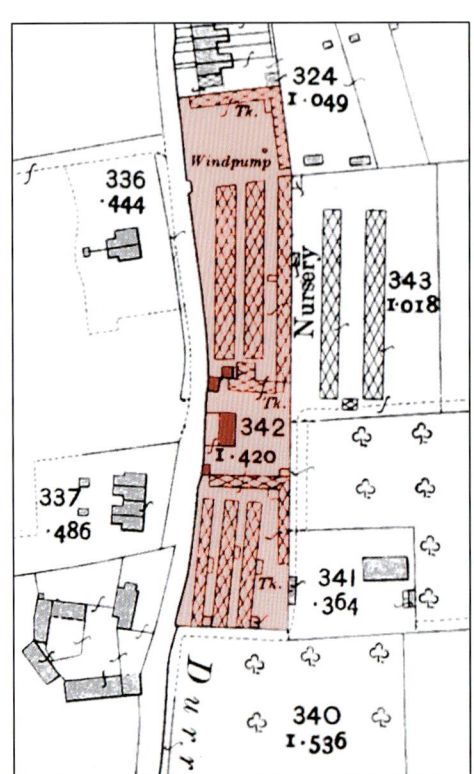

Excerpt taken from OS 25":1 mile Sheet LXIV: 9 3rd Edition 1912 (NTS)

Thomas Bushby (b.1842) was born in Sompting and married his wife **Annie** (nee Clifford) in Brighton in 1866. Although he owned the nursery and land in Durrington, he did not live on the site of the nursery, we find him listed living in the Heene area, where he owned and managed another nursery. *Bushby's Cottage* was being rented out to tenants throughout the period.

The 1901 census does not list all house names but it is probable that the cottage was occupied by a cowman, **George Brown** (b.1878).[35] The 1911 census tells us that the 4-roomed cottage was the home of **James Lish** (b.1884), his wife **Ethel Mary** (b.1888) and their young daughter **Ethel Nellie** (b.1909).[36] James was the younger brother of **Albert Lish** one of the Durrington blacksmiths who was living in Franklin Road.

The cottage and nursery have both disappeared and modern bungalows now stand on the site.

Modern bungalows standing on the site of *Bushby's Cottage*. © Dave Pryce 2015

5. Highdown View Terrace, Durrington Lane
(Now No's 88, 90, 92, 94 & 96, Durrington Lane)

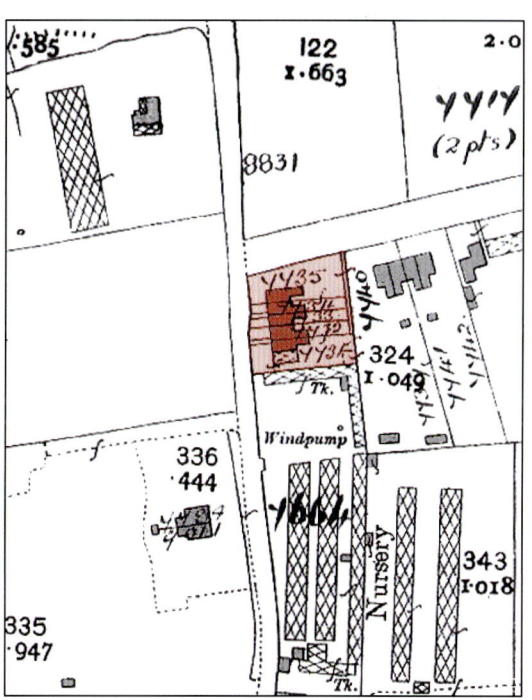

Excerpt taken from OS 25":1 mile Sheet LXIV: 9 3rd Edition 1912 (NTS)

This is a terrace of five properties, all of which were owned by **Mrs A Brake** of Worthing. She was the wife of a plumber and lived in South Farm Road. The properties were probably built around 1909 for a cost of £175 each and fetched a rent of between £12 and £15. They were built slightly raised from the road level, which must have helped with the very muddy roads that plagued Durrington and Salvington throughout the Edwardian period.

No 1 - This property is on the south corner of Durrington Lane and Greenland Road. Here, the 1911 census tells us that the village policeman **Ernest Jays** (b.1882) lived with his family.[37] He had been born in Tangmere and married his wife **Emily** (b.1889 nee Lawrance) in 1909. Their son **Ernest George H** was born the following year in Durrington.

His work as a village police constable was carried out from this house. We read in the local papers that law-breakers, including the poacher **James Voak** of *Pond Lane Cottage*, had been brought to this house when arrested.[38] In the newspaper report, the house is called *Durrington Police Cottage*.

The Inland Revenue Valuation has a previous occupant by the name of **H. Goble** crossed out and PC Jays name pencilled in.[39] Mr Goble has not yet been identified.

No 2 Highdown View Terrace was the home of Henry Wratting who according to street directories for 1907, had previously lived in Stone Lane, Salvington. He was listed as the occupier at No. 2 on both the 1911 census[40] and Inland Revenue Valuation.[41] **Henry Wratting** (b.1856) and his wife **Caroline** (b.1857) occupied the house with their three teenage children, **Frederick** (b.1892), **Albert** (b.1896) and **Agnes** (b.1897). They also had a step-daughter **Annie Hampshire** (b.1886). Henry and Frederick were both gardeners. Curiously only Agnes' birth can be confirmed from birth indexes.

Benjamin John Dennis (b.1870), originally from East Meon in Hampshire, was listed as the head of the household on the 1911 census for *No 3 Highdown View Terrace*.[42] He was a general labourer living in Durrington with his London born wife **Euphemia Frances** (b.1879) and four children, **Winifred** (b.1902), **Gladys** (b.1904), **Georg**e (b. 1907) and **William** (b.1910). They had been living in Durrington from as early as July 1904, as this is the date that their second child Gladys was baptised in the village.[43] The Inland Revenue Valuation has his name crossed out and the surname of Linberry as the new occupant.[44] This confirms that by May 1913, the date of the valuation, he had already moved. His last listing on the electoral register is 1912.

The fourth of the houses was the home of a market gardener and his family. **William Harwood** (b.1872), his wife **Sarah** (b.1871) and their two daughters **Alexandre Irene** (b.1903) and **Florence Daisy** (b.1905) had already been living in Durrington for some years before they moved to the new house. William and Sarah were listed in Durrington Street on the 1901 census and in street directories from the same date, but the exact address is unclear.[45]

In 1909, William had a disagreement with one of his neighbours from *No 4 New Cottages*, a little further up the lane. The neighbour was **Thomas Elliott** and it appears that the disagreement ended up with blows being struck and both men having to appear in court on a charge of assault. The case was dismissed as the newspaper report outlines. [46]

> **TWO CASES DISMISSED.**
> A Durrington man, named *Thomas Elliott*, was summoned by William Harwood for assault. There was also a cross summons, and both cases were taken together.
> Harwood stated that Elliott met him in Durrington-lane and asked him "what he had done to his mate," and then struck him in the face.
> This was denied by Elliott, who alleged that it was the other way about, and that Harwood had struck him.
> Each case was dismissed, and defendants were ordered to pay their own costs.

Worthing Gazette April 1909

In 1911 the last of the terrace, No 5, was the home of **Eli Greenyer** (b.1841) a retired station master. In the home with him were his wife **Sarah** (b.1842 nee Tench) and her older sister **Mary Ann Tench** (b.1835). The sisters were originally from Bridgenorth, Shropshire, while Eli was a local man born in Goring.

Eli had made his career working for the railways, and he is first listed on the 1861 census as a railway porter in Barcombe.[47] In 1863 he married **Sarah Tench** and by 1881 he was working at Battersea Station as a Station Master and the couple were living with Sarah's elderly father **Edward Tench**. Their next move was confirmed on the 1891 census when they were living in the station master's house in Battersea.[48] Here they stayed until around 1903 when Eli retired and returned to the area of his birth, moving first to *No 1 Southview Terrace* and in early 1911, to this address where he is listed on the census[49] and the Inland Revenue Valuation.[50]

Photograph showing *Highdown View Terrace*. Worthing Library

Modern view of *Highdown View Terrace*. © Dave Pryce 2015

6. Claremont Nursery, Durrington Lane
(Now No 121, Durrington Lane)

The land for this house and nursery was purchased in October 1905 by **Zoe Irene Wilton** (b.1875) the youngest daughter of a family from Shropshire. Her father **Frederick** had held the post of Solicitor Registrar of the County Court of Gloucestershire but had died when Zoe was very young. The 1901 census lists Zoe in Ewell, Surrey where she is working as a district nurse alongside another district nurse named **Emily Godard** (b.1870) and Emily's mother **Winifred** (b.c1836).[51] Around 1905, both Zoe and Emily had made the decision to change profession and the two ladies plus Winifred moved to Durrington where Zoe purchased the land, built the house and began a new career as a nursery woman. This, as Malcolm Linfield describes, was an unusual situation:

> *'A significant first for Durrington is the fact that one of its pioneer fruit growers under glass was a woman – Zoe Wilton – who owned and managed Claremont Nursery at Lamb Pond, situated on the western side of Durrington Lane, slightly to the north of the junction with Greenland Road. With just over 2 acres of land, Zoe bought the site in October 1905 for £400, subsequently investing £700, much of which was presumably spent on the building of four glasshouses, amounting to just over 500ft of glass. She planted vines in the houses, although she also had two pigsties and a shed for mushrooms. There was also a large barn on the site, a windpump and a house.'* [52]

As well as the cost of the nursery buildings described above, Zoe had paid a further £325 to have the house built. The 1911 census lists Zoe, Emily and Winifred in the house along with some of Emily's family who were visiting, namely **George Godard** (b.1869) and his daughter **Dorothy** (b.1898).[53] George is listed as a fruit grower, and it is very possible that it was the influence of the Godard family which started Zoe on the path of fruit growing. Emily, at this time, gives her occupation as a 'sick nurse', but she must have worked in the nursery as well, as 'Wilton & Godard' are advertising themselves as specialist chrysanthemum growers in January 1912.[54]

Worthing Gazette January 1912

The house is described in the Inland Revenue Valuation as having *'small rooms but well decorated'*, perhaps reflecting the very female influence on this property.[55] From the photograph opposite it can be seen that the house is completely rendered which was not common practice in Durrington at this time. The story in the village is that the house was built from brick batts purchased from the brickfields further down the road. Brick batts are broken and damaged bricks which would inevitably be cheaper to purchase, and it may have been the uneven brick lines which necessitated the walls being rendered.

The photograph shows a small building attached to the southern side of the house, possibly being the *'small 1 room bungalow'* Zoe advertised for sale in April 1912.[56]

Advert for bungalow at Claremont in April 1912

At the time of writing, this small annexe has just been demolished to create a building plot. The house itself is still standing.

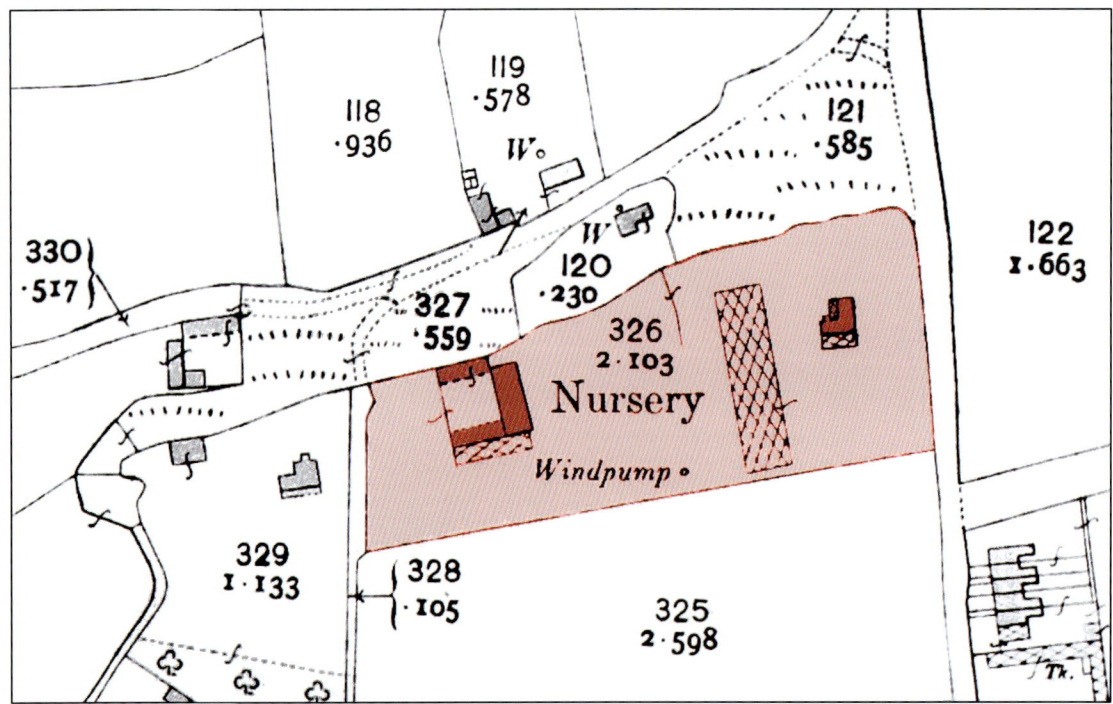

Excerpt taken from OS 25":1 mile Sheet LXIV: 5, 9 3rd Edition 1912 (NTS)

Modern photograph of the house at *Claremont Nursery*. © Tony Jeffrey 2015

7. Thatched Cottage, Pond Lane
(Now Thatch Cottage, Pond Lane)

This is a very old, very small thatched cottage, situated on a site adjacent to where a pond once stood which gave the cottage and lane its name. It is one of the last buildings in Durrington to have retained its thatched roof. Described in the Inland Revenue Valuation as a *'Very old boulder & thatch, situate very near pond. Very damp site. No footings.'*[57]

The cottage was built in the 18th century and is a Grade II listed building where the following description of the building is given:

> *'Probably C18, possibly with earlier interior features. Painted flint with brick dressings. Thatched, hipped at west end. 2 storeys. Irregular fenestration*
> *One window in east end. North front: left-hand porch with thatched gable and small windows in sides. One window in upper floor, 4 below (including to extension under roof slope at right end). Small chimney at top of hip. All windows are modern casements.'*[58]

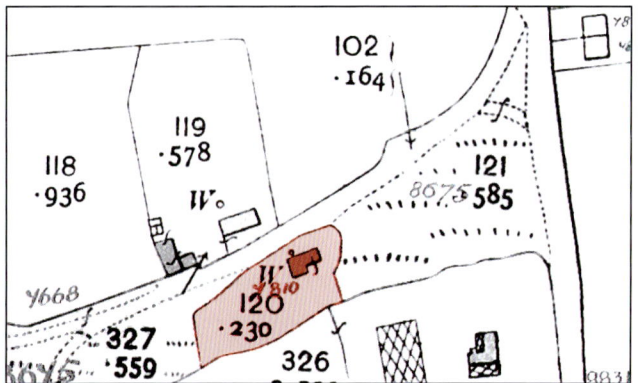

Excerpt taken from OS 25":1 mile Sheet LXIV: 5, 9 3rd Edition 1912 (NTS)
Inland Revenue Valuation numbers added

13

The cottage is marked on the Durrington Tithe Map having had various names during the Edwardian period. In 1905 it was sometimes called *Lamb Pond Cottage,* whilst on the 1911 census it was *Woodbine Cottage*[59] and by 1913 on the Inland Revenue Valuation it was being listed as *Durringmere.*[60]

Photograph dated around 1920 showing the pond and its proximity to the cottage. Worthing Library

The old photograph above confirms its close proximity to the pond which was fed by water which bubbled and ran from many springs that surface around the site. One can only imagine the living conditions inside this small four roomed cottage especially during wet weather. The property had no proper footings and was regularly water-logged making it particularly unhealthy.

The occupiers of the cottage at the time of the 1901 census were **Frederick Hamilton** (b.1873) and his wife **Fanny** (b.1878 nee Lovelock) who came from Hampshire.[61] He was a cowman on the farm and they lived in the cottage with four children whose birth places give a good indication of the period when they arrived in the village: **Percy** (b.1894) was born in Goring, whereas **Ernest** (b.1897) was the first to be born in Durrington, followed by **Ethel** (b.1899) and **Frederick** (b.1900) also born in Durrington. They therefore moved to the cottage around 1894, and we know they left in 1904 or 1905 when the next occupants took possession.

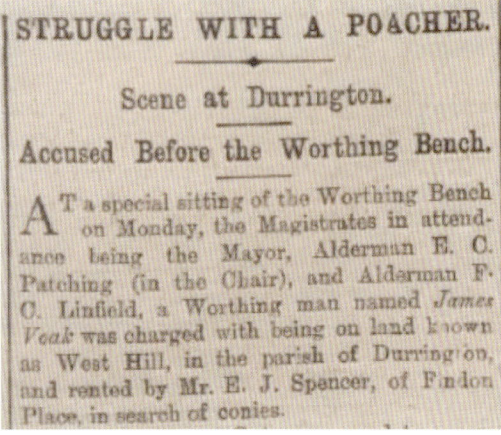

Worthing Gazette March 1911

The name of the new inhabitant was **James Voak** (b.1874) who is listed at this address in the street directories from 1905-1911. James was the son of a painter named **George Voak** and his wife **Emily** who lived in Tarring. In 1898 he married **Ellen (Nellie) Mary** (b.1880 nee Sayers**)**, and they went on to have at least six children during the Edwardian years. **Archibald** (b.1898) born in Angmering, **Emily** (b.1899), **Dorothy** (b.1901) and **James** (b.1903) born in Salvington, and finally **Percy** (b.1907) and **Sydney** (b.1910) born in the cottage in Durrington.

Photograph of James Voak. Owned by Owen Atfield

In July 1907, the cottage was sold to **Mr Thomas Wood** of Broadwater for £56 and continued to be rented out to various tenants, of which the Voak family were the first, as they were already living in the property. James Voak was an interesting character not averse to a little poaching to help keep food on the table for his family, as reported in the local newspaper.[62]

It was only some months after this incident that the family left the cottage. The Durrington Council School registers show that Nora (Emily), Dorothy and James were 'removed' from the school in June 1912 when the family moved on.[63]

T. Ibeson is named as the next occupant on the Inland Revenue Valuation in June 1913 and it is here that the cottage is called *Durringmere*. Apart from one advert in the Worthing Gazette where Mr Ibeson is selling some egg-laying ducks in January 1914, and one entry in the 1914 street directory, he is not named elsewhere so presumably did not spend many years at the cottage.

The cottage is still standing as the modern photograph shows

Modern photograph. © Dave Pryce 2010

8. Durrington Farmhouse, Pond Lane
(Now Durrington Farmhouse, Pond Lane)

In the 1901 census this house was called *The Farm* and was the home of **Horace Overington** and his wife **Caroline**.[64] The property had been sold as part of the sale of the Durrington Estate in 1895 where it was described in the sale catalogue as a 'flint-built cottage'.[65]

At this time, it was a much smaller dwelling than the extended building standing on the site today. The Inland Revenue Valuation describes it in the following terms;

> *'Old Cottage, boulder built, many settlements appear in walls, these have been cemented up ………… cowshed ………… This land has been and is liable to flooding.'*[66]

As already stated, the occupant at the beginning of the century was **Horace Overington** (b.1848) who was the eldest son of **Edgar Overington** of the *Forge* in Salvington Road. On the 1901 census Horace's occupation was given as 'Wheelwright and coachbuilder' a profession learned from family members no doubt. In 1874 Horace had married **Caroline Charlotte** (b.1847 nee Cox) in Steyning, and they were living at the house with their nephew **Herbert Edgar Tweed** (b.1870). Herbert's father **Charles Tweed**, was the blacksmith in Beeding, and his mother **Harriett** (nee Cox) was Caroline's sister.

In 1910 Caroline died and Horace left the house to live in *Durrington House*, Salvington Road, a property he had purchased in 1906.

By the time of the 1911 census, the occupants of *Durrington Farmhouse* are **Leonard Charles Linberry** (b.1858) and his wife **Selina** (b.1858 nee Stow), along with their three children **George** (b.1891), **Barbara** (b.1894) and **Albert** (b.1895).[67] Leonard Linberry was the son of George and Ellen Linberry who had run the *Half Moon Inn* in Salvington for some years.

The 1911 census gives the occupation of Leonard and his two sons as dairymen which may explain the pasture land to the north of the house Leonard was occupying at the time of the Inland Revenue Valuation.[68] The site of this field is now part of *Pond Lane Park*. The farmhouse still stands with more modern extensions and alterations.

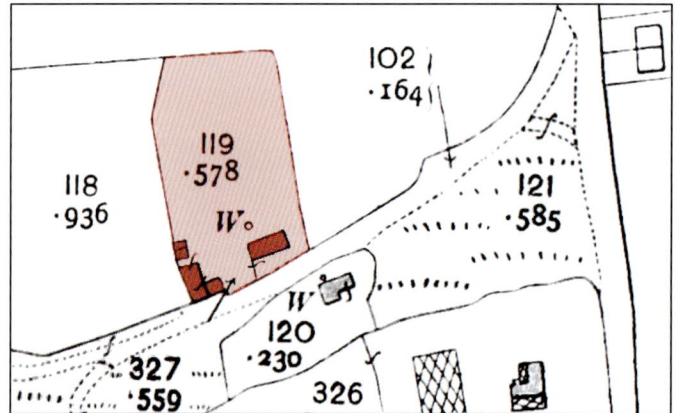
Excerpt taken from OS 25":1 mile Sheet LXIV:5, 9 3rd Edition 1912 (NTS)

Photograph of the period showing part of *Durrington Farmhouse* on the left and *Pond Lane Cottage* on the right.
Worthing Library

Modern Photograph of *Durrington Farmhouse* showing the extensions on the building. © Dave Pryce 2015

9. The Bungalow, Pond Lane
(No longer standing)

The electoral registers and street directories first list this property in 1908, when the name of **Charles Edwin Faull** is given as the occupier. Nothing else is known of Mr Faull except he did not stay at the address for very long.

The next occupants were **Arthur J Moore** (b.1880), a poultry farmer, with his wife **Ann** and son **Alfred** (b.1910). On the 1911 census, Alfred's birth place is given as Durrington which confirms the family were living here around 1910.[69] The Inland Revenue Valuation details a sale of the plot in December 1909 for the sum of £260.[70] The purchaser was **Alfred Taylor** from Worthing. In the census it states they had been married for one year, so it is probable that this was when they took up residence. *The Bungalow* itself was not large and was partly built of galvanised iron, as the valuation description confirms:

> '*Bungalow, one storey, gal iron roof & walls*'.[71]

Arthur J Moore was born in Sturminster, Devon, the son of a coal merchant's carter named **Henry Moore** (b.1845). It is interesting to note from the 1881 census that Arthur's mother, **Maria** and at least 2 of his siblings were born in Newfoundland.[72] *The Bungalow* they lived in is no longer standing.

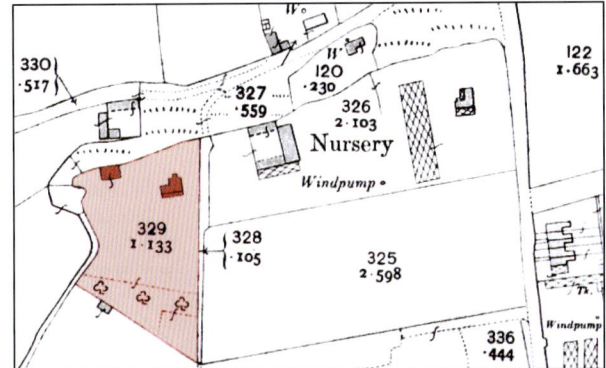

Excerpt taken from OS 25":1 mile Sheet LXIV: 9 3rd Edition 1912 (NTS)

10. New Cottages, Durrington Lane
(Now No's 112, 114, 116 & 118, Durrington Lane)

The following is written by Jean Hull the granddaughter of one of the occupants of No. 1 New Cottages:

'In 1896, George Jonathan Mills gave permission for builders Edward Henry Binstead and John Curtis to build, at their own expense, a pair of semi-detached cottages on a piece of land in Durrington Lane measuring 60 feet by approx. 180 feet below the Lamb Inn see plan below. In November of that year, when the houses were completed, the land and houses were sold to Thomas Green Baker - £60 paid to George Jonathan Mills for the land and £390 to the builders Messrs. Binstead and Cutler. On the death of Thomas Baker in 1897 and his wife in 1900, both cottages were sold by the Executor to Robert Smith of Clapham, Sussex for £620.

The cottages were built to a high standard in flint and brick with a pitched tile roof, a living room, kitchen/living room and scullery on the ground floor, with 3 large bedrooms, with fireplaces, on the first floor. In the back there was a well and space for a large vegetable and fruit garden. In 1901, my grandparents Sarah Ann Thomas (born in Cardiff) and Henry Thompson (born in Horsham, Sussex) married and moved into Elmbank Cottages. Then in 1902, with their daughter Edith, they moved into 1 New Cottages. The move had been suggested by Sarah's sister Elizabeth, who was the wife of Walter White, the licensee of The Lamb Inn. Very sadly Elizabeth died in June 1902. Sarah and Henry had further children, Elizabeth in 1903, William in 1905 (he sadly died in 1908), John (my father) in 1908, Henry in 1910 and Nell in 1913. In 1920 Sarah and Henry purchased No 1 and the property remained in the family until 1998 when Nell died.'

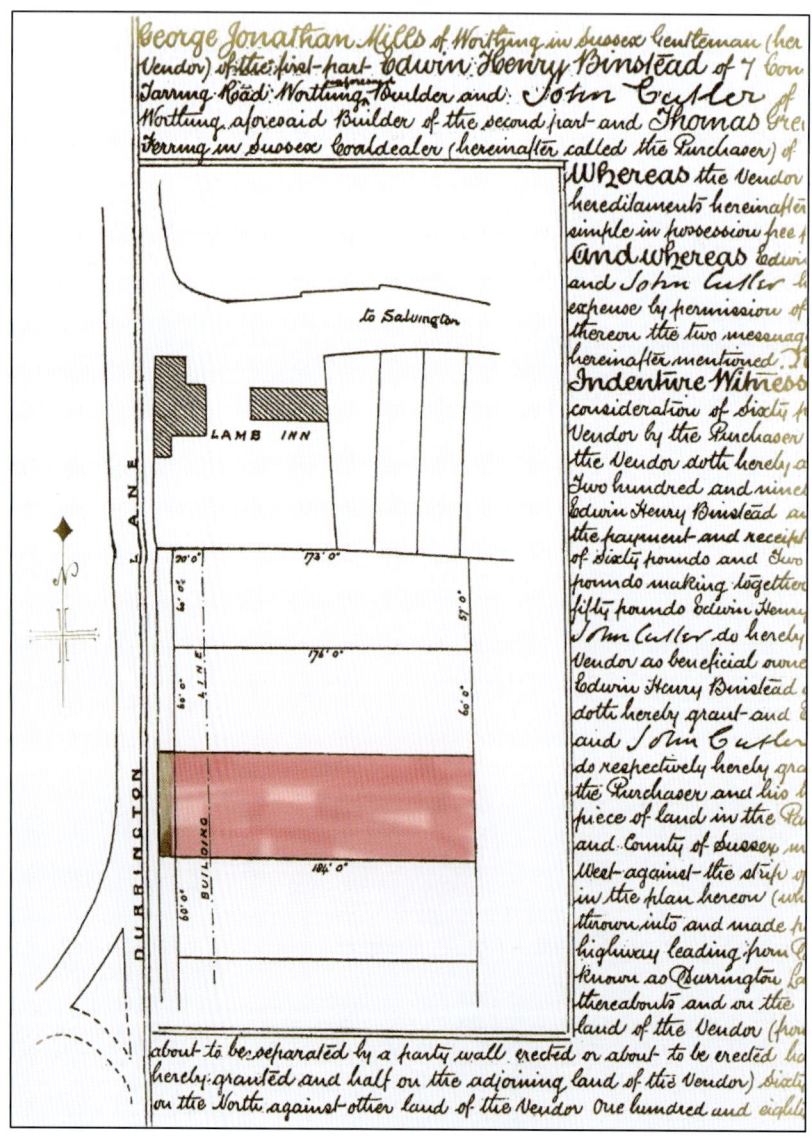

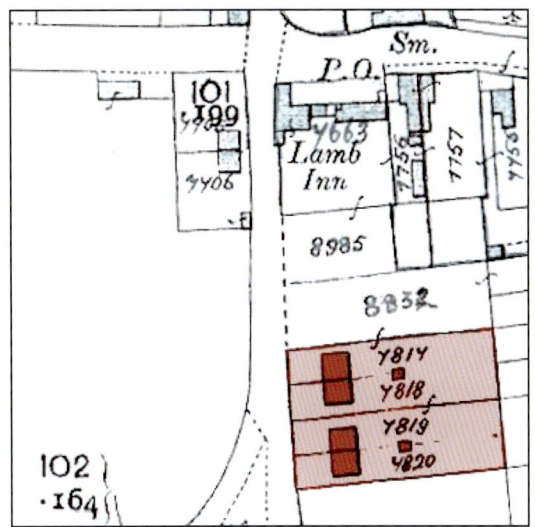

Excerpt taken from OS 25":1 mile Sheet LXIV: 5 3rd Edition 1912 (NTS)
Inland Revenue Valuation numbers added

The 1901 census informs us that the Thompsons were not the first occupants of *No 1 New Cottages*.[73] A widower named **Thomas Lambourne** (b.1841) lived in the property with his children, **Charles Daniel** (b.1873), **Albert** (b.1889) and **Millicent Emily** (b.1891). These houses were of a good size so he also shared the house with his older married daughter **Susannah**, her husband **Frederick J Hoare** and their four children. Susannah is interesting as the only place her name appears is on the marriage index for Frederick Hoare where her name is given as **'Susannah Harriet Standin'.**

The family did not stay long after the census, as Jean Hull has explained above, her family moved into the house in 1902. It was only from 1905 however, that **Henry Thompson** is listed at the address in street directories. His wife Sarah was the sister of Elizabeth White who resided with her husband at *The Lamb Inn* until she died. *No 1 New Cottages* became a family home for many years with details being added on the 1911 census.[74]

The first occupants of No 2 were, according to the 1901 census, **Frederic Henry Holden** (b.1850), his wife **Mary** (b.1851 nee Putick) and their seven children, **Ellen** (b.1876), **James** (b.1879), **Harvey** (b.1884), **John** (b.1886), **Levi** (b.1887), **Grace** (b. 1890) and **Dionysia (Dinina)** (b.1891).[75] Frederic is listed at the house until around 1906 when, according to the electoral register, he moved to Salvington.

The next occupiers of *No 2 New Cottages* were the Netley family which consisted of **Charles Netley** (b.1863), his wife **Matilda** (b.1865), originally from Hampshire and four of their six children, **Rhoda** (b.1894), **Gertrude** (b.1898), **Jessie** (b.1900) and **Georgina** (b.1903).[76] The family had previously lived at *The Row* until around 1905 and then moved to this much larger house. The Netleys seem to have been a troubled family. Their eldest child, **Charles** had been found guilty of theft in September 1907 when the policeman giving evidence at his trial appeared to know the family well from previous convictions. He had his own opinion as to the cause of some of the family's problems:

'Supt. Bridges said there was no doubt he had his mother to thank for his present position'.[77]

Further problems were attached to the girls who were continuously being removed from school over the issue of head lice, the school log book tells the tale:

June 11th 1909: *'....Have had to send the Netley's home again this week to have their heads cleaned'*[78]

June 24th 1909: *'In spite of promises (made only the day before yesterday) by a mother to keep her girls heads clean I had to send her girls home again to-day on account of vermin. The family has been complained of continually & I have sent the children home again & again.'*[79]

In the month of April 1910, their son **Alfred** was up before the bench for two charges, stealing eggs and pick pocketing.[80] A week later, his father Charles was accused of stealing a *'pair of gaiters'* at Durrington and was sent to prison for 21 days hard labour. In the case of Alfred, his mother had given him a character reference at the trial, which may or may not have helped his case!

The Netley family in the news

A MISSING BRIDLE

A lad of eighteen, named Charles Netley, was charged with stealing a bridle, valued at 1s., the property of Thomas Green, of Angmering.

The prosecutor left the bridle in a tin outside his stable, and missed it the next day.

A little boy named Sidney Norman said he found part of the harness in a ditch on Clapham Common.

William Heryett, of Durrington, said that the rest of it was brought to him by defendant, and he exchanged one of his brasses for it.

Walter White said he bought the brasses from defendant.

Defendant, against whom there is a previous conviction, said he was very sorry, and Supt. Bridger said there was no doubt he had his mother to thank for his present position.

He was fined £1, or, in default, fourteen days' hard labour.

Worthing Gazette 18th September 1907

FIVE HOURS IN THE POLICE COURT.

The Pickpocket in Beach House Park.

Dishonest Hotel Porter.

LAST week's sitting of the Beach, at the Petty Sessions, was of a protracted nature. The business was in progress when we went to press that afternoon, and the last case was not disposed of until just upon four o'clock. Mr. H. R. P. Wyatt presided at this stage of the proceedings, and with him on the Bench were the Mayor (Councillor J. G. Denton) and Mr. J. B. Dore.

When the Durrington youth, Alfred Reginald Netley, eighteen years of age, was again placed in the dock an additional charge was preferred against him. It was alleged that he had stolen eleven eggs, of the value of elevenpence, belonging to John Wetherall, a farmer at Durrington. It seems that eggs had been missed for a month past, and in consequence

A Pencil Mark

was placed upon some in the fowlhouse. P.C. Jayes kept watch, and saw the accused go up to the nests and take the eleven eggs away.

In the other charge—that of attempted pocket picking in Beach House Park on the evening of Easter Monday—evidence was given by a domestic servant named Gertrude Drake, Harry Wells, George Cheal, Alfred Swain, and P.C. Gibbons; and the accused, who was given a good character by his mother, was sentenced to fourteen days' hard labour for each offence, the sentences to be served separately.

Worthing Gazette 6th April 1910

STOLEN GAITERS AT DURRINGTON.

A farmer named Frederick Charles Collins, of Durrington, was the complainant in a case in which Charles Henry Netley, also of Durrington, was summoned for stealing a pair of gaiters, valued at 4s.

After hearing the evidence the Magistrates committed defendant to Prison for twenty-one days with hard labour.

Worthing Gazette 13th April 1910

Numbers 3 and 4 were an identical set of semi-detached properties, although they were built at least a year later than the first two properties. It was most probably to the same plans and by the same builders. When **Robert Smith** had purchased numbers 1 & 2 in 1900, he purchased these two as well, resulting in him owning all 4 identical properties.

The 1901 census lists **Noah Searle** (b.1862) with his family living in No 3.[81] Noah had been born in Clapham and on 31st March 1883 had married **Ellen Caroline Lillywhite** (b.1863). They had had three children but only two had survived by the 1911 census, **Fanny** (b.1884) and **Albert** (b.1885).[82] Noah was listed in the electoral registers and some street directories right through the period at this address and was named as occupant on the Inland Revenue Valuation.[83] Noah was related to Clement Searle who was lodging across the road in *Elder Tree Cottages*.

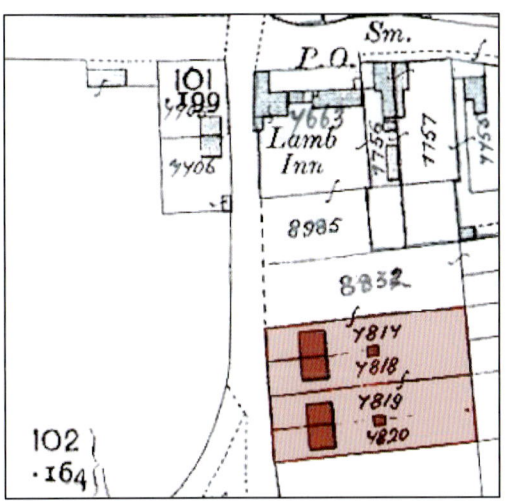

In 1901 there was also an interesting lodger in the Searle household whose name was **George Herbert Varley** (b.1873). He was a horticulturalist who ran a nursery in Greenland Road where, in the following years, he built a house and named the nursery *Downsview*. His story is included in Greenland Road.

No 4 New Cottages was the home of **Thomas Elliott** (b.1852) and his wife **Ellen** (b.1849). According to the 1911 census they had six children.[84] In 1901 the census only records one of those children, a son named **Thomas** (b.1885) living with them as well as a granddaughter named **Alice Victoria** (b.1899).[85] By 1911 the couple were living alone except for their granddaughter Alice who was still living with them.

Excerpt taken from OS 25":1 mile Sheet LXIV: 5
3rd Edition 1912 (NTS)
Inland Revenue Valuation numbers added

Photograph shows *New Cottages* on the right. Worthing Library

Modern photograph showing the four *New Cottages* on the right. © Dave Pryce 2015

11. Elder Tree Cottages, Durrington Lane
(No longer standing)

Elder Tree Cottages consisted of three small cottages sited on the top corner of what is now Pond Lane Park directly opposite *The Lamb Inn*, exactly where the entrance to the park is in modern times. They were originally owned by the Durrington Estate and as such were put up for sale in 1895 when a large part of the estate was sold.[86] The pair were sold for £200 at that time.

LOT 8.
(COLOURED YELLOW ON PLAN.)

A Pair of Flint and Tile Freehold Cottages,

Situated in the Centre of the Village of DURRINGTON.

Each containing Three Bed Rooms, Kitchen, and Scullery. Good GARDENS adjoining, enclosed with Walls, and in which is a good Well.

POSSESSION WILL BE GIVEN ON COMPLETION OF THE PURCHASE.

The 1901 census[87] and street directories list Thomas Saunders in Durrington Street and although it does not name the cottages it is most likely in *Elder Tree Cottages*. Indeed it is probable that this was the address he was living in as far back as the 1891 census.[88] **Thomas Saunders** (b.1846) shared this small cottage with his wife **Fanny** (b.1848), their nephew **William Saunders** and four boarders. The boarders were brothers **Albert & Cephas Mills** both brickmakers, **George Dunlop**, a blacksmith from Scotland who would have been working at *The Forge*, and the inevitable market gardener **Albert Standing**. Albert Standing later married and was living at *No 2 Southview Terrace*.

By 1911 Thomas and Fanny were still living here as was their boarder **George Dunlop**, who was now 85 years old. George was working as an *'Odd Man Labourer'* by this time, not the much more physical work of a blacksmith. They have another boarder named **George Drummer**, who was born in Eastbourne so may have been a relation of Fanny's as she had been born there.

Next door, in 1901, the Harwood family were living in the middle cottage.[89] The cottages are as previously stated, not named on the census, but the Saunders family are confirmed through street directories from 1901, we can assume their neighbours also lived in *Elder Tree Cottages*. **William Harwood** (b.1871) was the occupier with his wife **Sarah** (b.1868 nee Smith) and three boarders; **William & Frederich Love**, both wheelwrights from Hampshire and a farm carter named **Henry Butcher** from Dorset.

The last of the three cottages was occupied by the Norris family according to the 1911 census.[90] **Silas James Norris** (b.1871) and his wife **Lucy** (b.1868 nee Richman) were in the house with four of their five children, **John** (b.1895), **Heber William** (b.1898), **George Arthur** (b. 1904) and **Charles Richard** (b.1907).

The other interesting story illustrated by the 1911 census, is the identity of the two lodgers living with the Norris family at the time, namely **Clement Searle** along with one of his sons, **Thomas**. There had been a family breakdown and separation in the Searle household and although the family were still in the same neighbourhood they were not together. Clement had married **Mary Jane Northeast** in 1891 and had together previously lived in the family home in Coate Street with their six children. Changes had occurred in the couple's lives and they were now living apart. **'Jane' Searle** was claiming to be the wife of **Charles Henry Freeman**, although no marriage was recorded, and they were living with other Searle children and a small child of their own in *Hill Cottages*, Salvington Hill. Clement and Thomas were lodging here in *Elder Tree Cottages*.

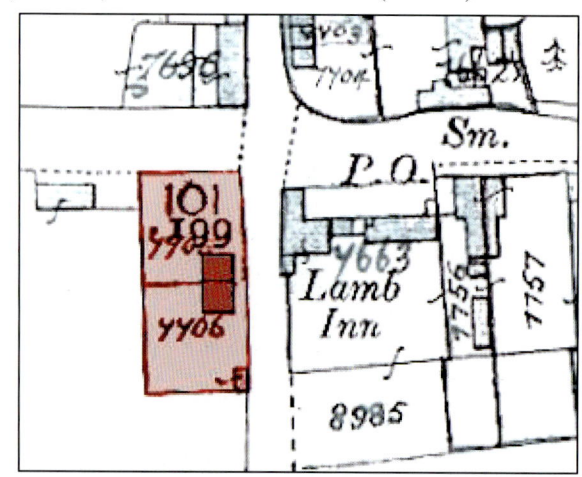

Excerpt taken from OS 25":1 mile Sheet LXIV: 5
3rd Edition 1912 (NTS)
Inland Revenue Valuation numbers added

Photograph showing part of *Elder Tree Cottages* on the right. Owned by Owen Atfield

Later photograph showing the outside of *Elder Tree Cottages*. Owned by Owen Atfield

Modern photograph of the site of *Elder Tree Cottages*. © Dave Pryce 2014

12. Southview Terrace, New Road
(Now No's 28, 30, 32, 34, 36 & 38, New Road)

This terrace comprises a set of six properties in three sets of semi-detached houses on the north side of New Road. We know from the Inland Revenue Valuation that the land upon which No's 2 – 6 was built, was originally purchased in 1907 for £22 a plot, and the building of the houses which would have happened very soon afterwards, cost £200 each.[91] The ownership of the original six properties is a little confusing; No. 1 is listed as being owned by *'Mathew. Seaview Nursery'*.[92] This was **John Kenneth Mathews** who ran his nursery in Salvington Road. The other five are, according to the Inland Revenue Assessment, owned by **Thomas Wood**, who is listed as a fruit grower in Durrington street directories 1901-1905 but who lived outside of the village firstly in Broadwater and a little later in Amberley, Sussex. However, the electoral registers only list **Thomas Wood** as the owner of No 3 – 6, which means the ownership of No 2 is unsure.

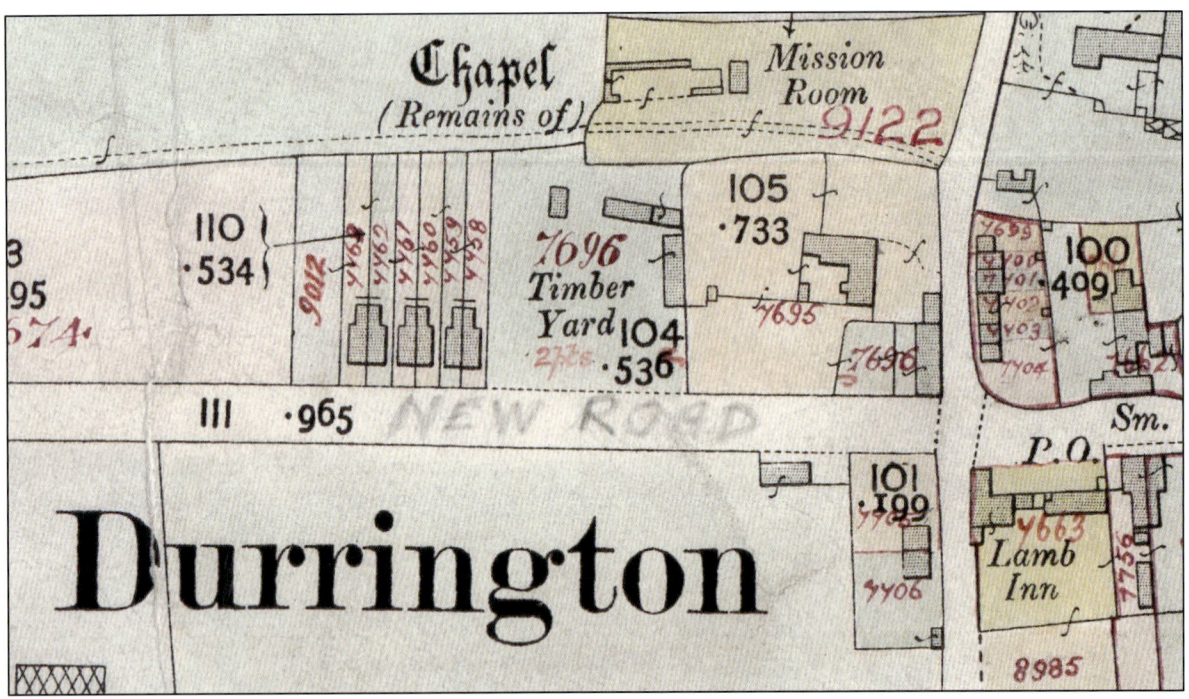

Excerpt taken from OS 25":1 mile Sheet LXIV: 5 3rd Edition 1912 (NTS)
Inland Revenue Valuation numbers added

The occupancy for the period is as follows:

The first of the properties was the home of **Eli Greenyer**, who lived here up until shortly before the 1911 census, when we know he moved to *5 Highdown View Terrace*. The next occupants were **Edwin Thomas Foster** (b.1885), his wife **Katherine** (b.1883) and their daughter **Ida Caroline** (b.1910).[93] Edwin was a nursery gardener.

No 2 Southview Terrace, according to the 1911 census,[94] was the home of Albert **James Standing** (b.1878) and his wife **Harriet** (b.1878). Living with them were their two sons, **Ernest Gordon** (b.1905) and **Maurice Leslie** (b.1906) along with a step-son from Harriet's first marriage **Stanley Albert Knight** (b.1896). Stanley was also working in the market gardens of Durrington.

No 3 was a home shared by two families; any earlier occupants have not so far been traced. The Kent family had three rooms in the house, while the Cook family were listed as lodgers and only had two rooms. This must have made living conditions a little cramped. The Kent family consisted of **Frank Kent** (b.1873) a market gardener, and his wife **Alice** (b.1882 nee Dearlove) with their two children **Alice** (b.1908) and **Rose Mary** (b.1910).[95] The family had moved here shortly after Rose's birth, as they are first listed in directories for 1911 and appeared on the 1911 census. They may have moved here from Littlehampton as Rose's birth was registered there. The second family who lodged with the Kents was headed by a jobbing gardener from Worthing named **Charles Cook** (b.1897) and his wife **Ada** (b.1886), along with their new born daughter **Hilda Alice** (b.1911) and a little nephew named **Norman Nickolas** born in 1898 in Brighton according to the census returns but no birth of that name was registered anywhere in England so he remains something of a mystery.[96]

No 4 South View Terrace is listed as 'unoccupied' on the 1911 census and any earlier occupants have not been identified.

James Henry Holden (b.1879), his wife **Charlotte** (b.1877) and their four sons **Harold** (b.1903), **John** (b.1904), **Frederick** (b.1906) and **Albert** (b.1907) are listed at No 5 on the 1911 census.[97] It is unlikely that they had lived here from the building of the property as their last two sons were born in Broadwater. They must have moved to Durrington around 1911 as the electoral register also lists his return to the village at this time. He was a nurseryman by profession as was his father. James was the son of **Frederick** and **Mary Holden,** who had lived in Durrington for over 20 years, originally moved to the village from Storrington. The 1901 census had previously listed James with his parents in *2 New Cottages*, Durrington Lane.[98]

The last of the semi-detached row of houses became the home of Walter White and his family.[99] Walter had been the landlord of *The Lamb Inn* for many years with his first wife Elizabeth and had moved here with his young second wife Harriett and the children in 1906 after he gave up the licence for the Inn. He continued to run his carter business, which he had begun when he was living at *The Lamb*, from these premises.

Modern photograph of *Southview Terrace*. © Dave Pryce 2016

---

[1] 1911 census RG14/5342 sch 131 (TNA)
[2] IR58/94204 No. 7694 (TNA)
[3] Linfield, p3
[4] Worthing Gazette 10th December 1902 p6
[5] Worthing Gazette 22nd March 1911 p7
[6] IR58/94206 No. 7801 (TNA)
[7] Lindfield p12
[8] 1911 census RG14/5342 sch 148 (TNA)
[9] IR58/94204 No. 7665 (TNA)
[10] Beswick, p192
[11] Beswick, p43
[12] Worthing Gazette 24th September 1902 p5 & 1st October 1902 p5
[13] IR58/94205 No. 7757, 7756, 7765 and IR59/94217 No. 8985 (TNA)
[14] IR58/94205b No. 7779 (TNA)
[15] 1901 census RG13/957 ff.78 (TNA)
[16] 1911 census RG14/5342 sch 142 (TNA)

[17] 1901 census RG13/957 ff.79 (TNA)
[18] 1911 census RG14/5342 sch 141 (TNA)
[19] 1901 census RG13/957 ff.79 (TNA)
[20] 1891 census RG12/835 ff.39 (TNA)
[21] 1911 census RG14/5342 sch 140 (TNA)
[22] IR58/94205 No. 7781 (TNA)
[23] 1901 census RG13/957 ff. 79 (TNA)
[24] 1881 census RG11/1118 ff. 22; 1891 census & 1891 census RG12/835 ff. 39 (TNA)
[25] 1901 census RG13/957 ff.79; 1911 census RG14/5342 sch 138 (TNA)
[26] Worthing Gazette 5th April 1905 p5 & Worthing Gazette 12th April 1905 p6
[27] 1911 census RG14/5342 sch 137 (TNA)
[28] 1901 census RG13/957 ff. 60 (TNA)
[29] 1901 census RG13/957 ff.79 (TNA)
[30] 1911 census RG14/5355 sch 197 (TNA)
[31] London Gazette 18th May 1923
[32] IR58/94204 No.7664 & 7666 (TNA)
[33] Durrington Estate Sale Catalogue July 1895, Lot 4. SC/WSL/000123a (Worthing Library)
[34] Linfield, p 1
[35] 1901 census RG13/957 ff. 78 (TNA)
[36] 1911 census RG14/5342 sch 143 (TNA)
[37] 1911 census RG14/5342 sch 132 (TNA)
[38] Worthing Gazette 22nd March 1911 p7
[39] IR58/94205 No. 7735 (TNA)
[40] 1911 census RG14/5342 sch 133 (TNA)
[41] IR58/94205 No.7732 (TNA)
[42] 1911 census RG14/5342 sch 134 (TNA)
[43] Durrington Parish Register
[44] IR58/94204 No. 7733 (TNA)
[45] 1901 census RG13/957: ff.79 (TNA)
[46] Worthing Gazette 28th April 1909 p5
[47] 1861 census RG9/585 ff.101 (TNA)
[48] 1891 census RG12/439 ff.6 (TNA)
[49] 1911 census RG14/5342 sch 136 (TNA)
[50] IR58/94204 No. 7731 (TNA)
[51] 1901 census RG13/582 ff.86 (TNA)
[52] Linfield. p10
[53] 1911 census RG14/ 5342 sch 125 (TNA
[54] Worthing Gazette 24th January 1912 p8
[55] IR58/94204 No. 7786 (TNA)
[56] Worthing Gazette April 10th 1912 p8
[57] IR58/94204 No. 7810 (TNA)
[58] www.britishlistedbuildings.co.uk (No. 432849) viewed 3/7/2012
[59] RG14/5342 sch 122 (TNA)
[60] IR58/94205 No. 7810 (TNA)
[61] 1901 census RG13/957 ff.79 (TNA)
[62] Worthing Gazette 22nd March 1911 p7
[63] Durrington Council School Admissions Register (Held at the School)
[64] 1901 census RG13/957 ff. 79 (TNA)
[65] Durrington Estate Sale Catalogue July 1895, Lot 4. SC/WSL/000123a (Worthing Library)
[66] IR58/94204 No. 7668 (TNA)
[67] 1911 census RG14/5342 sch 123 (TNA)
[68] IR58/94204 No. 7710 (TNA)
[69] 1911 census RG14/5342 sch 124 (TNA)
[70] IR58/94204 No. 7787 (TNA)
[71] IR58/94204 No.7787 (TNA)
[72] 1881 census RG11/2086 ff.39 (TNA)
[73] 1901 census RG13/957 ff.77 (TNA)
[74] 1911 census RG14/5342 sch 118 (TNA)
[75] 1901 census RG13/957 ff. 78 (TNA)
[76] 1911 census RG14/5342 sch 119 (TNA)
[77] Worthing Gazette 18th September 1907 p.5g
[78] Durrington Council School Log Book 1908-1928. June 11th 1909 p.26
[79] Durrington Council School Log Book 1908-1928 June 24th 1909 p27
[80] Worthing Gazette 18th September 1907 p.
[81] 1901 census RG13/957 ff. 78 (TNA)
[82] 1911 census RG14/5342 Sch 120 (TNA)
[83] IR58/94204 No. 7819 (TNA)
[84] 1911 census RG14/5342 Sch 120 (TNA)
[85] 1901 census RG13/957 ff. 78 (TNA)
[86] Durrington Estate Catalogue July 1895. Lot 8
[87] 1901 census RG13/957 ff. 79 (TNA)
[88] 1891 census RG12/837 ff. 134 (TNA)

[89] 1901 census RG13/957 ff. 79 (TNA)
[90] 1911 census RG14/5342 sch 117 (TNA)
[91] IR58/94204 No's 7758-7763 (TNA)
[92] IR58/94205 No. 7758 (TNA)
[93] 1911 census RG14/5342 sch 110 (TNA)
[94] 1911 census RG14/5342 sch 111 (TNA)
[95] 1911 census RG14/5342 sch 113 (TNA)
[96] 1911 census RG14/5342 sch 112 (TNA)
[97] 1911 census RG14/5342 sch 114 (TNA)
[98] 1911 census RG13/957 ff. 78 (TNA)
[99] 1911 census RG14/5342 sch 115 (TNA)

Chapter 2
Durrington Lane (North - Durrington Hill)

Introduction

This chapter continues the northwards journey of what was called either Durrington Lane, Durrington Street or, in more modern times, Durrington Hill. It runs from the junction with Salvington Road and New Road northwards until it reaches the Arundel Road at the top. In the Edwardian period the road included some of the larger properties including the *Manor House* and the field almost opposite which contained the site of the ruins of the old parish church, where *St. Symphorian's Church* now stands.

Undated drawing of the ruins of the old parish church in Durrington.
Worthing Library

View looking north up Durrington Lane with *Holly Grove* on the right and *Elm Bank Cottages* on the left. Worthing Library

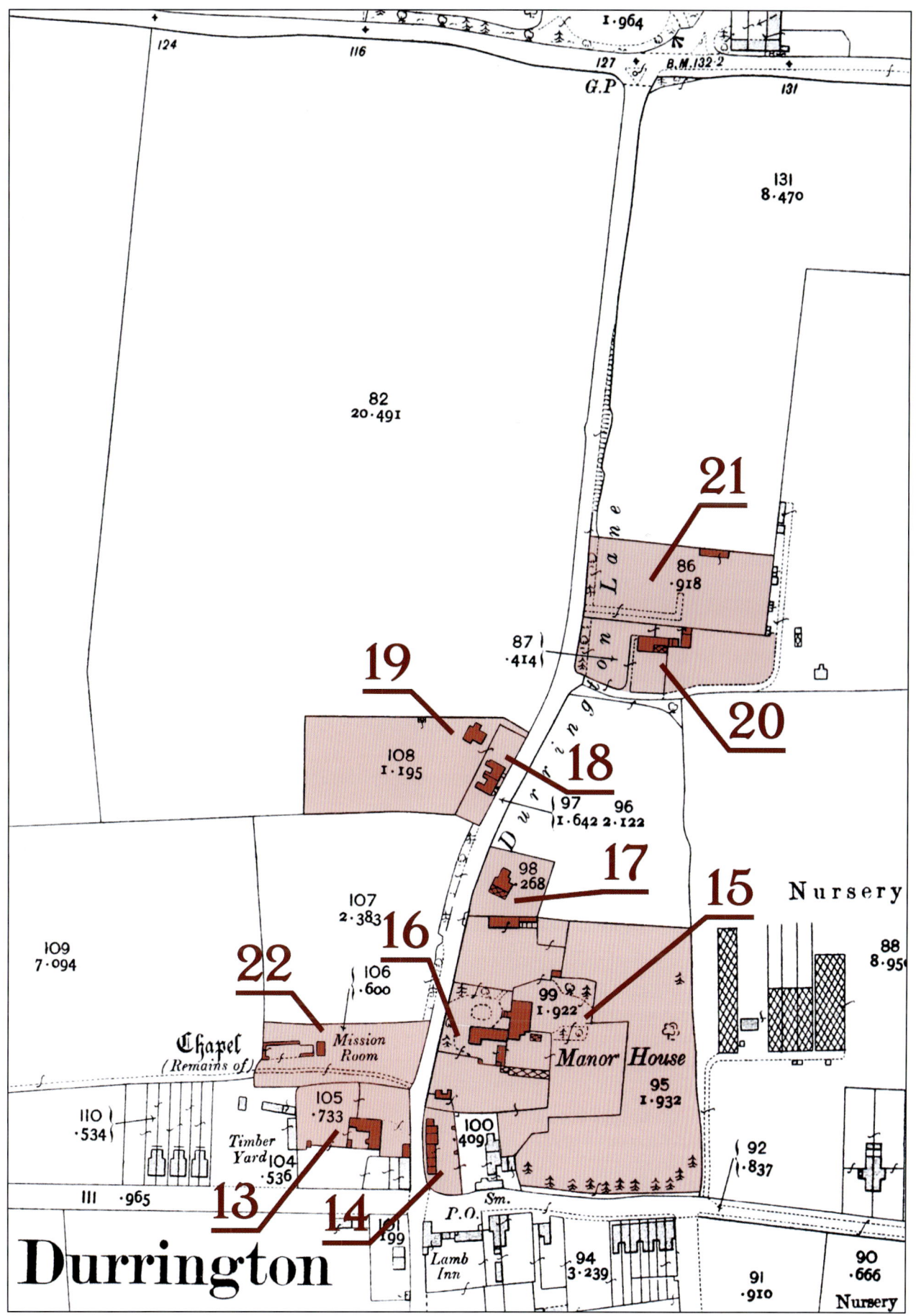

Excerpt taken from OS 25":1 mile Sheet LXIV: 5 3rd Edition 1912 (NTS)

13. Greenstede, Durrington Lane
(Now Greenstede House, Durrington Hill)

Greenstede is the first property on the western side of the road sited on the corner with New Road. It is a Grade II listed building described as follows:

> *'Probably early C18. 2 storeys. Very steep slated roof, taller than the house below, with upturn over plain wooden eaves. 5 evenly-spaced casement windows, the lower ones camber-headed. Both slightly left of centre are a ridge chimney and the porch, which is a later addition. (with pointed opening and jutting shoulders.)'* [1]

The house was owned by Henry Overington and although the house was not listed by name on the 1901 census the names of **Alfred & Amy Overington** are listed just before the *Manor House* so this is most probably *Greenstede*.[2]

The 1911 census and street directories for the period list **Amy Booth** as the next occupier.[3] **Caroline Amy Booth** (b.1863) came originally from London and moved to Durrington a short time before the census when she rented the property and began to run a boarding house. In 1891 Amy was working as a 'cook' in Beckenham, Kent, in the house of a builder **Howard Trollope** and his family. Here she would have honed the culinary and organisational skills enabling her to run her boarding house in Durrington.[4]

The 1911 census lists her, aged 48, as head of the household at *Greenstede*. She had three boarders staying with her: an 84 year old widowed lady from Blackfriars in London named **Emma Beckham** (b.c1827), **Sarah Jane Bursell** (b.c1854) from Birmingham and a seven year old girl from Southwark named **Constance Josephine G. Hornsey** (b.1903). Why such a young child is on her own and a long way from home is unclear, maybe she was sent to recuperate from an illness, but we do know that in the 1911 census, she was recorded as *'School'*. The admissions register for the school shows that she became a pupil in June 1911 and left the school again in March the following year with no reason given. It may be she returned home.[5]

Emily Beckton, another of the boarders in 1911 was not so fortunate. On the 3rd December 1911 she died while still boarding at *Greenstede*. Her death notice appeared in The Times confirming that she had died in Durrington.[6]

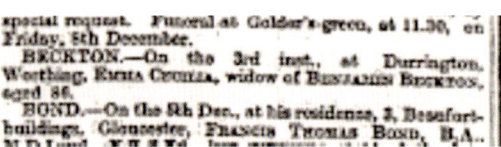

Death notice of Emily Beckton in The Times

The Inland Revenue Valuation for this property tells us that it had three bedrooms and the added luxury of *'1 dressing room'*. It also states the existence of a *'Walled in garden'* which is still clearly visible in the modern photograph of the rear of the property.[7]

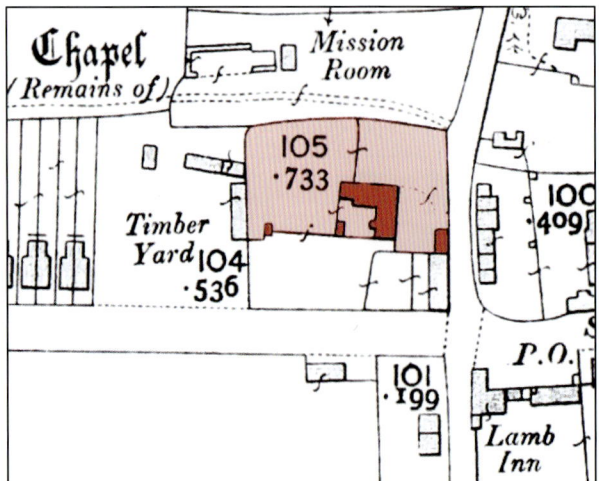

Excerpt taken from OS 25":1 mile Sheet LXIV: 5 3rd Edition 1912 (NTS)

Greenstede with ivy covered wall at the front and the rebuilt parish church, *St. Symphorian's* next door. © Dave Pryce 2013

Photograph of *Greenstede* showing the house during the period.   Worthing Library

Modern view of *Greenstede* showing walled garden. © Dave Pryce 2015

14. The Row/Terrace, Durrington Lane
(Now No 2, Flint Cottage and No 4, Willow Cottage, Durrington Hill)

This is a row of six cottages built on a small plot of land situated on the corner of Salvington Road and Durrington Hill. They were variously called *The Row* or *The Terrace* during different periods and in different sources, although locally they were nicknamed *Beetle Alley* owing to the damp conditions which drew many insects and beetles to the properties. The whole row had been sold in 1895 along with the *Manor House* to Edward Mills. In 1902 he again sold both the *Manor House* and *The Row*, the latter being sold to **W. Royal** of Warwick Road, Worthing who rented the cottages to various occupants.[8]

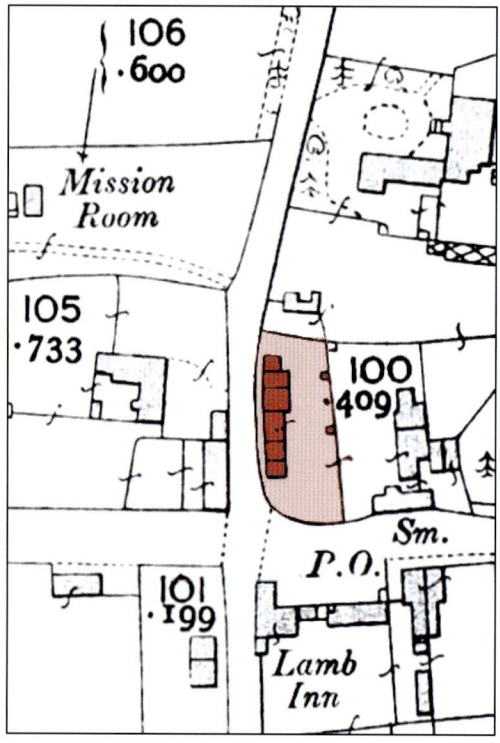

Excerpt taken from OS 25":1 mile Sheet LXIV: 5 3rd Edition 1912 (NTS)

The first of the cottages, travelling from the south up the road, was the home of a long term resident. In 1901 **John Norris** (b.1832), a retired shepherd, was already living at No 1 with his wife **Ann** (b.1843).[9] They continued in the cottage throughout the whole period also being listed on the 1911 census.[10] This plot had one of the largest pieces of garden stretching round the corner towards *The Forge* in Salvington Road.

John Joseph Tree (b.1868) and his wife **Eleanor** (b.1867 nee Heather) were the occupants of No 2 at the beginning of the century.[11] By 1903 they had moved on to *Cutler's Cottages* in Ashacre Lane. **Arthur James Varndell** (b.1875), his wife **Ellen** (b.1873 nee Moseley) and their children **Ernest James** (b.1900) and **George Charles** (b.1902) took up residence in the cottage around 1903. They had their third child **Elsie May** here in 1907 and are listed at the address in the 1911 census.[12] An entry in the school log-book in 1908 regarding the boys illustrates the health issues children faced during this period:

> *'Mrs Varndell sent a note stating that her two boys had heavy colds & sore throats. These symptoms are significant in the light of the others case of sickness.'*[13]

The state of the cottage they lived in would not have been helpful in recovery from illness but with other diseases around at the time it was a necessary precaution to exclude the children from mixing with others and spreading potentially deadly infections. Both influenza and scarlatina had been reported at the school in the previous week and obviously no-one was sure what illness the boys may have caught.

The occupant listed for No 3 on the 1901 census is **Mary Heather** (b.1851).[14] She was the mother of Eleanor Tree who was living next door at No 2. By 1909 **Louis James Knight** (b.1881) a roadman and his wife, **Winifred Frances** (b.1883 nee Wood) had left their previous home in *Duffield Cottages*, Stone Lane and moved into No 3 where they were to live for some years. They had three daughters, **Florence Winifred** (b.1903), **Adeline Mary** (b.1906) and **Alice Edith** (b.1910).

No 4 was unoccupied in 1901 with the first listed occupant being **Peter Woolgar** from 1905–1910 according to the electoral register; nothing else is known about this resident. The 1911 census lists **Charles (Chad) Richards** (b.1881) with his wife **Florence Annie** (b.1881 nee Norris) and son **Alfred** (b.1908) but this family also moved on very quickly to live in *Elm Bank Cottages* where Charles is listed on the electoral register from 1912.[15]

No 5 was the home of **Charles** (b.1863) and **Matilda Netley** (b.1865) in 1901[16] with their children. Charles was listed as a market gardener and we know from the previous chapter that they later moved into one of the *New Cottages* around 1905. The next resident to move into this cottage was **Harriet Saunders** (b.1836) with her son **William** (b.1859) and it is they who are registered on the 1911 census.[17] William was working in the market gardens as a carter, no doubt one of the carters who took the produce to *Durrington Station* where it was transported by train to London and elsewhere.

In the sixth and most northerly of the cottages was another family whose home it was throughout the whole period. On the 1901 census we find a lady, **Mary Bean** (b.1859), who was sharing the cottage with her husband **Charles** (b.1833) and their family.[18] Charles died in 1909 and Mary continued living in the cottage with **Thomas** (b.1890) her son, who was a nurseryman by occupation. We find Thomas' name appearing regularly in the local newspaper as a member of the Durrington cricket team during 1911. It is interesting to note that the cottages with the continuous occupiers were at each end of the terrace. Looking at the plots they both had larger areas of land attached to them rather than the tiny plots of the middle cottages which may have made living conditions slightly more favourable.

The Inland Revenue Valuation lists each cottage with a separate number but does not add any further details except to name the owner and a few financial details.[19] Other names have appeared in directories at *The Row* but which of the cottages has not been identified. In 1901 **William Henry Boxold** is listed in the street directory at *The Row* whereas he is at *Rose Cottage* in Stone Lane on the 1901 census, William died in 1903 aged 26 but we do not know where his widow moved to. Street directories for 1903 list **George Lillywhite** and **G. Langham** at the address but again we do not know which cottages they were living in.

A photograph of *The Row* taken around 1930. Worthing Library

Modern photograph showing the two new cottages built on the site of the original six cottages. © Dave Pryce 2015

4

LOT 2.
(COLOURED PINK ON PLAN).

A

VALUABLE FREEHOLD PROPERTY

EMBRACING AN AREA OF NEARLY

146 ACRES,

OF

VERY SUPERIOR ARABLE & PASTURE LAND,

Lying well together, intersected by good hard Roads, and well suited for a Pedigree Stock or Pleasure Farm, or more especially

For Market Garden and Fruit Cultivation,

Which forms a large and rapidly increasing industry in this locality.

The Manor House

Is a very comfortable Old-fashioned Residence of moderate size, part of which has been reconstructed in recent years, and is pleasantly situated in the VILLAGE OF DURRINGTON, about a mile-and-a-half from WEST WORTHING STATION. It stands a short distance from the Road, with gravelled Carriage Sweep in front, and comprises—

On the UPPER FLOOR,—Two Bed Rooms.

FIRST FLOOR (reached by Front and Back Staircases),—Five Bed Rooms, w.c., and Housemaid's Closet.

GROUND FLOOR,—Porch and Entrance HALL, with Passage through to Garden Entrance, DINING ROOM, DRAWING ROOM, and STUDY or SMOKING ROOM, Kitchen, Larder, Two Store Rooms, Scullery, and Large Cellar in Basement.

PLEASANT LAWN AND FLOWER GARDEN,

Well protected with Shrubs and Plantations, and adjoining is

Capital walled Kitchen Garden with Greenhouse

In which is situated a SMALL COTTAGE, now used as Store Rooms.

THE STABLING

Comprises Paved Yard with Double Coach-house having Loft over, Stable of Two Stalls, Loose Box, and Harness Room with Three good Grooms' Rooms over, and another Gig House. In the Paddock adjoining the House is a Cow Stall for Four, Tool House, Store Room, and Three Pigstyes. **TWO SETS OF FARM BUILDINGS**, Nos. 72 and 75 on Plan, the former comprising Enclosed Yard with Two Cattle Sheds, and the latter comprising Barn, Corn Store, and Enclosed Yard with Cattle Shed. Also

A ROW OF SIX LABOURERS' COTTAGES,

(No. 45 pt. on Plan), each containing Four Rooms, with Good Allotment Gardens (No. 42 pt. on Plan). Also a WORKSHOP and YARD (No. 51 pt. on Plan).

The Lands are large and convenient for working, and in addition to being of a capital deep Soil are in a good state of cultivation, having been in the occupation of the present Tenant, a noted Breeder of Pedigree Southdown Sheep, for some 40 years.

The following is a Schedule—

No. on Plan	Description	Area A. R. P.	Total Area A. R. P.	No. on Plan	Description	Area A. R. P.	Total Area A. R. P.
	LANDS (part of Manor Farm).				Brought forward...		137 1 25
28	Arable	44 0 20			THE MANOR HOUSE AND GROUNDS.		
40	Ditto	30 0 32		46	Garden	0 0 26	
42 pt.	Allotments	0 2 0		47	House and Grounds	1 1 33	
45 pt.	Cottages	0 0 29		48	Pasture	2 1 30	
52	Arable	21 0 8		50	Pasture	0 0 29	
53	Arable	26 0 12		51 pt.	Pasture	4 1 34	
72	Buildings	0 0 30					8 0 12
74	Arable	4 1 6			Mr. OVERINGTON'S Holding.		
75	Buildings	0 0 16		51 pt.	Workshop	0 0 5	0 0 5
76	Arable	2 2 33					
77 pt.	Ditto	7 3 39					
			137 1 25		TOTAL...	A.	145 2 2
	Carried forward...		137 1 25				

The Manor House and Meadows adjoining, containing 8 A. 0 R. 12 P., are at present let to Mr. GEORGE SAUNDERS at a Rent of £75. per Annum, upon a tenancy which can be determined at Lady-day next.

The Lands forming part of Manor Farm are at present let with the Farm, but the present tenant is quitting at Michaelmas next, so that Possession of that portion may be obtained on Completion of the Purchase.

The Workshop and Yard (No. 51 pt. on Plan) is let to Mr. HORACE OVERINGTON, on a yearly tenancy, at a Rent of £5. per Annum.

NOTE.—The late Owner of the Property entered into covenants with Mr. ROBERT HOLMES, the Owner of the Land adjoining No. 28 on Plan, respecting the Right of Way through Nos. 33 and 38 pt. as shown on Plan, and as to a new Road in lieu thereof along the Southern boundary of Nos. 28 and 48, as shown on plan, between the points marked A, B and C, and as mentioned in the Sixth Condition of Sale.

The Land Tax upon this Lot has been redeemed, with the exception of about 15 Acres (Nos. 72, 74, 75, 76 and 77 on Plan), which are still subject thereto.

Excerpt taken from the Durrington Estate Sale Catalogue July 1895 (page4) Listing the *'Row of Six Labourers Cottages'* which was *The Row*

15. The Manor House, Durrington Lane
(Now The Manor House, Durrington Hill)

This is a Grade II listed building[20] with an 18th century frontage, although the property itself is based on a much older manor house. The house was part of the Durrington Estate sold to **Edward Mills** in 1895, along with *The Row* and other land and property for £7,000. The *Manor House* was again sold in 1903 to **James Newham** who maintained ownership throughout this period. The property was, and still is, *'approached by carriage drive.'* according to the Inland Revenue Valuation. It was further described as an *'Old residence of good appearance'*.[21] As the photograph clearly shows, it was built of red brick with a Horsham slate roof. The ground floor comprised of three reception rooms, a kitchen and store rooms, while there were four bedrooms and a dressing room upstairs, as well as other attic and adjoining rooms. The house had a cottage standing to the side of the carriage drive, which throughout the Edwardian period was called *Manor Cottage*. It has also been listed as *Maun Cottage*, and in modern times is known as *The Dower House*. The whole of the site including house, cottage and other land covered 3 acres.

During the Edwardian period it was the home of various tenants. The first were named on the 1901 census as **Edward Otto Van der Medon** (b.1863), his wife **Florence (Frances) Daisey** (b.1863 nee Bruff), their three sons **Harold** (b.1891), **Reginald** (b.1893) and **Geoffrey** (b.1895) plus two servants.[22] Edward was from a family of bankers and solicitors born in London but originating from Germany. While they were living in the *Manor House* they had a little girl named **Louisa May** (b.1901). The street directories list them living here until around 1903 when we know the house was sold.

The next occupant was the new owner, **James Newnham** (b.1849). The Inland Revenue Valuation confirms that he purchased the house and surrounding land on 9th June 1903 for £1950. James and his family lived in the property for some years before he built and moved into a new house which he named *Holly Grove*. This house had been erected on the northern part of his land, a little further up Durrington Hill. He vacated the *Manor House* around 1909 to move into his new home and the street directories and electoral registers begin listing the new occupant as **William L. Robinson** of whom nothing else is known.

In 1911, a very interesting American born widow **Ellen Greppo**, had moved into the *Manor House* according to the census returns.[23] Why such a lady should choose Durrington to live in for a short period may be explained by the events that were happening in her family in the months leading up to her arrival in Durrington

Ellen Douglas Bateman was born in the United States in 1844, the daughter of theatrical parents. Her father was the actor and theatre manager **Hezekiah Linthicum Bateman** from St. Louis, and her mother **Sidney Frances Cowell** (b.1813) was the daughter of an English actor, **Joseph Cowell**. Sidney Cowell may not have been a great actress herself, but she raised her children within the theatrical world. Three of her daughters **Kate** (b.1843), **Ellen** (b.1845) and **Virginia** (b.1853) became actresses. The two oldest daughters had become child stars in the USA and England, known as 'The Bateman Children', when they were only seven and eight years old. However, Ellen ceased acting very early in 1860 when at 16 years of age she married a Frenchman, **Claude Greppo**. Claude was a silk merchant who ran a successful business in the United States. They spent the next years further developing the business and travelling many times between the USA and Europe including the United Kingdom. They had five children, **Claudie** (b.1861), **Theo** (b.1868), **Robert** (b.1870), **Ellen** (b.1873) and **Francis** (b.1875).

The connections with this theatrical family and the United Kingdom were strengthened when Ellen's father, Hezekiah, moved from America to England to manage The Lyceum Theatre in London. Ellen's youngest son, Francis also moved to England and began to work as an actor and manager. By 1910 Francis had been appointed as the stage manager at The Garrick Theatre and it is at this time a small paragraph appears in The Times which may give us a clue to the reason behind Francis' and his mother's occupation of the *Manor House*. Francis Greppo was reported as missing............[24]

MISSING LONDON STAGE MANAGER.—The relatives and friends of Mr. Francis Greppo, stage manager of the Garrick Theatre, are making inquiries as to his whereabouts. Mr. Greppo was last at the theatre on Friday, September 23. On the following morning he had breakfast at the Garrick Hotel, Charing Cross-road, where he had been staying, and subsequently went out. He has not returned since, although he left his personal belongings behind. No reason for his absence is known. His relatives, and those associated with him at the theatre, are without any information which might form the basis of inquiries. Mr. Greppo is about 40 years of age.

Times article reporting the missing Francis Greppo in 1910

Francis had married an English actress named **Irene Rooke**, although the marriage appears to have been unsuccessful. Was it an unhappy marriage or the stress of running a large London theatre that caused him to go missing as reported? We may never know, as the newspapers do not give any further information. All we can safely confirm is that shortly afterwards he is living with his mother in Durrington.

They did not stay for very long but the pace of life, the climate and its distance from the hustle and bustle of theatrical life in London may have helped in Francis' recovery. I have traced no mention of the stir and interest having such a colourful pair of Americans in Durrington living in the village may have had on the villagers. They do not seem to have had any great impact on Worthing either, as nothing is mentioned in the Worthing Gazette of them attending any functions in the town. If Francis was here for his recovery they may have lived very quietly away from the social scene of the town.

Whatever the reality behind the facts, Francis appears to have decided to change his life completely. He left England, probably alone, leaving his wife and family and went to Australia. On 30th August 1914, he joined the Australian army using the name 'Francis Greville' on his military papers.[25] He returned to Europe to fight in the First World War as a soldier and was killed in August 1918. He is buried in Heath Cemetery, Harbonnieres.

The next occupant was named on the Inland Revenue Valuation as **Percy Lovell**. Lovell was a nurseryman and fruit grower who lived at the *Manor House* and ran *Manor Nurseries* on land behind the house which was accessed from Salvington Road, for many years. Malcolm Linfield describes this nursery:

*'Also on the northern side of Salvington Road, at its western end, and quite close to the Lamb Inn, was the nursery established by **Percy Lovell** at Manor House in 1911. Originally an architect in London, Lovell specialised in growing carnations and made quite a name for himself.'*[26]

At the time when these glasshouses were erected, they were allegedly the largest in the county. No doubt Lovell's knowledge of buildings from his early career as an architect was a real asset in this venture.

The glasshouses of *Manor Nurseries*. One of the men standing outside is probably Percy Lovell.
Worthing Library

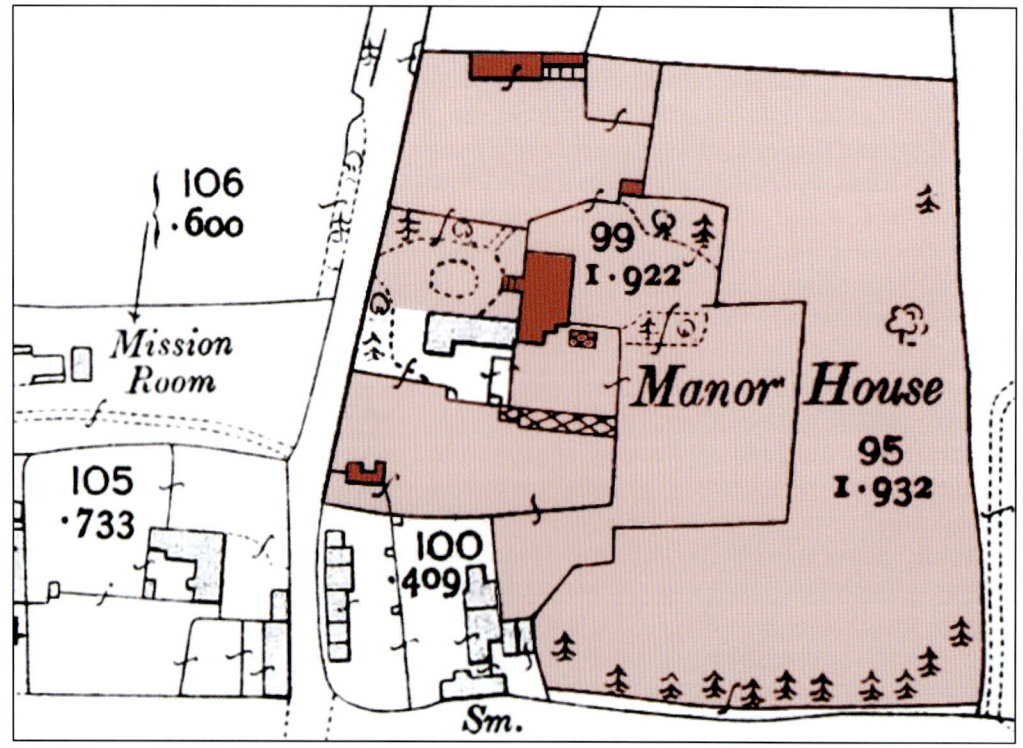

Excerpt taken from OS 25":1 mile Sheet LXIV: 5 3rd Edition 1912 (NTS)

Modern Photograph of *The Manor House*. © Dave Pryce 2016

16. Manor Cottage, Durrington Lane
(Now The Dower House, Durrington Hill)

This is a small cottage originally on the same plot of land as *The Manor House* sitting to the side of the front carriage drive. According to the Inland Revenue Valuation it consisted of three rooms and a scullery in 1913.[27] It was listed on the 1901 census as the home of a groom and domestic gardener **James Doick** (b.1865), his wife **Fanny** (b.1868 nee Whittington) and six of their nine children.[28] Three of these children **Winnifred** (b.1895), **Walter Harold** (b.1898) and **Maud** (b.1899) had been born in Durrington. How long James had been working as a groom and gardener at *The Manor House* is unknown, but he was listed as living in Durrington Street, most probably at this address, in electoral registers and street directories up to 1902. We do know that his daughter Maud died very young in 1901.

The next documented occupant was **George Lillywhite** (b.1838), who is listed on the 1911 census as a 75 year old farm carter.[29] He is in the cottage with his wife **Mary Ann** (b.1853 nee Wedge/Widge) who originally came from Fishbourne. In 1901, George had been boarding in or near *The Lamb Inn*,[30] and then according to the electoral register, he had moved to *The Row* before taking up residence at *Manor Cottage* not long before the next census was taken. This leaves the possibility of other occupants between the censuses but none have so far been identified.

Modern photograph of *Manor Cottage*. © Dave Pryce 2014

17. Holly Grove, Durrington Lane
(No longer standing)

The owner and occupier of this property was James Newnham. The house was built around 1908-1909 by James Newnham as his new family home. James was not a complete newcomer to Durrington, having started to purchase land and property in the village some years earlier. He owned the *Manor House* and cottage situated just south of *Holly Grove* and for some years the house had been the Newnham family home, only moving to *Holly Grove* when the building work was completed. The Inland Revenue Valuation from 1913 states that the house had cost £400 to build, and describes it as a *Modern villa*.[31]

James Newnham was born in Fletching, Sussex in 1849, the eldest son of James and Ann Newnham. In 1874 James married **Eliza Scott** whose father was the farm bailiff at Perriman's Farm in Buxted. Although James father was listed as an agricultural labourer, it is clear that James began to make his way in the world and improve his financial situation, as by 1871, he and Eliza were living in Fletching, and James was the owner of 4½ acres of land. Eliza at this time is listed as the school mistress, so it is probable that with two wages and careful planning they were making the most of their income.[32] By 1881, James has become a *'Coal Merchant'* employing one boy,[33] and by 1891 he was listed as a *'Coal Merchant and Farmer'* in Fletching with Eliza, four children and a servant.[34] By the 1901 census, the family are still to be found farming and running the business in Fletching.[35] Things began to change for James and by 1903 he had begun to purchase land and property in Durrington, including *The Manor House,* where he and his family lived between 1904 and 1909 until they made the move to *Holly Grove.* James had bought a plot of land to the north of *The Manor House* and attached part of the land to the old house, whilst he developed the other part and had *Holly Grove* built. The Inland Revenue Valuation also mentions that around 1909, he erected some new glasshouses on the site.[36]

James was a respected farmer in Durrington as well as being a landowner. He was elected to serve on the Parish Council in 1910, which he did for some years.

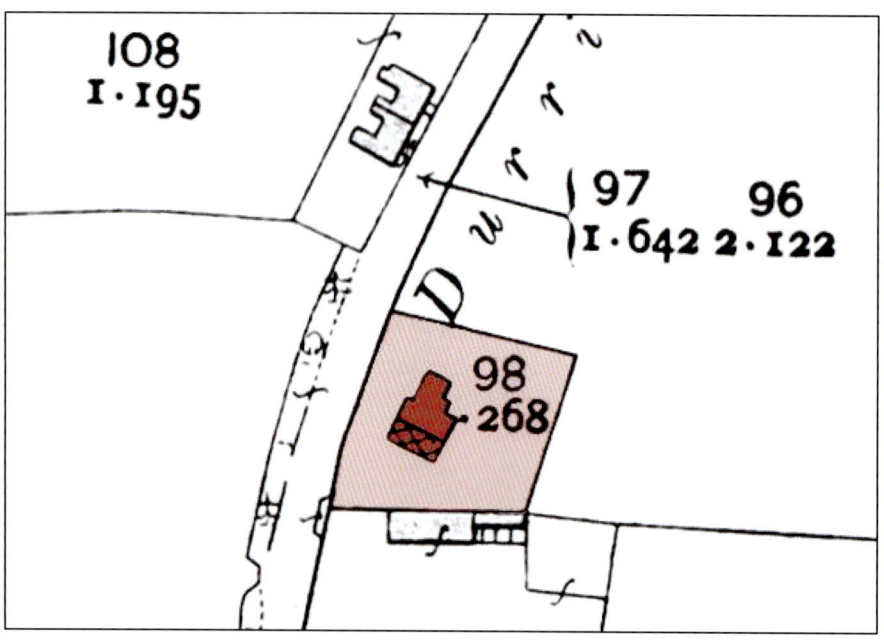

Excerpt taken from OS 25":1 mile Sheet LXIV: 5 3rd Edition 1912 (NTS)

18. Elm Bank Cottages, Durrington Lane
(Now No's 1 & 2 Elm Bank Cottages, Durrington Hill)

Elm Bank Cottages had already been standing for some years before they were sold as part of the Durrington Estate Sale in 1895.[37] In the catalogue, they are described as *'A Pair of Modern Freehold Cottages'* suggesting they were not very old. By the time of the Inland Revenue Valuation, however, in October 1912, they are described as *'Old Boulder built cottages'*. Both cottages were purchased a couple of years after the original sale by **W. R. & Mrs. Mills** of Gratwicke Road in Worthing at a price of £370 for the pair.

The earliest inhabitants have not been identified, but we do know that soon after the 1901 census, **Henry and Sarah Thompson** moved into one of the two cottages. This was to be their first home when they moved to Durrington. Henry had previously worked as a brickmaker in Rustington, but on marrying **Sarah Ann Thomas** in 1901 they chose to move into *Elm Bank Cottages* to begin their life together. Village memories tell of him being crippled in one leg due to an accident and travelling around the village on a specially adapted bicycle. This may be the reason he left brickmaking in 1901, as an accident would have left him unable to do the work.

In 1902 they moved to a larger cottage, *No 1 New Cottages*, which was just a little further down the road. The Inland Revenue Valuation of 1912 identifies a later occupier of one of the two *Elm Bank Cottages* as **E. H. Pelling**.[38] This would be **Edward Henry Pelling** listed on the electoral register from 1908 – 1911, but he was not in the cottage at the time the 1911 census was taken and is so far unidentified.

By 1911, only one of the cottages was inhabited and this was No 2 where **Henry Warland Bell** (b.1856) lived with his younger daughter **Elsie** (b.1889). Henry had been a widower since the death of his wife, **Fanny** in 1907. According to the electoral register, he moved into one of the cottages around 1910, and is listed as the occupier on the Inland Revenue Valuation.[39]

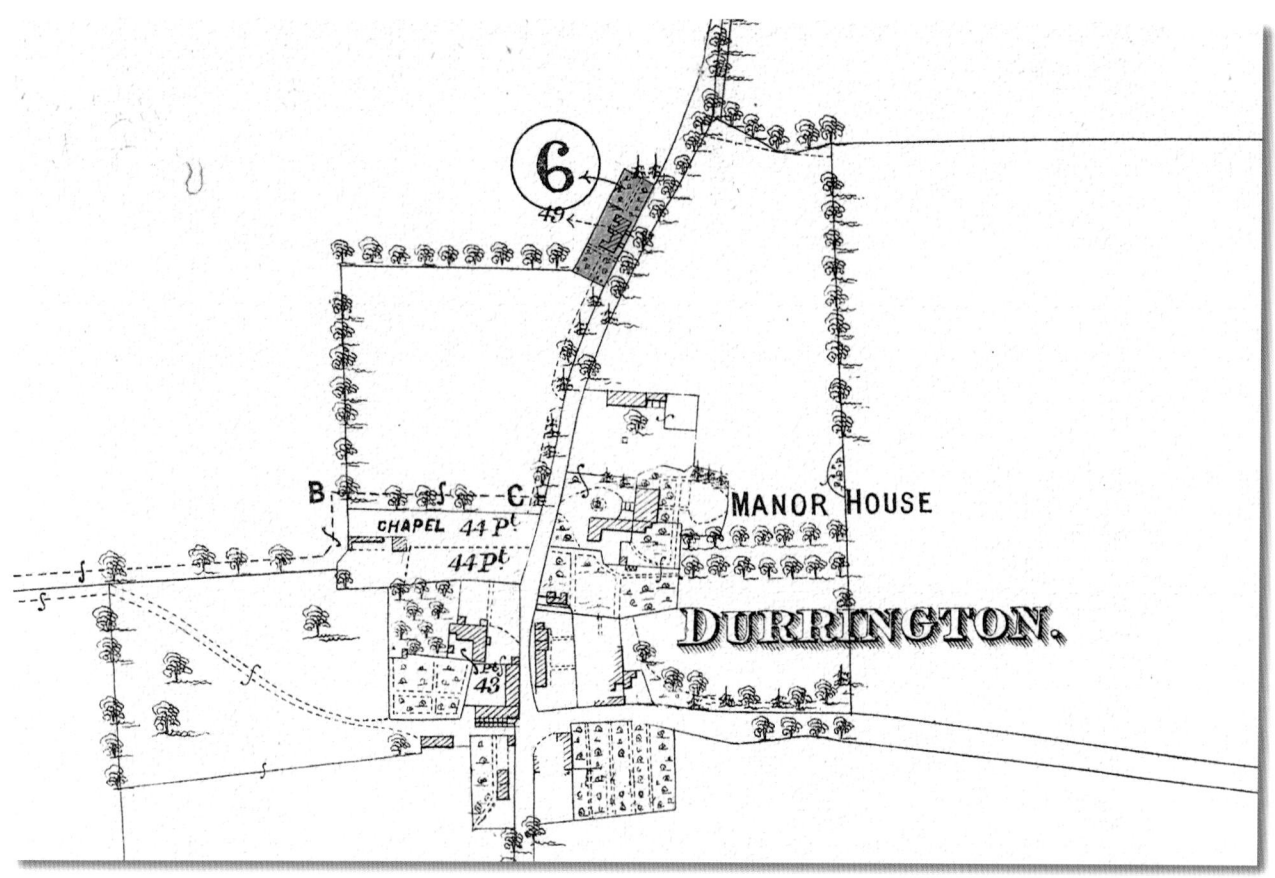

Map portion showing them as Lot 6 on Sale Catalogue 1902

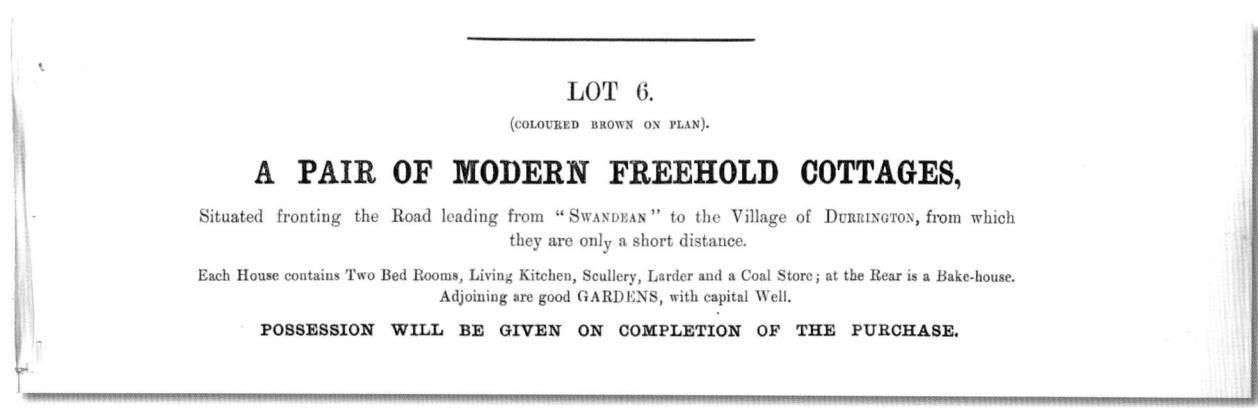

Extract from the sale catalogue describing Lot 6

Photograph showing *Elm Bank Cottages* c.1930. Worthing Library

Modern photograph *Elm Bank Cottages*. © Dave Pryce 2014

19. Bethany, Durrington Lane
(Now The Orchard, 1 Bramble Lane)

In May 1913 when the Inland Revenue assessed the property, it was described as *'Red Brick, double fronted, pretty garden'*.[40] This 3-bedroomed house was situated just behind *Elm Bank Cottages* and was the home of the **Helsdon** ladies. The entrance was originally in Durrington Street, but later it was moved and the property is now the first house in Bramble Lane.

The four Helsdon sisters, one of whom was married and living at *Bethany* with her husband, were using the one acre of land the site covered as a poultry farm. The earliest listing for them at the address was in a 1905

Old photograph of Elizabeth & Jane Helsdon. Owned by New Life Church

street directory; although the Inland Revenue Valuation records that the plot was not actually purchased by **E & J Helsdon** until Sept 1907 for £120, with a further expenditure of £400 to build the house. Maybe they rented the property for a while before they actually purchased it.

The 1911 census lists **Elizabeth Helsdon** as the head of the household.[41] She was the fourth child in her family, born in 1848 in St George in the East, London. The other members were **Ruth** (b.1843) who according to the census page was *'mentally weak from birth'*, **Jane** (b.1850) and a married sister named **Mary Anne** (b.1849) along with her husband **John Moulton** (b.1848). The ladies were all daughters of **Langley Helsdon**, and his wife **Esther** (nee Betts). Langley was a cabinet maker who, although born in Norfolk, had made his home in London. Langley's birth had been listed in Baptist registers for Norwich and this non-conformity was passionately shared by his children. The Helsdon household in Durrington were members and great supporters of the *Free Church* in Salvington Road, not only attending the church and holding prayer meetings in their house, but also donating finance for the building of the new chapel. Their names are engraved on a stone in the foundations of the church.

The whole family were already in their sixties at the time of the 1911 census, so the running of the poultry farm must have been hard work. They obviously had time to develop a garden at *Bethany*, as the Inland Revenue Valuation makes the unusual comment that the property contained a *'pretty garden'*. It also tells us that by May 1913, the family had left the property as a **Miss Wilson** is listed as the occupier. This may explain their name being used on the Inland Revenue Valuation for *Elmshurst,* Franklin Road,[42] but no further documentary evidence for change of address has been traced.

Modern photograph of *Bethany*. © Dave Pryce 2015

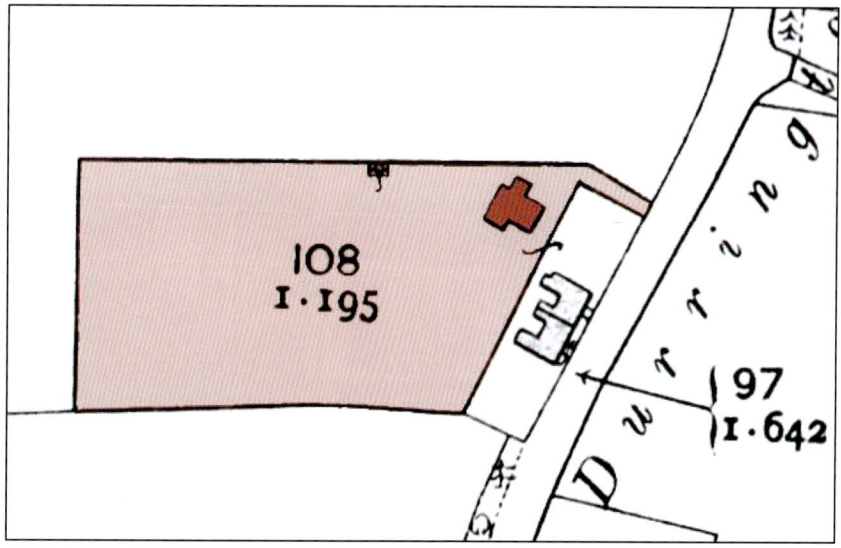

Excerpt taken from OS 25":1 mile Sheet LXIV: 5 3rd Edition 1912 (NTS)

20. Elm Bank (Elm Croft), Durrington Lane & Gardener's Cottage at rear
(Now Elm Bank House, Durrington Hill)

This property was built on land previously owned by **Rev. Springett,** the Rector of Tarring. In October 1905 the house and some land to the east of the house was purchased by **Ethel K. Kemp-Potter** of Rugby Road in Worthing. The land was rented in 1913 by the dairy farmer **Albert Linberry** of *Durrington Farm* and was worked as a market garden. It was described as a *'modern well-built residence'*.[43]

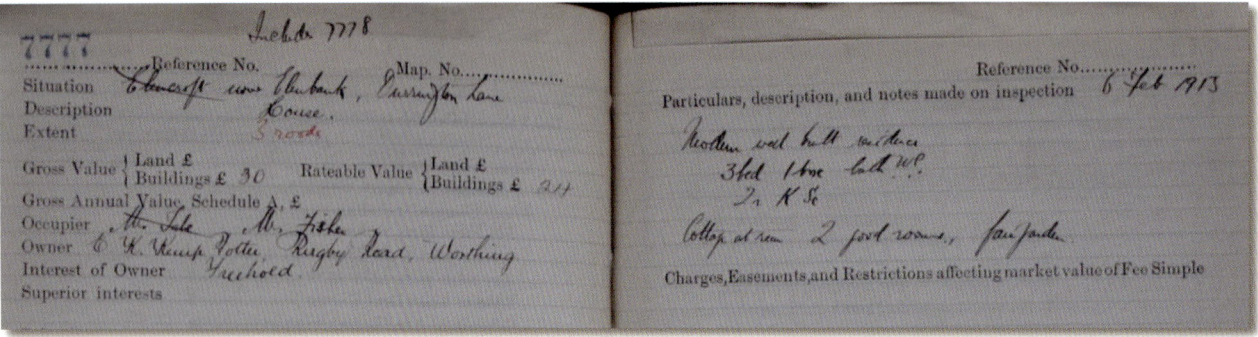

As well as the house there was a small two-roomed cottage at the back which was called *Elmcroft Cottage* rented for 3/- a week to **W. Clark** in 1913. The electoral register for 1910 lists **William Clark** and gives the address as *'Gardener's Cottage, Elm Croft'* an alternative name for the cottage. It was registered as *'Uninhabited'* on the 1911 Census.

The occupation order and length of each tenancy is unclear and at times confusing but there are names of people who lived here at different times. The Inland Revenue Valuation lists the previous occupier as **Mrs. Sale**, but this name appears on no other documents.[44] It states that from 1909 a five year tenancy was agreed by **Mrs. Fisher** but again there is no other documentation. We can say for certain that the 1911 census records **John Weatherell** (b.1857) living here with his daughter **Sarah Annie** (b.1885). John was a farmer and a widower.[45] They did not stay for many years and according to the electoral register moved to *Purley,* Salvington Road in 1913. This date suggests they may have occupied the house between the two ladies listed above.

Modern photograph of *Elm Bank*. © Lyn Tiller 2015

21. White House, Durrington Lane
(Now White House Place, Durrington Hill)

The *White House* was owned and occupied by **Walter Gardiner** (b.1862), a prominent member of society in both Worthing and Durrington. He held political office in Worthing, in later years becoming Mayor, as well as being an important photographer in the town. His reputation as a photographer is described by another Worthing photographer, David Nicholls:

> *'In the early 20th century, many notable moments of personal family history and the social development of Worthing as a community were captured through the lens of local photographer Walter James Gardiner.*
> *Important family portraits, scenes of local life and photographic caricatures of local characters were all recorded for posterity by the Gardiner family business and can still be seen in many homes and by visitors to Worthing Library'.*[46]

Walter Gardiner c.1901.
Worthing Library

Annie Gardiner, wife of Walter.
This photograph was taken c1897.
Worthing Library

Walter Gardiner had been born in Kent in 1862 and after some years spent in Australia, he returned to England in 1893 with his growing family, establishing a highly successful photographic business in Worthing. He had married his wife **Annie Elizabeth** (b.1864 nee Jenkins) in England before the move to Australia and they went on to have eight children: **John (?)**, **Frank Burrell** (b.c1890), **William Raphael** (b.1892) and **Ernest Freemantle** (b.1893) were all born in Australia. Sadly Ernest died in 1894 not long after they returned to England. The youngest four were all born in Sussex: **Gladys** (b.1891), **Joyce** (b.1897), **Hubert James** (b.1901) and **Mark** (b.1906).

In 1910 Walter Gardiner purchased a plot of land in Durrington Lane and on this land he built the *White House*. The 1911 census shows Walter and Annie living in the house with six of their children.[47] The photograph opposite shows the family gathered on the verandah of the *White House*.

The Gardiner family were staunch supporters of the Baptist movement both in Worthing and in Durrington. Annie Gardiner was particularly active in helping to fund the building of the *Free Church* in Salvington Road. In November 1911 where a stone laying ceremony was being

The *White House* viewed from the road in 1910.
Worthing Library

Modern road and housing now on the site of the *White House*.
© David Nicholls 2014

held at the site of the new church building we find Annie Gardiner fully involved and being honoured by having a stone with her name engraved on it laid during the ceremony. It is interesting to see this stone which is still visible by the side entrance to the church as the name on it reads 'Mrs Walter Gardiner'. It was obviously not considered appropriate to have her Christian name on the stone but only that of her husband. This ceremony was reported in the local newspaper of the time.[48]

The house was demolished in 2003 to make way for new housing although the *White House* is still remembered in the naming of the close where the original house and garden stood. It is called 'White House Place'

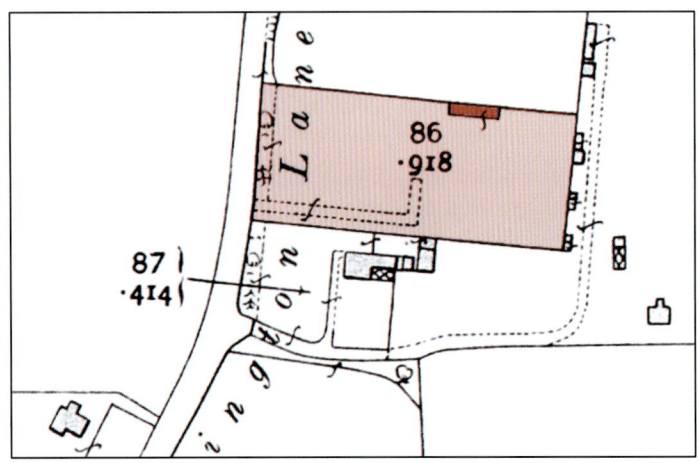

Excerpt taken from OS 25":1 mile Sheet LXIV: 5 3rd Edition 1912 (NTS)

22. Durrington Mission Room, Durrington Lane
(Now St Symphorian's Church, Durrington Hill)

The village of Durrington was a parish with its own chapel as far back as the Domesday Book where a building is mentioned. However, unlike many of the village churches in England which date back to the early Saxon and Norman period, this one did not survive the English Civil War when passions were high and people and clergy chose to support different sides.

The story began around 1638 when Rev. William Stanley had become the Rector of Tarring. As a passionate politician and a Royalist, as well as a man of God, he found himself in dispute with the people of Durrington who stood firmly in the Parliamentary camp. Disputes and arguments erupted over various issues; failing in his duty to the parish, payment of tithes and most prominently he was accused by the people of recruiting men to fight for the Royalist cause. The people refused to back down and so did their Rector. The result was that the chapel was abandoned or destroyed and by around 1651 it was in ruins. It would be over 400 years before the Anglican witness in Durrington could again be expressed by a permanent parish church building.

A postcard view of the old chapel ruins on Durrington Lane

In 1680 the inhabitants of Durrington gained permission to attend West Tarring for services and it was agreed at that time that the people would not be expected to rebuild the chapel. The village was poor and they would never have been able to afford the building costs.

In 1890 the then Rector of Tarring, Rev. Canon Bailey, personally financed the erection of a small metal hut known as the *Mission Room* and it was in here that some services began to be held in the village again. The hut stood against the eastern wall of the old chapel ruins and Edgar Overington was appointed as the first Church Warden. It was the next Rector of Tarring, Rev. Dr. Springett who began the task of raising money to re-build a permanent church, but nothing had actually been started by the time he left the parish in June 1898.

This was the situation in Durrington during the Edwardian period with the metal *Mission Room* being used for various meetings and gatherings of the congregation. Many of the church events were still held at West Tarring, but the people in the village would also gather in this little room on occasions. By 1910 the *Mission Room* was showing signs of deterioration and financing had to either go towards repairs or towards the building of a permanent new parish church. It was decided that plans would be put together, and more funds raised to build a new parish church. This new church was indeed built, dedicated to *St Symphorian's* in 1915 and consecrated in December 1916. A selection of cuttings from the Worthing Gazette from the period, included on the next page, show the discussions that were being reported.

Photograph's of the small *Mission Room*

New Parish Church needed for Durrington

A CHURCH FOR DURRINGTON.

Interesting Proposal.

WHEN the members of the Durrington Parish Council next meet, in the course of the current week, they will be invited to consider the possibility of erecting a Church in the village, to provide for the needs of the parishioners. Quite appropriately, the subject is to be introduced to the notice of his colleagues by Mr. Church.

Worthing Gazette 15th March 1911
Church for Durrington proposed by Mr Church

DURRINGTON AND ITS CHURCH.

Question Again Discussed.
Difficulties of the Existing Situation.
What Will Happen?

THE question of the provision of a Church at Durrington, which is one of the ambitions that the residents of that village hope to see realised in the near future, has been further discussed on two occasions during the past week. The matter was introduced again at the annual meeting of the Parish Council on Thursday evening, on a letter from the Rector of West Tarring (the Rev. C. Lee), and it also formed one of the chief topics for discussion at a Vestry meeting which was held in the village on the following evening.

Worthing Gazette 26th April 1911

THE DEMAND FOR A CHURCH.

The question of erecting a Church in the village was next introduced by Mr. CHURCH, who said he believed they already had a piece of consecrated ground near the old Mission Chapel, and that if they were to appoint a Committee to make inquiries they might find out where this was. Durrington was growing very fast, and better facilities than they now possessed were certainly required.

The CHAIRMAN remarked that there was a fund in the Diocese called the Bishop of Chichester's Fund, which did a great deal in the way of building or assisting to build new Churches where there was a real necessity for them; and he certainly thought the best plan would be to appoint a small Committee to make inquiries. There was no doubt the parish was

Greatly on the Increase,

and the present seemed an appropriate time to move in the matter. It had been said that they would never get a Church in the village, but the same thing was said concerning the School, and after all, the difficulties ought to be overcome if they were tackled properly.

Mr. BRAKE agreed that the proper course for them to pursue at this stage was to appoint a Committee to look into the matter, and it was eventually decided that the Chairman and Messrs. Brake, Church, Saunders, and Trim should form the Committee, and that the Rector of Tarring (the Rev. C. Lee) and the Clerk (Mr. E. W. Bartlett) should also be invited to serve on it.

Worthing Gazette 22nd March 1911
Durrington wants a Church

DURRINGTON AND ITS PAROCHIAL NEEDS.

AN INCUMBENT'S STIPEND GUARANTEED.
PROGRESS OF THE NEW CHURCH BUILDING FUND.
SEPARATE ECCLESIASTICAL PARISH PROPOSED.

Worthing Gazette 18th September 1912

1. www.britishlistedbuildings.co.uk (No. 302254) viewed 21.06.2012
2. 1901 census RG13/957 ff. 76 (TNA)
3. 1911 census RG14/5342 sch 109 (TNA)
4. 1891 census RG12/625 ff.41 (TNA)
5. Durrington Council School Admissions Register
6. The Times, 7th December 1911 p1a
7. IR58/94204 No. 7695 (TNA)
8. Sale Catalogue 'Tarring Durrington and Worthing Freehold Villas………' 30th September 1902. Lot F1. SC/WSL/000443a (Worthing Library)
9. 1901 census RG13/957 ff. 76 (TNA)
10. 1911 census RG14/5342 sch 103 (TNA)
11. 1901 census RG13/957 ff. 76 (TNA)
12. 1911 census RG14/5342 sch 107 (TNA)
13. Durrington Council school Log Book 1908-1928 23rd October 1908, p8
14. 1901 census RG13/957 ff.76 (TNA)
15. 1911 census RG14/5342 sch 105 (TNA)
16. 1901 census RG13/957 ff.76 (TNA)
17. 1911 census RG14/5342 sch 104 (TNA)
18. 1901 census RG13/957 ff. 76 (TNA)
19. IR58/94204 No.7699 and IR58/94205 No.7700-7704
20. www.britishlistedbuildings.co.uk (No.302252) viewed 21.06.2012
21. IR58/94205 No.7789 (TNA)
22. 1901 census RG13/957 ff.76 (TNA)
23. 1911 census RG14/5342 sch 101 (TNA)
24. The Times, October 1st 1910 p14
25. National Archives of Australia. Attestation Paper of Persons enlisted for Service Abroad. viewed 03/07/2014
26. Linfield p6
27. IR58/94205 No.7790 (TNA)
28. 1901 census RG13/957 ff.76 (TNA)
29. 1911 census RG14/5342 sch 102 (TNA)
30. 1901 census RG13/957 ff.77 (TNA)
31. IR58/94205 No.7791 (TNA)
32. 1871 census RG10/1055 ff.48 (TNA)
33. 1881 census RG11/1055 ff.43 (TNA)
34. 1891 census RG12/786 ff.128 (TNA)
35. 1901 census RG13/902 ff.129 (TNA)
36. IR58/94205 No.7791 (TNA)
37. Sale Catalogue 'The Durrington Estate near Worthing' 10th October 1895. Lot 6. SC/WSL/000132a (Worthing Library)
38. IR58/94206 No.7815 (TNA)
39. IR58/94206 No. 7816 (TNA)
40. IR58/94205 No. 7709 (TNA)
41. 1911 census RG14/5342 sch 98 (TNA)
42. IR58/94205 No. 7730 (TNA)
43. IR58/94205 No. 7777 (TNA)
44. IR58/94205 No.7778 (TNA
45. 1911 census RG14/5342 sch 97 (TNA
46. Nicholls, David. Durrington Project Research. Unpublished notes and research. (Worthing Library)
47. 1911 census RG14/5342 sch 96 (TNA)
48. Worthing Gazette 22nd November 1911 p7b

Chapter 3
Salvington Road

Introduction

Salvington Road runs east to west connecting the two areas of Durrington in the west and Salvington in the east. The route is based on an ancient pathway that joined the original Saxon settlements and still remains the main thoroughfare.

The road is marked at each end by a public house. At the Durrington end on the south side is the *Lamb Inn*, whilst on the north side of the road at the Salvington end, is the later public house, the *John Selden*. This public house was built and opened in 1910 replacing an earlier hostelry on the site named *The Spotted Cow*. Opposite both public houses during the Edwardian period were important establishments. On the north side of the road at Durrington, was *The Forge* run for many years by the Overington family. Salvington had the impressive *Salvington Lodge* on the south side, the home of Miss Bromfield and later Patrick Wisden, a member of the Wisden family from *The Warren* in Broadwater.

The land between the two Saxon settlements was still predominately farmland at the turn of the century. *Salvington Farmhouse* with its various barns and outbuildings was the most prominent dwelling along the road. As the decade unfolded, large tracts of the land were sold for nurseries, new homes, a bakery, a free church and the village school. By the beginning of the First World War, the road was a busy and bustling area, where already the demarcation of two separate villages was disappearing.

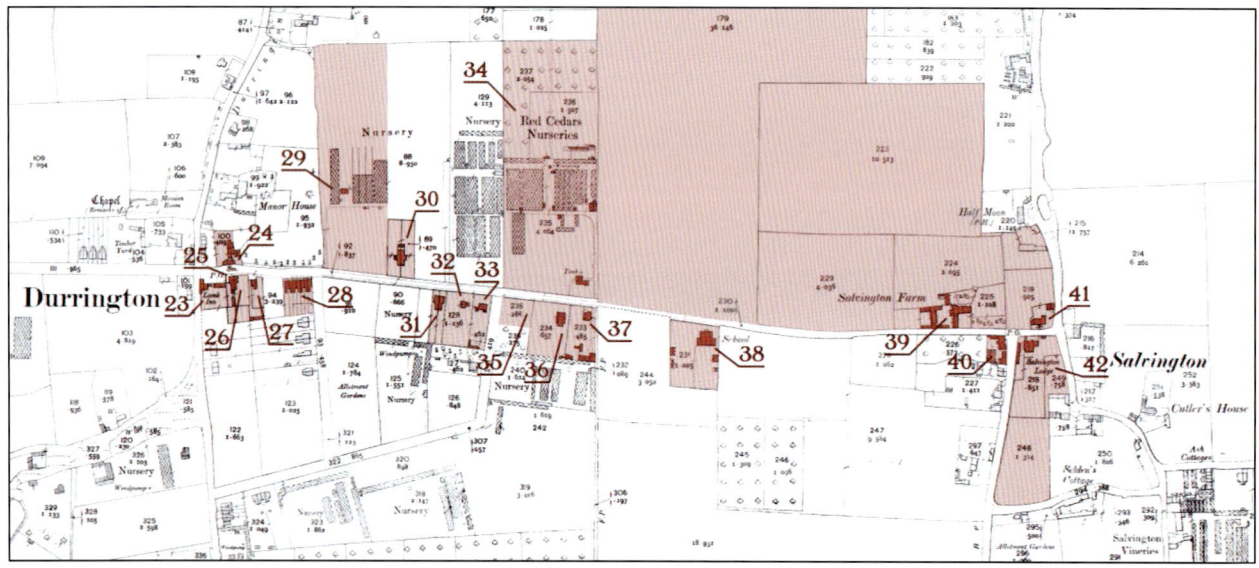

Excerpt taken from OS 25":1 mile Sheet LXIV: 5,6,9&10 3rd Edition 1912 (NTS)

Looking down Salvington Road to the east.
The *Lamb Inn* and *Durrington Post Office* are on the right.
Worthing Library

Looking down Salvington Road to the west.
With *Salvington Post Office* on the left on the corner of Stone Lane.
Worthing Library (cropped)

23. Lamb Inn, Salvington Road
(Now The Lamb, Salvington Road)

*'One of the main centre points of any village is its local inn and in Durrington this was, and still is, the Lamb Inn. In the late 1890's, a new licensee and his wife had arrived whose name was **Walter White**. Originally from Bromley in Surrey, Walter had married a Welsh lady, **Elizabeth Ann Thomas** from Cardiff in 1889. They had two sons, **Walter** (b.1891) and **Sydney George** (b.1897) who were born some years later in Littlehampton.*

Walter was a former groom and domestic coachman who was very fond of horses. So as well as running the Lamb Inn, he developed a hire carter business based at the Lamb Inn with stabling and a coach house. It is possible that the carts shown in the photograph below belonged to his business.

This is a view from the *Lamb Inn* looking down Salvington Road to the east.
Rock Cottages are visible in the background. Worthing Library

Here is the same view taken in 2015. © Dave Pryce

*Walter's wife Elizabeth (Lizzie) had been delighted when her young sister **Sarah** had married **Henry Thompson** and moved into Elm Bank Cottages in 1901. Sadly, Elizabeth died in 1902 from a combination of broncopneumonia and influenza brought on by advanced consumption. William was devastated but continued to run the Lamb Inn and his carter business. In 1904 he married again to a young lady of 17 named **Harriet Saunders**, who lived in Durrington Street very close to the Lamb. Shortly afterwards, she gave birth to a daughter **Ethel Nellie** (b.1904).'* [1]

(The description above was written by Jean Hull, the great niece of Walter and his wife.)

From a photograph dated around 1890 (see below), we can see that the building standing on the corner site today is not the original *Lamb Inn* building. Sometime around the turn of the century the inn was rebuilt further back from the road although details on the rebuilding have not so far been confirmed.

Photograph dated c1890 showing the different *Lamb Inn* building from that on the site today.
Worthing Library (cropped)

The Inland Revenue Valuation describes the inn and its adjoining buildings in May 1913:
> '*Village Inn in good position*
> *Poor appearance rendered & boulder built. Good pull up in front of house....*
> *.....Good stabling at side, 3 shops, and coach house'.* [2]

As well as the carter's business, mentioned by Jean Hull above, Walter ran a grocer's shop from the premises, both would have been based in these small shops and although they are listed at this address in 1901[3] they had moved by 1911. In 1910 Walter gave up the licence for the *Lamb Inn*, and moved to *6 South View Terrace* in New Road, although he continued to run the grocer and carter business for some years.

The next Licensee, **George Sargeant Arnold** (b.1863), arrived at the *Lamb Inn* in December 1910 and it is this family that we find on the 1911 census.[4] He was a former policeman and licensed victualler from the Croydon area. In 1902, he had married the daughter of a publican, **Julia Alexandra Smith** and they had one son **Harold George** (b.1903).

DURRINGTON.

TO AND FROM SWANDEAN.— In the printed proceedings of the Sanitary Committee, presented to the Worthing Town Council at the monthly meeting yesterday, it was stated that, in consequence of the receipt of a letter from the Durrington Parish Council, the Town Clerk should be instructed to write to Mr. Stent and request that the driver of the ambulance used for the conveyance of patients to Swandean should be directed to discontinue stopping outside the Lamb public-house when going to or returning from the Hospital, and to use the upper or Arundel-road, instead of passing through the village, on all such occasions.

Worthing Gazette reports on the story of the ambulances taking a short cut through Durrington

The inn was always a very busy place with local groups using some of the rooms as their meeting place. The Durrington Slate Club had regular gatherings and annual dinners within its walls. The Durrington Cricket Club also held various official meetings here, and probably many times met for a drink and chat after the cricket games held in the village. The inn also proved a great temptation to the ambulance drivers who drove their ambulances to and from *Swandean Hospital* and Worthing, as there was a complaint and request that they cease from stopping 'outside' the inn in the middle of their journeys.[5] One can only hope they never did so with patients on board!

Modern photograph of *The Lamb* taken from Salvington Road. © David Nicholls 2013

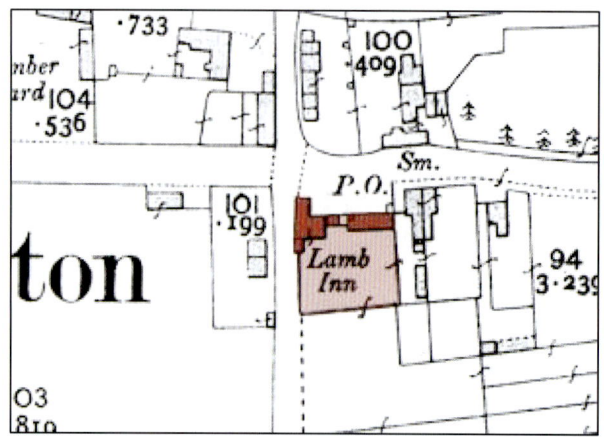

Excerpt taken from OS 25":1 mile Sheet LXIV: 5 3rd Edition 1912 (NTS)

24. The Forge, Rose Cottage & Blacksmith Cottage, Salvington Road
(Now No's 198, 200, 202a & 202 Salvington Road)

In 1901, the death of a well-known citizen of Edwardian Durrington was reported in the Worthing Gazette. The death had occurred on 31st July and reported in the next issue of the paper.[6]

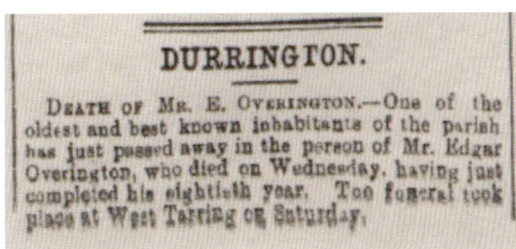

Worthing Gazette reporting the death of Edgar Overington in 1901

The name of the deceased was **Edgar Overington** (b.1821). As well as being the village blacksmith for many years he had held various leadership roles in the village. One of these roles was that of Churchwarden for Durrington, where according to Evans he was affectionately known as the 'Bishop'.[7] Edgar ran the family blacksmith business which he had inherited from his parents **Henry** and **Avis Overington**. According to the outside board, seen in the photograph below, the business had been established in Durrington in 1791 by the family who had moved here originally from Hampshire. By the Edwardian period they were one of the most prominent families in the village. The business itself was varied in the services it could offer, the list being quite extensive according to the sign board below:

'Shoeing and general smith. Heavy and light tyreing. Hot and cold water cisterns. All kinds of iron fencing supplied. Lawn mowers ground and repaired.'

By 1861 Edgar is listed on the census as a blacksmith at *The Forge* working with his father and this is where he stayed until his death.[8] He was married to **Elizabeth** (b.c1826 nee Unwin) and they had nine children; **Horace** (b.1848), **Fanny** (b.1850), **Ida** (b.1852), **Edith** (b.1855), **Laura** (b.1857), **Jessie/Luke** (b.1860), **Elizabeth** (b.1865), **Minnie** (b.1868) and **Alfred** (b.1871). The forge was a very successful business, the farms and growing number of nurseries in the area meant there was always plenty of work for a blacksmith and his associated skills.

On Edgar's death it was his youngest son, Alfred, who took over the running of the business. He continued to live on the site with his wife **Amy** (b.1873 nee Treagus) and their children: **Margaret** (b.1901) *(seen in the photograph holding her father's hand)*, **Benjamin** (b.1904), **Joan** (b.1905), **Iza** (b.1907) and **Janet** (b.1910). Alfred continued his father's village involvement in the Parish by holding positions of importance, including Durrington Parish Council and Church Parish Council. He is also regularly named as a member of the cricket team.

Overington's Forge, Salvington Road, Durrington, Worthing. Standing in front of the forge building are (left-to-right): unidentified man, George Dunlop, smith Margaret Overington and her father Alfred Overington; Albert Wratten, resident of Pond Lane, holding the head of a Coote's Bakery delivery horse; and Albert Lish, smith.
Worthing Library

As the photograph shows *The Forge* opened directly onto Salvington Road giving easy access for horses and carts as well as people. Directly behind and attached to the building were two cottages. The first, usually in this period called *Rose Cottage*, was occupied by the Overington family themselves as listed on both the 1901[9] and 1911 censuses.[10] Even today, the cottage retains many of the early architectural features as the photograph below shows.

This 2013 photograph shows the fireplace still exists inside the cottage. © Dave Pryce

The Inland Revenue Valuation gives this description of the forge and *Rose Cottage*:
*'Smithy's workshop on main road……..Good position for business.
At rear is a cottage boulder & slate. Old fair repair.'*[11]

Behind and attached to *Rose Cottage* was the smaller cottage named *Blacksmith Cottage* (Note: the 1911 census lists both of these cottages as *Blacksmith Cottage*). Here **William Godwin** and his wife **Alice** lived with three children; **Charles** (b.1894), **Victor** (b.1897) and a small three year old 'boarder' named **Ralph Jupp** (b.1901).[12] In 1911 William is listed as a bricklayer, but by 1912 in the directories he has become a blacksmith, presumably working at the forge. The Inland Revenue Valuation description for this property tells us more about the access to this cottage:

'Situated at back of Rose Cottage & approached only through two gardens.[13]

Today, as the modern photograph shows, *The Forge* with the smaller buildings to the east and the two cottages behind are all separate dwellings.

Modern photograph of the site. © Dave Pryce 2015

25. Post Office, Salvington Road
(No longer standing, now the site of shops and car park)

The *Post Office* for Durrington was housed in one of a pair of semi-detached properties owned by **W & M J Smith** & **R Piper** of Newland Road, Worthing.

The shop also traded as a grocers selling many of the staple foods needed by the people in this part of the village. It appears to have had a fairly rapid succession of five post masters throughout the period.

Photograph showing the *Post Office*. Worthing Library (cropped)

Between 1900 and 1901 both the directories and the 1901 census list **Robert William Painter Gay** (b.1865) at the *Post Office*. Living with him were his wife **Elizabeth** (b.1864 nee Walder) and their two young daughters, **Ada Elizabeth** (b.1897) and **Ellen Margaret** (b.1898).[14] He was appointed to the post of sub-postmaster on 24th April 1900 at a salary of £10-5-0 a year.[15]

From 1902 through to 1904, the street directories list **Frederick Sayer** at the *Post Office* and then by 1906 **John Carey** was running the business. **Charles Mills,** who is listed on the 1911 census at the *Post Office*, first appears in a 1910 street directory.[16] The census return tells us a little more about him. He was born in Northchapel in 1886 and married **Annie Hall Lampard** (b.1880) from Horsham in 1909. By the time of the Inland Revenue Valuation in 1912, Charles and Annie had moved again, the street directories suggest they had transferred to *4 Greenland Road* and the new postmaster was **F K Tavenner.**[17]

26. Harness & Saddle Makers, Salvington Road
(No longer standing, now the site of shops and car park)

Next to the grocers and *Post Office* was the home of a harness and saddle maker named William Bursnall. This would have been an ideal location for such a business as it was situated directly opposite the forge.

William Henry Bursnall (b.1881) was the proprietor of the shop and resided at the property. His father, **Edward Bursnall** was at various stages of William's young life, a butler, a groom and later a coachman in Clapham. William had chosen an occupation as a harness maker and by 1903 he was appearing in the local street directories for Durrington. What connection he had with Durrington or what prompted his journey south is not known. The Inland Revenue Valuation states that he took up the tenancy of the property and shop on 11th March 1902 for an annual rent of £16.[18] William remained single working from his home in Durrington for some years until in the last months of 1912 he married **Nellie Floyd Rudd** (b.1887). They never had any children, and lived together at this address for many years. Stories around the village suggest that William was a favourite with all the children. They would travel down the pathway at the side of the house to visit his workshop. It was not actually William they wanted to see, but the parrot he kept hanging in a cage in the shop that intrigued and amused them.

Photograph showing the *Harness Makers* shop.
It also shows the butchers shop to the left and the *Post Office* to the right with the words 'Grocery' visible.
Worthing Library

Both properties were demolished to make way for the parade of shops which now stands on the site.

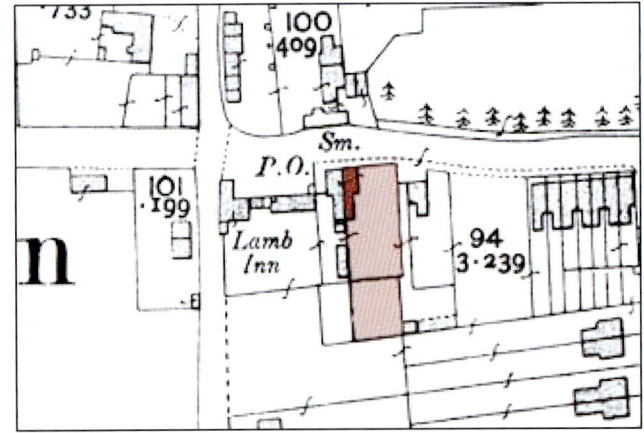

Excerpt taken from OS 25":1 mile Sheet LXIV: 5 3rd Edition 1912 (NTS)

27. Butchers Shop, Salvington Road
(No longer standing, now the site of the shops and car park)

George Church, so the Inland Revenue Valuation informs us, had purchased this plot of land in 1904 for £155, and consequently spent £500 on building the house and shop.[19] Planning permission was given for the complete set of buildings on 1st November 1904, and by the 4th April the following year the water certificate was issued.[20]

56

William George Daniel Church, to give him his full name, was born in Nottinghill in 1877. In the later months of 1905 he married **Lizzie Newnham** (b.1883) and brought his wife to his new home and shop in Durrington to begin their married life. Lizzie was the daughter of a coal merchant and farmer from Fletching in Sussex. They went on to have two daughters while in Durrington, **Ruby Elizabeth** (b.1906) and **Eileen Carmen** (b.1911) who were listed at the address on the 1911 census.[21]

George was very involved in the affairs of the village. In March of 1911 we can read the newspaper report of him voicing an opinion that the village should pro-actively move towards having a parish church again. At the same meeting, he was elected as a member of the committee who would work towards this goal.[22]

Mr Church introducing discussions in the village about a new parish church in March 1911.

A few months later, he appeared again in another article, speaking against a slaughter house being proposed for Durrington to be situated on land near Pond Lane.[23]

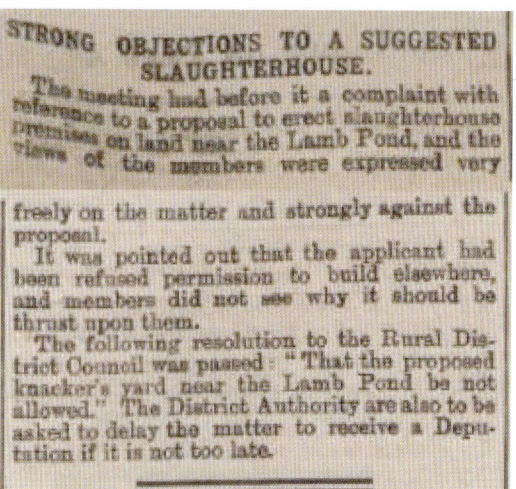

A meeting that George Church was present at when the issue of a proposed slaughterhouse was discussed in September 1911

How this would have affected his business is never stated, but he would have been ideally suited as a butcher to understand the effect of such a business on the village. How the argument and deputation progressed we are not told but no slaughter house was ever built near Pond Lane.

The Church family had left Durrington around 1912-1913, as by the Inland Revenue Valuation **Mr Jay** is listed as the butcher living at the address.

28. Rock Cottages & The Laurels, Salvington Road
(Now No's 147, 149, 151, 153, 155 & 157 Salvington Road)

These properties were built around 1905 as a row of six cottages and a slightly larger house named *The Laurels* on the western end, all built of red brick and tile. The properties were called *Rock Cottages* or sometimes *Rock Terrace* throughout the period. The Inland Revenue Valuation for each property reveals that the complete row was sold in 1907 to **R. Smith** of Clapham for £250 each.[24]

The cottages were all occupied as follows:

The first of the terrace known as No 1 stood on the corner of Franklin Road and Salvington Road and was occupied by **Richard Henry Coote** (b.1880) and his family. Richard was the eldest son of **Rhoda Coote** who was the head of the family bakery business, Coote & Sons, based in Salvington Road. Richard was listed on the 1911 census as a *'baker'*, clearly working in the family bakery business.[25] With him were his wife **Alice** (b.1881 nee Kent) and young son **Bernard** (b.1910). The property is the modern home of *Durrington Post Office*.

The next cottage was No 2 and this was the home of **Frederick Smith** (b.1851) and his wife **Emily** (b.1849). They were recorded as making the move from *Blacksmith Cottage* to *Rock Cottages* in 1905, which makes them one of the earliest families recorded as moving into the cottages. Frederick was a fruit grower and market gardener who ran a market garden on the south side of Greenland Road in the first years of the twentieth century. Two of his sons, namely **Arthur** (b.1894) who had been listed with them in *Blacksmith Cottage* on the 1901 census,[26] as well as **Edward** (b.1897) who was still living with them in 1911, were also listed as market gardeners probably working in the nursery with their father. The 1911 census lists an eight year old granddaughter, **Dorothy Buckland** (b.1903) living with them as well.[27] This little girl was born in Littlehampton, but must have spent some periods of time with her grandparents as she is listed in Durrington School Admissions Register twice during the Edwardian period. She firstly enters the school on 5th July 1908 only to be removed on 23rd July 1909. She later returns from Henley in Middlesex to attend the school again on 6th February 1911, leaving on 21st May the following year.

The 1911 census registers the occupants of *No 3 Rock Cottages* as the home of **Thomas Charman** (b.1879) and his wife **Annie Mitchell** (b.1877 nee Madgwick).[28] The electoral register lists Thomas at this address from 1909, but they may have been here even before that date, as no other occupier has been traced. Thomas was the son of **Charles** and **Mary Mitchell Charman** from *Nell (Knell) House, Harrisons Farm* in Littlehampton Road. They have two boarders living with them, a pastry cook named **Albert Budd** and a fruit grower named **William Smith** (b.1869), the brother of Frederick Smith living next door. William was most probably working in his brother's market garden.

No 4 is listed as *'Uninhabited'* on the 1911 Census. The Inland Revenue Valuation dated May 1913 records the previous occupier as **W. Spillis** and the present occupier as **Stenning**.[29] These two names are not listed elsewhere, so probably were only tenants for a short period.

The 1906 electoral register is the earliest document giving us any information on the occupant of No 5 and records the householder as **James Cunnell** (b.1841). The 1911 census gives his age as 70 and his occupation as a retired police officer from Croydon.[30] He is listed in Croydon on the 1881 census where he had reached the rank of sargeant.[31] His wife **Victoria Elizabeth** (b.1838 nee Haselwood) was 72 in 1911, the census confirms that they had been married for 45 years and had no children. A few months after the census, tragedy struck the elderly couple. Victoria was obviously ill and her husband had been struggling to cope with her. The result was that Victoria was removed to Greylingwell Hospital. Tragically James, maybe struggling with the loss of his wife, committed suicide in the July of 1911 as reported in the local newspaper, which gave fairly graphic details of the event. Mrs Annie Charman, from No 3, revealed in her evidence that she had been trying to help Mr Cunnell by providing plated meals for him. When she gave evidence at the inquest, she told of a conversation she had with the old gentleman the night before. When he had returned his empty plate, he told her to *'Come round and see if anything has happened. Something is going to happen but I tremble to think what!'* The jury decided he had committed suicide *'while of unsound mind.'*[32]

The occupants of the last cottage were another retired couple, **George Rogers** (b.1844) and his wife **Mary Ann** (b.1848). George was a retired printer's engineer from Shoreditch. The electoral register lists George in Durrington from 1909, so he may not have been the first tenant of the house.

The Laurels is the slightly larger house on the western end of the terrace. In August 1912, the Inland Revenue Valuation stated that the property had been owned by George Trim, of Franklin Road.[33] George Trim was a Durrington builder so it is probable that he was also the builder. The valuation mentions that the property had been sold to George Bush for £250, although no date for the sale is given. The house was occupied by **Alfred Coote** (b.1881) and his family. Alfred was another trained baker working in the family business run by his mother Rhoda Coote further down Salvington Road. Alfred's family were **Sarah** (b.1877 nee Denman) his wife, whom he had married in 1905 and their daughter **Muriel** (b.1907). Alfred's brother, Richard, was living at the other end of the terrace in No 1.

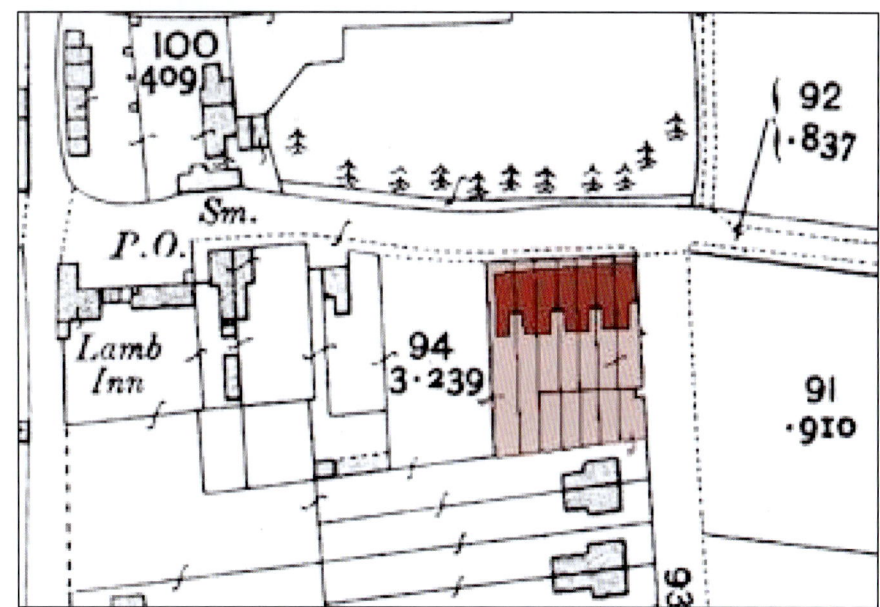

Excerpt taken from OS 25":1 mile Sheet LXIV: 5 3rd Edition 1912 (NTS)

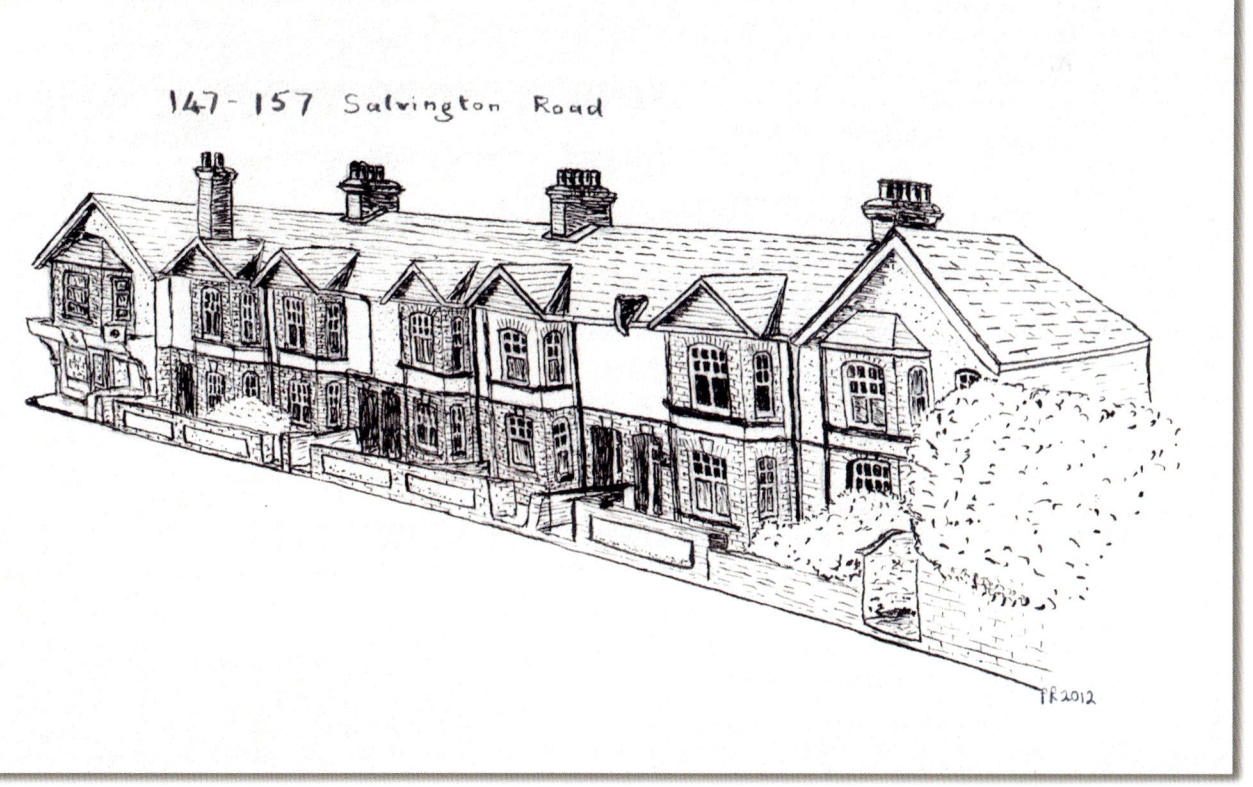

Line drawing of *The Row*. © Peter Rowe 2012

This picture shows *Rock Cottages* and *The Laurels* around 1905 fairly soon after they were built.
Worthing Library

This photograph shows *Rock Cottages* as they look today. © Dave Pryce 2015

29. Seaview Nursery, Salvington Road
(No longer standing)

On 29th September 1899, a 50 year tenancy was taken out on this land at an annual rent of £32 16s 4d. The owners were the Horticultural Travelling Structures Co. Ltd. whose address was 2-3 White Street, Moorgate Street, London EC.[34] The electoral registers and street directories lists a **Charles Barter Pyke** as a fruit grower in Durrington between 1902-1906 but does not give the name of the nursery. However, an advert in the Worthing Gazette confirms that Pyke was based at Seaview Nursery.[35]

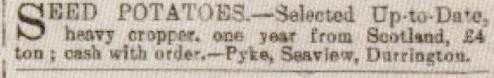

Advert from Worthing Gazette showing Pyke at Seaview Nursery.

This nursery was purchased in Durrington around 1906 or 1907 by **John Kenneth Matthews** (b.1884), who was the eldest of two brothers, both nurserymen in Durrington during this period. John Matthews was born in Harlow, Essex, the son of a gentleman farmer named **Thomas Matthews**. He had been to boarding school in his home county and then in Brighton, before embarking on a career as a nurseryman and working in Durrington at Seaview Nursery. John and **Harold Matthews**, his brother, are listed on the 1901 census living in *'4 caravans'* probably on the site of the nursery, making it likely that they worked for Charles Pyke for some time before John took over the business. Malcolm Linfield describes the nursery:

> *'...Seaview Nurseries, owned and managed by **John Kenneth Matthews**. On nearly three acres of ground, there were seven glasshouses recorded in 1913, although they are described as being in poor condition and the 'travelling type'.(LT 7771) These were glasshouses fixed on runners which could be moved to cover a different piece of ground, thereby enabling a more flexible growing regime and earlier crops. This was an innovation which became popular with a number of growers in the Worthing area......'* [36]

It is interesting to note the type of glasshouses that were being used on the nursery. The original owners of the land were a company making just the type of moveable glasshouses used by John Matthews. It is probable that Matthews inherited the glasshouses with the nursery when he took over the running of *Seaview*. The same company also owned the piece of land to the north of the nursery, but in 1913 this is listed as 'vacant land' suggesting it had not been cultivated by Pyke or Matthews.

By 1911, John and his younger brother, Harold were lodging in Broadwater.[37] Also lodging in the same property were another set of brothers **Frank and George Cotching** from Horsham. Harold Mathews and Frank Cotching were to form a partnership and work another nursery in Durrington based in Greenland Road. Although John was lodging in Broadwater, he was clearly taking part in Durrington village life, as he is listed as a member of the Durrington Cricket team around May 1908. This was always an important part of village life, with the teams and match scores being published in the Worthing Gazette. A photograph of the local cricket team taken around 1910 may have included him, but names have not been confirmed.

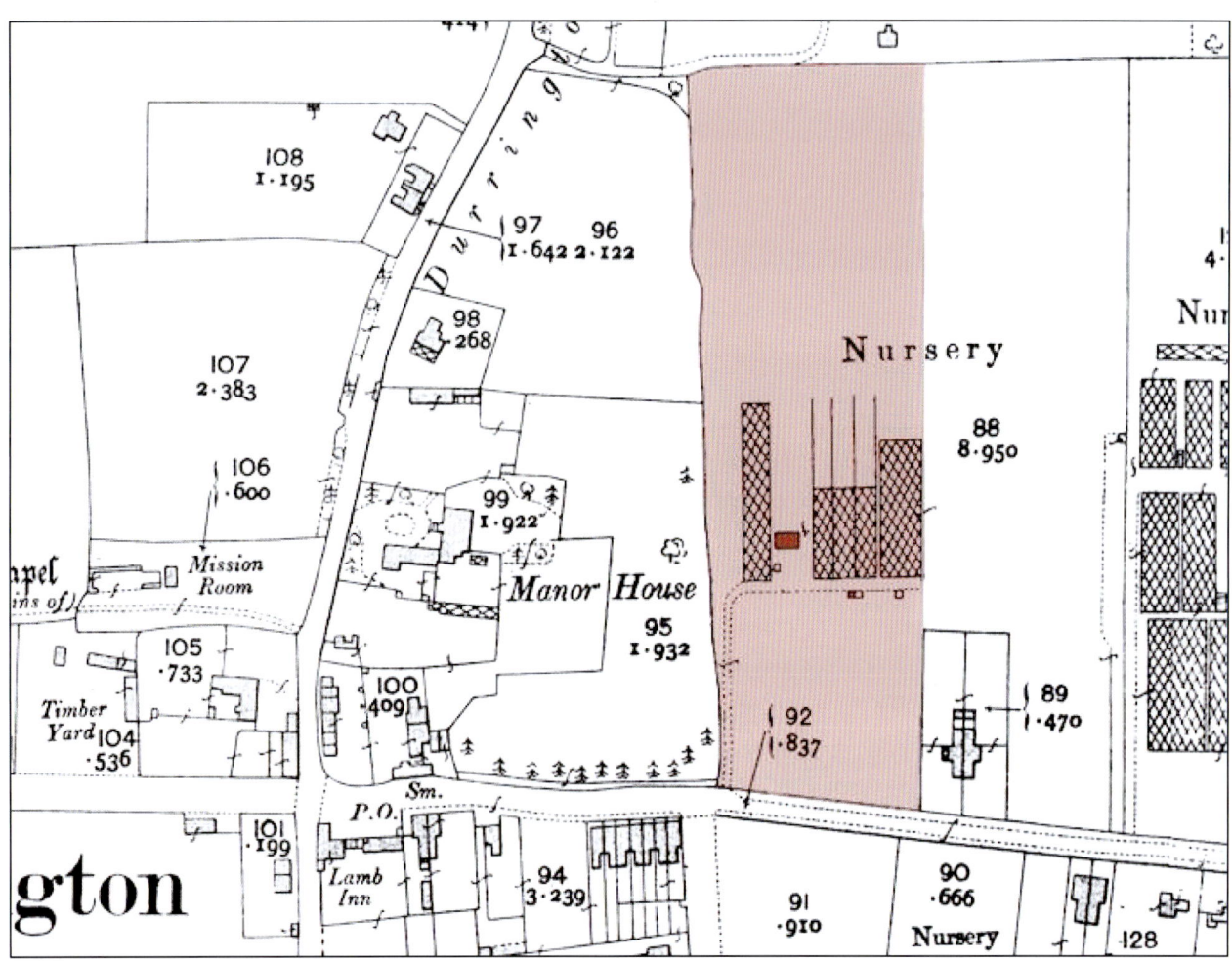

Excerpt taken from OS 25":1 mile Sheet LXIV: 5 3rd Edition 1912 (NTS)

Photograph of cricket team from c1910. Worthing Library

Modern bungalows situated on the corner of Exmore Crescent, previously the site of *Seaview Nursery*. © Dave Pryce 2016

30. Purley (Sydney Villa) & Thornberry (Avoca), Salvington Road
(Now The Heathers Nursing Home, Salvington Road)

Photograph of the houses in modern times now converted into a nursing home. © Dave Pryce 2014

These were a pair of red-brick semi-detached properties built around 1902-1903. *Avoca* is the house on the right hand side of the pair, and had some very interesting occupants for the first few years of its existence. The house was purchased in 1904 for £1100 according to the Inland Revenue Valuation which was carried out in June 1913 and describes the property. It had four large bedrooms on the first floor whilst downstairs there was a W.C., 2 rooms, kitchen & scullery and some out buildings. The purchase in 1904 also included four acres of land clearly marked on the map.[38] The owner of the property and land was **F. Martin** from Worthing.

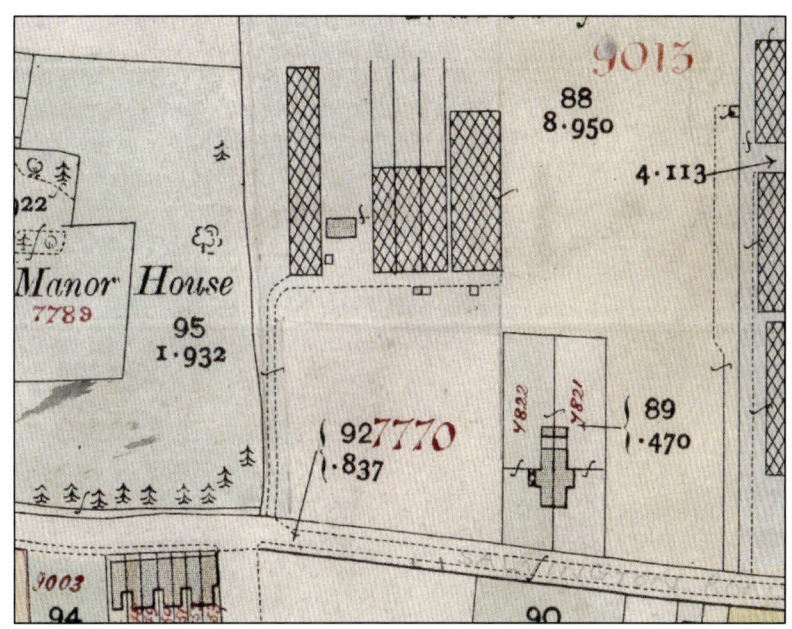

Excerpt taken from OS 25":1 mile Sheet LXIV: 5 3rd Edition 1912 (NTS)
Inland Revenue Valuation numbers added

In a street directory for 1905, the first occupant is given as **Major Willson Arno.** This name does not appear on any other census, but he is listed at the address in directories from 1905-1911, with one listing during this time on an electoral register in 1910-1911. There was a marriage in 1910 where the surname Arno appears on the certificate used by both parties of the marriage. The bride was a French lady **Leonie Catherine Lagadere (also Arno),** the groom is clearly shown as **John George Moore** otherwise Major Willson Arno.

Copy of marriage certificate

By the 1911 census, the whole family are living in Worthing and have reverted to calling themselves 'Moore'.[39] John George Moore is the name which also appears on his birth certificate, Royal Navy documents (he was a paymaster in the Royal Navy), the 1911 census and his death certificate. Changes of name were not uncommon and not illegal, but the reason for the name change is not known. What is clear, is that during their stay in Durrington they used the surname of Arno.

There are a multiple number of birth registrations for their children with some double entries appearing a few years after their birth. **Jack Jean Arno** was born in France in 1907 according to the census, so is not registered in England. **Carmen Willson Arno** is first registered in 1908 and re-registered in 1915 with the name 'Lagadere' added. **Henry (or Harry) Fellowes Arno** is also registered twice, in 1909 and 1915 with 'Lagadere' added. Their fourth child **Robert Pyatt** was registered in 1910 with the surname 'Moore'. The last three children were all born in Durrington. Around 1910-1911, Major Arno and his wife left the property for their new home in Worthing and reverted to using their other surname.

The next occupant is shown on the 1911 census where **Mrs Alice Webb** is listed and the house has been given a name change to *Thornberry*.[40] Alice was the widow of **Allen Webb** from *Salvington Farm* who had died in 1908. More details about Mrs Webb can be found with *Salvington Farm*.

The other half of these two semi-detached properties stood on the left hand side, shown in the photograph with a conservatory attached, being called *Orpington House*. The first purchase date is given on the Inland Revenue Valuation as November 1902 when **Thomas Saunders** bought the house for £450.[41] By January 1904, Thomas is advertising *'Buff Orpington laying pullets'* for sale in the local newspaper.[42]

The Buff-Orpington poultry were developed in Kent in the late 1890's and clearly are the reference for the house name. Thomas Saunders did not live at the property for long. Between 1904 and 1906 the street directories and electoral registers give the occupier as **Henry Dyer**. The next occupants were **William Rice** and his wife **Hannah**. They were retired lodging house keepers from Bermondsey, and another example of people who retired to Durrington. During their occupancy, the house changed its name to *Purley* which is how it is listed on both the electoral register and the 1911 census.[43] By 1913, the Inland Revenue Valuation records that **John Weatherell** is now owning and living in the property. He was a widowed farmer who had been born in Brighton in 1857. He had been living in *Elmcroft* in Durrington Lane with his unmarried daughter **Sarah** and moved into this property in 1913.

31. The Briars & Fernbank/Villa (Avondale), Salvington Road
(Now 119 & 121 Salvington Road)

Modern photograph. © Philip Amos 2016

This pair of semi-detached houses were already built and occupied by the time of the 1901 census. *Fernbank*, on the left of the pair, was the home of the **Douglas** family. The family consisted of **Clare Henry** (b.1875), his sister **Violet** (b.1881), and two of his brothers **James Sholto** (b.1882) and **Edwin** (b.1886). The brothers and sister were all children of **Edwin James Douglas**, a Scottish born figure and animal painter who had made his home in the Worthing area. The three brothers were fruit growers who ran nurseries in and around Durrington at the time. They included the appropriately named *Douglas Nurseries* almost directly opposite on the northern side of Salvington Road next door to *Red Cedars Nursery*. The relationship with the Saunders family, who ran *Red Cedars Nursery*, was further enhanced by the marriage in 1903, of **Clare Henry Douglas** to the eldest daughter of William Saunders, **Edith Emily Saunders** (b.1881).

In May 1910, *Fernbank* and its neighbour *The Briars*, were purchased by the Lewes Co-operative Building Society.[44] The Douglas family, which by now had grown a little with the birth of two children **Dorothy Christine** (b.1904) and **Kenneth Gordon** (b.1907), moved to *Birklands* in Greenland Road. Another of the brothers, James, had moved to Findon to live with his widowed father.

The next occupant was **Herbert Edgar Tweed** (b.1870), his wife **Annie** (b.1876 nee Newbury) and their son **Herbert** (b.1909). The Tweed's changed the name of the house to *Avondale*. He had been born and raised in Upper Beeding where his father was the blacksmith. There is a short interlude in Herbert's life where it appears he is taking a career break from being a wheelwright. The Worthing Gazette names him in January 1908, being issued with a temporary licence at *The Coach and Horses* in Clapham.[45]

THE COACH AND HORSES.

A temporary transfer of the licence of the Coach and Horses Inn, Clapham, was granted to Mr. Herbert Edgar Tweed, of Durrington; the outgoing tenant being Mr. Wakeham.

The Briars was the other semi-detached house of the pair, and in 1901, was the home of **William** and **Mary Hazell** and their niece, **Rebecca Shipp**.[46] The couple never had any children. William was another Durrington fruit grower who had come to the area from Windsor. He had worked firstly in Heene where he is listed in 1891[47] as a nurseryman living at *The Rosary*, Mill Road and then later moved to Durrington to work as a fruit grower where, as an employer, he is sometimes found advertising in the Worthing Gazette for staff. [48]

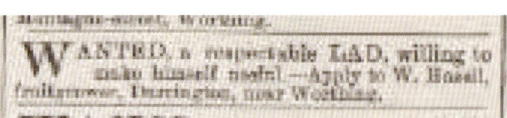

April 1901 advert

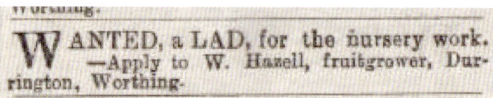

July 1902 advert

William was the first person in the village to put himself forward for nomination as a councillor on the newly created Parish Council in 1902. Unfortunately he did not secure enough votes to win a place on the council.[49] In 1906 William died, leaving the childless Annie a widow, although she continued to live in the house alongside her niece who was listed as a housekeeper or domestic on the censuses.

32. Alleyne Cottage, Salvington Road
(Now the site of Ellison Court)

The first mention of *Alleyne Cottage* is in a street directory for 1910, although the Inland Revenue Valuation suggests the timber-built poultry houses which surrounded the back garden were erected around 1909. The house was described in less than favourable terms by the Tax Assessor:

> '*Modern red brick 2 storey detached villa…..rather unattractive design…..ranged all round garden at back are fowl houses, timber built…..appear to have been erected since 1909*'[50]

The first occupier was listed in 1910 as **John H Jones**, a poultry farmer. Nothing else is known of Mr Jones until his sudden death was reported in the local newspaper.[51]

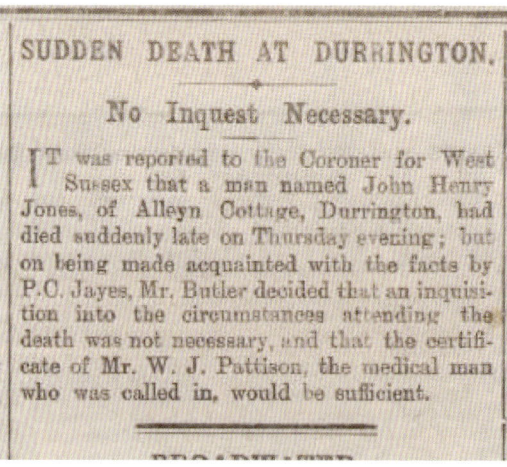

Worthing Gazette recording the inquest of
John Henry Jones in February 1911

Whatever the cause of his sudden demise, the decision was made that it was not suspicious and there was no need for an inquest.

The next occupants purchased the house for £600 and nursery land to the north of Salvington Road, around February 1911, for another £750. They were a young family from London, **John and Alice Neal** and their young son also called **John** (b.1906). There were, confusingly, at least three generations of John's in the family. John Jnr, so named in the Worthing street directories for 1911, was born in 1886 in Battersea where his parents John and Henrietta (Harriet), were coal merchants. John was an only child and joined his father in the family business. In 1904, he married **Alice Mitchell** (b.1883 nee Livie) in Battersea and by 1906 they had a son, also called **John**. In the early months of 1911, the decision was made by the whole family to move south. John's parents, John and Henrietta had retired and moved into Ash Grove in Worthing. John Jnr purchased *Alleyne Cottage* plus the four acres of land on the north side of Salvington Road which was worked as a market garden.[52] The 1911 census gives his occupation as Poultry Farmer, and the directories of the period call the property *Alleyne Poultry Farm*.[53] Although John had purchased the house, poultry farm and nursery in February 1911, it was not to be a long occupation for him, if indeed he actually worked the business himself, as he may have employed others to do the work in the poultry farm. By June 1911 he was renting the whole business to **Mr F W Clarke** for £50 a year.

It is possible that John did not have good health and the work would have been very physical. We do know that he died at *Alleyne Cottage* very suddenly from Cardiac Disease on 12th August 1911 as his death certificate confirms.

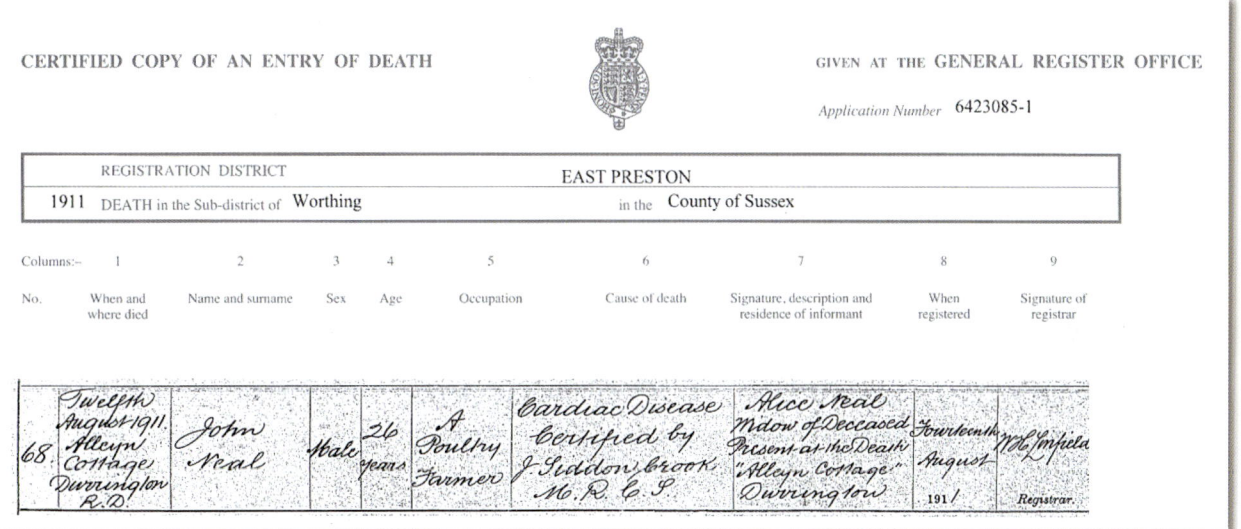

Portion of Neal death certificate showing cause of death.

His wife and young son continued to live in *Alleyne Cottage* for some years after his death.

It is interesting to note that this house and poultry farm saw the sudden death of both of its occupants during the Edwardian period. No photographs of the original cottage have been traced and the property has since been demolished. *Ellison Court* stands on the site today.

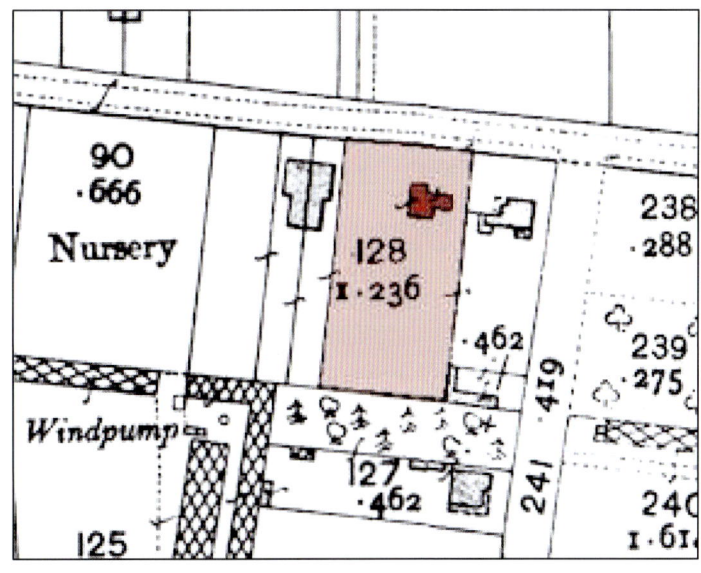

Excerpt taken from OS 25":1 mile Sheet LXIV: 5,6 3rd Edition 1912 (NTS)

Ellison Court now stands on the site of *Alleyne Cottage*. © Dave Pryce 2015

33. Durrington House, Salvington Road
(No longer standing)

This was a three-bedroomed detached house standing on a plot of land on the corner of Salvington Road and Greenland Road. The Inland Revenue Valuation of June 1913 described it as *'Red brick, tiled roof, pretty elevations'*.[54] Obviously this was deemed at the time to be an attractive property. The grounds of the house included two glasshouses and two timber built sheds which appear from the map to have been at the bottom of the garden.

The occupants first listed during the Edwardian period appear on the 1901 census as **Edward Parry Davies** (b.1858) and his wife **Amelia** (b.1858).[55] They were not Sussex born and lived in the village having come originally from London where Edward had been in the clothing trade. Electoral registers and street directories suggest they were already here in 1900 and left the house around 1905. When Durrington had its first Parish Council in 1902, **Edward Davies** unsuccessfully stood for election, where we see him listed as a 'gentleman'.[56]

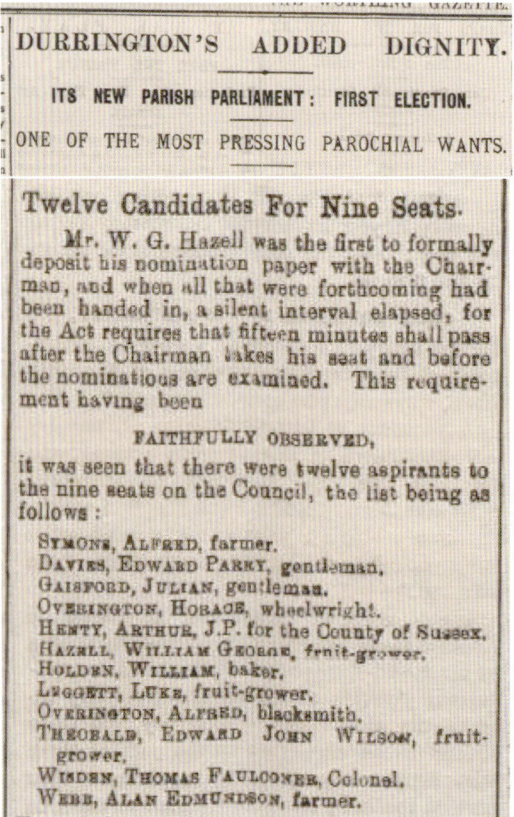
The first election of a Durrington Parish Council in December 1902

Previously, Durrington had only a large enough population to merit a Parish Meeting but with the growth of population they could now go forward with a full Parish Council.

The next occupant, **John Allen**, is only listed in street directories for 1905-1906, and apart from one advert in the paper we know nothing more about him. In June 1906 he was advertising a Cob and Cart plus some hosepipes for sale. As this was around the time he left the house, he may have been disposing of unwanted items.[57]

In 1906 *Durrington House* was purchased by **Horace Overington**, the eldest son of **Edgar Overington**. Horace had until this time been living in Pond Lane at *Durrington Farmhouse*. He became the owner of various properties around Durrington; among them was *Greenstede House*, the *Timber Yard* in New Road next door to it and one of the cottages in *The Forge* complex run by his family. The cost of purchasing *Durrington House* was £450 with only a small further outlay, which suggests the property was still in good condition.

Arthur Henry Symonds is the occupier from 1907-1909, and then the owner **Horace Overington** moved into the house after the death of his wife, **Caroline** in 1910. He only stayed at the address for a short time as the 1911 census lists **Harry Pearless** (b.1876) with his wife **Kate** (b.1876) and their young son **Ronald** living at the address.[58] Harry was a carpenter and joiner originally from East Grinstead.

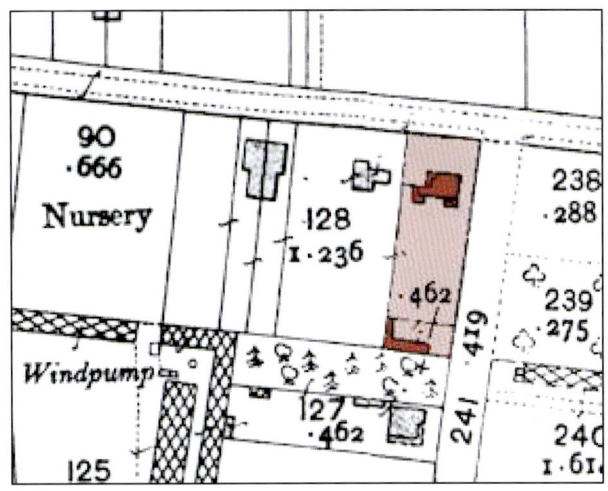

Excerpt taken from OS 25":1 mile Sheet LXIV: 5,6 3rd Edition 1912 (NTS)

This row of modern houses has been built on the site of *Durrington House*. © Dave Pryce 2014

34. Red Cedars Nursery & House, Salvington Road
(No longer standing)

The house known as *Red Cedars* stood in the grounds of the nursery of the same name, which was owned and run by William Nathaniel Saunders during the Edwardian years, and became noted for its lavender fields and grapes.

Lavender fields much like those at *Red Cedars* nursery in the period

William Nathaniel Saunders was born in Preston, Sussex in 1853 and worked as a 'map mounter' both in Sussex and in London for the first years of his working life.[59] In 1879 while still in London, he married **Mary Ann Pocock,** a lady born in Brighton around 1844. The couple went on to have three children, all born in the Lambeth area where William had his business, **Edith** (b.1881), **Florence** (b.1882) and **William Hoad** (b.1886).

By 1901 William is still on the census in London working as a 'map mounter' but he is also listed on the 1901 electoral register for Durrington as a landowner so obviously he had brought land and plans were being made for the move south.[60] The Inland Revenue Valuation outlines the purchase and further expenditure of almost £5000 on the land and buildings enabling *Red Cedars* to begin to function as a nursery and the family to have a house to live in.[61] By 1902 they have made the move and the name of William Saunders is appearing in the street directories for Durrington. William and Mary had made the decision to change occupation and move south and we know from a family source that this journey was a long and arduous undertaking. His granddaughter, Marjorie Parker wrote about the journey in a letter she sent to local school teacher, John Green, in March 1987:

> *'The house was called 'Red Cedars' and my Grandparents moved there from London – in a pea soup fog, the furniture vans in those days were horse drawn and the move apparently took three days!'*

By 1904 they were well established in Durrington, and adverts begin to appear in the paper with livestock and produce for sale. By June 1904, a letter appears in the Worthing Gazette singing the praises of Mr Saunders grapes which had been spotted in no less a place than West Hartlepool![62]

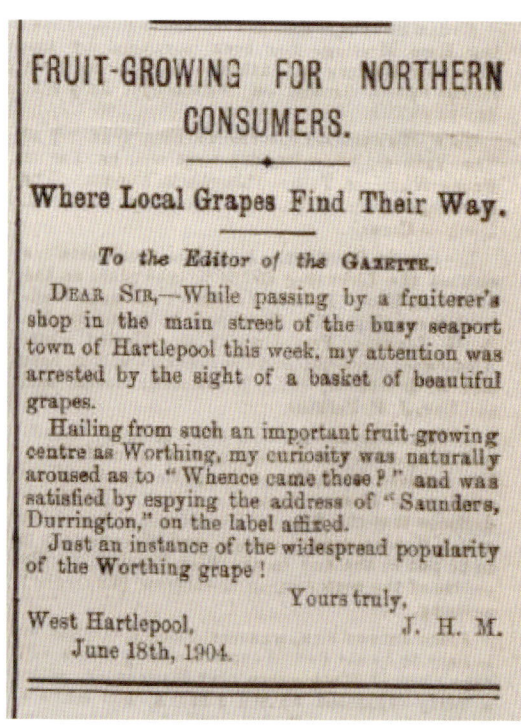

Letter from the Worthing Gazette regarding Mr Saunders grapes in West Hartlepool in 1904

A newspaper article in April 1906 tells the story of a bicycle owned by William's son, William, who was living at *Red Cedars* with his parents. The said bicycle had been stolen from Worthing by a German gentleman, **Robert Boje**. The chase to find the thief and the bicycle was undertaken by a Worthing policeman, **Sergeant Payne** who followed the trail and recovered the bicycle in Findon. Not satisfied with just recovering the stolen bicycle a trail through to Polegate and finally Eastbourne was followed and the German stable lad was finally captured. The result was regarded as a *'Commendable Capture'* in the local press.[63]

The house and nursery land stretched from Salvington Road as far north as the Arundel Road, but both have been lost and replaced by the modern telephone exchange and the housing in Mendip Road and Cheviot Road.

Photograph of the site where *Red Cedars* house originally stood. It is now the entrance to the British Telecom exchange building.
© Dave Pryce 2015

35. Durrington Free Church, Salvington Road
(Now New Life Church, Salvington Road)

Durrington Free Church has been researched and written by Lyn Tiller, one of the project volunteers and a member of staff at the church.

At the turn of the century the only religious congregation in Durrington was Anglican. The Church itself was still in ruins and services were conducted in a small tin hut called the *Mission Room* which stood beside the ruins. There was no non-denominational meeting place either in Durrington or Salvington.[64]

In 1905, **George Hide** of High Street, Tarring, rented an upper room in a house in Stone Lane to conduct non-denominational services for his own family and a few friends.

This continued for four years until the owner of the property terminated the tenancy. Undeterred, for about three months during the summer of 1909, they held open-air services outside *The Spotted Cow* (now the *John Selden*) at the eastern end of Salvington Road and mid-week prayer meetings were held at

Worthing Gazette reporting on the Undenominational meeting in Salvington in 1906

Bethany Durrington Hill (now *No 1 Bramble Lane)*, the home of **Elizabeth and Jane Helsdon** who were two of the founder members of the Church.

SALVINGTON.

THE MISSION.—The first anniversary of the Salvington Mission took place on Monday, the proceedings consisting of a tea and meeting. There were about fifty present. Mr. Brooks presided over the meeting, and after his opening remarks addresses were given by Messrs. G. Hide and G. Hills. Solos were sung by the Misses Violet and Lily Hide. There is one thing needed in connection with the Mission, and that is a Mission Room. Anyone who would like to help with this is requested to communicate with Mr. G. Hide, High street.

Worthing Gazette, 4th April 1906

SALVINGTON.

MISSION ANNIVERSARY.—Wednesday evening saw the completion of two years' work at the Salvington Mission, and a tea and anniversary gathering were held to celebrate the event. About forty-five were present at the tea, and the place was fairly well-filled for the after-meeting. Mr. George Hide presided, and gave an account of the work which had been carried on for the past two years, during which time most satisfactory progress has been made. It was also suggested that, as the villagers are taking such a large amount of interest in the work, it was quite time there was a better and more permanent place provided to meet in. A most helpful address on the necessity of the use of the Christian armour as a shield against sin was given by Mr. George Hills, and the proceedings also included solos by Master E. Scutt and Mrs. McClean.

Worthing Gazette 10th April 1907

MISSION WORK AT SALVINGTON.

Interesting Presentation.

THERE have been interesting doings at Salvington in connection with the Gospel Mission during the past week. A New Year's Tea to all the people of the village and neighbourhood was given on Wednesday, about fifty-five accepting invitations.

The meal, which was thoroughly satisfactory, received full justice, and subsequently Mr. G. Hide, the energetic Secretary of the Mission, presided over the evening gathering.

The meeting had only been in progress a few minutes when Mrs. W. Holden asked permission to speak to the Chairman. This was accorded, and she read to him an address signed by a large number of the worshippers at the Mission which was in the accompanying terms:

"To Mr. George Hide,—We, the undersigned, being the adult worshippers and children of the Salvington Undenominational Mission, ask that you will be pleased to accept, as

A Token of Appreciation

of the services you have so very kindly rendered for nearly two years past to the Mission, a gold-mounted umbrella from the adult section, and a water-bottle and glass for the desk from the children; and in doing so we trust that you may be spared for many years to continue your labour amongst us, and that God will bountifully bless your voluntary efforts to do good."

The CHAIRMAN, who was quite taken by surprise by the presentation, accepted the gifts with a few grateful words of thanks.

Messrs. G. Hills and J. Burse gave short addresses, and solos were sung by Mrs. McClean, Miss Ella Ansfield, and the Misses Lily and Violet Hide.

On Thursday night about sixty children of the village sat down to a similar tea, and spent a most enjoyable evening in singing solos, etc. A short address was given by Mr. J. Burse, who also presented to each of those children who could read, and who attend the Sunday School on Sunday afternoons, a New Testament.

As they left the building each child received an orange.

Worthing Gazette 30th January 1907

THE BAPTIST CAUSE.

Sunday Evening Services at Durrington.

AMONG the reports presented to the West Sussex Education Committee, at a monthly meeting at Horsham on Wednesday, was one from the Finance Sub-Committee. This stated that the Committee's Inspector had reported upon the letting of the Durrington Council School out of Public Elementary School hours; and it was now agreed, on the recommendation of the Sub-Committee, that the application of the Rev. W. D. Ross for the use of a room in the School for Sunday evening services, at a charge of £10 a year, should be approved.

Worthing Gazette reports on the permission given for the Undenominational Mission to meet in the school buildings in October 1909

In November 1909, this small group of people began to rent the newly opened *Durrington Council School* in Salvington Road and for two years, held their Sunday evening services there.

With the help of other churches in Worthing, efforts were made to establish a free church in the village of Durrington. A building committee was formed and in 1911 they succeeded in purchasing a plot of land on the corner of Salvington Road and Greenland Road, for the princely sum of £70. Plans were made to build a small chapel to seat 70 people. They were helped by the Free Church Council who underwrote the cost of £450 for this building project and the debt was cleared in 7 years – no small feat for such a small group of people!

The hall was built on the southern end of the plot of land, reserving the space on the northern end facing the main road, for a larger building in the future (which was accomplished in 1939). Today the completed church still stands on this site, the original small chapel forming the southern part of the building now known as 'The Coffee Shop'.

On 15th November 1911 the stone laying ceremony took place for the new chapel. Afterwards, tea for 70 people was served at *Downsview*, the home of **Henry Capel and Mabel Saunders** in Greenland Road, who had married just three weeks earlier in Reigate, Surrey where Mabel came from. Their house in Greenland Road was part of *Downsview Nursery* which Henry Capel Saunders owned and ran. It also became the venue for the Sunday Services pending the completion of the Chapel, which took 3 months to build.

Photograph of Henry and Mabel Saunders taken around the time of their wedding in 1911. Owned by New Life Church

The building was completed early in 1912 and the opening ceremony was held on 21st February.[65] On 25th February, they held their first service in the new chapel. The 12 founder members sat around the communion table and held hands to receive each other into membership of the newly established church. There were 12 adults and also 12 children in the Sunday School who were originally taught by their parents. The 12 founder members were; Mrs. Annie Elizabeth Gardiner, Mr. Ernest & Mrs. Alice Gough, Miss Elizabeth Helsdon, Miss Jane Helsdon, Mrs. Mary Ann Moulton, Mr. Henry Capel & Mrs. Mabel Saunders, Mr. William Thomas and Mrs. Caroline Tunstall, Mr. John Weatherell and Miss Sarah Annie Weatherell.

Photograph of the new church building opened in February 1912.
Worthing Library

Henry Capel Saunders was very influential in the life of the church serving as Treasurer, Church Secretary and Deacon for around 40 years. Mabel Saunders equally played a significant part in starting a regular women's meeting which she ran for 33 years and was attended by 50-60 local women. She also started a children's club which ran on Tuesday evenings, which was very popular and attended by many of the children from the village and area who filled the hall week by week.

During the first four years, while this fledgling church had no minister of its own, the church was greatly helped by **Rev. John Onions** who lived in Rowlands Road, Worthing. Other ministers of various denominations from Worthing also came and helped. Across the years the Church continued and grew and still stands on the corner of Salvington Road and Greenland Road. It is now known as *New Life Church*.

New Life Church photographed in 2013 © Dave Pryce

NEW CHAPEL AT DURRINGTON.

ITS FORMAL DEDICATION.

FIRST INSTALMENT OF A MORE AMBITIOUS SCHEME.

FREE CHURCH UNITY.

ORIGIN AND HISTORY OF THE MOVEMENT.

WHEN the plans and intentions of the Federated Free Churchmen in that direction are fully accomplished, Durrington will find itself placed in possession of a block of buildings the extent and character of which are indicated in the accompanying illustration. For some time past a movement has been in progress to provide a building in which undenominational services may be conducted, and the completion of the first section of the scheme was witnessed on Wednesday, when the building was formally dedicated. A commencement has been made with a Mission Hall, the modest part of the structure which is depicted on the extreme right of our photographic reproduction; and when circumstances favour a more ambitious project the promoters will proceed with the erection of the larger building.

Unlocking the Door.

It was intended that Mr. Jasper Cowell, of Steyning, whose services are so often in request in connection with religious movements in this neighbourhood, should perform the opening ceremony, but illness prevented his attendance, and he sent a cheque for £5 for the funds. In his absence the door was unlocked by Mr. F. J. Norman, who occupies the position of President of the Free Church Council.

When those who were identified with the movement were admitted to the building they the record in the porch of West Tarring Church.

The Rev. W. BAMPTON TAYLOR reminded those present that there would be a need for the exercise of a great deal of charity in the carrying out of the work at Durrington; but he was quite sure that the work would

Go On Very Nicely And Smoothly

if they exercised that charity which covered a multitude of sins, and saw not the worst in people but the best (applause). And they must remember that they would also have to exercise a good deal of perseverance, for they were not going to have gala days and picnics every day. In the days to come they would have difficulties, and discouragements, and stress, and strain; and in those days, when the work began to get thankless and went against the grain, he wanted them to exercise the grace of patience, the grace of perseverance, the grace of pegging away.

The Rev. J MAYLES said he was asked by Mr. Willoughby to supplement the statement already made by Mr. Norman. If the larger building on that site was not erected and paid for within ten years from that date, then the house which he now offered would revert to the Primitive Methodist Church at Worthing, to be sold by auction and the proceeds given for the reduction of the debt on

The Building at Worthing.

He hoped the debt would be liquidated by that time, though he could assure them they had a live monkey on it at the present time (laughter). Such a contingency as he had spoken about would be something in the nature of a God-

HOW THE COMPLETED BUILDING WILL APPEAR.

found that, though modest in its proportions, it was admirably adapted to its present purpose, and will continue to fill a position of usefulness even when the more ambitious part of the scheme is carried out. Mr. J. E. Lund was the Architect, and the building was erected by Mr. F. A. Moat; each of these divisions of the work having been accomplished in a manner which has given

Complete Satisfaction

to those immediately concerned. The building is bright and cheerful, and those associated with the movement seem very pleased with it.

Among those who were present were the Rev. W. Bampton Taylor, Rev. J. Moyles, Rev. G. Kaines (Honorary Secretary of the Free Church Council), Pastor J. Onions, and Messrs. E. A. Smith, M. Willoughby, J. Blackman, G. Hide, H. C. Saunders, etc. Mrs. W. J. Gardiner presided at the harmonium, and played the accompaniments to the several hymns that were sung in the course of the inaugural proceedings.

After the formal opening a service was held, the sermon being preached by the Rev. W. Bampton Taylor; and subsequently tea was provided for the numerous company.

The Later Proceedings.

The final event of these commemorative proceedings took the form of a public meeting presided over by Mr. J. R. C. Palmer, and attended by a company that took possession of the whole of the accommodation available, a few additional chairs having, indeed, to be procured. At the request of the Rev. G. Kaines (the Honorary Secretary of the Worthing Free Church Council),

A statement of the position was presented by Mr H. C. SAUNDERS, who remarked that the one feeling they had was one of thankfulness that they had now a roof over their heads. The work was begun by Mr. George Hide, who, in April, 1905, rented a room at Salvington, and took over the whole responsibility, financial and otherwise, with the occasional help of a few friends. This continued for about four years, when, owing to the action of the owners, the room had to be given up. For about three months they were

Without a Building,

and had to carry on their work in the open air. In November, 1909, the Free Church Council at Worthing undertook to rent the Council Schools for Sunday evening services, and that work was carried on for two years and two months, which brought them up to last Christmas. In January last year a Committee was formed from the different Churches to see if something could be done to provide a permanent place of worship. The land was obtained, the size of the site being seventy feet by a hundred feet, for the price of £70. Mr. Mark Willoughby promised the first £5 as a contribution, and he had made the promise to them that if, within five or ten years, they built a Chapel on the northern part of the site, he would give them at his death—which they hoped would not be for a good many years—(hear, hear)—a house on the adjoining plot, worth at least £300. The condition was that the Chapel should be

Opened Free of Debt;

send to the Trustees at Worthing; but he thought he could rise above considerations of that sort, and he did hope that they at Durrington would be able to avail themselves of Mr. Willoughby's offer; and that in the years to come they would carry on in the larger building a work which would bring glory to God and great blessing to the people of that locality (applause).

The substantial sum of £56 was contributed during the day, and £220 is now available for the fund.

AT THE WINTER HALL.

The Noble Art.

Representation of a Boxing Match.

AN effective illustration of the art of boxing was furnished to large and appreciative audiences at the Winter Hall on Saturday evening, and the film was retained in the list as the star subject until last night. The West supplies us with many popular pictures now, and this is one of them. The producers were the Nestor Company, and a love story was seen to have been deftly interwoven with the more serious part of the subject.

The Plot Fails.

The story, briefly summarised, concerns itself with one Edwin Baxter in a little Western town. He is a clever boxer, but as his sweetheart, May Sutton, does not approve of such a course, he declines to accept a challenge issued by a Theatrical Company to box a pugilist who forms one of the attractions. But as May consents, owing to poverty, to marry a certain Samuel King, Baxter determines to try to obtain the promised two hundred dollars.

King becomes acquainted with this arrangement, and approaches the professional pugilist, to whom he offers any sum he cares to mention if he will only defeat Baxter. But the plan miscarries, for after a very vigorous and realistic exhibition Baxter is proclaimed the winner, and earns the gratitude of his sweetheart and her parents.

So long a time has elapsed since it was seen here that the Biograph film, "The Country Doctor," was warmly welcomed on its return on Saturday. It is

A Singularly Pathetic Picture,

showing a doctor's devotion to duty, for whilst he is able to cure the child of a widowed mother, his own little one dies whilst he is absent on his mission.

The spectacular film included in the list that evening consisted of a representation of a Cossack Regiment engaged in a number of exercises, which they carry out with characteristic dash; whilst amongst the remaining subjects we may mention a very diverting picture showing some sportive Kentucky girls who place a matrimonial message in some tobacco which they are packing, and as it is not discovered until many years later, the result is most unexpected and amusing.

Dedication of the new chapel in Durrington part (2 of 2)

> and the work, he might add, was to be carried on upon undenominational and unsectarian lines (hear, hear). To himself it was an eye-opener when he first came there, to see the need for such a work, and to see how ignorant and degraded were some of the people living there.
>
> Mr. F. J. NORMAN said he was desired by Mr. Willoughby to explain that he did not regard his offer as his own gift. If it had not been given to that particular work, its equivalent would have gone to the Primitive Methodist Church in Worthing; so that Mr. Willoughby wished it to be understood from the commencement that this cottage was given as the gift of the Primitive Methodist Church. The total cost of the building in which they were now assembled was, in round figures, about £450; and by the end of that evening he hoped they would be in possession of £300 of that money. He wanted to thank quite a number of friends for all the help they had given, and especially did he wish to acknowledge with gratitude the work of Mr. Saunders (applause). He could remember the time when it would have been
>
> **Impossible To Have Such a Meeting**
>
> as they were holding that night. And for the change that had been brought about he thanked God for the Free Church Council. It had its faults and its weaknesses, for it was a human institution; but he thanked God for the spirit that had taken possession of men and women, and caused them to unite in bringing about such a result as that (applause).
>
> The CHAIRMAN based his observations upon the second chapter of the First Epistle of Peter, pointing out that more than two hundred and fifty years ago John Selden, born in an old thatched cottage at Salvington, knew the Lord; and he was sorry that so few people knew the testimony he bore, as contained in

Worthing Gazette 28th February 1912 (Part 3 of 3)

36. Victoria Bungalow, Salvington Road
(No longer standing)

We find the earliest mention of this property in the street directory for 1905. The owner and first occupier was **Joseph Edward de Vere Mills** (1871-1916). Born in Islington, London, he is listed at the property from 1905-1911 according to the directories and appears on the 1911 census.[66] He was a leather manufacturer who had retired to Durrington with his wife **Mary Maud (nee Moores).** According to the census, they had been married for eight years, although no registration of a marriage has been found on the indexes. Listed on the census they have a young Spanish servant, **Emilienne Vidal,** living with them which suggests they may have travelled and possibly married abroad. They had no children.

The property was purchased by **Joseph Mills** on September 29th 1908 for £600, so the couple may have rented their home for a period before they purchased it. The Inland Revenue Valuation describes the house having five rooms, kitchen, scullery, bathroom and other buildings.[67]

By May 1913 when the Inland Revenue Valuation was taken, three cottages had been added on the land around *Victoria Bungalow*. One was built behind the property as a detached cottage, now demolished, while the other two were a pair of semi-detached properties still standing, now *149 and 151 Salvington Road*.

Joseph died in 1916. His widow Maud eventually went to New Zealand where she sadly died in a Psychiatric Hospital in Auckland in Sept 1958. In 1960, notices appear in the newspapers in England asking for next of kin, especially her elder sister, to come forward as no relatives could be traced.

Victoria Bungalow has since been demolished.

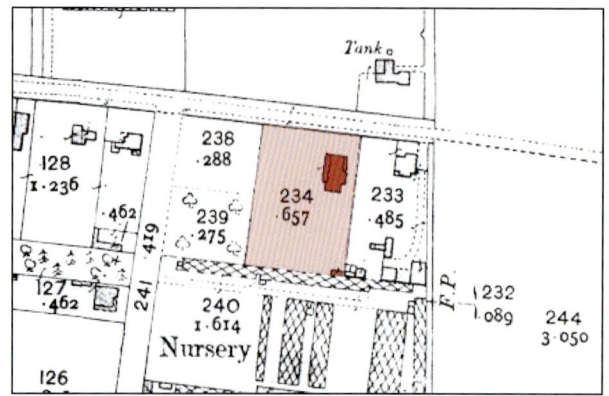

Excerpt taken from OS 25":1 mile Sheet LXIV: 5,6 3rd Edition 1912 (NTS)

Modern photograph showing the site where *Victoria Bungalow* stood. © Dave Pryce 2015

37. Coote & Sons Bakery, Salvington Road
(No longer standing, now Bakers Court, Salvington Road)

During the Edwardian period, this bakery was run by one family, the Coote family. The head of the business and indeed of the family was **Rhoda Coote.** Rhoda had been born in Devon in 1851, and in 1878 had married a miller named **Alfred Samuel Coote** (1855-1898).

During Alfred and Rhoda's years of marriage, they moved to various mills to work. The birth places of their children, illustrate the journey the couple had taken before arriving in Salvington. It was only after Rhoda was widowed, that she blossomed as the head of a thriving bakery business.

They began their journey in Houghton, Hampshire, and it was here that the first three of their eight children were born. The 1881 census lists the couple with two children living at Houghton Mill where Alfred was the miller.[68] Their first son was **Richard** (b.1879), who was later to marry and settle in Durrington working in the business with his mother. The second son to be born at Houghton was **Alfred** (b.1881), he also later married and settled very close to his older brother in Durrington and joined the family business. Sometime after Alfred was born the family moved to Lyminster in Sussex, where **Cecil** (b.1883), **Ganey** (b.1885), **Samuel** (b.1886) and **John** (b.1889) were born. The family then moved again to *Ashington Water Mill* in Sussex where **Charles** (b.1890) was born. They must have moved again to *Salvington Mill* before 1894, as their last child **Alice** (b.1894) was born the same year in Salvington.

Salvington Road in 1910 showing the bakery on the left. Worthing Library

In November 1898, Alfred died leaving Rhoda a widow with eight children. With some of her children, she then embarked on a career running her own business and *Coote & Sons* was born. She is first listed in her own right as a baker in a 1900 Kelly's Directory, and again appears as head of the family in the 1901 census, where she is registered as living *'on her own account'*.[69] The Inland Revenue Valuation taken on 23rd May 1913 gives clear details about the site.[70] It was purchased in 1900 for £140. This was only a short time after Alfred had died and as no property is shown on the 1890's OS map, this was probably the price of purchasing the land. In the ensuing months, a sum of £1100 was spent, reflecting no doubt the cost of building the house and bakery buildings. When Alfred had died, he had left his widow the sum of £401 10s 6d, which it would appear she wisely invested in the land and development of a business along with her sons. The Inland Revenue Valuation further describes the completed site as:

'Well-built house & Shop. Red brick & rough cut & half-timber work…….'

The photograph of the period inserted above clearly shows this decorative work. The OS map shows the house, which included the shop at the front of the plot, and further buildings at the rear, one of these being where the bread and cakes were baked, described in the Inland Revenue Valuation as a *'Bakehouse. Well built. Good modern ovens, tile walls, loft area.'* The mention of tiled walls is obviously of note and does not appear in other assessments for the area making this a very modern, stylish and up to date property.

Coote & Sons were regularly contracted to provide flour, bread and cakes to *East Preston Workhouse*, and rarely seem to have taken out any advertisements to boost their workload.[71]

During this period the house seems to have been known as *Durrington House*. A confusing name, as a few yards down the road, there was another property named *Durrington House* which stood on the corner of Salvington Road and Greenland Road. By 1911, Rhoda was living in the house with two of her younger sons, John and Charles who were both listed as bakers, and her daughter Alice.[72] We know that four of her sons were living in the Durrington/Salvington area, and all working at the bakery making this a truly family venture.

In June 1911 the Worthing Gazette reported Coote & Sons having their tender accepted to provide bread & cakes to East Preston Workhouse

79

The business was eventually sold to *Knowles Bakery* and ran as such until it closed in 1978. The buildings were demolished to make way for retirement flats, retaining the original business in its name and known as *Bakers Court*.

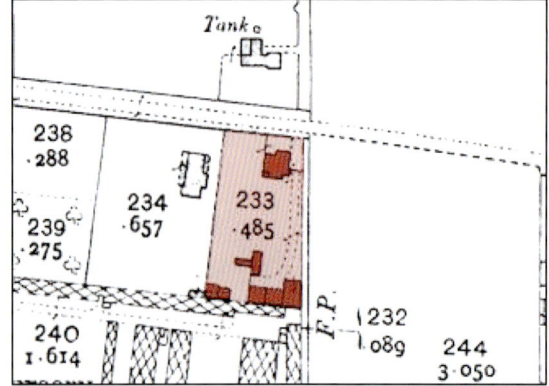

Excerpt taken from OS 25":1 mile Sheet LXIV: 6 3rd Edition 1912 (NTS)

Modern photograph showing the flats now standing on the site of *Coote's Bakery*. © Dave Pryce 2015

Picture of *Coote's Bakery* horse being attended to at *The Forge*.
Worthing Library (cropped)

38. Durrington Council School, Salvington Road
(Now Durrington First School, Salvington Road)

Durrington Council School has been researched by a group of pupils from the school in 2014 with their teacher, Mrs Sarah Rickwood. The children each produced a piece of creative writing and one of these has been reproduced in the book after the story of the school which is based on the work of Sarah Rickwood.

'School began with 45 children...' wrote the school's Headmaster; Mr Laban Boorer on 3rd July 1908 in the old School Log Book.[73] Would its future pupils realise that the school had first opened its doors to children on May 10th 1909 with Mr Boorer as Head Master, so many years ago?

The intention to build a much needed elementary school was the subject of a public inquiry by West Sussex County Council in March 1907.[74] The first discussions of cost were submitted to the County Education Authority on the 15th July 1907 when the estimate for the site, its buildings, fixtures and fittings came to a total of £2,667. However it would appear that even in Edwardian times every penny had to be accounted for as a revised final tender from Mr A. Crane of Worthing for £2,056 13s 9d was finally accepted.

A proposal to buy an acre of land from Mr Arthur Henty at the price of £350 was reported in a letter brought to the council dated 16th January 1908, and final approval from East Preston Rural District Council[75] was reported in the Worthing Gazette in 8th April 1908.[76]

The situation became even more urgent when in April 1908 the Worthing Gazette reported that decisions were being made by the Worthing Council Education Committee to close West Tarring School.[77] This could have resulted in educational disaster for the Durrington children who had nowhere to go to school. The Worthing Gazette reveals the efforts made to provide for the children until the school building was completed. Temporary premises were obtained[78] and rent issues were variously dealt with as the interim period continued.[79]

The Public Inquiry into the need for a school as reported in the local papers.

Attendance issues and the non-availability of enough school places were illustrated by an entry into the School Log Book on 17th September 1908:

> *'The ill-effects of non-attendance was remarkably exemplified today. Only four children could spell the word 'Who'.'*[80]

In a further edition of the paper it reported *'Mr Edwin Burns, of Stone's-Lane, Salvington (note the slight road name change), is to be paid the sum of ten shillings a week for the rent of Durrington Temporary School.'*[81] The temporary Durrington Council School opened June 29th 1908, but it seems the government soon stepped in with policies to be obeyed; it was soon visited by an inspector, who required urgent alterations to the paths, floors and offices. This work was carried out at a sum of £14 1s.

The desperate need for a school seems proven with L. Boorer reporting less than a month after opening *'We are full already and several other children have sought admission'.*[82] Mr Boorer was joined by Miss Mary F. Pigrome, a certified teacher, and he noted that *'additional help was required!'*[83]

Eventually the building of the school was completed, the children moved in and although there have been many changes through the years Durrington school still stands in the middle of the community that it serves.

Part of the children's project for their study of the school during the Edwardian period was to write a piece of work reflecting the life of a pupil at the school when it first opened. Included below is one of those essays.

<u>My day in the life of a Edwardian child.</u>

This morning when I woke up I looked out of my dusty, paned window. It was pouring with rain. Wind and rain whipped the air quicker than I had ever seen. I struggled into my cream coloured knee length frock and fitted my feet delicately into my black, highly polished shoes.

By the time I was ready to go the rain had eased slightly so I forced my way to school, dragging my brown and leather satchel in the puddles. When I eventually arrived at school Betty, my friend, was waiting there eagerly for me. She peered anxiously at my sodden pinafore.

First we had Arithmetic I had Miss Pigrome as Miss Scales was off with a swollen face. Arithmetic was really hard because we were laboriously writing vulgar fractions. I don't really understand vulgar fractions so I looked out of the window, watching the rain instead. After a bit, the rain stopped so I carried on with my work. Miss Pigrome had asked for at least 5 vulgar fractions but I had only done 3. When I handed my work in she looked at me through her rounded glasses. Miss Pigrome (unlike Miss Scales) had a kind, gentle sort of face so I was not worried that much when I handed my in short piece of work.

The rest of the day flew by. We had English and writing with Miss Rideout. English and writing were my favourite as we have Miss Rideout, who is friendly, and clever.

When it was time to go home, I went to the gate to meet Betty. Betty was unfortunately in a different class to me so when she told me the way she had been learning and drawing plants I had been listening in awe. I don't do nature because only the year above me does can do nature and sadly Betty is in that year.

Soon I got home and swung the door open. It was no longer pouring with rain but it did not matter as I was home.

By Lila Hite

The children outside the school on Coronation Day 22nd June 1911. Worthing Library

39. Salvington Farmhouse & Farm, Salvington Road
(Now, Old Sussex Cottage, Salvington Road)

This Grade 2 listed farmhouse, also known as *Salvington Letts* and *Old Sussex Cottage,* was built in the 18th century of flint and brick. It forms part of a group of buildings and out-buildings original to the farm. The buildings still have many original features, including a cock-pit in the attic of the farmhouse. The description given in their listing text is as follows:

> *'Salvington Letts………….(This is the real name of the house, but in the Rate-books it is entered as Old Sussex Cottage). C17. 2 storeys. 4 windows. Squared flints with red brick dressings and stringcourse. Red tiled roof. Modern Casement windows. Extension to 3 windows to west. All the listed buildings at Salvington Letts form a group.'* [84]

Salvington Farm was owned by **Frederick Wisden** from Henfield. He was a son of **Thomas Wisden** of *The Warren*, Broadwater. A younger brother of Frederick's, **Patrick Wisden** was living in *Salvington Lodge* near the farm in Salvington in 1908. The farm had been worked for many years by **Allen Webb** and his wife **Alice**, being listed at the farmhouse as early as the 1891 census.[85] Allen died in June 1908 and although Frances, his wife, continued to stay at the farmhouse for some years, she eventually moved further down Salvington Road to *Thornberry*. The ownership of the farm then passed to **Mr Edwin Lephard**. He was a well-known dairy farmer and political figure in the area, being a member of the first Worthing Town Council. The picture on the right is extracted from the town council photograph dated around 1890.[86]

Salvington Farm produced very high quality milk owing to the richness of the pasture land the cows grazed on. Adverts in the local paper weekly throughout the whole period, not only praised the milk, extolling its beneficial properties for *'infants and invalids'*, but it also listed other products which included butter from the Jersey herd as well as cream and clotted cream.

The farm was obviously an expensive outlay, even for Mr Lephard who owned land in Salvington and West Tarring, although he actually lived in *The Manor House, West Worthing*. The Inland Revenue Valuation of June 1913 reveals that the rent on the farm had risen and Mr Lephard decided he could not continue:

> *'Rent many years ago was £350. Mrs Webb recently paid £225. Lephard finds present rent too high and has given notice to quit.'* [87]

He was at the time being charged £325 annually for the farm and £50 for the buildings and the meadow.

The farmhouse itself was occupied by tenants other than the farmer of the land. The 1911 census lists a poultry farmer and market gardener from Kent named **Arthur Banks** (b.1867).[88] He lived here with his wife **Eda Georgiana** (b.1878 nee Bradford), and their two young sons **Alfred** (b.1908) and **Lionel** (b.1910). Eda's father was an architectural sculptor named **Alfred Bradford**. He had been born in Framfield, Sussex around 1846 and worked in the area for some years before moving to live and work in London.[89]

Modern photograph of the farmhouse. © Dave Pryce 2015

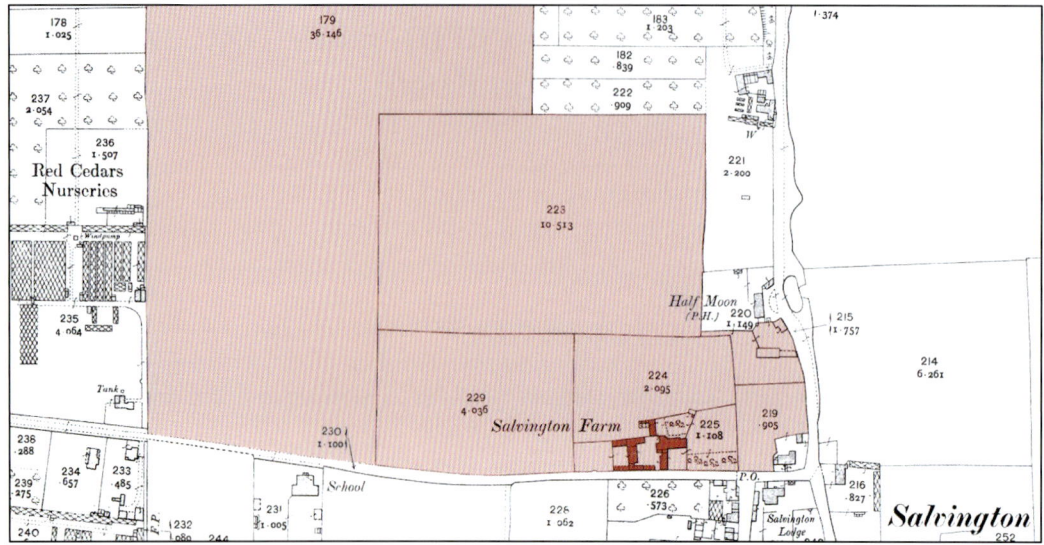

Excerpt taken from OS 25":1 mile Sheet LXIV: 6 3rd Edition 1912 (NTS)

40. Beta House & Alpha Cottage, Salvington Road
(No longer standing)

Drawing by Arthur Elliot. 1908   Worthing Library

Beta House was situated on the corner of Salvington Road and Stone Lane, and had a small adjoining cottage called *Alpha Cottage*. The interesting use of Greek alphabet words for the buildings is not repeated elsewhere in Salvington during the period, the derivation is unknown. Beta House and the adjoining cottage were both owned by **William Holden**.

William had been born in West Tarring, and it was there in October 1878 that he married a lady named **Callista Augusta de Liancourt** (b.1841). While William was the son of **John Holden**, a shoemaker from Tarring and his wife **Frances (Fanny),** Callista stated on her marriage certificate, that she was the daughter of '**Callistus Augustus Count de Goddes Liancourt'** (1806-1890). No birth certificate under that name can be traced but there is a child born in 1851 in Camden Town whose name was registered as Augusta Neopolia Goddes Nash and I believe this to be the lady in question.[90] Her mother was given as **Harriett Nash** and no father was named on the birth certificate. A few months before her birth, when the 1851 census was taken, Harriett Nash was living as servant/housekeeper to **Count Liancourt** in Port Hill, Hertfordshire, making it very possible that he was her father.

Tragically, her mother died early in 1852[91] and during the ensuing years Callista lived with relatives and friends using variations of her name: **Augusta Park** in 1861,[92] **Augusta Liancourt** in 1871[93] and by the time of her marriage - **Callista Augusta de Liancourt.**

After their marriage, William and Callista ran the *Salvington Post Office* from *Beta House* from 1882-1912. The business also included a grocery and bakers shop. In 1913, the Inland Revenue Valuation describes the property they lived in as:

> '*Large House of old style, valued with very small shop at corner of premises, shop is badly lighted, low roofed and too small for the work of a PO* '[94]

The property included a number of other buildings on the site including a bake house and flour loft, presumably used for the baking of bread sold in the shop. William and Callista had 4 children, **Callistus Augustus de Liancourt** (b.1879) who never married and lived with his parents assisting them in the business, **Arthur Stanley** (b.1881) who was often known as 'Stanley Holden' and was regularly before the magistrates for various offences. **Callista Augusta Godda Sophie May de Liancourt** (b.1884) was their only daughter, and in 1910 she married **Alic William Basil Taylor** from *Salvington Nurseries*. The last child was **William Alexander Holden** who was born in September 1888 but died the following June. William was involved in the affairs of the parish during his lifetime and was one of the elected members of the first Parish Council in 1902.[95]

The Holden's lived in *Beta House*, running the *Post Office* and shop until March 1912 when William suddenly died. An inquest was held on 6th March 1912 at the *John Selden Inn* just across the road.[96] This revealed that William had been suffering from *'chronic asthma for the last 28 yrs. and lately from influenza'*. He had been regularly using laudanum and had evidently overdosed. His wife, giving evidence, revealed that for *'years he had prayed to die; but he had never threatened to take his life.'* The inquest also gave some interesting details about internal family issues. Mrs. Holden was asked if her husband was depressed. *'Yes, very much depressed''* she had replied. The inquest recorded a possible reason for some of his unhappiness, *'One of his sons had been a lot of trouble to him, but notwithstanding that he was passionately fond of him and could not see his faults until too late.'* His second son Arthur, or Stanley as he was known, is often reported in the Worthing Gazette for drinking, fighting and other small misdemeanours. These included throwing water over a prospective parliamentary candidate and using abusive language in January 1906.[97] The jury's verdict in the inquest of William's death was, *'"Death by misadventure," in accordance with the medical evidence.'*[98]

SENSATION AT SALVINGTON.

Startling Discovery.

Mr. W. Holden's Tragic Death.

QUITE a painful sensation has been created in the adjacent village of Salvington by the death, under tragic circumstances, of Mr. William Holden, an old and highly respected resident of the district, who has for many years held the position of Sub-Postmaster there, in addition to carrying on the business of a baker.

The widowed Callista Holden continued to run the *Post Office* for some months but finally moved to *Beaconsfield Terrace*, Ashacre Lane where she continued to live.

Postcard c.1910 looking west down Salvington Road featuring the *Post Office* on the left.

Alpha Cottage was a tiny cottage attached to the western side of *Beta House*, clearly visible in the photograph above. Various tenants were listed there during the period, some for only a short period. The name of **Henry Smith** is listed in street directories in 1912 and **Wyatt, H** and **Batchelor** appear on the Inland Revenue Valuation, although no further details are recorded.[99] Occupants on the census have not been identified for this address.

Excerpt taken from OS 25":1 mile Sheet LXIV: 6 3rd Edition 1912 (NTS)

41. The Spotted Cow/John Selden, Salvington Road
(Now Ye John Selden, Salvington Road)

The original name for the public house standing on this site was *The Spotted Cow*. The tithe map of 1838 simply calls this site a *'House and Garden'* owned by a man named **Soutton Waterman.** Its occupants being **George Henson** (b.1781) and his wife **Elizabeth** (nee Holder) who were listed as agricultural labourers not innkeepers. George died in 1850, and his wife then changed the use of the house giving herself a means of income. By 1851, she was running the property as a beerhouse and her occupation listed as *'Brewer and Ale Seller'*.[100] The site of this beerhouse was only a few yards away from an even older inn, in Half Moon Lane, yet it is clear that these two establishments co-existed very close to each other for some years. One of the reasons for this may be that *The Spotted Cow* was run as a beerhouse and not a fully licensed public house. Beerhouses were only permitted to sell beer and ale, no spirits could be sold from the premises.

Photograph of *The Spotted Cow* before it was demolished to make way for the new *John Selden*.
Worthing Library

The Inland Revenue Valuation for this property reveals some more information. In 1909, it had an unlicensed value of £250, but by the date of the valuation the old building had been demolished and a new public house erected, the one we see today, which was given a full licence and a *'Licensed Value as per Mr Fleck's report, £750.*'[101] The origin of Mr Fleck's report is not known, but it is obvious that as a fully licensed property it was worth a great deal more for tax purposes.

The beerhouse keeper at the beginning of the Edwardian period was **Frederick Ansfield** (b.1859). In 1881 Frederick had married **(Frances) Ellen Linberry** (b.1862) and together they lived at *The Spotted Cow* for many years. This was an interesting marriage as Ellen was the daughter of **George and Ellen Linberry** who were the innkeepers of the *Half Moon Inn*, the second of the public houses, round the corner in Half Moon Lane. Presumably there was no animosity between the two establishments. Frederick died in 1904, and Ellen continued to run *The Spotted Cow* on her own until 1909, when she moved to *Beaconsfield Terrace*.

Newspaper reports reveal a little of what was happening behind the scenes during this period. In February of 1909 it was announced that the licences for *Half Moon Inn* and *The Spotted Cow* would not be renewed as changes were about to happen.[102]

AN IMPROVEMENT AT SALVINGTON.
Mr. E. B. Wannop applied on behalf of Messrs. Lambert and Norris for a renewal of the licences of the Half Moon Inn and the Spotted Cow at Salvington, explaining that it was proposed to erect on the site of the Spotted Cow, before the next Licensing Meeting, a new house, at a cost of about £1,000, if the Bench would consent to the full licence of the Half Moon being transferred to the new house, the licence of the latter house being given up, and no compensation or monopoly value being asked for.
To this the Bench assented.

Report of the plan to erect a new 'house' on the site of *The Spotted Cow*

By March 1909 there was a request to renew the full licence to the *Half Moon Inn* and the lesser licence to *The Spotted Cow*, with the agreement that the full licence would be transferred from the *Half Moon Inn* to the *'new house'* with full agreement of all parties.[103]

On 12th April 1910 plans were passed by the East Preston Rural District Council for permission to build on the site.[104] The cost of this re-building was given in an application for licensing by the owners, **Messrs Lambert & Norris** as £1000. By November 1910, a *'Temporary protection of the licence of the Spotted Cow'* was issued for **Mr Sandham**.[105] This was **Samuel Sandham** (b.1855) from Funtington, Sussex who would become the new proprietor of the *John Selden,* as the new public house was to be called. Mr Sandham is the name we find for the publican on the 1911 census along with his wife **Harriet Jane** (b.1850 nee Thorpe).[106] By December 1910 all is settled, the new building completed and the new licence granted.[107] We know that at this time the *Half Moon Inn* ceased working as a licensed public house and became a tea room and laundry.

A little puzzle remains for this period. The Inland Revenue Valuation Field Book page is undated but lists **Ansfield** as the previous occupier, although this has been crossed through. No mention is made of Samuel Sandham, but the new name inserted is **E Schooley.** The identity of this person is as yet unknown.[108]

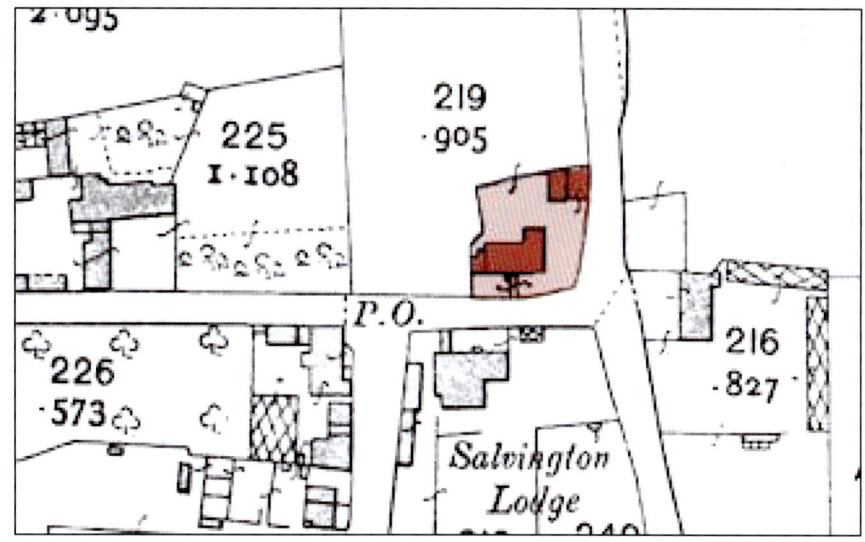

Excerpt taken from OS 25":1 mile Sheet LXIV: 6 3rd Edition 1912 (NTS)

The *John Selden* as it looked shortly after it was built.

The *John Selden* as it looked in 2014. © David Nicholls

42. Salvington Lodge, Salvington Road
(No longer standing)

This was a five bedroomed detached house owned by the **Wisden family** of The Warren, Broadwater and Henfield. The property had already been standing for many years before the Edwardian period as a large house with over four acres of land surrounding it.

The occupant of the house at the beginning of the century was **Ellen Worth Bromfield** (b.1844). She had been listed at the property continuously in the street directories from 1886 – 1908. Ellen's family originated from Causton in Warwickshire where her father was a prosperous farmer. She never married, spending much of her early life with her father on the farm until he died in 1883, and within a few years she had moved to *Salvington Lodge*. Her younger brother **George** (b.1842) was a clergyman in Lambeth. They must have been a close family as the census reveals that she spent periods of time with him in London. Both the 1891[109] and 1901[110] census lists her staying with him in Lambeth at his home. Around 1907, she left *Salvington Lodge* and moved a short distance down Ashacre Lane into a house she named *Causton*, after the place of her birth.

The next occupant was a younger member of the Wisden family who owned the property. **Patrick Wisden** and his family took up residence at *Salvington Lodge* on a 14 year lease from 29th September 1908. The house seems to have undergone renovations around 1907, when on 20th August plans were passed for alterations and additions to the building.[111] These building works must have taken some months as Patrick Wisden and his family did not take up residence until a year later.

Arthur Patrick Wisden (1875-1922) was the second son of **Thomas Faulconer Wisden** (b.1867) of *The Warren* in Broadwater who had died in 1904. The estate had passed to the eldest son, **Frederic (Frank) T Wisden** (b.1870) who had inherited *Salvington Lodge* as part of the estate leasing it to his younger brother. His own residence being in Henfield.

Patrick, as he seems to be generally called, had married **Ethel Charlotte Pigott Court** in London in 1900. The 1911 census informs us that they had been married for ten years and had three children all still living.[112] Only two of these children were with them at *Salvington Lodge* on the night of the census: **Thomas** (b.1904) who was born in Kent and **Richard** (b.1910) who was born in Durrington.

No photographs of *Salvington Lodge* have been discovered. The site is now completely covered in houses and a row of shops fronting onto the corner of Salvington Road and Ashacre Lane shown in the photograph below.

Modern photograph showing the shops on part of the site where *Salvington Lodge* once stood. © Dave Pryce 2015

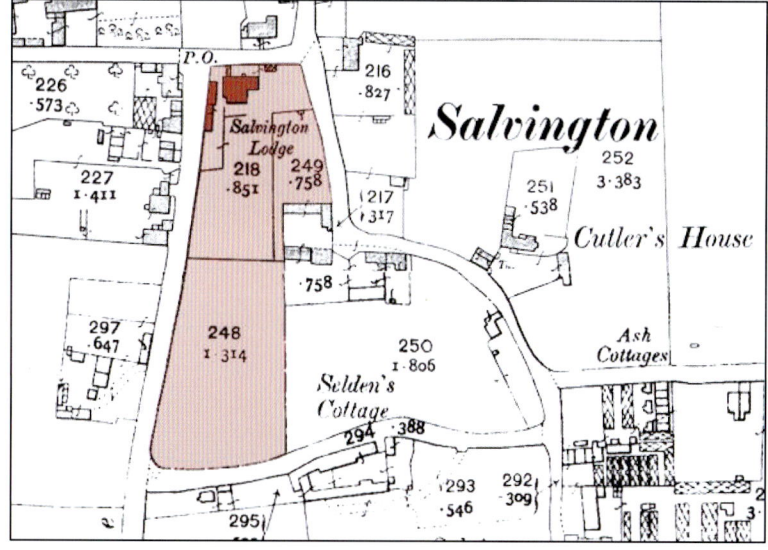

Excerpt taken from OS 25":1 mile Sheet LXIV: 6, 10 3rd Edition 1912 (NTS)

[1] Hull, Jean, Durrington Project Research, unpublished notes (Worthing Library)
[2] IR58/94204 No.7663 (TNA)
[3] 1901 census RG13/957 ff.77 (TNA)
[4] 1911 census RG14/5342 sch 149 (TNA)
[5] Worthing Gazette 8th August 1906 p7
[6] Worthing Gazette 7th August 1901 p5
[7] Evans, p31
[8] 1861 census RG9/614 ff.2 (TNA)
[9] 1901 census RG13/957 ff.76 (TNA)
[10] 1911 census RG14/5342 sch 151 (TNA)
[11] IR58/94204 No.7662 (TNA)
[12] 1911 census RG14/5342 sch 150 (TNA)
[13] IR58/94204 No.7661 (TNA)
[14] 1901 census RG13/957 ff.77 (TNA)
[15] Walker, Vol 4. unpaged (Worthing Library)
[16] 1911 census RG14/5342 sch 152 (TNA)
[17] IR58/94204 No. 7756 (TNA)
[18] IR58/94204 No. 7757 (TNA)
[19] IR58/94204 No. 7755 (TNA)
[20] EPRD Mins 1904 p125
[21] 1911 census RG14/957 sch 155 (TNA)
[22] Worthing Gazette 22nd March 1911 p7
[23] Worthing Gazette 13th September 1911 p7
[24] IR58/94205 No's 7748-7753 (TNA)
[25] 1911 census RG14/957 sch 161(TNA)
[26] 1901 census RG13/957 ff.77 (TNA)
[27] 1911 census RG14/5342 sch 160 (TNA)
[28] 1911 census RG14/5342 sch 159 (TNA)
[29] IR58/94205 No.7751 (TNA)
[30] 1911 census RG14/5342 sch158 (TNA)
[31] 1881 census RG11/817 ff.32 (TNA)
[32] Worthing Gazette 5th July 1911 p6
[33] IR58/94205 No.7754 (TNA)
[34] IR58/94205 No. 7770 & 7771 (TNA)
[35] Worthing Gazette 21st February 1906 p8
[36] Linfield, p7
[37] 1911 census RG14/5342 sch 88 (TNA)
[38] IR/94206 No.7821 (TNA)
[39] 1911 census RG14/5337 sch 239 (TNA)
[40] 1911 census RG14/5342 sch 170 (TNA)
[41] IR58/94206 No.7822 (TNA)
[42] Worthing Gazette Jan 13th 1904 p3
[43] 1911 census RG14/5342 sch 169 (TNA)
[44] IR58/94205 No. 7746 & 7747 (TNA)
[45] Worthing Gazette 8th January 1908 p5
[46] 1901 census RG13/957 ff.77(TNA)
[47] 1881 census RG11/837 ff.98 (TNA)
[48] Worthing Gazette 24th April 1901 p3 & Worthing Gazette 2nd July 1902 p2
[49] Worthing Gazette 10th December 1902 p6
[50] IR58/94214 No.8663 (TNA)
[51] Worthing Gazette 1st February 1911 p7
[52] IR58/94218 No.9013 (TNA)
[53] 1911 census RG14/5342 sch 172 (TNA)
[54] IR58/94205 No. 7743 (TNA)
[55] 1901 census RG13/957 ff.77 (TNA)
[56] Worthing Gazette 10th Dec 1902, p6
[57] Worthing Gazette 6th June 1906, p8
[58] 1911 census RG14/5342 Sch 146 (TNA)
[59] 1891 census RG12/399 ff.157 (TNA)
[60] 1901 census RG13/414 ff.72 (TNA)
[61] IR58/94205 No.7768 & 7773 (TNA)
[62] Worthing Gazette 22nd June 1904 p6
[63] Worthing Gazette 12th April 1906 p5
[64] Worthing Gazette 10th January 1906 p2
[65] Worthing Gazette 28th February 1912 p3
[66] 1911 census RG14/5342 sch 176 (TNA)
[67] IR58/94205 No.7720 (TNA)
[68] 1881 census RG11/1228 ff. 64 (TNA)
[69] 1901 census RG13/957 ff.77 (TNA)
[70] IR58/94205 No.7719 (TNA)
[71] Worthing Gazette 21st June 1911 p5

[72] 1911 census RG14/5342 sch 178 (TNA)
[73] Durrington Council School Log Book 1908-1928 3rd July 1908, p1 (Held at the school)
[74] Worthing Gazette 27th March 1907 p7
[75] EPRD Minutes 18th February 1908 p355 (WSRO)
[76] Worthing Gazette 8th April 1908 p7
[77] Worthing Gazette 1st April 1908 p6
[78] Worthing Gazette 15th July 1908 p7
[79] Worthing Gazette 19th August 1908 p7 & 17th February 1909 p7
[80] Durrington Council School Log Book 1908-1928 3rd July 1908, p5 (Held at the school)
[81] Worthing Gazette 19th August 1908 p7
[82] Durrington Council School Log Book 1908-1928 21st June 1908 p2 (Held at the school)
[83] Durrington Council School Log Book 1908-1928 17th July 1908 p2 (Held at the school)
[84] www.britishlistedbuildings.co.uk No. 432946 – 432950 (viewed 21.06.2012)
[85] 1891 census RG12/836 ff.120 (TNA)
[86] Worthing Library PP/WSL/P007174 (cropped)
[87] IR58/94206 No.7855 (TNA)
[88] 1911 census RG14/5342 sch 68 (TNA)
[89] 'Alfred Bradford', Mapping the Practice and Profession of Sculpture in Britain and Ireland 1851-1951, University of Glasgow History of Art and HATII, online database 2011 [http://sculpture.gla.ac.uk/view/person.php?id=msib1_1277886282, accessed 25 Jan 2016]
[90] GRO Index. Sept Q 1851. St Pancras, Vol 1, p350 (TNA)
[91] GRO Index. Mar Q 1852. St Pancras, Vol 1b, p71 (TNA)
[92] 1861 census RG9/802 ff.83 (TNA)
[93] 1871 census RG10/1348 ff.8 (TNA)
[94] IR58/94206 No.7851 (TNA)
[95] Worthing Gazette 10th Dec 1902 p6
[96] Worthing Gazette 6th March 1912 p5
[97] Worthing Gazette 31st January 1906 p5
[98] Worthing Gazette 13th March 1912 p7
[99] IR58/94206 No.7853 (TNA)
[100] 1851 census HO107/1651 ff.262 (TNA)
[101] IR58/94206 No. 7861 (TNA)
[102] Worthing Gazette 3rd Feb 1909 p5
[103] Worthing Gazette 3rd March 1909 p3
[104] EPRD Mins 12th April 1910 p83 (WSRO)
[105] Worthing Gazette 23rd November 1910 p5
[106] 1911 census RG14/5342 ff.64 (TNA)
[107] Worthing Gazette 21st December 1910 p5
[108] IR58/94206 No. 7861 (TNA)
[109] 1891 census RG12/394 ff.52 (TNA)
[110] 1901 census RG13/408 ff.69 (TNA)
[111] EPRD Mins 20th August 1907 p 319 (WSRO)
[112] 1911 census RG14/5342 sch 65 (TNA)

Chapter 4
Franklin Road

Introduction

This road leads from Salvington Road to the southern part of Greenland Road, often being referred to as 'Frankland Road' in documents. It was being developed throughout the Edwardian period, having no buildings at all in 1902 when the plots of land were first being sold. By the time of the 1911 census, the road only had properties on the western side, whilst on the east it was being used as allotment gardens.

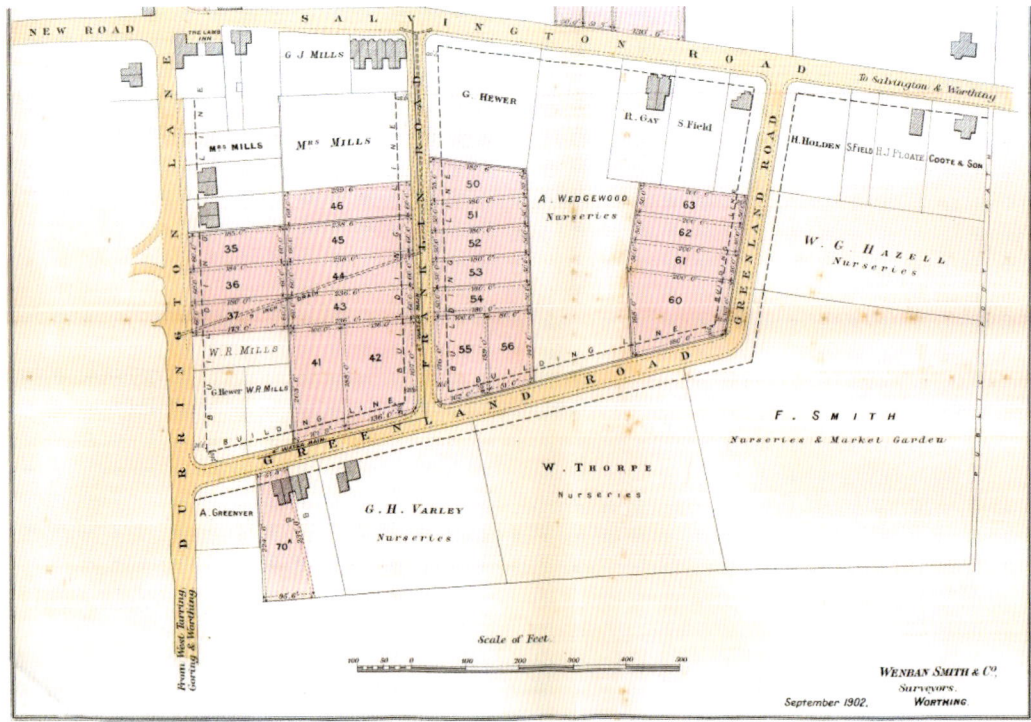
Sale Catalogue map for the plots of land in Franklin Road sold in 1902 (Original held at Worthing Library)

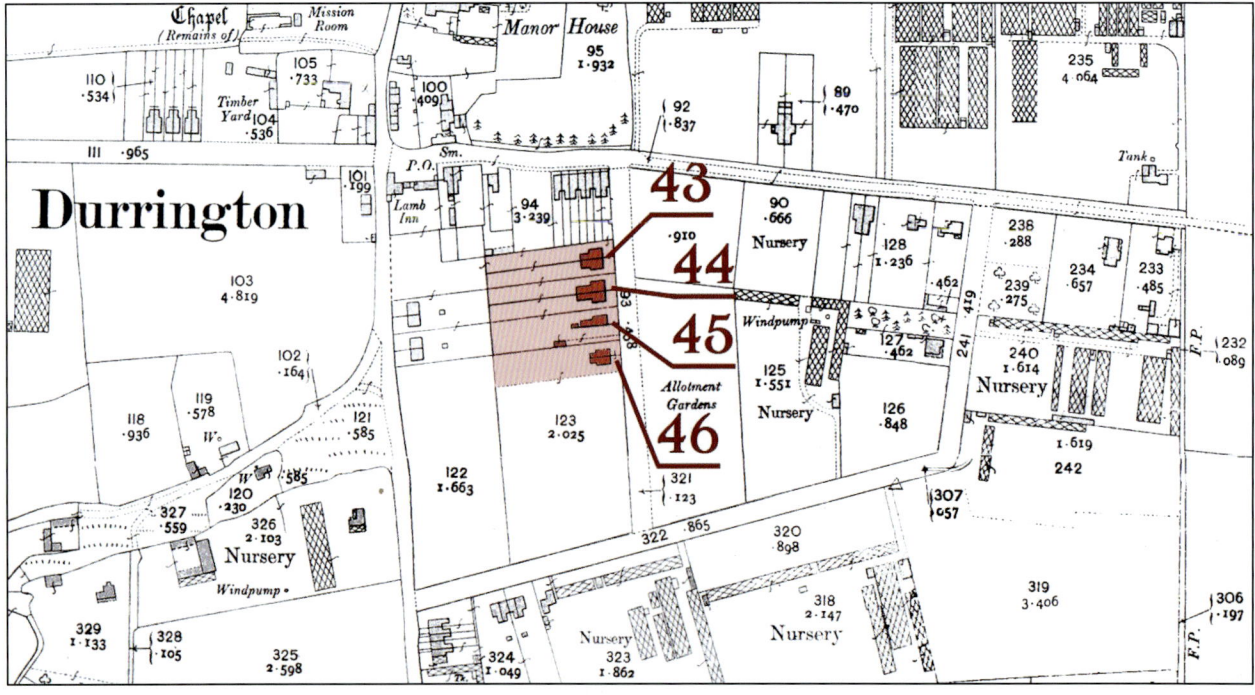
Excerpt taken from OS 25":1 mile Sheet LXIV: 5,6,9,10 3rd Edition 1912 (NTS)

43. No's 1 & 2 Franklin Road
(Now No's 37 &35 Franklin Road)

The first two semi-detached properties were owned by **William Tunstell**, a french polisher from Lambeth, Surrey. The two plots of land had been purchased in July 1904 for £46 15s per plot according to the Inland Revenue Valuation, with a very exact figure of £354 11s, spent on the building of each three-bedroom house.[1] The East Preston Rural District minutes record permission for William Tunstell to build two houses in Franklin Road in November 1904.[2]

The first occupant of No 1 is unknown, but street directories list inhabitants from 1909-1913 as **Walter Martin** (b.1864) a gentleman of private means from London. The 1911 census lists his wife, **Margaret Letitia** (b.1869 nee Arthur) who he had married in 1892, living in the house with him.[3] On the 1901 census, the couple had been living in Fulham and Walter gives his occupation as a "Ship booker Agent".[4] They had no children. This was quite a large house and they had two boarders living with them, **Alfred Edser** (b.1872), a bread maker and his son **Alfred** (b.1905). Alfred was a widower and would have been working at one of the bakeries in Durrington, most probably Coote's, as this was the largest. Alfred junior was registered at Durrington Council School from November 1911 but removed later the following year.

The second of the properties was owned and occupied by William Tunstell. The 1911 census records the family details. **William Tunstell** (b.1855) was living here with his second wife **Sarah Caroline** (b.1863 nee Whitehead) and their daughter **Hilda Grace** (b.1905).[5] Hilda was, according to the Durrington Council School Admissions Register, placed in the school in 1910 when she was five years old. William's first wife, **Mary Elizabeth** (b.1856 nee Ingram) had died in 1899 leaving him with six children, although none of them were living in Franklin Road with their father. According to the electoral register, the Tunstell family moved from Worthing to this house in Durrington in 1907 and continued at the address through to 1913.

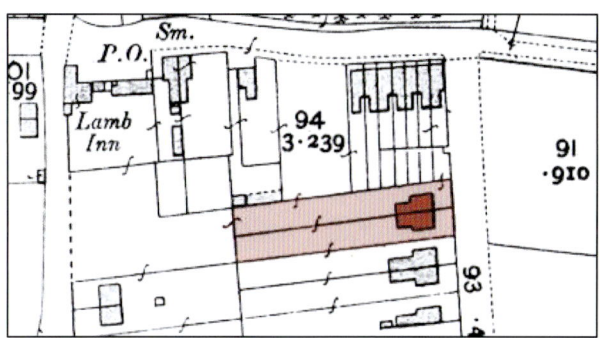

Excerpt taken from OS 25":1 mile Sheet LXIV: 5 3rd Edition 1912 (NTS)

Modern photograph showing No 1 (now 37) on the right and No 2 (now 35) on the left as they stand today © Dave Pryce 2016

44. Bisham (No 3) & Irene (No 4) Franklin Road
(Now No's 33 & 31 Franklin Road)

Photograph showing *Bisham* on the right and *'Irene'* on the left as they stood in 2014. © David Nicholls

The next two semi-detached properties were owned by the Trim family. One was called *'Bisham (No 3)'* and was the home of the established Durrington builder **George Trim** (b.1853) originally from Dorset. The Inland Revenue Valuation gives the owner as **Frederick Trim** of Three Kings Yard, Davies Street, London; who was George's younger brother.[6] It records that this plot was purchased *'about 1900'* although it's other semi-detached property, lying south of the pair, *'Irene (No 4)'* states 1905 as the date of purchase.[7] It may be that the two plots were acquired at different times and only built on at a later date when, perhaps, both properties were erected.

The Trim family were newly established in Durrington. In 1901 George had been listed as a *'Grocer, Shopkeeper & Bricklayer'* living in Heene, Worthing. Obviously he was a multi-talented business man even at this stage.[8] Interestingly, his wife **Emma** (b.1853 nee Richardson) was also listed as a grocer on her own account on the same census.

The houses must have been built by October 1907 as a curious advert was placed in the newspaper:

> *'I, George Trim, of Bisham, Franklin Road, Durrington and of West Tarring, Builder, hereby give notice that I am not in any way connected to any other builder in Worthing or district of the name of Trim.'*[9]

This little excerpt confirms that at this date the house was already being lived in by George and that something had prompted him to defend his reputation as a builder. Whatever the reason, he continued to own and build properties in Durrington and Salvington, including four houses in Ashacre Lane, *Hillview, The Dean, Twyford* and *Wilburton*. George and Emma had seven children but three had died before the 1911 census. Only **Reginald James Douglas Trim** (b.1892) was living with them in 1911, he was working as a carpenter.

The neighbour to *Bisham* was No 4 Franklin Road, a house called *Irene*. Identical to its neighbour, it was also built by George Trim who lived next door. The only occupiers identified are listed on the 1911 census as **George Thomas Grant** (b.1862) and his second wife **Margaret** (b.1871), both born in Angmering. George's first wife was **Ann Venn** whom he had married in 1884; no birth for her has been confirmed. They had three children, the youngest of which was **Norman Venn Grant** (b.1896). Ann had died around the same time that Norman was born, suggesting she may have died in childbirth. George was left with three children to raise and was fulfilling the role alone in 1901 when he was still living in Angmering.[10] The 1911 census tells us that he had been married for one year and so was obviously making a new life in Durrington.[11] He was a carpenter by trade, but the property was also worked as a poultry farm, according to the street directory of 1912, perhaps by his wife.

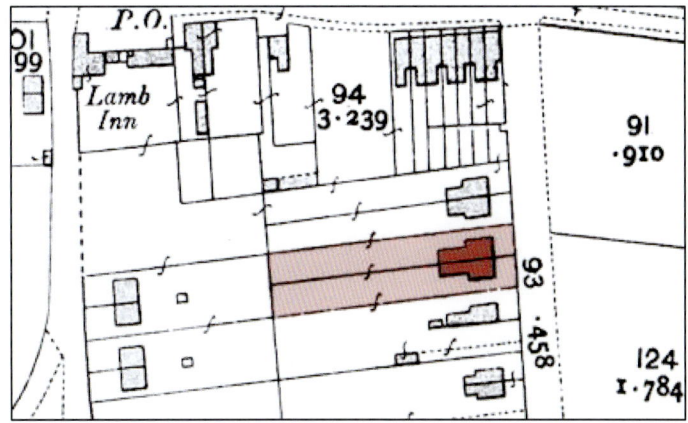

Excerpt taken from OS 25":1 mile Sheet LXIV: 5 3rd Edition 1912 (NTS)

45. Elmshurst, Franklin Road
(No longer standing)

This property was a detached house with a stable owned by **H. Strong** of Pavilion Road in Worthing. Permission for the building of a house was given in July 1905 by East Preston Rural District Council,[12] with the property first being listed and occupants named in 1909, when street directories and electoral registers list **Ella Mary Willicombe** living there. She stayed until just before the 1911 census was taken, when she moved to Salvington.

The 1911 census records a widow named Mrs Betteridge, of private means, occupying the property with her son.[13] **Ellen Mary Betteridge** (b.1862 nee Hooker) had married **Edward Betteridge** in 1893. He was much older than she was and died, aged 74, in 1900, leaving her with one son **Edward Charles** (b.1893) who was living at *Elmshurst* with his mother. They had come from Kent with no known connection to the village. Their stay in the property was of a short duration, so much so that they are missed off of the Inland Revenue Valuation altogether where Willicombe is registered as the previous occupant. His name is crossed out and the surname 'Helsdon' is written in.[14] The only reference to this surname at the time is the **Helsdon** sisters who were living in *Bethany,* Durrington Street. The electoral registers and street directories from 1912, however, list **Ernest F. Gough** as the occupant of *Elmshurst*. Ernest and **Alice Gough** were both founder members of Durrington Free Church in Salvington Road and this may hold a clue to the Helsdon connection, as they were also founder members of the church. Perhaps in some way the Helsdon ladies were connected with the renting of the property.

Excerpt taken from OS 25":1 mile Sheet LXIV: 5 3rd Edition 1912 (NTS)

Modern photograph showing the site of where Elmshurst stood. © Dave Pryce 2016

46. Cottages, Franklin Road
(Now No's 23 & 21 Franklin Road)

The two cottages as they appear in Franklin Road in 2014. © David Nicholls

These are two three-bedroomed cottages, unnumbered on the census in 1911 and in street directories, although we can trace their date of building and occupation. The cottages were built around 1909 on what is described as a *'very wet site'*. They were owned by **Mr. A. Brake** of South Farm Road, Worthing and built for a cost of £200 each.[15]

Two families had moved into the cottages on completion, renting them for the sum of £15 12s a year according to the Inland Revenue Valuation. **Kitty Williams** (b.1861) was a widow who was listed at the address in 1911 with her two sons: **George Albert** (b.1885) and **Frank** (b.1888).[16] Both the boys were gardeners, no doubt working in the nurseries which dominated Durrington's work force at the time. Kitty was the widow of **James Williams,** a builder and carpenter, who had moved his family into Durrington by the time of the 1901 census but had died in 1904.[17] Fortunately for Kitty, her sons had employment in the nurseries and they were able to move into the new cottage.

The other cottage was the home of a local blacksmith **Albert Edwin Lish** (b.1878), his wife **Rose Selina** (b.1880 nee Hillman) and their son **Albert Ernest** (b.1907). The photograph right shows Albert at work at *The Forge* in Salvington Road dealing with the horse from *Coote's Bakery* situated further up the road. Albert's brother James and his family were living in *Bushby's Cottage*, Durrington Street at the same time.

Albert Lish working at *The Forge* on one of the horses from Coote's bakery.
Worthing Library (cropped)

Excerpt taken from OS 25":1 mile Sheet LXIV: 5 3rd Edition 1912 (NTS)

---

[1] IR58/94205 No 7726 & 7727 (TNA)
[2] EPRD Mins 1st November 1904 p.125 (WSRO)
[3] 1911 census RG14/5342 sch 162 (TNA)
[4] 1901 census RG13/62 ff.60 (TNA)
[5] 1911 census RG14/5342 sch 163 (TNA)
[6] IR58/94205 No.7728 (TNA)
[7] IR58/94205 No. 7729 (TNA)
[8] 1901 census RG13/960 ff.77 (TNA)
[9] Worthing Gazette 10th October 1907 p4
[10] 1901 census RG13/961 ff.41 (TNA)
[11] 1911 census RG14/5342 sch 165 (TNA)
[12] EPRD Minutes 25th July 1905 p.187
[13] 1911 census RG14/5342 sch 166 (TNA)
[14] IR58/94205 No.7730 (TNA)
[15] IR58/94205 No. 7737 & 7738 (TNA)
[16] 1911 census RG14/5342 sch 167 (TNA)
[17] 1901 census RG13/957 ff.76 (TNA)

Chapter 5
Greenland Road

Introduction

This road runs from Durrington Lane eastwards until in bends sharply north and reaches Salvington Road. It was very much in the development stage at the turn of the century with very few houses. As the Edwardian period unfolded four houses were built on the south side whilst other dwellings were built on three of the five nurseries that straddled the road on both sides; to house the nurserymen and their families. Only the houses remain in modern times all the nurseries have long since been developed for further housing.

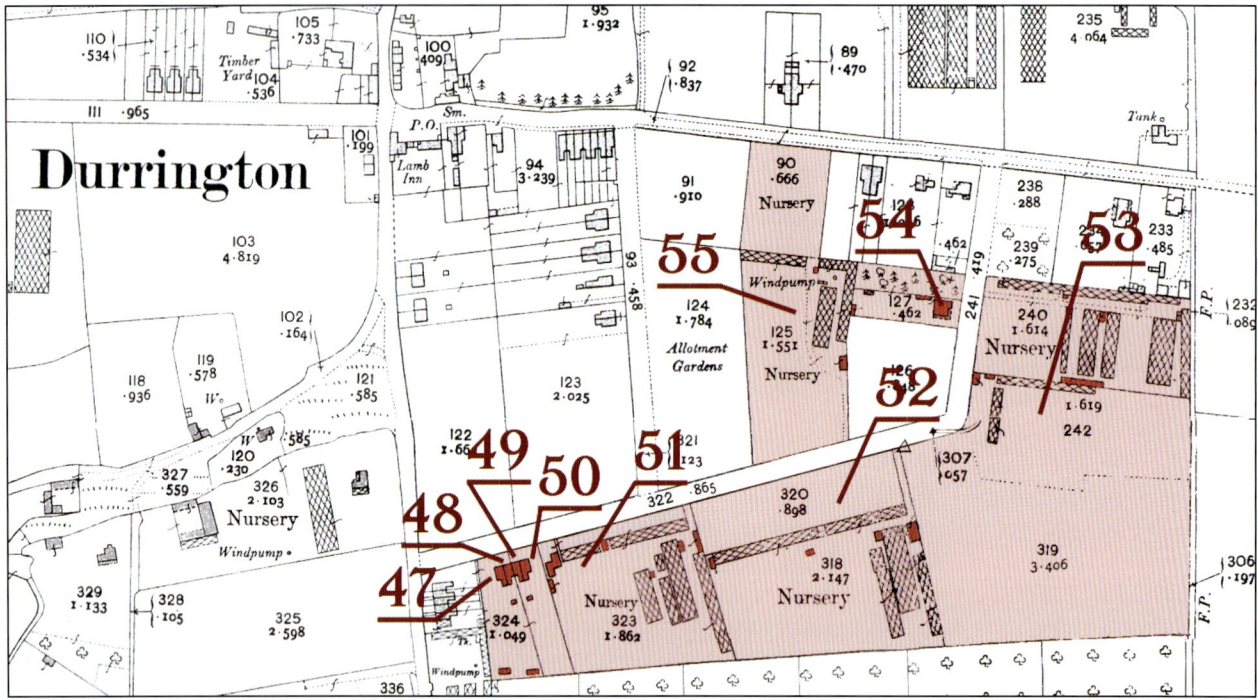

Excerpt taken from OS 25":1 mile Sheet LXIV: 5,6,9,10 3rd Edition 1912 (NTS)

This postcard shows *No's 1-4 Greenland Road* and the property next door *Downsview House*.
Owned by New Life Church

47. No 1 Greenland Road
(Now No 117 Greenland Road)

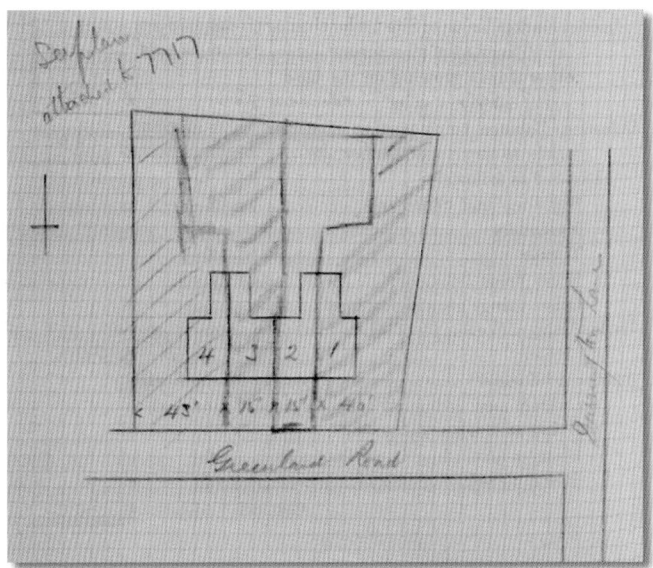

The plan shows the position of the first four houses in Greenland Road. Excerpt taken from Inland Revenue Valuation Field Book No. 7739

This is the first house on the southern side of the road as you enter Greenland Road from the junction with Durrington Street. It is part of a row of four terraced properties which first appear on a sale catalogue dated 1902 so must have been built a little earlier. The Inland Revenue Valuation gives a plan outline of the four houses and the land they occupied. This property has the largest plot of land of the four houses, attached to the side.

The first occupant so far discovered was **Henry Overington** who had previously lived in *Holly Cottages,* Littlehampton Road. The electoral register records that they moved from the cottage in Salvington to Greenland Road around 1907, which probably indicates that he was not the first occupier.

Henry lived here with his wife **Annie Elizabeth** (b.1862) and their two youngest sons: **Wilfred** (b.1895) and **Maurice** (b.1897). More of this family's story can be found with *Holly Cottages,* but we do know that by the time Henry filled out the census return in 1911, two of their children had died.[1] The eldest, **Henry Allan** had died age 12 in 1900 and their second son **Arthur Cecil** (b.1888), had been committed to the West Sussex County Asylum, known as *Greylingwell Hospital*, in March 1906 and died there in April 1910 (See the Notice of Death below). The cause of death was given as *'Melancholia and Tuberculosis'*.

Arthur Cecil Overington 1888 - 1910

Tragedy was again to strike this family when in July 1911 Henry himself died whilst being taken to Worthing Hospital for surgery in a taxi cab. After Henry's death, Annie continued to live at this address for some years.

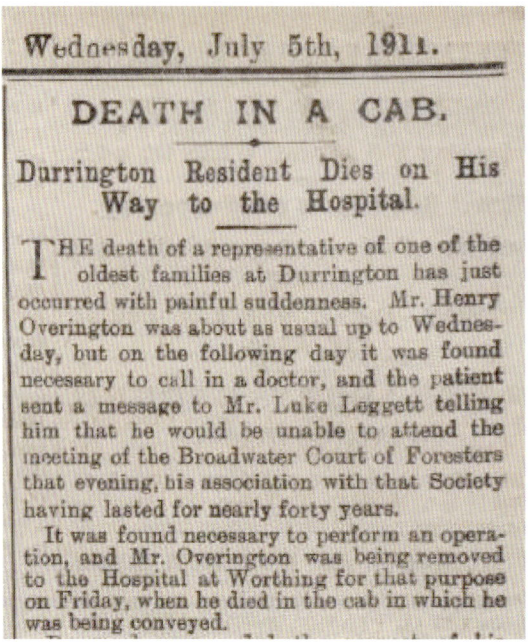

Report of Henry's death in a cab on the way to Worthing Hospital in July 1912

48. No 2 Greenland Road
(Now No 115 Greenland Road)

This was the home of **George Bush** (b.1849) and his wife **Mary Ann** (b.1843). George was a gardener who had purchased the house in January 1910 for £250. He may have rented it for some years before he bought it. Both he and his wife Mary, originally from Devon, had already lived for some time in Angmering, as on the 1901 census he was working there as a gamekeeper.[2] Exactly when the family moved we do not know, but he is listed in street directories for Durrington from 1905, but with no address given. His name is listed firstly in Greenland Road in the directories, census returns and electoral registers from 1911 onwards.[3]

49. No 3 Greenland Road
(Now No 113 Greenland Road)

Sarah Mills, a lady from Tarring, owned both this house and No 4 next door. The house was occupied by a hire carter by the name of **William Sivyer** (b.1864) who had been born in Eastergate. With him were his wife **Ann Eliza** (b.1863 nee Langrish) whom he had married in 1867. This was William's second marriage and of the three children living in the house at the time of the 1911 census, only the youngest **Albert** (b.1898) was Ann's son.[4] The other two members of the family were older children from William's first marriage; they were **Ellen** (b.1893) and **William** (b.1895). In 1901 they had been living in Durrington Street when William's father **James** (b.1852) was in the house with them.[5] The electoral registers show that they lived in Goring for a short period before returning to Durrington, probably to take up occupation in this house.

50. No 4 Greenland Road
(Now No 111 Greenland Road)

This house, as well as being owned alongside No 3, by Sarah Mills of Tarring, was actually the family home of her son **Edward H Mills** (b.1877) and his wife **Harriet** (b.1875 nee Saunders). Harriet was the daughter of **Thomas and Fanny Saunders** of *Elder Tree Cottages*. Before her marriage, Harriet had firstly been in service in Brighton and then had been employed at *Swandean* when it was still a private home owned by the

Dalbiac family. Edward had spent his childhood years at *The Lamb Inn* where his parents **Henry and Sarah Mills** had run the public house. Henry (b.1848) had died in 1895, and at this time Sarah moved to Tarring where in 1901 she is registered as a lodging house keeper. She obviously chose to invest some of her money into property in Durrington by buying the two properties.

Modern photograph of 111, 113, 115 & 117 Greenland Road. © Dave Pryce 2016

51. Downsview House & Nursery, Greenland Road
(Just house remains, now No 107 Greenland Road)

The first owner and occupier of this plot of land was **George Herbert Varley** (b.1875). He is listed as a fruit grower on the land from as early as the 1900 street directories although he did not live on the site at this time. He was shown on the 1901 census boarding a little distance away in *New Cottages* at the house of Noah Searle. His name is given on a 1902 sale catalogue as owner of a plot and the electoral register for 1903 lists him as having land and buildings but no house until 1904. It is possible that he had the house built soon after the 1901 census period when he married **Mary Louisa** (b.1875 nee Wilson) in London in 1902 and brought her to live in Durrington. We do know that George was offering tomato and cucumber plants for sale from the nursery between the years 1902-1905. Mrs. Varley had also settled into life in Durrington and is advertising chicks and hens in 1906, although neither source gives a home address, only *'Durrington'*. Even by February 1905 when Mrs. Varley is offering a reward for anyone who can find her sable collie *'Dolly'*, who had obviously got herself lost, the only address again is *'Durrington'*.[6]

The photograph left shows George in his glasshouse with vines growing – the photograph is not dated but he placed an advert for vines in Worthing Gazette in 1905, so the photograph must be around this period.

Early in 1910 it becomes clear that the nursery was not thriving and George began the process of declaring bankruptcy. Various entries in the London Gazette for the period, chart the process that George had to go through and this ended with the sale of

Downsview Nursery.[7] The family then moved to Essex where George worked as a managing clerk in a brick and tile manufacturer.

It is unclear who owned the house and nursery after George Varley sold it, as the site has two Inland Revenue Valuation numbers, both giving different owners.[8] The first was **Clark & Smith** from Wiltshire, while the other was, maybe in error, still recorded as being owned by George Varley.

Downsview Nursery and *Downsview House* were next occupied by **Henry Capel Saunders** who was a fruit grower originally from Clapham in London. Malcolm Linfield gives this description:

> 'During the Edwardian period, there was extensive nursery development in Greenland Road. At the turn of the century, there were no nurseries in the road at all, but by 1912 there were five new glasshouse growers. Starting on the south side from the junction with Durrington Lane, the first nursery was being managed by **Henry Capel Saunders**; at just under 2 acres, there were nine glasshouses with a total run of 1050 ft, at least one of which was a vinery. Saunders was living at Downsview House on the nursery site, a detached villa with 3 bedrooms. He was a nephew of Worthing grower **C. Douglas Crouch**, owner of Lyndhurst Nurseries between Lyndhurst Road and Church Walk. Crouch was also pastor of Worthing Tabernacle church, which he opened for public worship in 1908. Interestingly, Saunders was living at his uncle's house in East Worthing in 1901 and is described as 'Fruit Grower, own account'. Presumably, he learnt the business by working on his uncle's nursery before setting up on his own in Durrington. He also owned Rosslyn Nurseries in New Road.'[9]

Henry Capel Saunders (b.1875) had married his wife **Mabel** (b.1876 nee Swan) in Reigate late in 1911. He was already living at *Downsview* on his own on the 1911 census, which was taken earlier in the same year.[10] He brought his new wife to the house and they lived there and raised their family for many years. Henry Saunders was very involved in the new free church in Salvington Road, and continued to work his nursery and his activities at the church, as did his family, for many years.

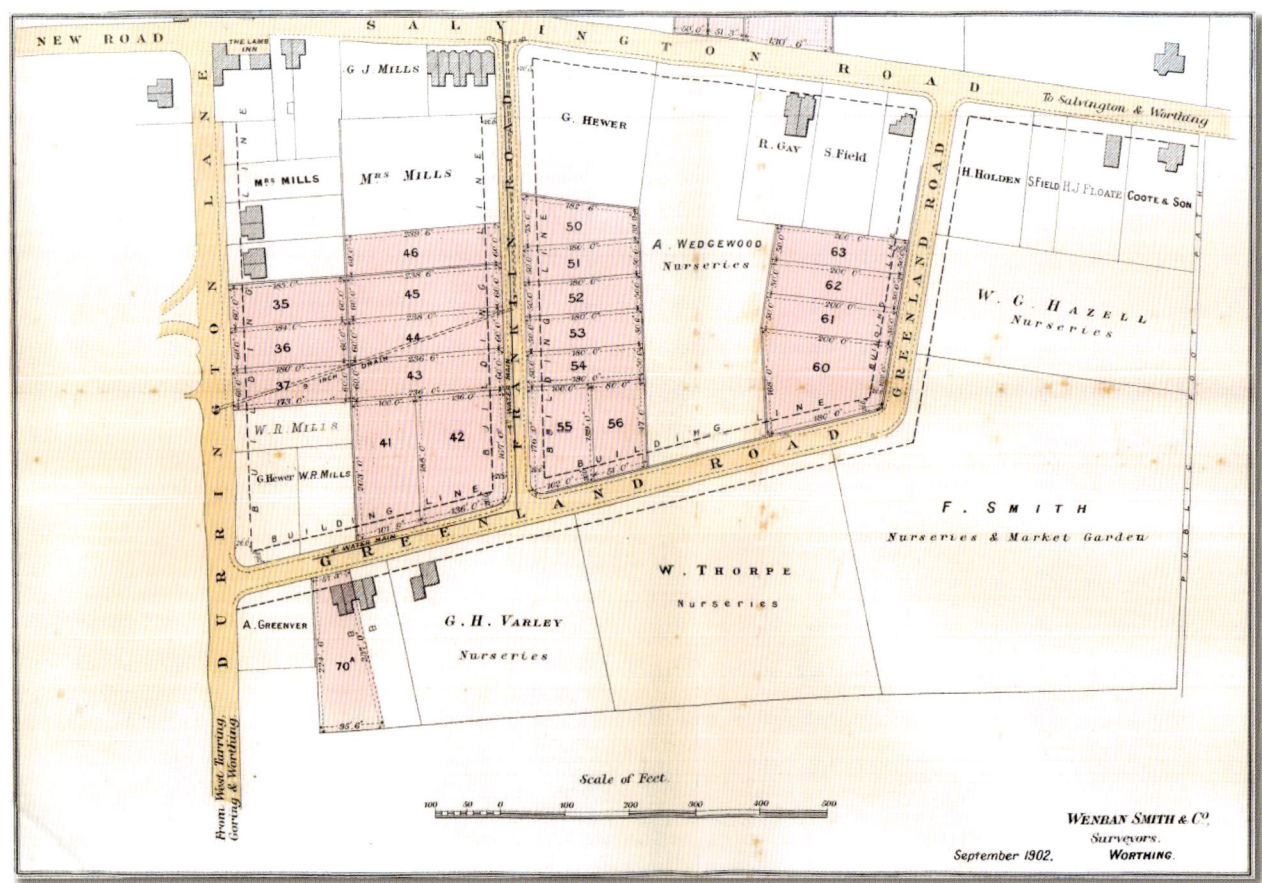

Map from 1902 sale catalogue of land in Durrington which clearly shows the position of the nurseries in Greenland Road and George Varley's name printed as owner. Original held in Worthing Library

Photograph showing *Downsview House,* on the left, as it looks today. © Lyn Tiller 2014

52. Glencoe Nurseries, Greenland Road
(No longer standing)

Malcolm Linfield describes this nursery:

> *'Just to the east of Saunders' Nursery, still on the south side of Greenland Road, was Glencoe Nurseries, set up by* **Harold W. Thorp** *during the early 1900s. Harold was born in 1866 in Preston, Lancashire and in the 1891 census is described as a 'Steam Engine Maker'. During the nineties, he moved to Chesswood Road in Worthing with his widowed mother where he presumably spent a year or two working at one of the local nurseries in the area before setting up on his own in Durrington. By 1901, he had already started his nursery where, by 1913, he had erected seven well-built glasshouses on 3 acres of land, amounting to 960 ft of glass. He had vines established in five and tomatoes growing in the other two, amounting to 800 ft of vineries.*[11] *He also grew prize-winning chrysanthemums, winning a silver medal at the Palace Show in 1909 for his new variety 'HW Thorp'.*[12]

Harold Thorpe of *Glencoe Nursery*.
Owned by Mary Steel

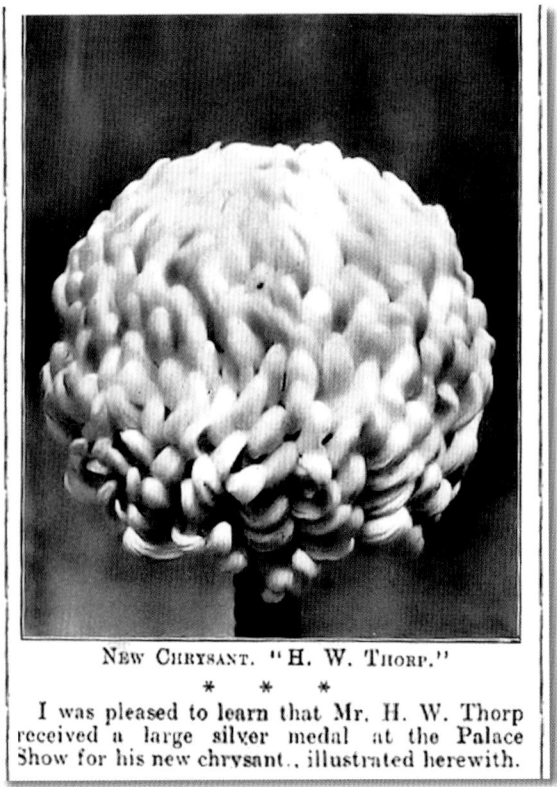

A black and white picture of the H.W.Thorp chrysanthemum[13]

Harold Thorp was obviously a man of some standing with his chrysanthemums, as another named variety he was responsible for developing was found in the pages of 'The Gardeners Chronicle' a magazine for the horticultural industry of the period. This magazine has various mentions of H. W. Thorp and among the pages gives details of a variety named *'Ethel Thorp'* describing its place in the show in fairly positive terms:

> *'Mr H.W.Thorp, Durrington, Worthing, showed Japanese and incurved Chrysanthemums of fine quality, prominent in the group being the new Ethel Thorp, an incurved flower of soft pink shade'*[14]

Unfortunately according to the Royal Horticultural Society none of the Thorp varieties has survived into cultivation today.

Harold and his family in High Salvington where they were living in 1915. © Owned by Mary Steel

Some years after the nursery was established Harold moved with his mother and sisters into a house in High Salvington called *Woodlands* where the photograph with the family in the garden was taken.

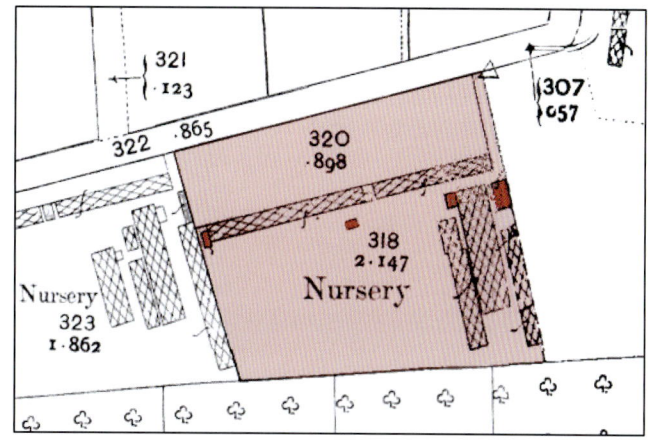

Excerpt taken from OS 25":1 mile Sheet LXIV: 9 3rd Edition 1912 (NTS)

53. Other Unnamed Nurseries, Greenland Road
(No longer standing)

Next door to *Glencoe Nursery* was yet another portion of land run as a nursery and market garden by **Frederick Smith** (b.1851). He is listed as a fruit grower in Durrington from the early 1900s possibly living firstly at *Blacksmith Cottage* and then moving to *2 Rock Cottages* when they were built in 1901.

The land was taken over at some point and run by nurserymen in a partnership registered as **'Cotching & Matthews'**. Malcolm Linfield has described this nursery:

> ***Cotching and Matthews*** *also had a nursery in Greenland Road, further east from Thorp's nursery, on the southern corner of Greenland Road as it curved northwards towards the junction with Salvington Road.* ***Harold Matthews*** *was the younger brother of* ***John Kenneth Matthews*** *of Seaview Nurseries, and he was working in partnership with* ***Frank Irving Cotching.*** *They rented the 2 acre site, and in 1910 erected 6 glasshouses, one of which was planted with vines (a south facing 180ft house) whilst the other five were used for growing tomatoes. These tomato houses provided 650ft of protected cropping space. A 130ft deep well was bored in 1910.*[15]

In 1911 **Harold Matthews** (b.1890) was registered on the census lodging in Broadwater with his older brother **John Kenneth** (b.1884).[16] Also lodging in the same house, were another pair of brothers named **Frank Irving** (b.1883) and **George Frederick** (b.1879) **Cotching** who had both been born in Horsham. Harold Matthews and George Cotching were to form the partnership that was named in the Worthing Gazette in January 1910 as '*The Nurseries, Durrington*'.[17]

The next nursery along on the eastern side, as it led up to Salvington Road, was run by **William George Hazell** (b.1851) who was living at *The Briars*, Salvington Road. He was already being listed as a fruit grower and employer on the 1901 census, so was obviously employing men to work at the nursery at that time.[18] By December 1903 however, he had left and the land was purchased by **Clare Henry Douglas** (b.1875) the younger brother of **James Douglas** who ran a nursery on the north side of Salvington Road.

54. Birklands, Greenland Road
(Now No 12 Kingfisher House, Greenland Road)

Crossing the road at this point onto the western side of Greenland Road was the next house & nursery known at the time as *Birklands*. The earliest traced occupier of the site was **Edward Rufus Martin** (b.1841), a retired tailor. In the 1901

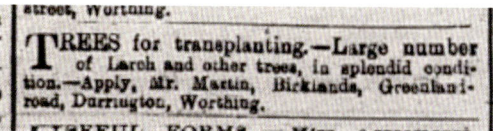

census, he is still a working tailor living in Worksopp, Nottinghamshire with his wife and daughter.[19] However by 1903, Edward has retired and the whole family had moved to Durrington where he appears in the street directories and later the electoral Rolls from 1904-1908. They quickly established the work of the nursery and were already advertising small trees ready for transplanting in the Worthing Gazette in November 1903.[20]

He left the property around 1908 and moved to West Tarring. The next occupier was **George Naldrett** who was only listed for one year in the electoral register. We have discovered no other information about George but we do know that **Mrs G E Naldrett** was advertising rooms to rent in *Birklands* in August 1907.[21]

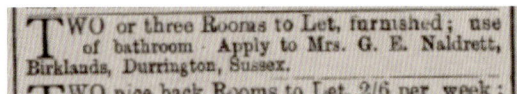

Mrs Naldrett advertising Rooms to Rent at *Birklands* in 1907

By the 1911 census, the house was being let to the fruit grower **Clare Henry Douglas** (b.1875) originally from Dorking in Surrey.[22] Clare was one of the three Douglas Brothers working as nurserymen and managing nurseries in Durrington under the company heading of Douglas Brothers. He had previously been living in Salvington Road with his two brothers. In September 1903 he had married **Edith Saunders** (b.1881) a member of another of the Durrington nursery families who ran *Red Cedars Nursery* in Salvington Road. One of their two children, **Dorothy** (b.1905) was listed as attending Durrington Council School in 1911 when she would have been six years old.

The house is listed on the electoral register for 1911 giving the owner as **Frank Martin** of *Sherwood,* Heene Road, Worthing. Frank was the son of **Edward Martin**, the first listed occupier of the house, but it is not known if he was also the original owner or his father had passed the property to his son. Frank was employed by Worthing Borough Council as an *'Assistant Overseer and Plate Collector'*. By the time of the Inland Revenue Valuation, the property was owned by **H. N. Fowke** of Red Hill House, Wollaston, Wellingborough.[23]

Today the house is still standing and is named *Kingfisher House,* it is described by Finlay who was a pupil at Durrington School during 2014 and lives in the house. He wrote…

> Kingfisher house
>
> The house was built in 1861. It has 3 floors including the attic and 7 rooms as well as a garage. In the garden there is a shed with three doors and we believe this was built with the house.
>
> I have lived here with my family for 3 years and when we moved in my dad found a picture of when it was built. The house also has a conservatory, but we think this is a later addition. The house has a kingfisher plaque by the gate and the same design on the front door, we are not sure whether these were around in Edwardian times. The roof looks quite old but we are not sure if it has been replaced.
>
> Finlay

Story of his house by Finlay, Kingfisher House, Greenland Road 2014

Photograph of Kingfisher House found by Finlay's dad.

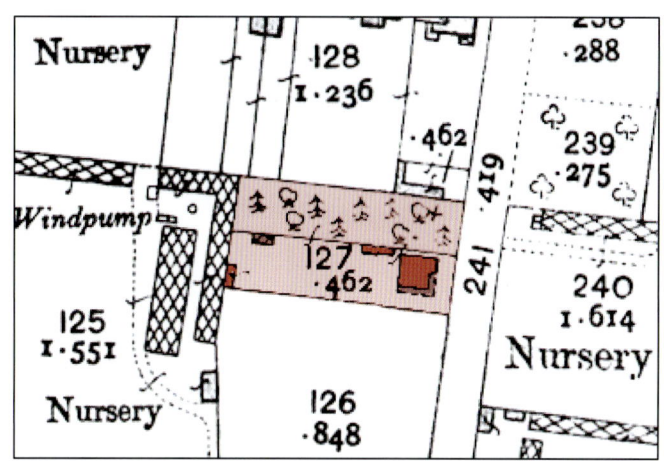

Excerpt taken from OS 25":1 mile Sheet LXIV: 5,6 3rd Edition 1912 (NTS)

55. Tirana Nursery, Greenland Road
(No longer standing)

The last nursery with a house in Greenland Road was *Tirana Nursery*. This was run by **Paul Lawson** and is described by Malcolm Linfield:

> *'Although Greenland Road saw extensive nursery building on its southern side, only one nursery was established on the north, which in 1909 was being run by Paul Lawson. He was probably responsible for building the 4 glasshouses on the two acre site, two if which were being used to grow tomatoes. At that time, rather intriguingly, the site was owned by a member of the famous Wedgewood family of Stoke on Trent. A rather ominous note states that "site lies low, and is subject to flooding by underground springs, mainly at site of glasshouses……….Water appears to come through hills from Pulborough, usually 6 weeks after floods at Pulborough, for these springs are active.".[24] These periodic floods created real problems for the grower, flooding the greenhouses and more critically extinguishing the fire in the stokeholds.'[25]*

There is no record of a Paul Lawson ever having lived in Durrington during the Edwardian years. His home was in Brighton and it is possible that he employed other people to work the nursery for him. A house (38 Greenland Road) was built on the land some years later and it is still standing today.

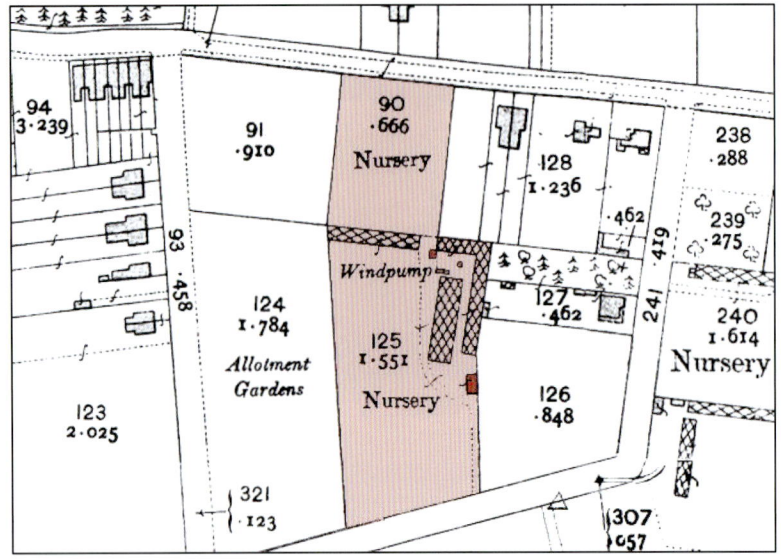

Excerpt taken from OS 25":1 mile Sheet LXIV: 5,6,9,10 3rd Edition 1912 (NTS)

Modern photograph of 38 Greenland Road. ©Dave Pryce 2016

---

[1] 1911 census RG14/5342 sch 126 (TNA)
[2] 1901 census RG13/5337 sch 53 (TNA)
[3] 1911 census RG14/5342 sch 127 (TNA)
[4] 1911 census RG14/5342 sch 128 (TNA)
[5] 1901 census RG13/957 ff.78 (TNA)
[6] Worthing Gazette 15th February 1906 p8
[7] London Gazette 25th February 1910 p1464, 1st March 1910 p1566, 8th July 1910 p4925 et al
[8] IR58/94205 No. 7723 & 7724 (TNA)
[9] Linfield p.8
[10] 1911 census RG14/5342 sch 130 (TNA)
[11] IR58/94205 No.7725 (TNA)
[12] Linfield p.8
[13] *Fruit, Flower and Vegetable Traders Journal.* November 1909
[14] *The Gardeners Chronicle* November 5th 1910 p.346 (www.forgottenbooks.com) viewed 26/09/2015
[15] Linfield, p9

[16] 1911 census RG14/5320 sch 88 (TNA)
[17] Worthing Gazette 26th January 1910 p6
[18] 1901 census RG13/957 ff.77 (TNA)
[19] 1901 census RG13/3124 ff.122 (TNA)
[20] Worthing Gazette 18th November 1903 p3
[21] Worthing Gazette 7th August 1907 p8
[22] 1911 census RG14/5342 sch 175 (TNA)
[23] IR58/94205 No.7738 (TNA)
[24] IR58/94205 No.7709 (TNA)
[25] Linfield p9

Chapter 6
Stone Lane & Selden's Way

Introduction

Stone Lane, or Stones Lane as it is sometimes written, is a roadway running from Salvington Road in the north to Littlehampton Road in the south. The only dwellings in the road during the Edwardian period were all nestled at the north end of the road just below *Beta House* on the left hand corner and *Salvington Lodge* on the right, which both had their entries in Salvington Road.

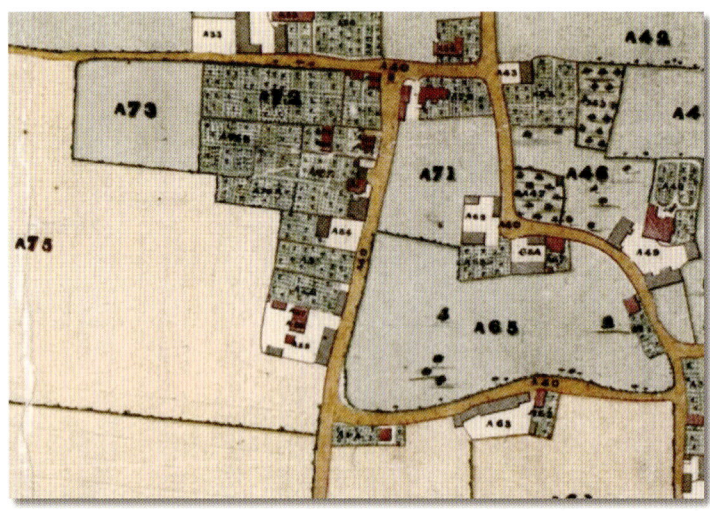

A short way down the road past the cottages and farm buildings, there is a short roadway we now call Selden's Way on the eastern side. This seems to have been unnamed in this period, and only included *Selden's Cottage* with some farm buildings plus one other small cottage occasionally referred to as *Evergreen Cottage*. The lane gave access at its eastern end to Ashacre Lane, where farm traffic would have moved back and forth connecting the fields and buildings from *Salvington Farm*. Clearly little had changed from that shown on the Tithe Map of 1838 for West Tarring[1] and what we see in the first decade of the twentieth century.

Tithe map showing Stone Lane with cottages and buildings around the northern junction with Salvington Road.

How Stone Lane looks today, looking north from Selden's Way 2016. ©Dave Pryce

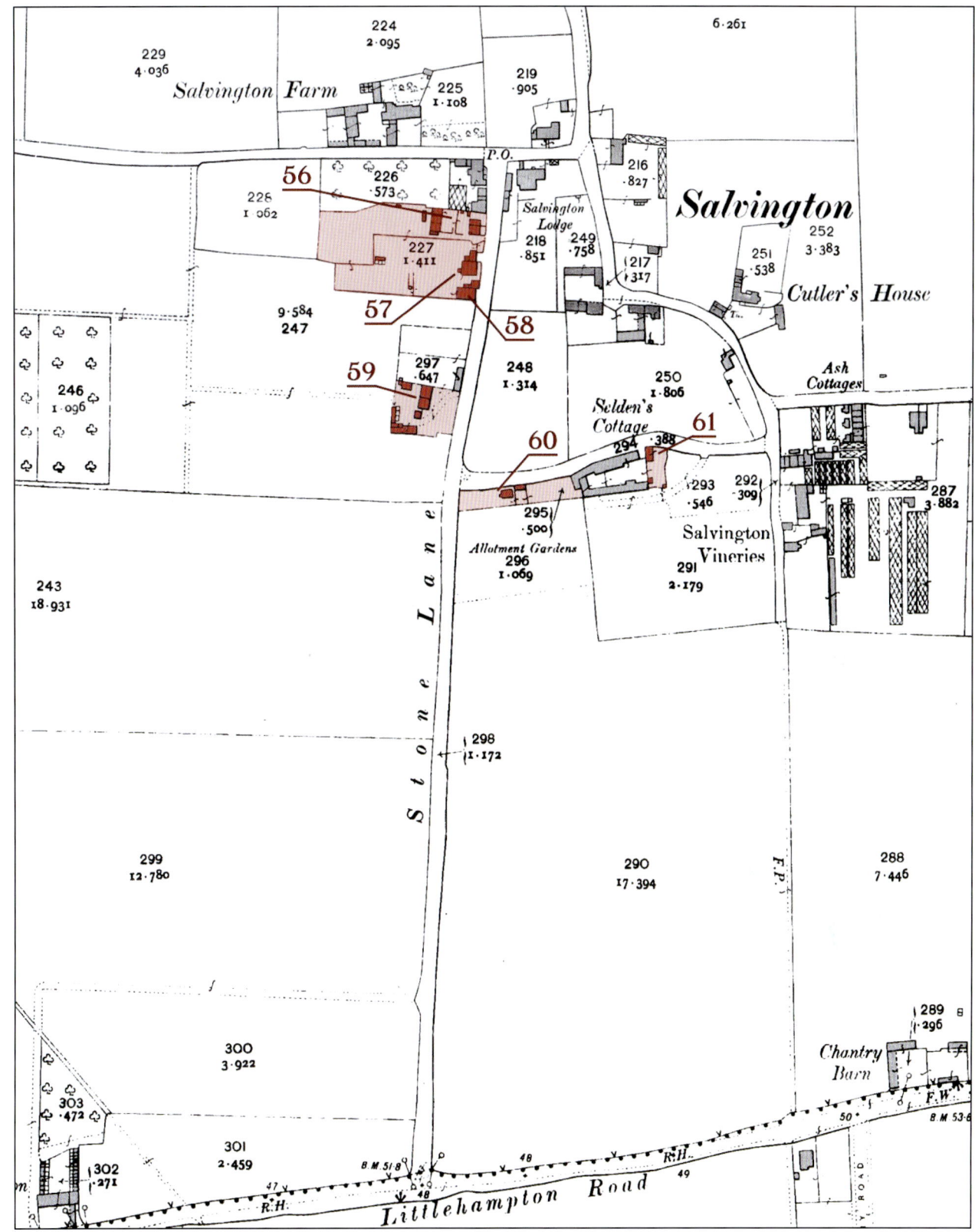

Excerpt taken from OS 25":1 mile Sheet LXIV: 6,10 3rd Edition 1912 (NTS)

56. Stone or Salvington Cottages, Stone Lane
(No longer standing)

This was a collective name for a group of five cottages situated at the top of Stone Lane, sitting just below the land at the rear of *Beta House* on the western side of the road. They were given various names in different documents, often reflecting that they were all part of the farm run by **Edwin Lephard** and owned by the Wisden Estate. The names *Cottage, Farm Cottages, Stone Cottages and Salvington Cottages,* are all used at different times to refer to these buildings. The first two cottages, numbers 1 and 2, stood on the actual roadside with very little land at the front, whereas the other three cottages sat as a small row on the land behind them as the map plan below shows. What we know of the occupancy is outlined below.

Excerpt taken from OS 25":1 mile Sheet LXIV: 6 3rd Edition 1912 (NTS)

No 1 Stone Cottages, Stone Lane

This was the first of a pair of red-brick, semi-detached, three bedroom cottages in Stone Lane.[2] We know that in 1908 this cottage still had a thatched roof as it is mentioned in a fire report relating to the cottages which stood behind *Stone Cottages*. The details of this serious fire are detailed below. In 1901 the cottage was the home of **John Saunders** (b.1869), his wife **Louisa Bessie M.** (b.1870 nee Hardy) and their children: **Lilian** (no birth record traced), **Winifred Elizabeth** (b.1896), **Percy Alfred T.** (b.1897) and **John Henry** (b.1899).[3] In 1904 John died age 34 leaving his wife and four children. Louisa married again in 1909 and moved next door to *Chez Nous* with her new husband **James Charman** (b.1869), her children and several of James' children.

The next occupiers of this cottage were, according to the 1911 census: **Silas Lewis** (b.1873), a market gardener, his wife **Esther Louisa** (b.1875 nee Titcombe then Lloyd) and his family which consisted of two step-sons as well as his own son and daughter.[4] This family moved around the *Salvington Cottages* area two or three times during the Edwardian period and it is not clear exactly the dates of their various moves. They were for one period living in *Selden's Cottage* and later, in the 1912 electoral register, they are listed at *Evergreen Cottage*. Both of these properties are situated in Selden's Way. Relationships with the Lewis family and workers at the laundry were not always harmonious and details of the court case involving Silas' wife Esther, is detailed with *Selden's Cottage*.[5]

The Inland Revenue Valuation lists a **C. Lewis** at the property in 1913 which maybe an error for Silas Lewis who had actually moved some time before, or it may have been another occupant.

No 2 Stone Cottages, Stone Lane

This was an identical cottage with No 1 although by 1913 it is noted that it had a larger piece of land with it.[6] The cottage was the home of **George William Penfold** (b.1871) on the 1901 census.[7] He lived here with his London born wife **Frances Ruth** (b.1871 nee Hall) and their three sons: **James** (b.1894), **William John** (b.1897) and **Percy** (b.1899). George Penfold does not appear in any electoral registers and is only listed once in a 1901 street directory.

We know however, that the family were still living at the address in 1908 when James, the eldest of their sons, was mentioned in the local paper as having been involved in an affray outside *The Spotted Cow*. James, who was around 16 years old at the time, had allegedly been fighting with some children whose surname was Henley. Whatever had caused the fight James had, in turn, been assaulted by the children's father who was no doubt coming to his children's defence. In the unfortunate incident an unidentified lady just known as **Mrs Churcher,** somehow found herself between the two combatants, and was on the receiving end of one of the punches straight to her jaw.[8]

A SALVINGTON DISPUTE.

Charges of assaulting Mrs. Churcher and James Penfold were preferred against *James Henley*.

The alleged offences took place near the Spotted Cow Inn, Salvington, and the evidence showed that in some dispute the accused struck at Penfold, and Mrs. Churcher, coming between them, received the blow on her left jaw. It was also stated that accused struck Penfold several times in the face.

Defendant alleged that Penfold had been striking his children, and explained that he lost his temper. He admitted striking Penfold, but he had no intention of hitting Mrs. Churcher.

After deliberating in private the Bench decided to dismiss the summons for the assault on Mrs. Churcher, on the ground that they thought it was done accidentally; and in the other case they considered there had been some provocation, and thought justice would be done by binding accused over in the sum of £5 to keep the peace.

Defendant also had to pay the costs.

The identity of the Henley family comes from newspaper reports of the fight, and a possibility that **James Henley** was a member of the local cricket team, as someone of that name is listed occasionally in the newspaper as a player. The other information we have of James and his children occurs with the reports of the fire in the rear three cottages which are detailed below.

The next occupants moved into the cottage around 1909 when they moved from *1 Beaconsfield Terrace* to Stone Lane. These occupants were **Thomas Tyrrell** (b.1865), a local man born in Salvington and his wife **Jessie Louisa** (b.1862 nee Stringer). They had three children living with them in 1911: **Jessie Louisa** (b.1891), **Frederick Thomas** (b.1894) and **Violet Mary** (b.1897). [9]

Photograph showing *Chez Nous* on the left and a little further up the road the cottages standing close to the roadside are visible. Worthing Library

No's 3, 4 & 5 Stone Cottages, Stone Lane

A row of three small cottages stood directly to the rear of the larger two semi-detached homes detailed above. They were also part of *Salvington Farm* and owned by the Wisden Estate. Edwin Lephard was their direct landlord and most of the occupants were working on the farm in some capacity.

It is difficult to pin-point how the numbering was used as it seems to change in different lists. For ease, the three cottages will be treated together. On the 1901 census, the first of the cottages was inhabited by **Walter White** (b.1839), his wife **Sarah Ann** (b.1839) and two of their sons, **Frank** (b.1876) and **Jack** (b.1884).[10] Walter was working as a carter and with the horses on the farm while both of his sons were agricultural labourers.

The second cottage was the home of the Wells family, who consisted of **James Wells** (b.1856), his wife **Fanny** (b.1856 nee Willard) and their two sons: **Thomas** (b.1890) and **Andrew** (b.1897).[11] According to the electoral register, James moved to Durrington in 1904, although the address is not confirmed.

The third of the row of cottages housed **Elias (Ellis) Evans** (b.1853), a widower originally from Pulborough, and three children: **Kate** (b.1885), **Percy** (b.1887) and **Ellis** (b.1893). Elias' wife **Ellen** had died at the time of Ellis' birth when they were still living in Pulborough. The only listing for Ellis senior is in the electoral register for 1903 and we do not know where or when the family moved again.

We also have **Luke Peacock** (b.1856) listed in a street directory for 1907. Luke lived in one of the cottages with his family for a short while until he moved to *Cutler's Cottages,* Ashacre Lane around 1908, when we know that a momentous event changed the lives of the inhabitants of numbers *1, 2 and 3 Salvington Cottages* who were in residence at the time.

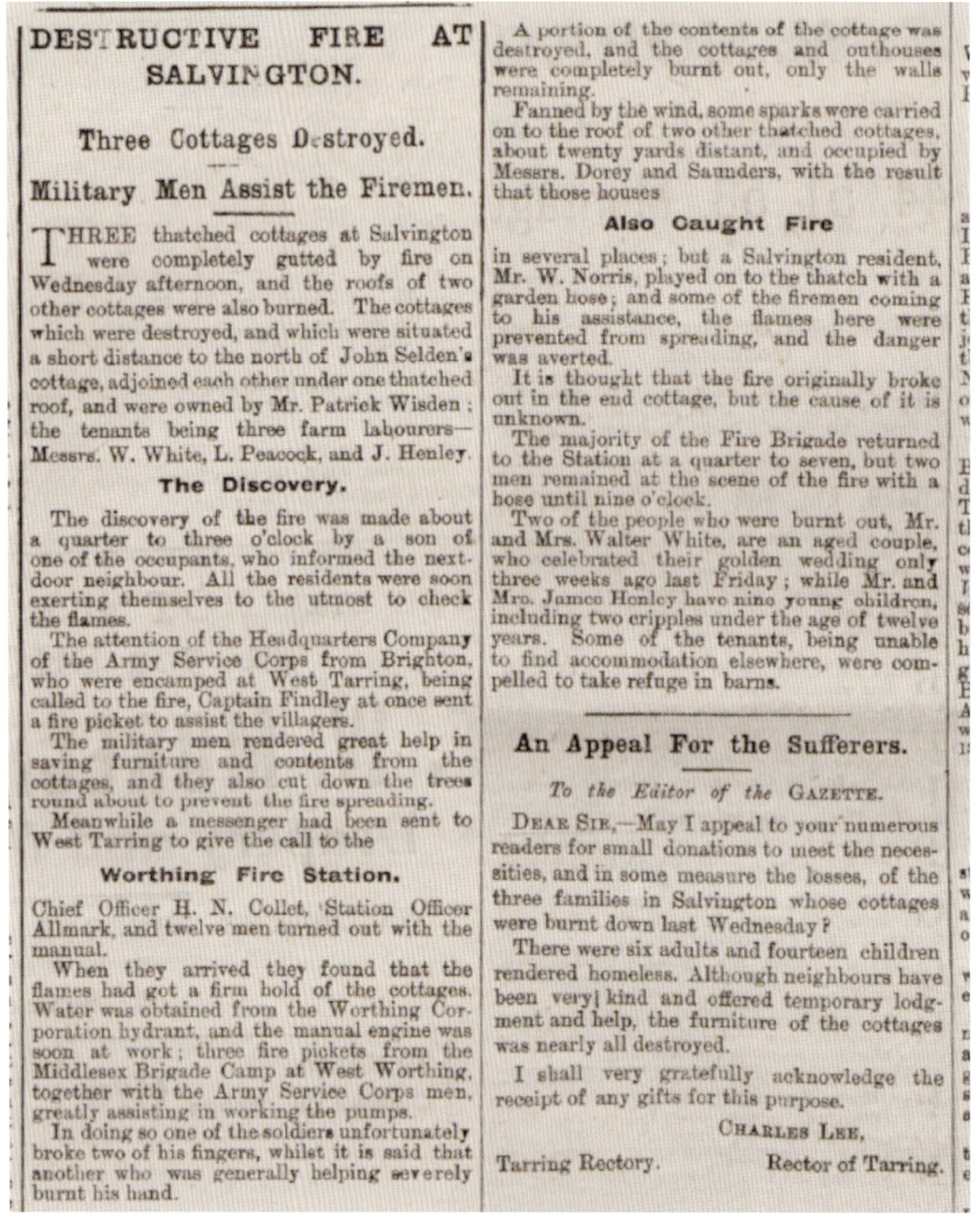

Fire at *Salvington Cottages* as reported in Worthing Gazette

It was on a summer afternoon in August 1908 when disaster struck as the cottages caught fire. From the newspaper report above, which in itself has some very interesting sub-stories, we learn that the cottages were completely gutted although fortunately no lives were lost.[12]

At some time in the afternoon of the 12th August 1908, a fire was noticed in the thatch of one of the cottages. Despite valiant attempts by the local people, a contingent of the Brighton based Army Service Corps staying at West Tarring, and a twelve man team from Worthing Fire Station, the cottages could not be saved. Due to a wind blowing sparks into the air, the thatch of the two cottages in front placed them in danger from the fire spreading, but this was averted by the judicious use of a hose, the newspaper explains:

> '...a Salvington resident, **Mr W Norris**, played onto the thatch with a garden hose; and some of the firemen coming to his assistance, the flames here were prevented from spreading.'[13]

The identity of Mr Norris is known, he was **William Norris** who was living a little further down Stone Lane in *Duffield Cottages*. Three families were made homeless on the day of the fire, which left only the walls standing. The first was **Walter** and **Sarah White,** the elderly couple from No 1, who went to live with their son **Frank** and his family at *6 Beaconsfield Terrace.* The second family was that of James Henley, also listed above. The newspaper report reveals some new information about this family; it tells us that *'Mr and Mrs James Henley'* and *'nine young children, including two cripples under the age of twelve years.'* were made completely homeless on that day in August. This must have been a real tragedy for the family, although the kindness of neighbours is reported as is a wider appeal in the form of a letter published in the newspaper at the same time. This letter was an appeal for donations to help the families, the result of which was the collection of £10 1s 6d to be distributed among them.[14] We do not know where the Henleys moved to, but six children with the same surname were removed from the school at the break of the summer season in July 1908, they had only been on the register for four weeks. The reason for their removal was not mentioned, they may have already been preparing to move on again, but as this was only two weeks before the fire it was just another upheaval for the young children.

The last of the three named families was that of **Luke Peacock,** who again is already mentioned above. He did find new accommodation for his family as, according to the electoral register in 1908, exactly the time of the fire, he moved to *Cutler's Cottages,* Ashacre Lane. These cottages were part of the *Salvington Farm* stock of buildings managed by Edwin Lephard, so this family at least, found another home in property owned by *Salvington Farm*.

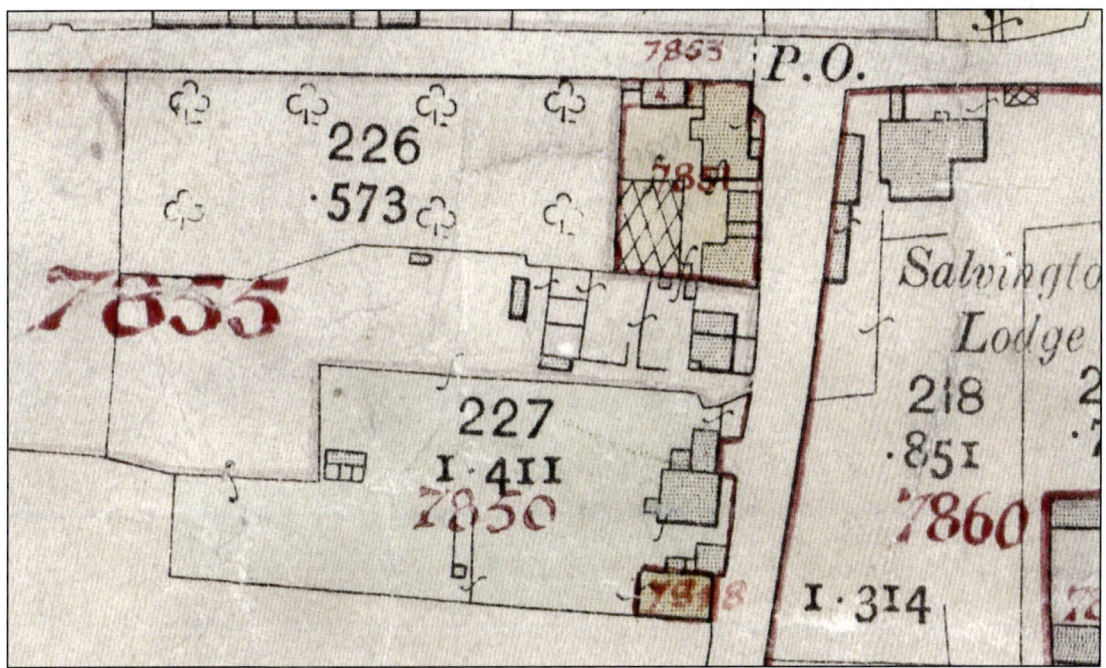

Excerpt taken from OS 25":1 mile Sheet LXIV: 6 3rd Edition 1912 (NTS)
Inland Revenue Valuation numbers added

An interesting little additional story to the fire was the allegations against one of the people who helped extinguish the flames. The gentleman had the surname of Pierre so was probably a relation of Leon Pierre who was the landlord of the *Half Moon Inn* at the time. The report reads:

'BAD LANGUAGE AT THE FIRE

> *It was alleged against a young married man named Albert Pierre, an ex-soldier, for whom Captain J Haywood appeared, that he used obscene language on the occasion of the fire at Salvington last Wednesday. P.C. Wood, Mr. H. N. Collet (Chief Officer of the Fire Brigade), and William Holden gave evidence showing that the accused was in a most excited condition, and*
> *Defendant, who did not deny the offence, but on whose behalf it was urged that he worked very hard in suppressing the fire and was then ejected, was fined 7s 6d.'*[15]

57. Chez Nous & Laundry
(No longer standing)

Chez Nous or *Chez Nory* as it was sometimes called was a large five-bedroomed property standing behind a low flint wall. The property stood at the front of the plot close to the roadside and included other buildings behind them. The site was listed as a *'house with garden'* as early as 1838 when it appears on the West Tarring tithe map.[16] On the 1901 census it was recorded as a *'Miller's Shop, Granary and Stores'*, with the head of the household named as Stephen Scutt, who had been the last miller at *High Salvington Windmill*.[17]

Stephen Scutt (b.1855) was the son of a butcher originally from Bolney in Sussex. He had begun his working life as an agricultural labourer but at some time between the 1871 and 1881 censuses he had joined the army and was a private in the 1st Battalion of the Royal Sussex Regiment in Egypt when they fought in the Second Egyptian War of 1882. This period of his life as a soldier was later to be cited as one of the root causes for his periodic drinking and family breakdown.

By 1886 we know that Stephen had left the army as in the July of that year he married **Elizabeth Fanny Castle** (b.c1855) in Lancing. They had a daughter named **Mary Elizabeth** (b.1886) not many months afterwards but the marriage was not to last as Elizabeth herself died in 1888 leaving Stephen alone with a small child.

The 1891 census shows Stephen living on his own in Lancing at *Mill Cottages* where he was working as a miller,[18] but of Mary, his young daughter, there is no sign at this time. Stephen did not stay single for very long, marrying **Fanny Armstrong** (b.1863) later in the same year. The couple stayed in Lancing for some years and it was here that their first son **Edwin (Edward) James** (b.1894) was born. The move to Salvington, where Stephen took up the post as miller at *High Salvington Windmill*, happened between 1894 and 1899 as their second child, **Arthur Allen** (b.1899) was born in Salvington. They also had a daughter **Gladys Ada** (b.1901) and we know from the 1901 census that the family were living at *Chez Nous* by this date.[19] The census tells us that Stephen's daughter, Mary, had joined the rest of her step-family and was with them in Salvington as well.

Stephen was the last miller to work at *High Salvington Windmill* where it has been suggested that he may have been employed by *Coote's Bakery* to provide the flour. He was certainly working there at the beginning of the century, with the commercial arm of the business being run from *Chez Nous*.

One of the ways the family supplemented their income was to rent rooms. On the 1901 census two young families are listed as lodging at *Chez Nous* each occupying two rooms. One was the family of a hire carter **Henry (Harry) Linfield** (b.1877), his wife **Mary** (b.1878 nee Cooper) and two sons **Eric Sydney** (b.1898) and **Henry Charles Vincent** (b.1899). The other family consisted of a young couple **William Henry Boxold** and his wife **Edith Rosalind** (b.1880 nee Brown). William's birth was supposed to be around 1877 at Arundel but no registration for that name has yet been confirmed. We do know that in 1899 he married Edith and sadly in 1903 at the age of 26 he died. He possibly did not live here for very long as a 1901 street directory lists **William Henry Boxold** at *The Row* in Durrington although we do not know which of the cottages he was living in.

However, the story for Stephen Scutt and his family is not one of either business or personal success. In the years after the 1901 census passed the mill failed, as did his marriage and an agreed separation left him struggling to cope. Despite various attempts at help from the village, where he seems to have been well thought of, he eventually committed suicide by drowning himself in a water tank at the nursery owned by James Lord in Ashacre Lane where Stephen had been working. We can learn more about the story from the inquest which was reported in the local newspaper soon after it had taken place.[20]

Photograph showing *Chez Nous* cropped from photograph on page 113. Worthing Library

SAD STORY OF DOMESTIC DISAGREEMENT.

A Husband's Suicide.

Coroner's Investigation at Salvington.

A PECULIARLY sad story of an unhappy married life was revealed at Salvington on Saturday evening, when an inquiry was held at the Half Moon Inn into the circumstances associated with the death of a man named Stephen Scutt, aged fifty-two years, who drowned himself in a tank in the nursery grounds of Mr. Lord on the previous evening. The deceased was an ex-soldier, and saw service in the Egyptian Campaign; and several members of the Jury, of which Mr. A. Taylor was appointed Foreman, bore testimony to his good character in general.

The Discovery of the Body.

The first witness who was summoned before the Jury, after they had proceeded to the deceased's former cottage to formally view the body, was JAMES LORD, a gardener, who stated that Scutt was employed by him for three hours on Friday, and promised to return on Saturday. From time to time, for several days at a stretch, he had been employed by witness. He did not notice anything unusual about him on Friday, except that he seemed rather dull. About ten minutes to six o'clock in the evening, witness, after returning from tea, saw deceased's clothes lying in the garden—his hat and two jackets—and then saw his head in the tank. The latter was about six feet deep and seven feet wide, and contained about five feet of water; and deceased was floating on the top. Witness went to the spot to attend to the stokehole, and that was how it was he came to discover the body. He fetched two young men, and within five minutes the body was taken out. It was about a quarter-past five when they parted in the roadway, going different ways. Deceased did not say "anything out of the way," but promised to return about seven o'clock on Saturday morning. He had known the deceased for ten years, and a nice quiet man he was. He had a glass of beer, the same as any other man; but it was not very often he got the worse for drink.

Domestic Differences.

FANNY SCUTT, widow of the deceased, deposed that her husband was a miller by trade, but the mill had been closed for some time, and for the past nine months he had been working at the Golf Links. He was fifty-two years of age. She last saw him alive about half-past five o'clock on Thursday evening; he had not slept at home since the previous Saturday or Sunday—she was not quite sure which. He told her he was going away, but he did not say where, and she did not exactly know why.

The Coroner: Were there differences between you?—Yes, sir.

Was that the reason why he was going?—Yes.

Has he ever left you before?—Yes; but not for so long.

Did you ask him to go away?—Yes, I did.

This last time?—Yes, I did. But I wanted an agreement drawn up.

You wanted a separation, in fact?—Yes.

In reply to further questions witness said she did not expect to see him back, as she thought he had gone to Canada. He had given her no money, and she did not know where she was going to get the money to make up the year's rent. When he came home on Thursday she knew he had drunk away the money which should have gone to pay the rent. She threw his things outside the house, and told him he might go too. He stayed about ten minutes, but she did not see him again. She did not know where he slept that night, or during the early part of the week. She had never heard him threaten to make away with himself. She could not say that he had a bad temper, except when he was the worse for drink, and she had been

Afraid of Him Lately,

as he had often been under the influence of liquor. Mr. and Mrs. Wyatt occupied part of witness's house.

Can you tell the Jury anything more than you have already said which could throw any light on the subject of his death?—I can't think what induced him to take his life, sir. I never thought he would do such a thing (here the witness commenced to cry).

I suppose it is just the fact that you have not led a happy life with him for some time?—Yes, sir; that is it.

ALBERT WHITTINGTON, of Farm-Cottages, Salvington, said he had known deceased for the past fifteen months. He worked with him all last summer, but had not seen much of him during the past week or so. Between half-past eleven and twelve on Friday he last saw the deceased alive. Deceased slept at witness's house on Thursday night. He came there asking Mrs. Whittington to cook some sausages for his supper, saying he did not dare go to his own house. When witness reached home he said he had come for a night's lodging, and witness said he should not turn him away. After talking for an hour they went to the Half Moon, where they remained until ten, and deceased was then "as nice as could be." All night long he was very restless, and a young man who slept with him said he kept talking about his wife, but they could not catch what he said. He had breakfast and dinner in the house, and witness left him in the Half Moon, after they had a drink together, deceased then stating that he was going to the Golf Links. He

Did Not Appear to be Depressed,

and showed no signs of making away with himself. Deceased seemed upset about his domestic affairs, but said nothing about the matter.

The CORONER briefly commented upon the unhappy circumstances revealed by the evidence, and

The Jury returned a formal verdict that deceased committed suicide whilst temporarily insane.

P.C. Carpenter, who had charge of the inquiry on behalf of the Coroner's Officer (Supt. Bridger), informed the Coroner that the deceased had £1 18s. in his possession.

Report of the inquest into the death of Stephen Scutt in March 1906

Only a few months after Stephen's death we find Fanny Scutt mentioned in the Wisden Estate sale catalogue which included *Chez Nous* among the plots to be sold. Lieut. Col. Thomas Wisden had died at the end of 1904 and according to the instructions of his will, some parts of the estate were to be sold. The sale catalogue entry used in an advert for the sale in the Worthing Gazette gives us even more details of the building and its tenancy.[21] It was rented on a quarterly basis to Mrs Fanny Scutt for the annual sum of £26. Obviously, either at the time of the original separation from her husband or at the point of his death in March 1906, she had taken on the renting of property for herself and was continuing with her business.

Wednesday, September 5th 1906.

Mr. HARRY JAS. BURT.

TO-MORROW.

By Order of the Trustees under the Will of the late Lieut.-Colonel T. F. Wisden, J.P., D.L.

BROADWATER, WEST TARRING, DURRINGTON, AND SALVINGTON, SUSSEX.

Important Sale of valuable FREEHOLD BUILDING LAND, the TARRING OLD FIG GARDENS, COTTAGES, MARKET GARDEN LAND, CORN MERCHANT'S SHOP and STORES, WHEELWRIGHT'S YARD and PREMISES, and the SALVINGTON WINDMILL, for investment or occupation.

HARRY JAS. BURT

Is instructed to Sell by Auction, at THE TOWN HALL WORTHING, ON THURSDAY, SEPTEMBER 6TH, 1906, At 3.30 o'clock, in six Lots the following valuable FREEHOLD (small part Copyhold) PROPERTIES:

Lot 1.—A FREEHOLD TWO-TENEMENT COTTAGE and WHEELWRIGHT'S YARD, WORKSHOP, and PREMISES, in BROADWATER STREET, BROADWATER. The Cottages are let to John Gould and Arthur Batchelor, weekly tenants, at 3s. per week each. The Yard and Premises are let to Mr. William Green at £20 per annum, on a seven years' lease, expiring Christmas, 1906.

Lot 2.—The TARRING FIG GARDENS, a valuable FREEHOLD DETACHED COTTAGE and large garden, in SOUTH STREET, WEST TARRING, known as the Ancient Fig Gardens, let to Mr. Daniel Humphrey, at £27 10s. per annum.

Lot 3.—The SALVINGTON WINDMILL (copyhold) and FREEHOLD COTTAGE, in the parish of DURRINGTON, forming a splendid site for the erection of a bungalow. The Mill is in hand. Cottage let to Mr. Walter Bailey, a quarterly tenant, at £10 per annum.

Lot 4.—A desirable DETACHED HOUSE, SHOP, CORN STORE, STABLE, PIGGERIES, and large garden, known as CHEZ NOUS, STONES LANE, SALVINGTON (copyhold), let to Mrs. Fanny Scutt, a quarterly tenant, at £26 per annum.

Lot 5.—A valuable piece of FREEHOLD MARKET GARDEN or BUILDING LAND, with good frontage, at SALVINGTON, let to Mr. James Lord, a yearly tenant, at £10 per annum.

Lot 6.—A FREEHOLD DETACHED COTTAGE, and large garden, with long frontage, situate at SALVINGTON, in the occupation of Mr. James Holden.

Particulars and conditions of Sale may be obtained of Harry Jas Burt, Auctioneer and Valuer, Steyning, Sussex; and of Messrs. Upperton and Bacon, Solicitors, 6, Pavilion-buildings, Brighton.

Advert in Worthing Gazette September 1906 giving information on the lots to be sold at the auction on the following day.
Chez Nous is Lot 4.

It is interesting to note that this property was not sold in 1906 as it was still offered as part of the Wisden Estate when another auction of holdings was held for sale some years later in 1923. This is confirmed as the Inland Revenue Valuation of 1913 still gives the owner as 'Wisden F. T. of Henfield'.[22]

Whatever the drama in the family life of the Scutts was, day to day life had to go on and Fanny enrolled two of her children, Arthur and Gladys, into the local school in June 1908, although they were removed again in the July with no reason given. The children had been moved to the school from Goring so maybe they returned there. Fanny and the family moved from *Chez Nous* around this time and moved to *8 Beaconsfield Terrace* where she continued living for the rest of the period.

In 1909 **James Charman** (b.1870) of *3 Yew Tree Cottages* had married **Louisa Saunders** (b.1870 nee Hardy). For both of them it was a second marriage and both brought children to their new marriage. According to the electoral register they then moved into *Chez Nous* and it was this move which also brought the change of the use of the property to that of a laundry as the street directories now list it as *Chez Nous Laundry*. Louisa had not moved far having been the previous occupant of one of the cottages next door where she had lived with her first husband, John Saunders, who had died in 1904.

The 1911 census gives us details of the household, the head being **Louisa Charman,** a son **Albert Charman** (b.1876) (probably the same as a step-child named Albert Skinner/Charman listed on the 1901 census)[23] and four of Louisa's children: **Winifred Elizabeth Saunders** (b.1896), **Percy Alfred T.** (b.1897), **John Henry** (b.1899) and **Dorothy** (b.1905). James and Louisa had also had a child of their own as **Joseph** was born in 1910.[24]

James is not at home on the night of the 1911 census being listed as a visitor at a house in Bramley, Surrey where he gives his occupation as *'Wood Sawyer'*.[25] This had given Louisa a little issue to think through when she was filling out the census form. She had first listed herself as *'wife'* and then maybe reading the instructions again had crossed this out and written *'Head'* still leaving the top line of the sheet empty where James' name should have been entered.

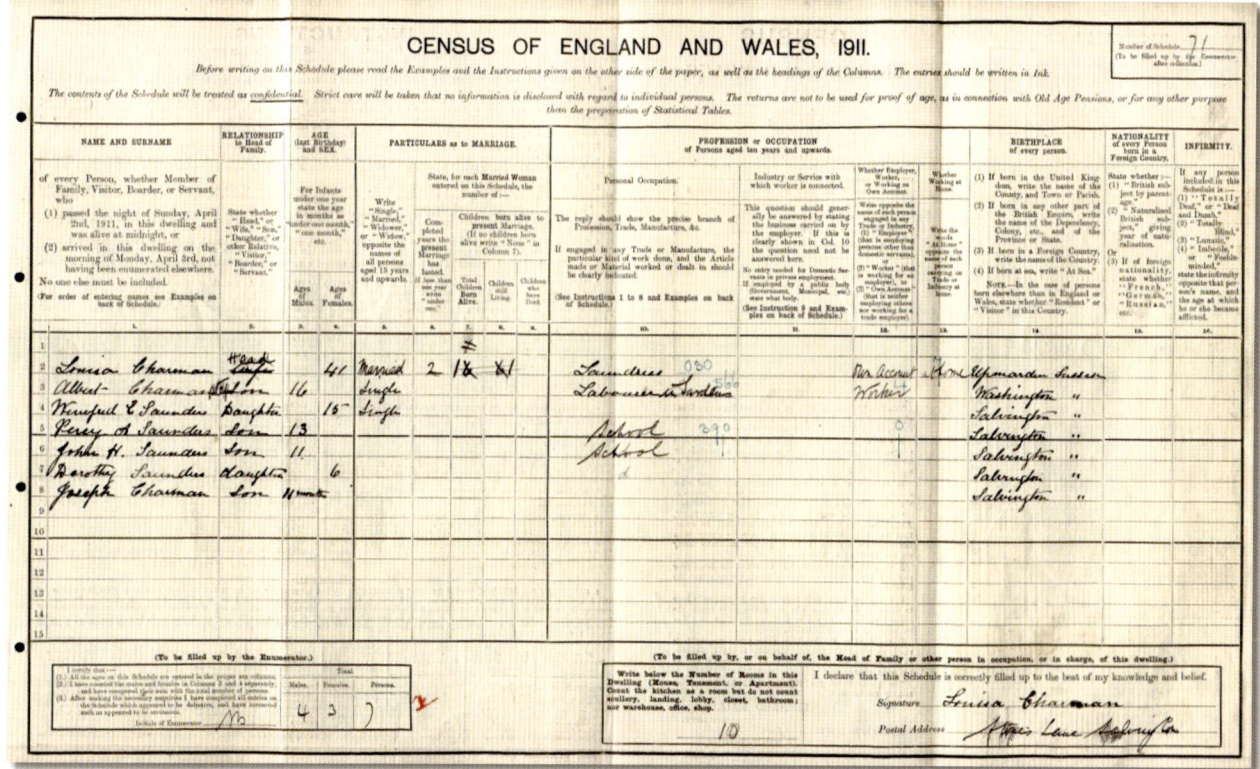

1911 census sheet for *Chez Nous* © The National Archives

The Saunders children, who were of the appropriate age, are listed in the Admissions Register for Durrington School, the three youngest not leaving until Christmas 1909, when Winifred left to work in domestic service, having enrolled the year only before. In 1911 the next child, Percy, left to become a bakers boy and in 1913 John Henry left to work in the market gardens. Louisa's eldest daughter, Lilian was not enrolled into school at all being listed as *'imbecile'* in 1901.[26] This unfortunate phrase was often used to describe any form of learning difficulty during the period. There is also no birth record yet traced for Lilian.

Albert Charman, as he is listed on the 1911 census, was obviously a very bright child referred to in the school log-books as *'top boy'* and did not get permission to leave the school until he was 14 years old. The headmaster records the reason:

> *'My top boy Albert Charman leaves today. He had been offered work before, but was not 14.'*[27]

The fact was that the need to work prevented many intelligent children from continuing with their education as the economic needs and expectations of the family had to come first. On the 1911 census we have it recorded that his occupation was by this time a *'labourer in garden's'* most probably one of the numerous market gardens in the area.

Excerpt taken from OS 25":1 mile Sheet LXIV: 6 3rd Edition 1912 (NTS)

58. Rose Cottage, Stone Lane
(Now No 93 The Old Coach House, Stone Lane)

According to the 1911 census further down the road from *Salvington Cottages* was a cottage named *Rose Cottage* which was the home of a retired cook **Thomas Hyde** born in Petworth around 1845 and his wife **Alice** (b.1844).[28] The cottage is still standing as shown in the photograph below and is now called *The Old Coach House*.

Modern photograph of *The Old Coach House*. © Dave Pryce 2015

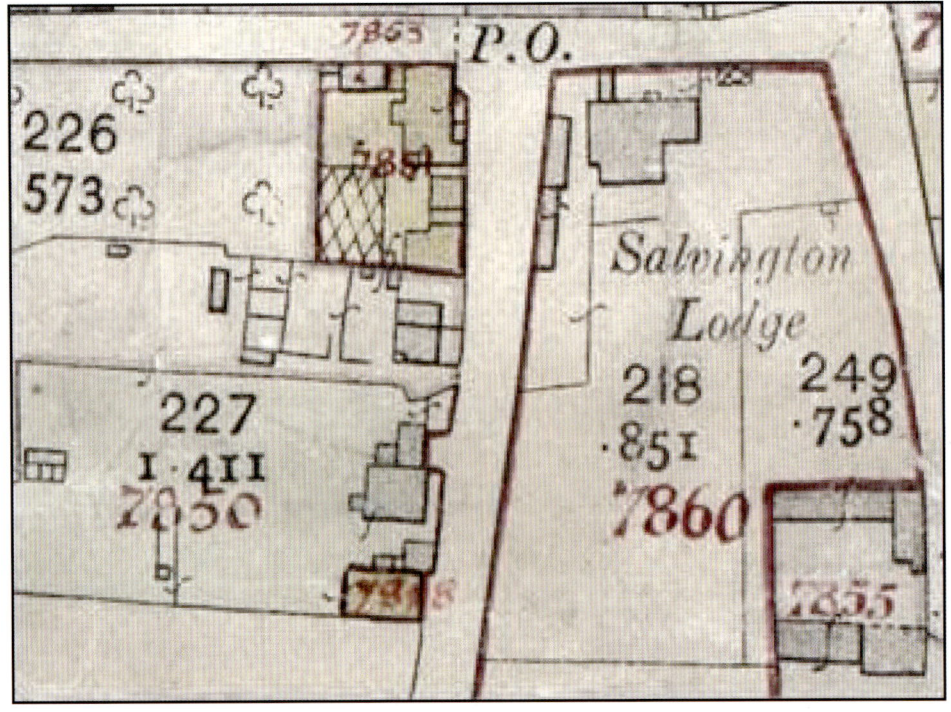

Excerpt taken from OS 25":1 mile Sheet LXIV: 6 3rd Edition 1912 (NTS)
Inland Revenue Valuation numbers added

59. Salvington or Duffield Cottages, Stone Lane
(No longer standing)

Duffield Cottages consist of a pair of semi-detached properties described in the Inland Revenue Valuation in May 1913, within the returns for a portion of land in Stone Lane, owned by the Wisden Estate.[29] The occupier at the time is given as H. P. Gray. In the electoral registers for the 1910-1913 years this person is identified as **Hubert Patrick Gray,** a fruit grower actually living in Victoria Road, Worthing.

The tenancy for the cottages had been taken up in September 1905 for 14 years by Mr Gray and both cottages were rented on, seemingly to occupiers who were already living in them at the time of their purchase. The Inland Revenue Valuation also has separate valuations for each cottage recorded in 1913 but they do not name the occupants.[30] We can, however, trace who was living there through census and other records.

The description of the land and the cottages is easily recognisable from the photograph which appeared in Country Life Magazine in May 1914.

Duffield Cottages as they appear in Country Life in 1914. © Country Life used with permission

The Inland Revenue Valuation recorded the site as:

> '*Good arable land. Part planted with fruit trees.*
> *2 old cottages, bad repair, thatch roofs, 1 granary,*
> *1 shed brick & thatch*
> *2 pigsties*
> *1 shed.*'[31]

This is the second time that a granary appears in the Inland Revenue Valuations for Durrington or Salvington, the other being at *Ham Farm* in Littlehampton Road.[32] The granary building can be clearly seen on the left of the picture with small wooden steps leading up to a small wooden door. The undergrowth around the base has obscured the familiar mushroom shaped straddle stones which the granary would have stood on. The shape of these stones was very effective at preventing rats and mice from getting into the stored grain and also kept the contents well away from the damp Salvington ground.

The cottages were thatched as mentioned and the curving path around the front is clearly marked on the 1912 Ordnance Survey map (see page 123). According to the 1911 census each property had only three rooms providing homes for the families to live in.

In 1901 the first of the cottages was the home of **John Knight** (b.c1836) who was already a widower.[33] Two of his children were living with him: **George Ernest** (b. 1869) and **Louis James (Jesse)** (b.1881) who married a few months after the census was taken and then he moved to 3 *The Row,* Durrington with his wife **Winifred Frances** (b.1883 nee Wood). John left the cottage some years later and moved to Withdean in Brighton to live with his eldest son also called John, who was a poultry farmer.

The 1911 census gives us the next occupant, a married lady by the name of **Amy Dean** (b.1856 nee World) who lived here with her son **Alfred Ernest** (b.1896).[34] They had previously lived at 1 *Ashacre Cottages, Ashacre Lane* with Amy's husband William Dean,[35] whose whereabouts is unknown at the time of the 1911 census. Amy is working as a laundress probably at *Chez Nous Laundry* a few steps up the road.

The second cottage was the home of **William Norris** (b.1862) and his family throughout the whole period. William shared the cottage with his wife **Sarah Jane** (b.c1865 nee Saunders) and four daughters: **Lucy Lily** (b.1889), **Edith Mary** (b.1891), **Mary Louise** (b.1892) and **Alice Maud** (b.1900). By the 1911 census the three older girls had all left home and only Alice remained with her parents.[36] She had been young enough in 1908, when the new school opened in the village, to transfer from Tarring where she had previously attended school, to the new school just round the corner in Salvington Road. She left in 1913 to be employed as a domestic worker.

We hear of the family again, when William Norris was mentioned in the newspapers in August 1908 helping with the serious fire which completely burnt out the three thatched cottages further up Stone Lane.[37] William and Sarah left the cottage in 1913 as the electoral register records a move from Salvington to Durrington.

Photograph of the original site of *Duffield Cottages* in 2015. © Dave Pryce

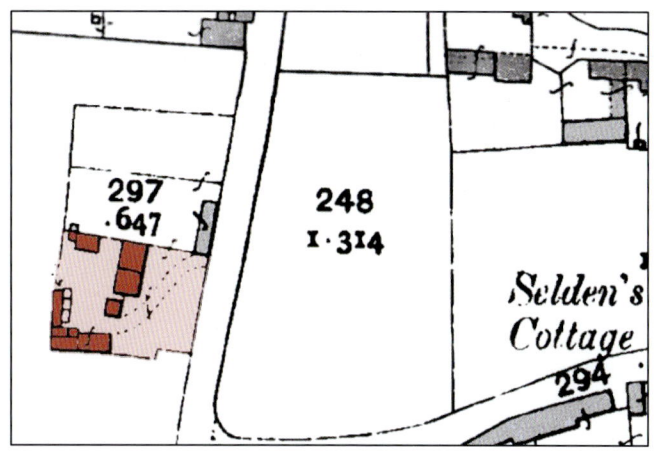

Excerpt taken from OS 25":1 mile Sheet LXIV: 10
3rd Edition 1912 (NTS)

60. Evergreen Cottage, Selden's Way
(Now No 33 Selden's Way)

This cottage stood on the southern corner of Stone Lane and Selden's Way and is another of the cottages called by various names or no name in different documentation. The 1901 census simply calls it *'cottage'*,[38] whilst the street directory for the same year lists it as *'Selden's Lane Cottage'*.

In 1901 the cottage was the home of **James Voak** (b.1874), his wife **Ellen (Nellie)** (b.1880 nee Sayers) and two children named **Archibald** (b.1897) and **Emily Norah** (b.1899). After the census had been taken they went on to have two more children: **Dorothy Kathleen** (b.1901) and **James William** (b.1903). Around 1905 the family moved to Pond Lane where they settled in the thatched cottage called *Woodbine Cottage* at the time and went on to have two more children. The occupants for the 1911 census have not yet been identified.

Photograph of *Evergreen Cottage* (No 33) Selden's Way in 2015. © Dave Pryce

61. Selden's Cottage (Lacies), Selden's Way
(No longer standing)

This was a very old cottage in Salvington which was the birthplace in 1584 of **John Selden**, hence the naming of the cottage and the reference to him in the naming of the *John Selden Inn*. Selden was a well-known politician and writer of the time who spent most of his life working life in London, although he had humble beginnings in this cottage in Salvington. His writings are well known and his interesting life was played out against the background of the English Civil War.

The cottage itself, in the Edwardian period, belonged to *Salvington Farm*, and was for most of its life variously occupied by farm workers, as were many of the other properties in and around Stone Lane.

The occupant of *Selden's Cottage* was already in residence as the twentieth century began and was listed on the 1901 census. The head of the household was **Edward Henry Lewis** (b.1864) along with some members of his family. In 1885, Edward had married **Mary Ann Leggett** (b.1864) and they went on to have at least five children, only four of whom survived into adulthood. **Edward Henry C.** (b.1886), **Rosa E.** (b.1887), **Frances Eleanor** (b.1889), **Daisy Alma** (b.1890) and **Alice Mary** (b.1893) are the five children listed on the census returns for 1901[39]. Their eldest son Edward sadly died in 1903 whilst they were living at the cottage.

Interestingly, on the night of the 1901 census, Mary Ann Lewis was not at home with her husband and children. She was registered in Lyminster, Sussex at the home of her mother-in-law **Frances Lewis**, where she may have just been visiting or possibly caring for her in some manner.

Between 1904 and 1907 Edward and Mary Lewis were to move from the cottage into a new property in Ashacre Lane called *East Villa*. This move may have reflected by the fact that Edward was by 1911, working in the more prestigious occupation of *'Farm Baliff'* at *Salvington Farm*.

The next occupant is first listed at this address in street directories for 1907 followed by a first entry in the electoral register in 1908. The name of this occupant was **Silas Lewis** (b.c1874) who may share the same surname as the previous tenants but appears not to be a relative.

Silas, another market gardener, lived in *Selden's Cottage* with his wife **Esther Louisa** (b.1875 nee Titcombe & Lloyd) and their two children, **Winifred Rosa** (b.1906) and **Ronald Silas** (b.1908). Life was not always calm in the Lewis household, illustrated by a situation which arose in the autumn of 1910 where tempers had flared and Esther found herself in court on a charge of assault. The story appeared in the Worthing Gazette in September 1910, and it outlined an altercation that took place in Salvington between Esther Lewis and a lady named **Mrs. Maud Denyer**. There is no record of a lady by this name living in the village, but a lady matching the name was living in Queen Street, Worthing on the 1911 census. This lady gave her occupation as *'laundry worker'* which makes it highly likely that she was working at the *Chez Nous Laundry* in Stone Lane. The newspaper article related the court proceedings, and outlines a *'wordy quarrel'* which resulted in a stick being used as a weapon, a carving knife being brandished and blood being spilled. The whole unseemly episode is told in the newspaper article, where there was obviously still a lot of anger with claims and counter claims being aired in the court house.[40] Mrs. Denyer claimed that the whole situation began when a son of Esther's threw stones at her doorway

> **A DISTURBANCE AT SALVINGTON.**
>
> A plea of "Not guilty" was tendered by Mr. A. Buckland Dixon on behalf of *Mrs. Esther Lewis*, of Salvington, who had been summoned for assaulting Maud Denyer on Wednesday afternoon, and there was also a cross-summons against *Mrs. Denyer*, in which Mrs. Lewis asked that the latter might be required to find sureties to keep the peace.
>
> The evidence of Mrs. Denyer showed that they had a wordy quarrel, in the course of which defendant struck her three times on the head with a stick, cutting her head open, and necessitating her going to the Hospital, where she was still being treated as an out-patient.
>
> Corroborative evidence was given by a boy named John Henry Saunders, and by James William Madgwick and Eliza Mosley.
>
> Addressing the Bench for the defence, Mr. Dixon did not deny the assault, but his version was that Mrs Lewis received very great provocation, and that she only struck Mrs. Denyer with the stick in self-defence when the latter ran after her with a chopper.
>
> Mrs. Lewis supported this account of the affair on oath, and Frederick Henry Lloyd and Thomas Searle corroborated.
>
> The Magistrates decided to convict Mrs. Lewis in the assault case, and the summons for using threats was then withdrawn.
>
> Superintendent Bridger was called as a witness to defendant's character, and
>
> The Magistrates then imposed a fine of 20s., including costs.
>
> A further summons was afterwards heard, in which *Mrs. Denyer* was alleged to have assaulted a boy named James W. Lloyd, son of Mrs. Lewis. Mrs. Denyer, who explained that she hit the boy because he threw stones at her door, was fined 2s. 6d.

so she may indeed have been living in the area at the time of the incident.

The Lewis family had originally taken a three year tenancy on *Selden's Cottage* beginning in September 1909, according to the Inland Revenue Valuation, at a rent of 2/- a week.[41] They must have moved to their next address, 1 *Stone Cottages,* a little before their tenancy agreement finished as by the 1911 census we have different occupants registered. As *Stone Cottages* was situated next to the *Chez Nous Laundry* it is probable that both Mrs Lewis and Mrs Denyer were neighbours in some way at that time. It is to be hoped that after the court case some semblance of friendly relations was re-established between the two families.

The 1911 census records that there were new occupants in *Selden's Cottage* where we find a young farm labourer, listed as a 'cowman', named **William James Marshall** (b.1887) registered with his family.[42] Although William's father and mother were both Sussex born and bred, William himself had been born in Sydney, Australia. The family must have been resident in Australia for some years before returning to England.

William Marshall had married his wife **Daisy Alma** (b.1890 nee Lewis) in 1908. She was a daughter of the previous occupant of the cottage, making it possible that her parents had vacated the cottage to make available a home for their son-in-law and daughter. By the time of the 1911 census, they had had two children, **William Edward** (b.1909) and **Daisy May** (b.1910) both born in Salvington

We do not know how long they stayed at the address, but they may have been the *'humble tenants'* mentioned in an anonymous letter written to The Times in February 1914, bemoaning the continuous deterioration of the famous cottage where John Selden had been born. From this letter we know that the cottage was now named *Lacies Cottage* and this name was to continue for many years. [43]

JOHN SELDEN'S BIRTHPLACE.

A PLEA FOR NATIONAL PURCHASE.

TO THE EDITOR OF THE TIMES.

Sir,—Your columns give almost daily evidence of awakened interest in England's notabilities.

December 16 next will be the 330th anniversary of the birth of John Selden, the great jurist, whom Dr. Johnson described as "the glory of the English nation" and Horsfield as "the conscientious defender of his country's liberties." His birthplace, The Lacies, Salvington, Sussex, a tiny timber-built thatched cottage, with exterior carved oak beams of great and rare beauty, still stands in a remote out-of-the-way country lane, well back from the main road, which has, providentially, so far acted throughout the centuries as a protecting shield from the curio-hunter. But from the ravages of time it has not been protected.

On the inside of the lintel over the humble entrance, sadly besmirched by the plasterer's lime-brush, is a Latin distich, composed and carved by Selden himself when but 10 years of age, which reads :—

"Gratus, honeste, mihi ; non claudar ; inito sedeque,
Fur, abeas ; non sum facta soluta tibi."

Johnson has translated this :—

"Walk in and welcome ; honest friend, repose.
Thief, get thee out ; to thee I'll not unclose."

But the thief Time cannot be kept out. More than 330 years have worked' superficial havoc on thatched roof, timbered walls, latticed windows, and carved beams. But substantially it is intact—indeed it is still in the occupation of humble tenants.

With the memory of the splendid restoration and preservation of the cottage occupied by Anne Hathaway (all will admit, at least, not greater than "the glory of the English nation"), cannot the 330th anniversary of Selden's birth witness his cottage the possession of the nation ? Failing this it may quite well be that our more appreciative Transatlantic cousins may acquire the same and transport it bodily to the land which, to our lasting loss, has carried away so many of the treasures of the old country.

What says the Selden Society to this ? A few hundreds would probably acquire from the patriotic owner the freehold of the cottage and its patch of garden ground, while a few more would sufficiently restore and preserve it for all time. Members of the Selden Society and London lawyers generally may be interested to know that a black marble tablet to Selden's memory may be seen in the choir of the Temple Church. Should the lawyers be unequal to the effort, would this not be a suitable case for the intervention of the Society for the Preservation of Objects of Historical Interest?

I enclose a photograph of the cottage showing in part the unique oak carving.

Yours, &c.,

February 21. MEDII TEMPII.

The Inland Revenue Valuation gives no description of the building at all just a few details recording that *'the farmer',* who we know was Edwin Lephard was renting the property to someone with the surname 'Ridgley'. This may be Charles Ridgley who is listed in the street directory for 1912 living in *Salvington Cottages* (this may be a reference to *Selden's Cottage*) and who had been a lodger at *Chez Nous* in 1901.[44]

The cottage was controversially demolished in 1956 after a fire had badly damaged the building.

Lacies Cottage, Salvington, also known as *Selden's Cottage*.
Worthing Library

Modern photograph showing the site of where *Selden's (Lacies) Cottage* once stood. © Dave Pryce 2015

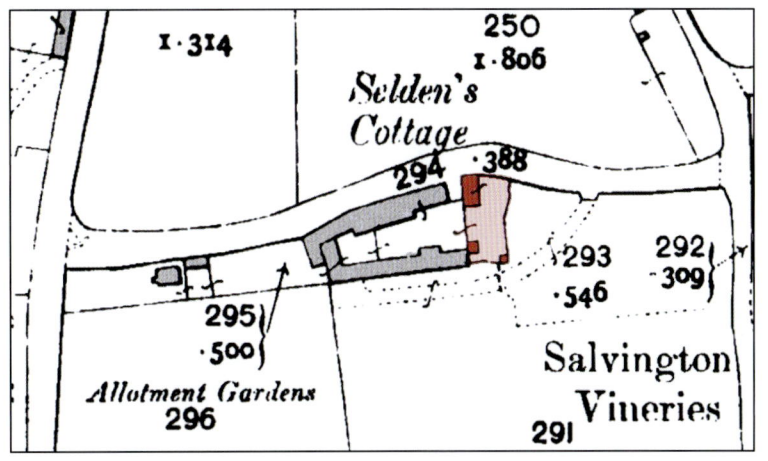

Excerpt taken from OS 25":1 mile Sheet LXIV: 10 3rd Edition 1912 (NTS)

---

[1] West Tarring Tithe Map 1838. Par 193/21/1 (WSRO)
[2] IR58/94205 No. 7890 (TNA)
[3] 1901 census RG13/957 ff.61 (TNA)
[4] 1911 census RG14/5342 sch 69 (TNA)
[5] Worthing Gazette 7th September 1910 p5
[6] IR58/94205 No. 7891 (TNA)
[7] 1901 census RG13/957 ff.61 (TNA)
[8] Worthing Gazette 17th June 1908 p5
[9] 1911 census RG14/5342 sch 70 (TNA)
[10] 1901 census RG13/957 ff.61 (TNA)
[11] 1901 census RG13/957 ff.61 (TNA)
[12] Worthing Gazette 19th August 1908 p7
[13] Worthing Gazette 19th August 1908 p7
[14] Worthing Gazette 26th August 1908 p5
[15] Worthing Gazette 19th August 1908 p5
[16] West Tarring Tithe Map 1838. Par 193/21/1 (WSRO)
[17] 1901 census RG13/957 ff.62 (TNA)
[18] 1891 census RG12/824 ff.94 (TNA)
[19] 1901 census RG13/957 ff.62 (TNA)
[20] Worthing Gazette 28th March 1906 p3
[21] Worthing Gazette 5th September 1906 p4
[22] IR58/94296 No. 7850 (TNA)
[23] 1901 census RG13.957 ff.60 (TNA)
[24] 1911 census RG14/5342 sch 71(TNA)
[25] 1911 census RG14/1358 sch 203 (TNA)
[26] 1901 census RG13/957 ff.61 (TNA)
[27] Durrington School Admissions Register 1908-1928. 31st March 1909, p.20 (Held at the school)
[28] 1911 census RG14/5342 sch 74 (TNA)
[29] IR58/94206 No. 7847 (TNA)
[30] IR58/94206 No. 7881 & 7882 (TNA)
[31] **IR58/94206 No. 7847 (TNA)**
[32] IR58/94204 No. 7690 (TNA)
[33] 1901 census RG13/957 ff.62 (TNA)
[34] 1911 census RG14/5342 sch 72 (TNA)
[35] 1901 census RG13/957 ff.77 (TNA)
[36] 1911 census RG14/5342 sch 73 (TNA)
[37] Worthing Gazette 19th August 1908 p7
[38] 1901 census RG13/957 ff.62 (TNA)
[39] 1901 census RG13/957 ff.62 (TNA)
[40] Worthing Gazette 7th September p5
[41] IR58/94206 No.7876 (TNA)
[42] 1911 census RG14/5342 sch 69 (TNA
[43] The Times (London, England), Tuesday, 24th February 1914 p 4
[44] 1901 census RG13/957 ff.62 (TNA)

Chapter 7
Ashacre Lane and Ashacre Way

Introduction

Ashacre Lane runs east to west through the middle of the hamlet of Salvington. It begins at Offington Lane and ends at the junction with Salvington Road by the *John Selden*. The road is named after the land which ranged along the north side, called *The Ashacre* and was a main pasture area for *Salvington Farm.* At the beginning of the Edwardian period, very few properties were situated on the northern side of the road with the exception of two or three dwellings near the *John Selden*, around the junction with Half Moon Lane. The south side of the road was beginning to be developed as *Beaconsfield Terrace* and other properties were built and lived in.

Photograph of cows grazing at Salvington Farm[1]

Photograph of Ashacre Lane from *Beaconsfield Terrace* looking east. Owned by Gerald White

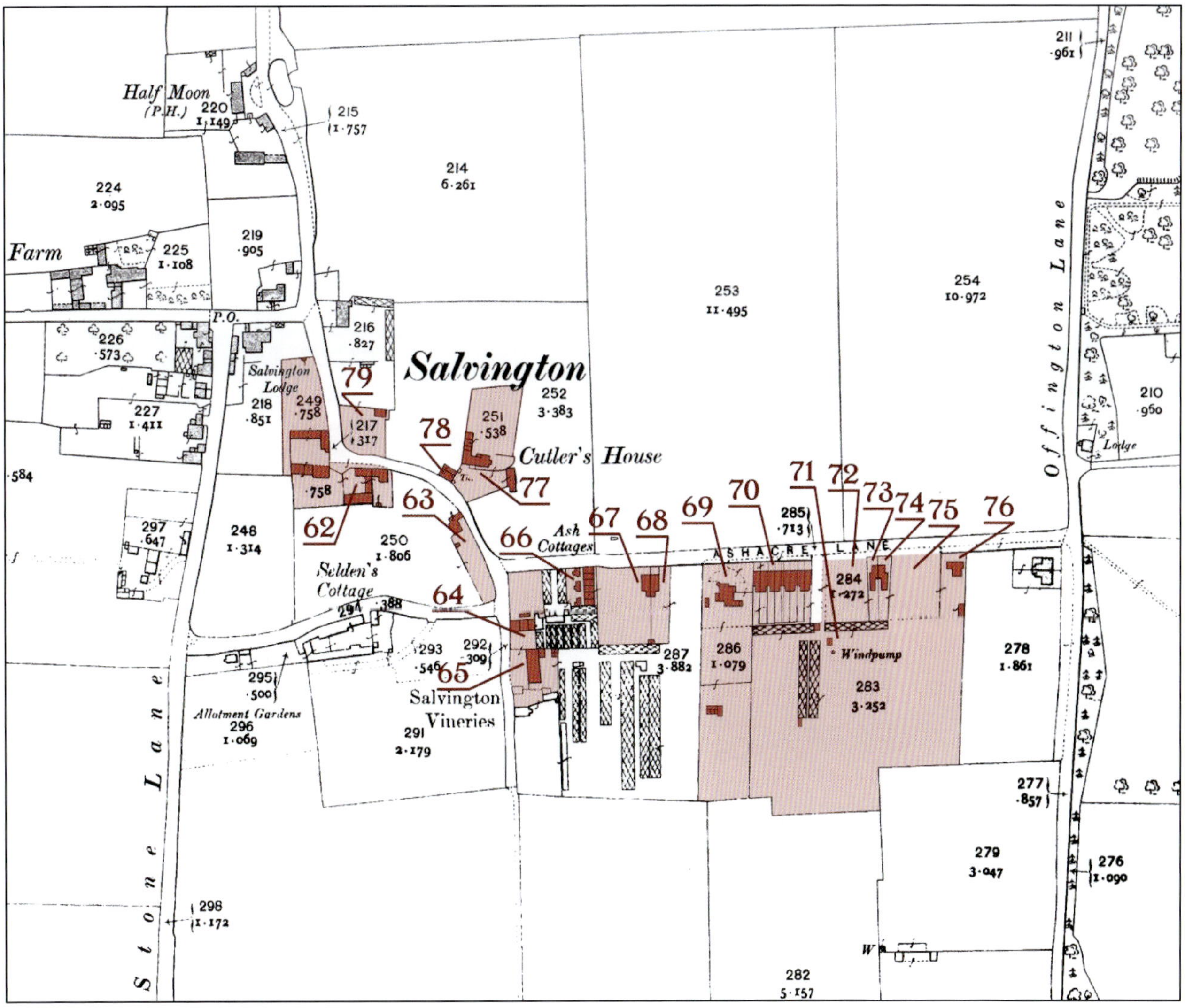

Excerpt taken from OS 25":1 mile Sheet LXIV: 6,10 3rd Edition 1912 (NTS)

62. Farm Buildings, Ashacre Lane
(Now No 87 The Old Cottage, Ashacre Lane)

This site of what is now a cottage sits very close to the road and was part of the collection of farm buildings belonging to Salvington Farm. It is now a Grade 2 listed building where it is described as dating from the late 18th century.[2]

The complex of buildings is described on the Inland Revenue Valuation as:

> 'Salvington Buildings: stables for 3, Cart Lodge, Barn, shed, piggeries etc.'[3]

No mention is made of a cottage indicating that it may not have been being used as a dwelling at the time. The complex of farm buildings is clearly seen on the OS map. Modern photographs show that it is now a cottage called *The Old Cottage*.

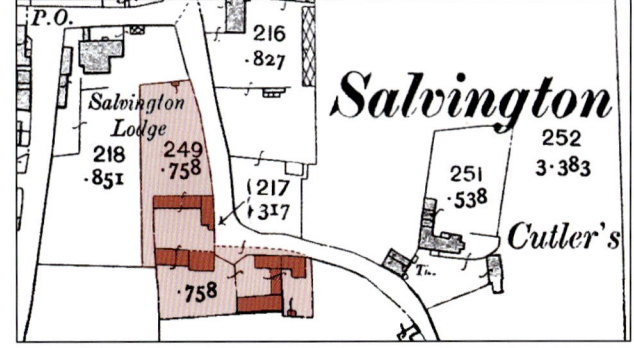

Excerpt taken from OS 25":1 mile Sheet LXIV: 6,10 3rd Edition 1912 (NTS)

Modern photograph of the *Old Cottage*. © David Nicholls 2013

Modern photograph of the barn complex now a cottage and workshops. © Dave Pryce 2014

63. Walnut Tree Cottage, Ashacre Lane
(Now Walnut Tree Cottage, No 79 Ashacre Lane)

This flint cottage is a Grade 2 listed building dating from around 1760 situated on the south side of Ashacre Lane, which at various times has been called *Gables Cottage*, *Pear Tree Cottage* and *Walnut Tree Cottage*. The description on its listing gives more details stating that it is:

> *'Dated 1762. Flints with red brick dressings and stringcourse. Small cornice with modillions placed slantwise below eaves. Red tiled roof.'*[4]

Stone plaque giving 1762 as the date of the building. © Dave Pryce 2013

The date is recorded on a stone plaque attached to the wall of the cottage shown in the modern photograph above. The cottage has been added to, even throughout its early life, with an addition at the rear of the building recorded as early as the 1860's. The Inland Revenue Valuation gives very few details only calling it a *'cottage'*.[5] It does, however, inform us that the property was owned by the trustees of **J Barker** of whom nothing else is known. The name of the occupant is given as **John Parker,** who lived there with his family throughout the Edwardian years.

John Parker (b.1833) came originally from Findon where he had married his first wife **Charity** (b.1837 nee Lisher) in 1859. Charity died in 1863, and in 1867 John re-married **Mary Ann** (b.1844 nee Holland). By 1891 when the census was taken, they were already living in Salvington with four of their eleven children: **Edward** (b.1869), **James** (b.1878), **Elizabeth** (b.1880) and **Grace** (b.1885).[6] Elizabeth, who was eleven years old at the time, was the first to be listed as born in Salvington which gives the date for their arrival in the village between 1878 and 1880. Sadly, by the 1911 census, the couple had noted on their census return that five of their eleven children had died.[7] They had also noted on both the 1901[8] and 1911 censuses that their oldest son, Edward, and youngest child, Grace, were *'feeble minded'*. They noted quite specifically on the 1911 schedule paper that Grace had been so from *'1yr old'*. One can only wonder if an accident or illness had caused some brain damage, or with such a full house of children had they not so easily noted lack of development.

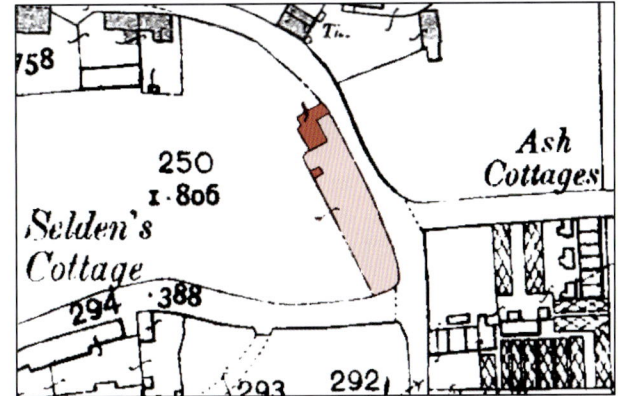

Excerpt taken from OS 25":1 mile Sheet LXIV: 6,10 3rd Edition 1912 (NTS)

For most of the censuses, John's occupation is either a farm or agricultural labourer, but in 1881 his occupation had been given as *'Traction Engine Driver (Farm)'* which must have been an interesting job to have in the early days of mechanised equipment on farms.[9] By 1911, and at the grand age of 79 years old, John was continuing to work on the farm according to the census returns.

The house is still standing today and over the years has had some very interesting further occupants. Modern photographs show many of the original features are still visible in the property.

Modern photograph of *Walnut Tree Cottage*. © Dave Pryce 2013

Inside the cottage. © Dave Pryce 2014   Original roof trusses. © Dave Pryce 2014

64. Yew Tree Cottages, Ashacre Lane
(No longer standing)

According to the Inland Revenue Valuation taken in April 1913, these cottages consisted of a row of three. Each dwelling had two rooms downstairs and two bedrooms upstairs, the middle cottage strangely had no front door. Presumably this meant that the cottage was entered either through one of the other cottages or only through a back entrance. The three dwellings were owned by **Raymond Potten** of Fox Hill, Patching as his name is on the Inland Revenue Valuation and in the electoral registers.

We know nothing more about the actual cottages as no further details or early photographs have been discovered, but they were probably thatched. The name *Yew Tree Cottages* is used in the 1891 census referring to six cottages but this is likely to be a reference to the row of six cottages later called *Ashacre Cottages* just a short distance away in Ashacre Lane.[10] The name changes of cottages during the Victorian and Edwardian period is not uncommon, however, these three cottages are listed as *Yew Tree Cottages* from the turn of the century and occupation can be followed through the censuses, electoral registers and street directories.

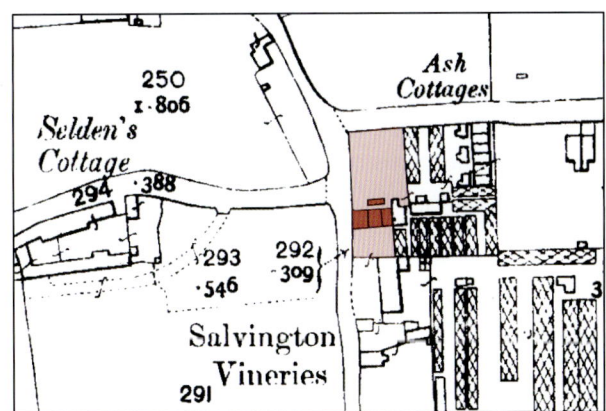

Excerpt taken from OS 25":1 mile Sheet LXIV: 6,10 3rd Edition 1912 (NTS)

No 1 Yew Tree Cottages

The first of the row was the home of a locally born man, **Daniel Ruff** (b.1879) and his wife **Maria** (b.1872 nee Utley) who had originally come from Norfolk. Daniel worked as a carter on the nurseries around the area, no doubt taking the daily journeys to the railway station to transport the produce grown in Salvington and Durrington on the first stage of its sometimes long journey around the country for sale. He is listed as living at this address right through the period, and by the time of the 1911 census he and Maria had two daughters: **Muriel Maud** (b.1902) and **Sarah Gladys Hilda** (b.1904).[11] Both girls were enrolled in the local school, Muriel in 1908 and Gladys in 1909 and when they finally left in 1916 and 1918 respectively they each went into domestic service.[12]

This property was just registered as *'cottage'* in the Inland Revenue Valuation with no further details about the building given.[13]

No 2 Yew Tree Cottages

The second of the cottages was situated in the middle of the row, and as already mentioned had no front entrance of its own. This was obviously not too difficult to live with, as again, the same family are recorded as living here throughout the whole period. **Maurice Lord** (b.1875) was a market gardener in the area and lived here with his wife, **Mary Ann** (b.1870 nee Richens) and daughter **Lena Mary** (b.1900) in 1901.[14] By the recording of the family's details on the 1911 census, they had had two more children, both boys who were born at the address: **Henry James Maurice** (b.1903) and **Sydney Herbert** (b.1908).[15] In the December of 1913, Lena, their eldest child, had finished her time at school and left to become a dressmaker. The boys however, continued their education for many more years, Henry transferring to St Andrews senior school in 1915 and Sydney not leaving until 1922 to work in the gardens.

No 3 Yew Tree Cottages

In 1901, the cottage was already occupied by **James Charman** (b.1870) and his wife **Clara**.[16] Clara (b.1870) is an interesting lady as her marriage to James was not her first. With the family in Salvington were three children all listed as step-children: **Edith** (b.1891) and **Mora** (b.1893) both had the surname 'Jones'. Edith had been born in Hampshire, the county where her mother had also been born, whilst Mora had been born in

Steyning. This was the area where the marriage between James Charman and Clara Jones took place. There was also another step-child in the home in Salvington, a little boy named **Albert Skinner** (b.1876) but nothing further about his background is known. James' younger brother **Charles Charman** (b.1880) is also living in the cottage. This mix of family must have made living and sleeping arrangements a little cramped. Clara died in 1905 at the age of 38, and some years later James made the move to *Chez Nous* in Stone Lane when he married Louisa Saunders, a widow who lived almost next door to his new home. Mora, the eldest of Clara's daughters eventually took up a domestic post as a servant at *Red Cedars,* Salvington Road.

The electoral registers show that James made the move from *Yew Tree Cottages* around 1910 and the next residents were a general labourer named **William Clevitt** (b.1879) and his wife **Elizabeth** (b.1868). They had both been born in Angmering and gave very few details on their 1911 census form.[17] It does not reveal how long they had been together and presumably they had no children. No marriage for them has been traced.

After the Clevitt's left the house there was a quick succession of inhabitants. The Inland Revenue Valuation of April 1913 names **Richardson** as the previous occupants, who had presumably already moved on, and the surname **Dean** was inserted as the new occupant.[18]

65. Burt's Cottage, Ashacre Way
(No longer standing)

This cottage was situated on the eastern side of what is now called *Ashacre Way.* The Inland Revenue Valuation describes the building as an *'Old House',* which contained two attics and three bedrooms. Downstairs it had two rooms, a scullery and a larder. Considering the size of the cottages to the north of this property it was a substantially larger home than those around it.[19]

The cottage had been occupied by the same family for many years. The 1901 census lists **George Goddard** (b.1834) and his wife **Mary Ann** (b.1836 nee Hyde).[20] They had married in West Tarring in 1860, and by the following year were already listed on the census in Salvington Village, most probably in this cottage.[21] When the Inland Revenue Valuation describes them as *'Old tenants,'* it is an apt description of a family who had been in residence for many years. It was in this home that they raised at least seven children: **Charles** (b.1862), **Elizabeth** (b.1864), **Charlotte** (b.1865), **Emily** (b.1868), **Fanny** (b.1870), **Alfred** (b.1873) and **William Walter** (b.1877), although by 1901 only Emily and William were still living with them.

The street directories list George Goddard until 1907 when the name changes to William Goddard. George and Mary had both died in 1908 and 1910 respectively. It was their youngest son, William, who continued to occupy the cottage with his wife **Emily Louisa** (b.1881 nee Dean). They already had two children by the time of the 1911 census: **Edith Emily** (b.1905) and **William Walter George** (b.1908).[22] William's older sister **Emily** was also living with them in 1911. She had been working as a servant in Broadwater in 1891[23] but had already returned to Salvington by 1901, where her occupation is given as a 'sick nurse'[24].

The cottage is no longer standing having been replaced with modern housing.

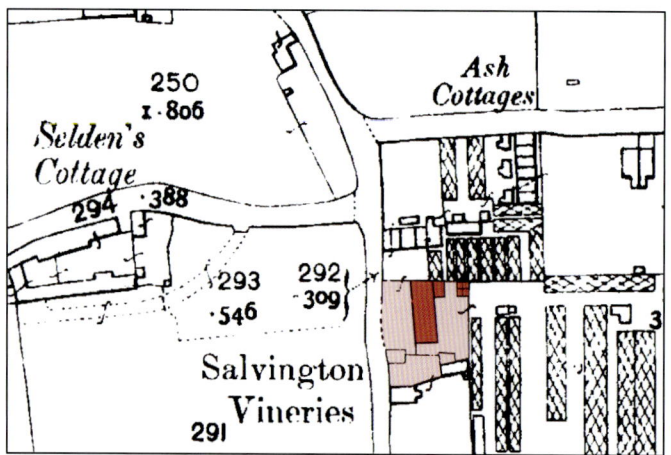

Excerpt taken from OS 25":1 mile Sheet LXIV: 10
3rd Edition 1912 (NTS)

Modern photograph showing the site of *Burt's Cottage*. © Dave Pryce 2015

66. Ash (Ashacre) Cottages, Ashacre Lane
(No longer standing)

This was a row of six small cottages, having two rooms downstairs and two bedrooms upstairs. The cooking area for these dwellings was a separate building, reached by crossing a path running along the rear of the cottages. The separate kitchens are clearly marked on the OS map. All of the cottages were part of *Salvington Farm* and in general they housed farm workers, the majority of whom worked with the dairy herds in the fields to the north of Ashacre Lane. This terrace of very small cottages seems to have had a fairly rapid succession of families in the majority of them and some of the families seem to have swopped cottages at intervals. Perhaps some had slightly more favourable conditions than others.

Modern photograph showing the site of *Ash Cottages*. © Dave Pryce 2015

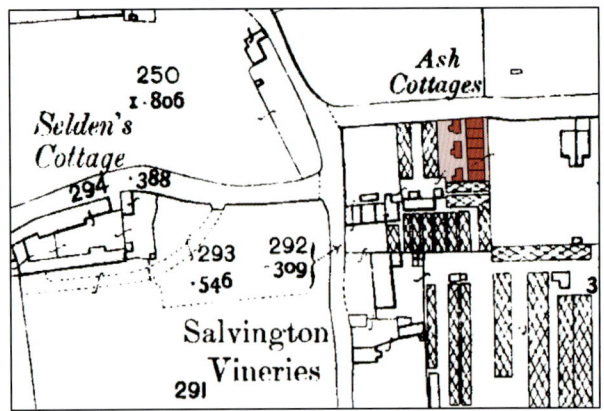

Excerpt taken from OS 25":1 mile Sheet LXIV: 10 3rd Edition 1912 (NTS)
Map showing cottages and the separate buildings serving as kitchens behind them.

No 1 Ash (Ashacre) Cottages

The first cottage in the terrace on the 1901 census was the home of **William John Dean** (b.1852).[25] He lived here with his wife **Amy (Emily)** (b.1856 nee World), his son **Thomas Henry** (b.1875) and their two youngest sons **Stanley Gordon** (b.1889) and **Alfred Ernest** (b.1896). The couple had come with their family from Poole in Dorset where William had worked as a *'Boatman on Sea'*.[26] Both **William** and his son **Thomas**, were working with the cattle on the farm, as was William's oldest son William Arthur, although he was living at *5 Ash Cottages*. Both father and son being named William is confusing as the directories variously list a William Dean at *1, 3 & 4 Ash Cottages* throughout the Edwardian period. In 1911, Amy is still listed as married but was recorded on her own at another address; *Salvington Cottages*, near the *Post Office* with her youngest son.[27] Her occupation is given as *'Laundry work'* so she was probably employed at one of the laundries in Salvington at the time.

A street directory for 1905 lists a **Richard Thomas Cooper** at this address, but whether he was a lodger or the next occupant is unclear.

The next family to live in the property were the Moseley family. The head of this family was **George Moseley** (b.1882), one of the farm workers, who is listed at the address in street directories from 1905 and electoral registers from 1908. In 1911, the census fills in his family details.[28] George's wife was called **Eliza** (b.1879 nee Elliott) and they had a son named **Frederick** (b.1906) who was admitted to Durrington School in September 1911.

No 2 Ash (Ashacre) Cottages

The second of the cottages was the home of **James William Lord** (b.1836). James had been born in Clapham, but lived most of his life in these cottages in Salvington being listed as early as 1871. He was a market gardener in Durrington on the 1901 census, having previously been working as an agricultural labourer.[29] He probably attained residence at the cottage by working on the farm, and was later being permitted to stay when he changed to market gardening. His wife **Frances (Fanny)** (b.1838 nee Walls) was also listed as a market gardener in 1901, although she died somewhere between April and June 1906. James and Fanny had three children, the youngest of which was **Maurice (Morris)** (b.1871).

The market garden James ran was the scene of the suicide of Stephen Scutt in 1906. Stephen was the last miller at *High Salvington Windmill* and as well as losing his place at the mill he was trying to deal with the breakdown of his marriage. Stephen and his wife, Fanny, had separated and he had left the family home at *Chez Nous, Stone Lane*. James had given him casual work in his nursery and it was here that he drowned himself in a water tank. Details of his death and the inquest that followed are included with the information on *Chez Nous*.

Malcolm Linfield writes of James Lord's discovery of the body:

One evening in March 1906, about 5.50pm, James returned to the nursery after his tea to check whether he needed to make any adjustments to the boiler, when he made a rather gruesome discovery. He noticed a human head at the surface of his water tank, which was 5ft deep. After checking the stokehole, he went to fetch some help to retrieve the body. He recognised the deceased as Stephen Scutt, whom he had been employing recently as casual help on the nursery...........'[30]

Results from the auction in September 1906 confirming James Lord's purchase of the land he had been previously renting

It is clear that this sad event did not deter James from continuing to work the plot as a market garden. The auction sale of the Wisden Estate in 1906, records the plot in Salvington coming up for auction. The advertisements in the Worthing Gazette, the week before the auction, revealed that the land was already being rented by James Lord at a rent of £10 per annum.[31] The following week another report in the newspaper confirmed that James Lord had purchased the plot for £250.[32]

By the time of the 1911 census James, now 70 years of age, was still working as a market gardener in Salvington on the same piece of land. He was recorded in the same cottage living alone except for a lodger named **Robert James Walls** (b.c1842) who was a road labourer.

No 3 Ash (Ashacre) Cottages

This cottage was the home of another farmworker **Stephen Ruff** (b.1876), his wife **Hannah Jane** (b.1867 nee Dumbrell) and their son **George Stephen** (b.1894). The whole family were living here for the years covering both the 1901[33] and 1911[34] census. Stephen first appears in a street directory in 1903.

No 4 Ash (Ashacre) Cottages

The 1901 census records **James Terry** (b.1859) originally from Southampton, as yet another cowman living in the cottages.[35] With him were his wife **Emily** (b.1859 nee Chalk) and four of their children: **Bertie James** (b.1888), **Alice Minnie** (b.1891), **Violet Rose** (b.1896) and **May Blossom** (b.1899). May was the only one of the children born in Salvington suggesting they had moved here to work on *Salvington Farm* around 1899. The street directories for 1903 list **W. Borold** at this address, but the name has not appeared anywhere else so could reflect either another short stay occupant or an error.

The next occupant was **William Arthur Dean** who lived here with his family until around 1908, and then moved into the cottage next door. (See *5 Ash Cottages* below)

By 1908, the street directories confirm that the Page family were the occupants and their stay was recorded on the 1911 census where we can find the family details.[36] The head of the house was **Joe Page** (b.1876) who lived with his wife **Henrietta** (b.1875 nee Bristow) and their five children: **Albert** (b.1900), **Alice Alexandra** (b.1902), **Henrietta** (b.1904), **Thomas (Arthur)** (b.1906) and **Florence May** (b.1910). The school admissions register records that the school aged children had arrived from Hurstpierpoint, where the family would have previously lived before arriving in Salvington. According to the electoral registers, the family moved next door to *5 Ash Cottages* in the early months of 1912.

By April 1913 when the Inland Revenue Valuation was taken, the new occupant's surname was given as **Wareham**.[37] We can discover details about the Wareham children before we can become acquainted with the parents, although an incident involving Mrs Wareham is found a little later in the newspaper. Of Mr Wareham, in the early period of their occupancy, we know nothing although we can presume that they moved into the farm cottage due to his being employed to work on the farm. His five daughters had enrolled in Durrington Council School, transferring from Thakeham on 1st May 1912. They were **Ellie** (b.1898), **Edith** (b.1899), **Emily** (b.1901), **Annie** (b.1904) and **Fanny** (b.1907). Life was never easy for these families, at least having five girls; the sharing of the second bedroom in the small cottage would have been slightly easier than for the mixed sex families. Education was a valuable asset for all children, but often had to be of the shortest possible duration. Ellie, the oldest, was removed from school to *'help at home'* in 1912, Edith to enter domestic service in August 1913 and the other three were simply *'removed'* in September 1913 with no reason given.

The identity of Mrs Wareham is revealed when she was named as a witness into the sudden death of **Ellen Willard** the licensee of the *North Star Inn,* Littlehampton Road in January 1913. Further details of this event are included with the details of the *North Star Inn.* The newspaper report confirms that her Christian name was *'Fanny'* and searching the marriage indexes we can find a possible marriage recorded in 1896 in the Westbourne district for **Fanny Smith** and **Alfred Wareham.**[38] How interesting that in a period when the head of the household, usually male, is the first to be named and traced, that this family is better known through the children at school and the reported kindness of Fanny Wareham in the newspaper.

No 5 Ash (Ashacre) Cottages

The fifth of the cottages was, according to the 1901 census, the home of **Frederick Charles Holden** (b.1872), his wife **Fanny** (b.1877 nee Warrington) and their son **Frederick William** (b.1897).[39] Frederick had been born in Sidlesham, dating their arrival in Salvington after 1897 and they were gone again by 1905 when the electoral register first lists **Robert Collard** at this address. He is listed here until 1909 when he moved to Broadwater but we know nothing else about him.

The family who next took up residency did not have far to come as they relocated from *4 Ash Cottages* next door. The 1911 census gives the details naming the head as **William Arthur Dean** (b.1874).[40] William Jnr was the son of William Dean who was living at *1, Ash Cottages.* He had transferred into this cottage with his wife **Ada Louisa Jane** (b.1879) and their son **William Arthur** (b.1906). They also had Ada's young brother **Ernest Burton** living with them. According to the electoral register, they had been living at *4, Ash Cottages* between 1907-1908 and then transferred to No 5 in 1909. Ada's husband William is interesting, as in 1891 he had been working in Standlinch, Wiltshire as a servant in the household of Horatio Nelson, the great nephew of Admiral Horatio Nelson who was killed at the Battle of Trafalgar in 1805 on his famous ship 'HMS Victory'.[41] The Dean family left the cottage and England in October 1912 when the Durrington Council School Admissions register records that they were emigrating to Australia.[42] By this period Ernest, Ada's brother, is using the name **Alfred Ernest Dean.**

No 6 Ash (Ashacre) Cottages

The 1901 census records that the last of the six cottages in the terrace was the home of a widow **Eleanor Dale** (b.1857) and her three children: **Alice Maud** (b.1886) who was a domestic servant, **Mabel Florence** (b.1889) and **Percy Charles** (b.1891).[43] The street directories list her here until around 1904 when she moved.

The next occupant we can identify is **George Long** who is listed in street directories and on the electoral register at this address around 1908. There is a 'Long' family associated with Salvington, and listed on previous censuses so we may presume that this is the same family. Three children with the surname 'Long' were admitted to Durrington Council School, where the two eldest, **Thomas** (b.1900) and **Edith** (b.1901) were admitted when the school opened in June 1908 although no address is given. Their sister **Dorothy** (b.1903) was admitted in the September of 1908 again with no address, simply listing 'Salvington' in the address column.

In October 1908 we discover more about this family from the school log book. Mrs Long had informed the school that her son had scarlatina and this would also prevent her daughters from attending. They would have to be excluded as a precaution against infection. Illness was a constant danger for young children in the damp and crowded conditions they had to live in, and again on 9th September 1909 we see the situation had not changed when the headmaster Mr Boorer had written in the school log book:

> *'I called to see Mrs Long and requested her to keep her 3 children away until they recovered from 'whooping cough'. Measles started at the home…………'*[44]

All three children were removed from school in September 1909 so maybe they never returned from this second bout of sickness. We do know they moved to another property in Salvington from the electoral register, but the address is not given and why they did not return to the school is as yet unsolved.

By the time the census was taken in 1911, the occupiers of the cottage were **Thomas Spooner** (b.1887), his wife **Louisa Ellen** (b.1882) and a daughter **Louisa Ellen** (b.1898).[45] They were sharing the house with Louisa's brother **Horace Golds** (b.1883) and both men were working as cowmen. Thomas and Louisa's marriage was registered in the Steyning district in 1908, some ten years after the little girl was born, which may indicate a second marriage for Mrs Spooner. Whatever the personal circumstances, they moved to work here on *Salvington Farm* shortly after their marriage.

67. West Villa, Ashacre Lane
(Now No 57 Ashacre Lane)

The 1907 street directory is the first source to list this property and reveals it as the home of **James Wares Dorey** (b.1868). We know the rest of the family from their 1911 census return, alongside James was his wife **Jane** (b.1876 nee Patching) and their son **James Reginald** (b.1910).[46] Jane's mother, **Sarah Ann Patching**, is also living in the house as well as two lodgers, a cowman named **George Brown** (b.1885), and a nurseryman, **Ernest Fucher (Tucher)** (b.1883). On first arriving in Salvington, James had lived with his parents in Stone Lane before later moving to *West Villa*. He had had a military career in the 19th Hussars before being finally discharged in July 1902 and coming to Salvington where he married and settled to work on *Salvington Farm* for a period.[47]

The Inland Revenue Valuation records that this house is one of a pair of three bedroomed cottages built in red brick. They were probably erected around 1907 when the first listing of the address appears. Although the houses themselves were identical, *West Villa* had been built on a bigger plot and therefore had the larger garden. By May 1913 when the house was assessed, the Dorey family had moved, as they were crossed out and **James Madgwick** had moved with his family from *5 Beaconsfield Terrace* to live in the property.

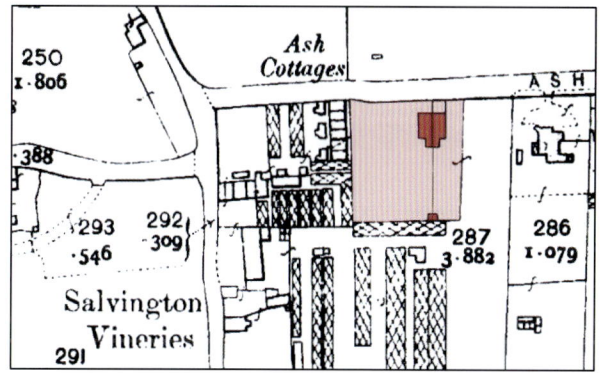

Excerpt taken from OS 25":1 mile Sheet LXIV: 10 3rd Edition 1912 (NTS)
West Villa on the left and *East Villa* on the right.

68. East Villa, Ashacre Lane
(Now No 55, East Villa, Ashacre Lane)

This property is a semi-detached house with its identical neighbour *West Villa*. The first occupants were the Lewis family who moved here around 1907 from their previous address in *Selden's Cottage*.

Edward Lewis (b.1864) had been working as a horse carter at *Salvington Farm* when he was listed on the 1901 census.[48] Ten years later, according to the 1911 census, he had become the farm bailiff, and moved his family to their new house in Ashacre Lane.[49] His occupancy, according to the street directories and electoral registers, began in 1907 and continued for many years.

Edward shared the house with his wife **Mary Ann** (b.1864 nee Leggett) and two of their daughters **Frances Eleanor** (b.1889) and **Alice Mary** (b.1893). Both of the girls were working as general domestic servants at the time.

The only other mention of Edward is an advert placed in the Worthing Gazette, where he is offering mangolds for sale in January 1914.[50] Mangolds were also called 'mangel-wurzels', and are a member of the beet family which includes sugar beet and beetroot. These root vegetables are edible for humans, but were usually grown for animal food and the crop would have added a little extra income into the family budget.

This is a photograph of both *East Villa* (Left) & *West Villa* (Right). © Dave Pryce 2016

69. Causton, Ashacre Lane
(No longer standing)

The first mention of this property is in a street directory of 1909 when the occupants name was given as **Ellen Worth Bromfield** (b.1844). Ellen had moved to this new four bedroomed house in 1908 from *Salvington Lodge*, where she had previously lived for some years.

The Inland Revenue Valuation describes the house as a *'Modern Red Brick detached'* property, and states it was owned by Thomas Cureton from Wolverhampton.[51] It was almost certainly Ellen, though, who named the house *Causton* as it was name of the village where she had been born and raised.

Causton was a small hamlet situated near Dunchurch in Warwickshire. Ellen had been born the second of the children of **Henry Jenkins Bromfield** (b.1806) and his wife **Helen (Ellen).** Henry owned and ran a large farm of 342 acres and along with his wife, children and various servants he worked and lived on the farm right up until his death. Henry and Helen had had three children, the eldest being a son **George Henry Worth** (b. 1842) whilst the youngest was **Emily Worth** (b.1847). There is an interesting story relating to the family farm which tells of a suspicious and potentially disastrous fire which occurred on the land when Ellen was only four years old.[52] This fire was most probably an arson attack and The Times gives some details of the event and possible perpetrator.

INCENDIARY FIRE.—RUGBY, Nov. 10.—Last night a fire of a most alarming character broke out on the premises of Mr. Henry Bromfield, of Cawston. A servant-man, in the employ of Mr. Bromfield, was going over the farm, about 5 o'clock in the evening, when his attention was attracted by a large glare of light; upon looking in the direction, the man saw one of the corn stacks, consisting of the produce of 14 acres of barley, in flames. A messenger was immediately sent to Rugby for the fire-engine, which was despatched as quickly as possible with four post-horses, from the Eagle Hotel, preceded by Mr. Bromwich, the superintendent of the Fire Brigade, who made such arrangements that no delay took place in getting the engine to work. This, seconded by a good supply of water, and the active co-operation of a large number of people from Rugby, Dunchurch, Cawston, Thurlaston, and Bilton, had the effect of confining the fire to the place where it broke out, but, had not assistance been so promptly rendered, the consequences must have been most disastrous, the dwelling-house and stack-yard being near the spot; and, even as it was, it required the utmost exertions of the assemblage to save them from destruction. During the time the fire was in its strength a stranger attracted the attention of Mr. Siggins, in consequence of his looking quietly on, and not attempting to give any assistance. Upon being questioned his replies were so unsatisfactory that he was given into the custody of police constable Broughton, by whom he was taken before Mr. J. Atty. The prisoner gave the name of James James, and said he was 27 years of age, a native of Canterbury, and connected with one of the most respectable families in the city. He was for some time a book-keeper in a highly respectable commercial house in Canterbury, but having formed some loose connexions he disgraced himself and lost his situation. Since that time he had become reckless, and he did not now care what became of him. Nothing, however, should induce him to give his real name, as he would rather suffer death than disgrace the other members of the family, two of whom held high official situations under Government. The prisoner was ultimately remanded till 11 o'clock on Saturday morning.

Article in The Time regarding a serious fire that occurred in Ellen's younger years at her home on the farm in Causton,

Ellen's father Henry died in 1883, by which time he had already been widowed. It appears that George did not take over the running of the farm from his father. Instead he chose a profession as a clergyman, and throughout his years in ministry he was largely based in Lambeth at the churches of St Mary and St Mary the Less. Whilst serving as a Vicar in Lambeth, in 1886 he preached during Holy Week at Westminster Abbey, a prestigious honour.

Ellen had been living with a cousin **Elizabeth Elsdale** in Moulton, Lincolnshire at the time of the 1871 census[53], but then had moved back to be with her elderly father and younger sister at the farm by 1881[54]. When he died in 1883 the sisters needed to make their home elsewhere, and this may have been when Ellen joined her brother in Surrey for a period. None of the siblings ever married but were always able to support themselves; the censuses always recording the sisters as *'Living on own means'*.

Ellen Bromfield remained in the house in Ashacre Lane for some years. The 1911 census records that she was living in *Causton* with her French companion **Madelaine Stuart** (b.1851), a cook **Annie Pack** (b.1853) and a young male servant named **Edwin Scull.**[55] Some time later she moved to West Tarring where she named yet another property after the site of her family home. When Ellen died in April 1928 her address was given as *Causton House,* South Street, West Tarring.

The house in Ashacre Lane later became known as *The Red House* and served as a private school. It has since been demolished and replaced by modern houses.

The plot of land to the rear of the house was used as a market garden occupied by *'Tullett'* according to the Inland Revenue Valuation, although it was noted on the pages of the valuation that the plot was *'Void in 1909'*, the meaning of this phrase is unknown.[56]

Modern houses built on the site of *'Causton'*   © Dave Pryce 2015

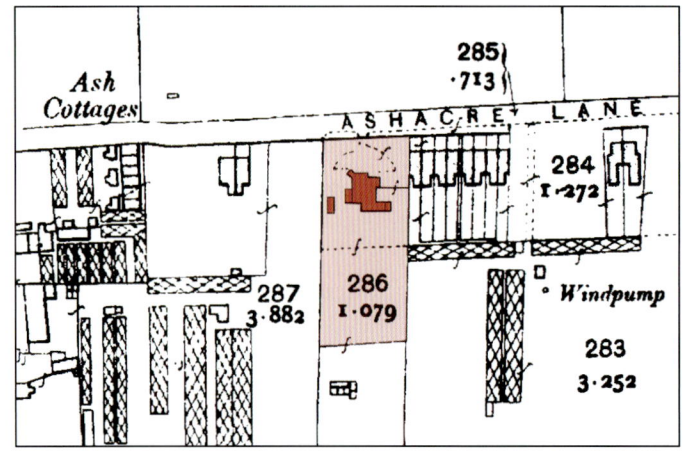

Excerpt taken from OS 25":1 mile Sheet LXIV: 10 3rd Edition 1912 (NTS)

70. Beaconsfield Terrace, Ashacre Lane
(Now No's 43, 41, 39, 37, 35, 33, 31 & 29 Ashacre Lane)

Beaconsfield Terrace has been researched and partly written by Sarah Godfrey one of the project volunteers.

Introduction

Plaque on the wall of *Beaconsfield Terrace* showing the date they were built. © Dave Pryce

Beaconsfield Terrace, Ashacre Lane, was built in 1906 as a terrace consisting of eight brick-built cottages. All were built to an identical specification except for number five which has an extra room built over a passageway. According to both the electoral registers from 1909 and the Inland Revenue Valuation of 7th April 1913, they were owned by **Mr Henry Alfred Streeter**.[57] Henry Streeter, according to the 1911 census, lived at 9, Upper Coombe Street, Croydon where his occupation is given as *'plumber'*.[58] This is confirmed by a Kelly's London Street Directory for 1913, where there is an entry, at the same address, for **Streeter H. A. J. & Sons, plumbers.**

It is not known when Henry first bought this land but the East Preston Rural District Council minutes record permission being given for *'eight cottages in Salvington for Mr H A Streeter'*[59] in December 1905. The properties were then built very soon after. Water certificates had been granted to Mr Street, which could be a mis-spelling for *'Streeter'*, for four of the properties on 17th April 1906[60] and for No's 5, 6, 7, and 8 on the 1st of the following month.[61] This suggests that the families began to move in in the latter part of 1906. The electoral register only shows numbers 1 and 4 as occupied by 1907, although the street directory for that year also had someone living in No's 2, 5 (with an incorrect name) and 8.

From the Inland Revenue Valuation it is possible to build up a picture of the cottages although the description is only recorded on the first property where it stated:

> *'One of a row of 8 cottages. 3 bed(rooms), 1 K(itchen). Sc(ullery) Brick built fronts, bay to gd floor only' (my brackets)* [62]

The size of each plot for seven of the cottages was roughly 14ft by 120ft each. No 5, having the passageway beside it, had a slightly wider plot. This passageway was a right of way used by all the adjoining cottages. The market value of the other properties in 1913 was £230 but the extra space made No 5 worth £243. The term of tenancy was weekly with rent of 6/- (6/6 *for No.5*).

Most of the cottages had several families living in them during the Edwardian period. According to the electoral registers none were occupied in 1906, although the Worthing Gazette for 12th September 1906 has an advert for prize tomato sauce that could be obtained from **Gulliver** at *8, Beaconsfield Terrace*.[63]

Advert for the splendid tomato sauce available from *Beaconsfield Terrace* in 1906

It is therefore likely that the families began taking up residence in the autumn of 1906. As the electoral registers and street directories do not show anyone with the surname of Gulliver it has not been possible to identify the purveyor of the tomato sauce.

By using the 1911 census, electoral registers, Inland Revenue Valuation and street directories, it has been possible to trace most of the occupants, although, unfortunately, in several instances, the records give conflicting information. It is, however, interesting to see the connections between the various families. Many of the men worked in market gardening, including two consecutive occupiers of No 4, **John Milner** (as well as his son) and **Edward Dinsdale**. Next door at No 5, **James Madgwick** and then **William Hazelgrove,** were also involved in the gardening trade, as were **Alfred Tulett** at No 8, **William Tyler** at No 3 and three of the **Ansfield** sons from No 1. Several worked on the *Golf Links (Worthing Golf Club),* including **Frederick Pratt** from No 2, who went on to become head greenkeeper. Sisters, **Mildred White** and **Sarah Hayes** lived next door to each other at No's 6 and 7 respectively. A father and son lived next door to each other, Alfred Tulett at No 8 and **Horace** at No 7. A brother moved in after his sibling had moved out, (**Frederick** followed by **Albert Pratt** at No 2). One last connection that can be made is that, in 1930, the Hayes' daughter at No 7 went on to marry one of the Hazelgrove sons from No 5.

Beaconsfield Terrace in Edwardian times. Owned by Gerald White

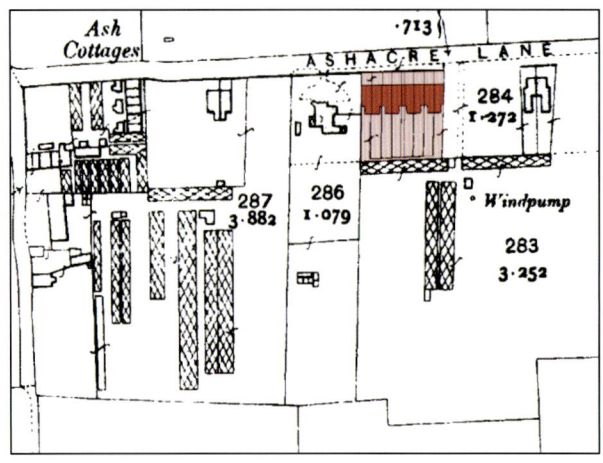

Excerpt taken from OS 25":1 mile Sheet LXIV: 10 3rd Edition 1912 (NTS)

No 1 Beaconsfield Terrace
(Now No 43 Ashacre Lane)

According to the Electoral Registers the first occupant of *1, Beaconsfield Terrace* was Thomas (Tom) Tyrell, who moved from Church Lane, West Tarring to *Beaconsfield Terrace* in 1907. He was still there in 1908, possibly leaving in 1909.

Thomas Tyrell (Tyrrell) (b.1865) had at least one daughter, **Violet** (b.1897) as she is recorded as one of the first pupils to attend the school when it opened on 29th June 1908. The address given in the Register of Admissions was simply 'Salvington.' Later in the year Violet became ill and Mr Boorer, the headmaster, made the following entry in the school logbook:

> *'Mrs Tyrrell saw me this morning & said that Violet was unwell. Symptoms suggested "Influenza".'*[64]

Violet happily recovered and left the school in 1911 to go in to domestic work.

According to the 1911 census the family in residence at the time were the Ansfields.[65] **Frances Ellen Ansfield** (b.1862 nee Linberry) was the widow of **Frederick Ansfield** (b.1859) and the daughter of **George and Ellen Linberry** who had run the *Half Moon Inn* in the 1870s and '80s. With her husband Frederick, who had died in November 1904, she had also managed *The Spotted Cow* in Salvington Road.

Frederick and Frances had had eleven children and although two had died in childhood six of them were living in this house with her: **George Frederick** (b.1882), **Henry Gordon** (b.1884), **Albert William** (b.1887), **Louise Annie E** (b.1894), **Dorothy Kathleen** (b.1896) and **Wilfred Clarence** (b.1899). Both Dorothy and Wilfred were enrolled in the new Durrington Council School on the day that it opened.[66]

There is, however, a rather sad story relating to this family. On the 1911 census **Ella May Ansfield** (b.1890), another of the Ansfield children, was not listed with her mother and siblings in Salvington. She was at the time a patient in the *West Sussex County Asylum* known as *Graylingwell*. There is very little other information given about her except that she was twenty years old, of no occupation and had been a 'lunatic at birth'. Nothing was registered on the 1901[67] or 1891[68] census to suggest that Ella had mental health issues. Thanks to the West Sussex Record Office, the repository for the *Graylingwell Hospital* records, it has been possible to fill in some of the background to Ella's life. According to the case book entry Ella's father had died in 1904 from consumption. Her mother was still living in Salvington in 1909 and Ella was recorded as having learning difficulties. She had been in *The Home for Feeble Minded* at Cumnor Rise in Oxfordshire for ten weeks in 1909 before being admitted to the *Berkshire County Asylum* on 13th May 1909. She was then transferred to *Graylingwell* two months later on 8th July. When *Graylingwell* became a

war hospital during WW1 the patients were transferred to other asylums. Ella was sent to the *East Sussex County Asylum* at Hellingly. She died there of influenza, possibly part of the pandemic, on 1st December 1918.

No 2 Beaconsfield Terrace (Now No 41 Ashacre Road)

Apart from a mysterious directory entry for a **Smith** in 1907 the first known occupant was Frederick Pratt who was listed in street directories from 1909 to 1913 as well as on the 1911 census.[69] **Frederick Pratt** (b.1883) was the head of the household and lived here with his wife **Jane Louise** (b.1882 nee Kinnard). They had two daughters: **Louisa** (b. 1905) and **Hilda Lilian A** (b.1908). Jane's brother **(Charles) Albert Kinnard** (b.1894) was also lodging with them and both men were working on the *Golf Links*. This was a term regularly used when referring to *Worthing Golf Club* which had been founded in 1905.

Frederick and Jane went on to have two more daughters: **Winifred C.** (b.1912) and **Gladys M.** (b1914) who sadly died the following year. Louisa, Hilda and Winifred all attended Durrington Council School at various times. Louisa in 1910, possibly before the family had moved in to as the address given is just 'Salvington'. By the time Hilda attended, in March 1913, the family was living at *Golf Cottages* in Broadwater.

Louisa was mentioned in the school logbook in March 1911:

> *'Edith Goddard & Louisa Pratt are both ill with the "measles". These are the first cases amongst the infants, but an outbreak has appeared imminent for some time.'*

Louisa and Hilda both left the school to take up work in domestic service. No leaving date, nor occupation, is given for Winifred.

No 3 Beaconsfield Terrace (Now No 39 Ashacre Lane)

There are four families known to have lived in No 3 between the building of the terrace and 1914. In 1909 **Douglas Faulkner** was listed at the property. It has not been possible to find any further information about him.

The 1911 census lists **Charles Cuckney** (b.1886), a carpenter, and his wife **Louisa** (b.1885 nee Grover) living at No 3.[70] They had named the house *Down View*, a name which only seems to have lasted for the occupancy of the Cuckneys. The couple had married in 1909 and celebrated the birth of their first daughter **Doris** a little later in 1911 while still in residence.

Later in 1911, according to the electoral register, Henry Gobel had moved in to No 3 from *Ivy Cottage,* Durrington where the family had been living for the previous two or three years. They did not stay in *Beaconsfield Terrace* for many years as by the time of the Inland Revenue Valuation in April 1913 their name had been crossed out and the new occupier was listed as **Tyler**. **William George Tyler** (b.1886) is confirmed as the new resident by his entries in street directories for 1912 and 1913 and electoral registers from 1914. He had moved from 34, Archibald Road, Worthing, where he was living in 1911 with his wife, son and sister. His occupation was given as nurseryman.

No 4 Beaconsfield Terrace
(Now No 37 Ashacre Lane)

There are only two families known to have been living at *4 Beaconsfield Terrace* during the Edwardian period – the Milners and the Dinsdales.

John Milner (b.1870), a market gardener, had moved from the *Reading Rooms* in West Tarring where he was living in 1901[71] to *4 Beaconsfield Terrace* in 1907. He moved into the house with his wife, **Kate** (b.1889 nee Cornwell), and their children whose names we know because they appear in the Durrington Council School logbooks between 1908 and 1912.

Harry Ernest Milner (b.1895) was the first to gain a mention on 10th October 1908:

> *'Attendance officer called to enquire if Harry Milner (13) had come to school – he came in yesterday after 15 months non-attendance.'*[72]

A daughter named **Edith Selina Milner** (b.1897) also warranted a mention in the logbook for 13th January 1909:

> *'Edith Milner aged 11, who was admitted on Monday, does not know her letters. She has not attended school for 2 years, owing to illness.'*[73]

A younger son **Frank Thomas John Milner** (b.1899) was also mentioned due to illness, although by this time the family had moved back to West Tarring. The first mention was on 29th October 1912[74] when he had mumps and then, following on from this, on 4th November 1912 the log-book records:

> *'Frank Milner came to school again the morning after only a week's suffering with Mumps. He was sent home again & his mark cancelled. Parents, in their ignorance, pay little regard to the safeguards of isolation and take little, if any, trouble to prevent the spread of infectious complaints.'*[75]

The Milners were replaced by the Dinsdale family in 1911[76]. The family included **Edward Arthur Dinsdale** (b.1880), his wife **Clara** (b.1884 nee Turner) and their son, **Arthur Stanley** (b.1906), who was four years old when they moved into the terrace. Edward was a nurseryman gardener in the fruit and flower growing industry who had originally come from New Southgate, London.

On the 1891 census Edward's mother, **Lucy** (b.1846 nee Berry), is shown as a visitor at 14 Bedford Row, Broadwater, living on her own means,[77] whilst Edward and his sister, **Ethel Violette** (b.1878), are living at the Freeman Orphan School, Ferndale Road, Brixton.[78] Why the two children are living as orphans separated from their mother at this time is not known. By 1901 Grandma Lucy was a border at 3 Bedford Row (boarding house), still living on her own means, along with her daughter Ethel, who by now was a school teacher.[79] Unfortunately, it has not been possible to find out where Edward was living at this time. By 1911 his mother had moved to Mayfield Lodge, Cobden Road, Worthing where she was again shown as a *'lady lodger'* and still recorded as having enough income to support herself.[80]

Edward Arthur Dinsdale
(19 Aug 1880 – 14 Sep 1913)
Owned by Joan Dexter

Arthur Stanley Dinsdale
(15 May 1906 – 5 Dec 1984)
with his mother Clara. Owned by Joan Dexter

Arthur Stanley Dinsdale about the age he became a pupil at Durrington Council School.
Owned by Joan Dexter

Edward and Clara's son Arthur, at just under five years old, was enrolled into Durrington Council School in February 1911 a short while before the census was taken. Against his father's name, in the parent/guardian column of the admissions register is the note 'deceased'. Presumably this was added at a later date, possibly when Arthur left the school as Edward didn't die until 14th September 1913. The family were living still at No 4 at the time as this is the address given on the probate.[81]

No 5 Beaconsfield Terrace
(Now No 35 Ashacre Lane)

Apart from some single entries under this address we do not have much information regarding early occupancy. A street directory entry of 1909 lists **Mary Searle** and electoral registers for 1910 and 1911 suggest James William Madgwick was living in the house for a short period. We do know that by the time of the 1911 census James Madgwick had already moved to *Cutler's Cottages*. This was the home of his father-in-law, Luke Peacock, and three of his children: George, Mabel and William. James had moved with his wife, **Alice** and their two sons: **Frederick William** (b.1906) and **Edwin James** (b.1910).

The 1911 census records that the head of the house was **William Hazelgrove** (b.1880) who, like many of the *Beaconsfield Terrace* inhabitants, was a nursery gardener. He was married to **Mary** (b.1882) although no marriage has yet been traced. On the 1911 census they state that they have four children, although only three: **Adelaide Emily** (b.1905), **Herbert William** (b.1907) and **Lena Annie** (b.1910) are listed on the census with them.[82] The missing child was **Henrietta** (b.1906), who appears on the 1911 census living with her grandparents **Jeremiah** and **Adelaide Hazelgrove** at Hermitage Cottages, Castle Goring.[83]

The Inland Revenue Valuation lists the current occupier as Maidment and the previous as Madgwick, there is no mention of Hazelgrove. This suggests that the residence of the Hazelgrove family was of short duration and lay between the original preparation of the field book pages and the date of actually visiting and taking the tax valuation in 1913. The 1911 census records that a *'labourer in a market garden'* named **Benjamin Maidment** (b.1886) was living at 97 Southfield Road, Broadwater with his wife, **Kate** (b.1885 nee Boniface), and five month old son. It is quite probable that this is the family that then moved in to No 5 within a year or so of the census. The house in Southfield Road only had three rooms so the move to *Beaconsfield Terrace* with its five rooms may have been made because of the growing family.

No 6 Beaconsfield Terrace
(Now No 33 Ashacre Lane)

Mildred White with one of her children. Owned by Tony Hayes

Number *6 Beaconsfield Terrace* is the most straightforward of the cottages as it was the home of one family throughout the whole of the Edwardian period. **Frank White** (b.1876), a carter working at a market garden, had moved into the property around 1908. He lived there with his wife, **Mildred Ethel** (b.1886 nee Collard), son **Frederick Maurice** (b.1909) and his parents **Walter and Sarah Ann White** (b.c1841 nee Hewlett). On the 1911 census page another son is listed named **Robert Walter** (b.1905), whose age is given as five but then his name has been crossed out. It transpires that Robert had died in 1906 aged one. One can only wonder why a child dead for some four years was named and given an age on the form.[84]

Frank was born and brought up in Sussex, although it has not been possible to confirm his place of birth as it is different on each of the censuses. In 1901 he was still living with his parents and younger brother, Jack, at *3 Stone Cottages,* Salvington.[85] In 1905 Frank married Mildred Ethel Collard and it must have been soon after that they moved into this house and continued living here for many years. On the 1901 census she had been living in Littlehampton with her family where her father, **Robert Collard** (b.1845), was a gardener whilst Mildred and two of her sisters were laundresses.[86] Mildred was one of four sisters all of whom married local men. One of them, her younger sister, Sarah, had married **Frederick George Hayes** and was living next door at *7 Beaconsfield Terrace* in 1911.

No 7 Beaconsfield Terrace
(Now No 31 Ashacre Lane)

Samuel Baker is the first name to appear at this address in the 1906 electoral register where the property is referred to as *Beaconsfield Cottages*. A later electoral register gives the address as *7 Beaconsfield Terrace*.

A street directory for 1907 gives the next occupant as G. Long. This is possibly **George Long** who was living in Salvington in 1908 and had three children who attended Durrington School. Thomas and Edith were in the first cohort of pupils at the new school along with their younger sister, Doris (Dorothy), who joined them just six months later. All three were removed in September 1909, with no indication as to where they then went to school. By the time of the 1911 census a George Long and his wife **Alice** (b.1869 nee Utley), along with five children: **Thomas George** (b.1900), **Edith Kate** (b.1901), **Doris (Dorothy) Mary** (b.1903), **Frederick Arthur** (b.1907) and **Maurice (Morris) Lesley** (b.1909), were living at 3 Elmswood Terrace, Elm Grove, Worthing.[87] As with so many at the time George was a nurseryman working as a fruit grower.

The 1910 and 1911 electoral registers give us the next resident, his name was **Percy Thair** (b.1886). In 1901 Percy was still living with his parents in Angmering where he was working as a woodman.[88] By 1902 he was working as a striker on the railways on the London, Brighton and South Coast line. Although it is not possible to give his occupation at the time of living at *7 Beaconsfield Terrace* it is interesting to note that, by 1911, he was a golf professional at St Neotts Golf Club in Huntingdonshire.[89] He had obviously only just moved to St Neotts with his wife, **May Harriett** (b.1876 nee Newhouse) and young family as both his children's places of birth were given as 'Worthing' and his youngest child was only nine months old. Also living with him was **Maurice Newhouse**, aged 11, his stepson.

The family living in the cottage on the 1911 census are the Hayes family.[90] Their residency in the property was fairly short lived. At no point does the electoral register give Frederick Hayes as the occupier! Nothing is known about any residents in 1912 as Frederick had moved to *Salvington Tea Gardens* by this time. The Inland Revenue Valuation also does not have Hayes listed. On this document the previous occupier is Thair and current given as Tulett. This is Horace Tulett who was residing there from 1913.[91]

Frederick George Hayes (b.1875) was married to **Sarah Jane** (b.1890 nee Collard), sister of Mildred living at No 6, so for a short while they were living next door to each other. Frederick and Sarah had married in 1908 and come to live in Salvington where he worked as a groom. They had two children: **Arthur Thomas** (b.1910) and **Naomi Agnes** (b.1909). Also living with them was Sarah's mother, **Agnes Collard** (b.1856 nee Palfrey) who was a laundry ironer. This was obviously a means of employment the family were familiar with as in 1901 Agnes's daughters had been laundresses in Littlehampton.[92]

Frederick and Sarah Hayes and a portrait of Sarah Hayes. Owned by Tony Hayes

Around 1912, according to the street directories, Frederick and his family moved to *Salvington Tea Gardens* in Half Moon Lane for a period. Living at the tea gardens was James Wyatt and his wife Agnes with their family. The two families were related as Agnes Wyatt was another of the four Collard sisters, being Sarah Hayes' older sister. This means that three out of the four Collard sisters were living near each other in Salvington, as Mildred White, another sister, was living at *6 Beaconsfield Terrace* with her family. The fourth of the sisters, Selina, was also married and living not far away in Shoreham.

After the Hayes family, **Horace Alfred Tulett** (b.1881), a house painter, moved in with his wife, **Eliza (Elizabeth) Mary** (b.1872 nee Bicknell) and their children: **Horace Alfred** (b.1904) and **Dorothy** (b.1905). Horace's father, Alfred lived next door at No 8.

No 8 Beaconsfield Terrace
(Now No 29 Ashacre Lane)

The last of the cottages is another property that housed several families during the Edwardian years. The first occupant, as mentioned in the introduction to the terrace, was probably a gentleman named **Gulliver.**

The street directories for 1907 list an **R. Cole** at the address with nothing further known except the name. The surname 'Cole' makes one more appearance in 1909 when the name **Mary Cole** appears at the address. It is possible that this was a later printing error that had not been changed as we know that by 1908 there was a new occupant.

The next named occupant was **Fanny Scutt** (b.1863 nee Armstrong) who was the widow of Stephen Scutt, the last miller at *High Salvington Windmill*. He had committed suicide in 1906 (further details are included with *2 Ashacre Cottages,* Ashacre Lane). Fanny lived at various addresses around Salvington including *Chez Nous* in Stone Lane where she was listed until 1907. Her two youngest children, **Arthur** (b.1899) and **Gladys** (b.1901), were amongst those attending Durrington School on its opening day not long after moving into this new address. Both only stayed for a month before being removed. The reason may have been Fanny's moving again to Princes Terrace in Tarring.

The next occupant was listed on the 1910 electoral register when **Alfred Tulett** (b.1854) moved to this address from Glebe Road in West Tarring and continued living here throughout the rest of the period. The 1911 census gives us the details of his family.[93] He lived here with his wife, **Elizabeth** (b.1855 nee Boniface), and four of his sons: **Herbert William** (b.1884), **Arthur Edward** (b.1891), **Leonard Victor** (b.1894) and **Percy** (b.1896) along with one grandchild, **Frank** (b.1905). According to the census Alfred and Elizabeth had eight children but only seven were surviving. All were sons. One of his older sons was **Horace Alfred** (b.1881), who was married and living with his family next door at *7 Beaconsfield Terrace* for part of the period.

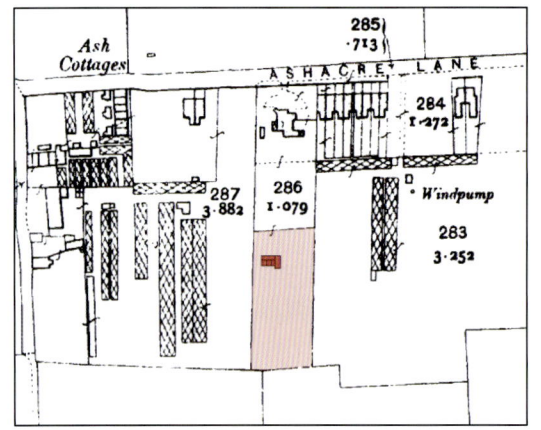

Excerpt taken from OS 25":1 mile Sheet LXIV: 10 3rd Edition 1912 (NTS)

Most of the family were gardeners of some sort. Alfred, along with Arthur and Leonard, were domestic gardeners whilst Herbert was a jobbing gardener. The odd one out was young Percy who, according to the 1911 census, was an errand boy, although, when he left school in 1910 he actually went *'to work in garden'*.

There was a plot of land behind *Causton,* which was the house next door, this land was rented by a Mr Tulett and used as a market garden (see marked on the map opposite). This is almost certainly Alfred as it reflects the occupation of both father and sons. On this plot of land, according to the Inland Revenue Assessment, there were *'3 brick built pigstyes in good condition'* no doubt adding to the family income and table as needed.[94]

Modern photograph of the terrace looking east down Ashacre Lane. © Dave Pryce 2014

71. Ashacre Nurseries & Glenside, Ashacre Lane
(No longer standing)

This nursery was situated on the southern side of Ashacre Lane on land behind *Beaconsfield Terrace*. In 1901 it was called *Ash Nurseries* and was being worked by **George Martin** (b.1877), a young market gardener, and his wife **Louisa** (b.1873) who were living in *1 Ash Cottages*.

In September 1905, they sold the nursery to **Charles Dorey** (b.1871) a Sussex fruit grower who already owned and ran *Seaview Nursery* in Lansdowne Road, Worthing. At the nursery in Worthing Charles already had a large house where he lived with his wife **Katherine** (b.1872 nee Sparkes) and their two daughters. He is, however, listed at this address on the 1911 census.[95]

He purchased *Ashacre Nursery* for £466 10s with four glasshouses already erected on the site, and a few years later he began to expand the nursery. Two more glasshouses were erected in 1911 at a cost of £350 adding another 300ft of glass to the site. There was an additional two more glasshouses in 1913 which gave yet another 300ft for exactly the same price. This gave a total of eight glasshouses which reflected the growing success Charles had brought to the nursery. He extended his land holdings into Ashacre Lane after 1909 when he purchased a plot of land on the south side just in front of the nursery and built the house calling it *Glenside*.[96] No-one is listed at the address on the 1911 census suggesting the building may not have been completed.

Old workshop still standing just behind *Beaconsfield Terrace*. © Dave Pryce 2015

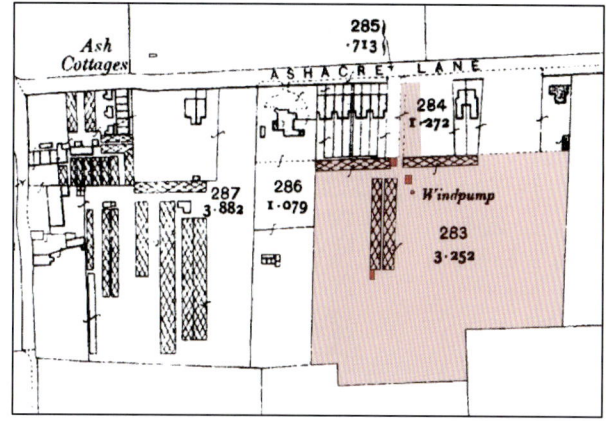

Excerpt taken from OS 25":1 mile Sheet LXIV: 10 3rd Edition 1912 (NTS)

72. Twyford and Wilburton, Ashacre Lane
(Now No's 19 & 17 Ashacre Lane)

The plot of land these two properties were built upon was empty until 1911, George Trim, the builder from Franklin Road, purchased the land in 1905 from Richard Cullen and in 1911 erected two properties on the site. In June 1913, by the time of the Inland Revenue Valuation, the site was described as:

> 'Vacant Land in Apl 1910
> 2 villas now stand with land erected 1911
> "Twyford" & "Wilburton" '[97]

The 1912 street directory list a **Thomas Peel** at *Twyford* but no occupancy for *Wilburton* during the same period has so far been traced.

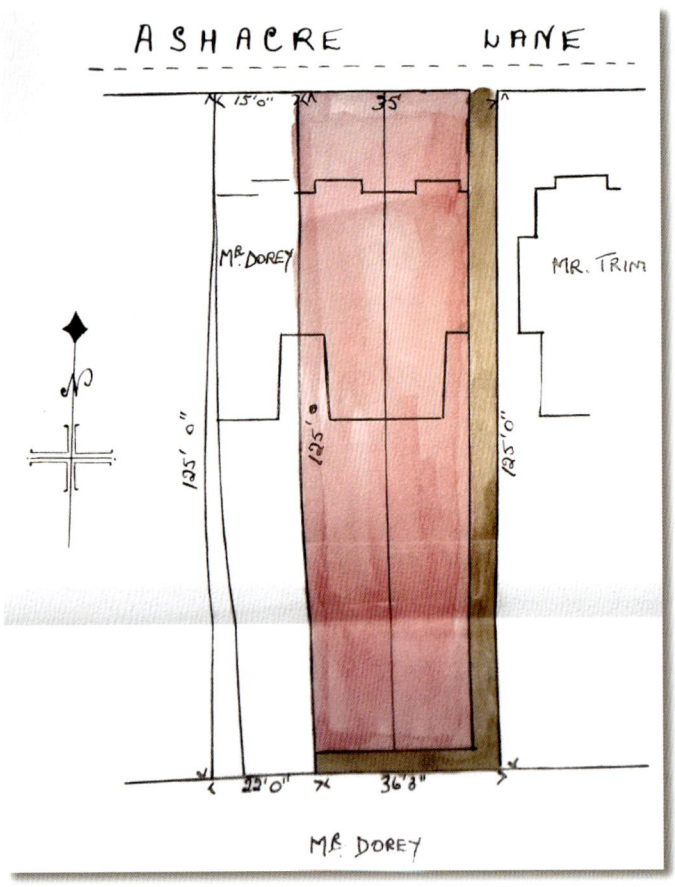

Extract from the Title Deeds of *Twyford* permission to use was kindly given by Kasia Watson

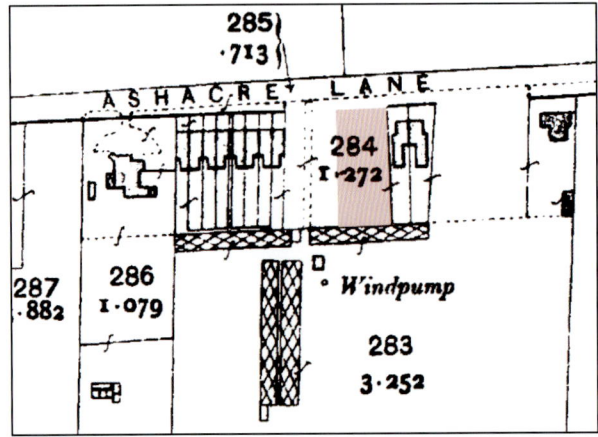

Excerpt taken from OS 25":1 mile Sheet LXIV: 10 3rd Edition 1912 (NTS)

Modern photograph of *Twyford* and *Wilburton*. © Dave Pryce 2015

73. The Dean, Ashacre Lane
(Now No 15 Ashacre Lane)

The Dean is a semi-detached property on the south side of Ashacre Lane which is one of an identical pair, the other being named *'Hillview'* (see below). Both properties were owned and built by George Trim, the Durrington builder who lived in Franklin Road. He purchased the plot of land in 1905 for the sum of £31.5s for each plot and spent £275 on the building costs. The rent for this property was £22 paid on a quarterly basis according to the Inland Revenue Valuation pages.[98]

The 1911 census gives us the first specific details about occupancy.[99] This was the home of **William Henry Dalgleish** who was born in Sudbury, Middlesex in 1883. By the time of the 1901 census, he was living in Hove with his widowed mother **Lucy J. M. F. Dalgleish** (b.1851) and his sister **Maude Lucy** (b.1879). Maude was listed as a *'professional musician'* who was obviously financing herself with her musical talent, as she is listed as living on her *'own account'*.[100] William, on the other hand, had chosen a different occupation and decided to become part of the banking world.

He lived for some years in Hove and in 1909 married a local girl **Emily Evelyn** (b.1882 nee Dockerill). It was at the time of their marriage or very soon after, that William and Emily made their home at *The Dean*, where street directories and the census list him in 1911 and the electoral register records him only for 1912. However, their stay was not very long as by the time of the Inland Revenue Valuation the property is recorded as *'Vacant'*.

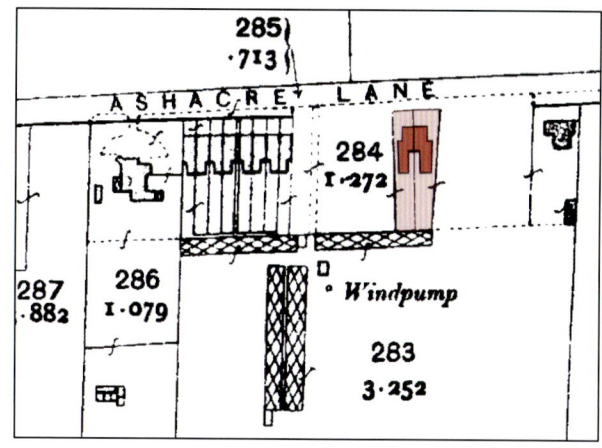

Excerpt taken from OS 25":1 mile Sheet LXIV: 10
3rd Edition 1912 (NTS)
Showing *The Dean* on the left and *Hillview* on the right.

Modern photograph showing *The Dean* on the right and *Hillview* on the left. © Dave Pryce 2015

74. Hillview, Ashacre Lane
(Now No 11 Ashacre Lane (there is no No 13))

This semi-detached property was owned and built along with its neighbour *'The Dean'* by Durrington builder, George Trim from Franklin Road.

The earliest traced occupiers of the house are the residents listed on the 1911 census. They were Irish born **John Ottley** (b.1855) and his Irish wife **Kate Coppinger** (b.1859 nee Thorne).[101] The Inland Revenue Valuation confirms that the land was purchased in 1905, with a further £275 spent on building the house. The street directories, electoral registers and 1911 census all confirm that 1911 was the earliest date the Ottleys are listed at the property, any earlier occupants are so far unknown.

The 1911 census page records John Ottley's occupation as a *'Retired Royal Navy Physician and Surgeon'*. His naval career must have seen him travelling in many ships and to many places in the world. In 1882, he had married the daughter of a retired Royal Naval paymaster, **Kate Coppinger Thorne** in Portsea.

John and Kate Ottley never had a family and it is clear from later events that their life was not an easy one. In 1897 things had come to a head and John found himself being court-martialled for being drunk on shore in Sheerness.[102] At the

NAVAL & MILITARY INTELLIGENCE

The Flora, cruiser, Capt. F. Hutchinson, arrived at Albany yesterday and will leave on Thursday.

Our Malta Correspondent telegraphs that the Algerine, sloop, Com. E. F. Domville, arrived yesterday from Gibraltar, and that the Hussar, torpedo gunboat, Lieut. and Com. C. G. Chapman, will leave on Friday for Port Said to relieve the Hebe, torpedo gunboat, Lieut. and Com. C. H. Umfreville.

The Wild Swan, sloop, Com. M. Napier, left Victoria, British Columbia, for Honolulu on Sunday.

A Court-martial was held on board the port guard-ship Sans Pareil at Sheerness yesterday for the trial of Staff-Surgeon John Ottley, of the Sans Pareil, who was charged with being drunk on shore at Sheerness on February 27, and also with being drunk on board the Sans Pareil on the same day. Capt. Robert F. Hammick, of the Pembroke, presided over the Court, and Mr. F. C. Alton, R.N., secretary to Vice-Adm. H. F. Nicholson, Commander-in-Chief at the Nore, officiated as Deputy Judge Advocate. Capt. J. L. Hammet prosecuted. The prisoner pleaded guilty to both charges, and in his defence stated that he had suffered of late from sleeplessness, and had also been in great trouble by reason of financial difficulties, from which he had now obtained relief, and from his wife's ill-health. The Court took into consideration the prisoner's services on the Niger in the operations of 1893, when he was mentioned in the despatches, also his services while in medical charge of the gunboats Herald and Mosquito for 16 months on the Zambesi river, for which he received the thanks of the Foreign Office. The sentence of the Court was that the prisoner should forfeit 12 months' seniority in the rank of staff-surgeon, be severely reprimanded, and be dismissed his ship.

time he was Naval Surgeon on board the port guard ship 'San Pareil'. His career and personal difficulties are revealed in the report. He had been mentioned in despatches in 1893 whilst serving in Niger, and had been in medical charge of two gunboats on the Zambesi River a few years later. However, financial difficulties due to his wife's ill-health had led to his being unable to sleep and resulted in the situation he found himself to be in. The result of the court-martial was seemingly unsympathetic to any external issues. He was punished by loss of rank, severe reprimand and the loss of his ship. This looks to have ended John Ottley's career in the Navy, and by 1898 he was placed on the retired list.

John then had various non-military jobs travelling on civilian ships as Surgeon, including at least two trips to Australia in 1904. We do not know what the state of his personal life was at this time, but he was living alone in Halesworth, East Suffolk on the 1901 census.[103] When he took up residence in Ashacre Lane around 1911, he was again living with his wife but they only stayed a short time, as by the 1913 Inland Revenue Valuation their name is crossed out and **Eldridge** is given as occupier.[104]

There may be one further post-script to the life of John and Kate Ottley. A man with the correct name, age and place of birth is registered as marrying a lady named **Ada Elizabeth Broughton Fairhead** in Adelaide, Australia on 24th October 1912. Had his wife died? Had he met another lady on his trips to Australia? It is not clear but the names of John & Kate Ottley have not been traced elsewhere in England. What is sad is that two months after John Ottley married in Adelaide, the same gentleman died in Australia.

75. The Rosary & Kimberley, Ashacre Lane
(Now No's 9 (Rosery) & 7 (Clovelly) Ashacre Lane)

These two properties were built at the end of the Edwardian period in July 1911 according to the Inland Revenue Valuation.[105] The plot of land is sited on the south side of the road and was owned by C. Skinner of 7, Wenban Road in Worthing as early as 1909, although the houses themselves had not been finally built and occupied until after the 1911 census had been taken.

Street directories for the 1912-1913 period tell us that *The Rosary* was occupied by **Alfred Dinnage,** and *Kimberley* was the home of **Charles King.** In both cases, this is confirmed by entries in the equivalent electoral register. These names were for new families moving into Salvington as Alfred Dinnage had previously lived in The Drive, Worthing according to his electoral register entry. We have no information at this time for the previous home of Charles King.

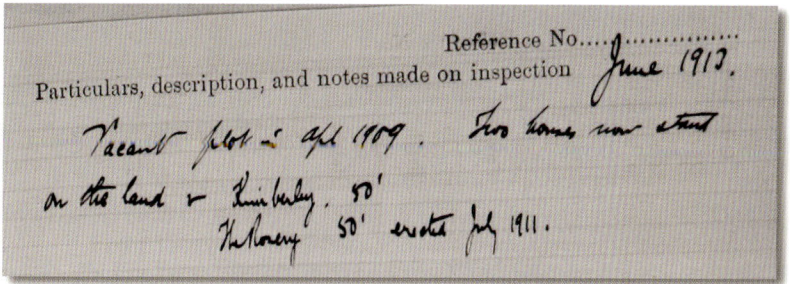

Excerpt from Inland Revenue Valuation Field Book No. 7829 giving the names of the two properties

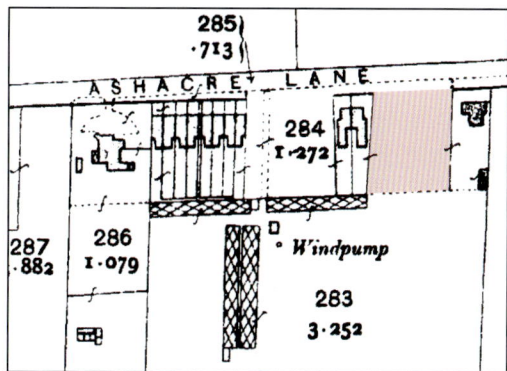

Excerpt taken from OS 25":1 mile Sheet LXIV: 10 3rd Edition 1912 (NTS)

Modern photographs of *The Rosary* (now *The Rosery*) above and *Kimberley* (now *Cloverly*) below. © Dave Pryce 2015

76. Lashburn Cottage, Ashacre Lane
(Now No 5 Ashacre Lane)

The plot of land upon which this property was built is on the south side of Ashacre Lane. It was purchased in October 1905 by a Worthing grocer **George Hill** (b.1842) and his son **Frederick George Hill** (b.1878). The Hill family owned and ran a grocer's shop in Newland Road, Worthing; (pictured below) where the p Frederick is shown standing in the front door of the shop.

Photograph of Frederick outside of his shop in Newland Road. Owned by Jane Dore

George had been born in Southwick, but by 1881 was already, according to the census, working in Worthing as a grocer.[106] The family were well established in Newland Road, and the property built in Salvington was to be the retirement home for George and his wife, **Mary Ann** (b.1848 nee Ingram). It was to become the family home for many years afterwards as neither Frederick nor his older sister **Florence** (b.1876) ever married.

The 1911 census details tell us that at the point the census was taken, it was George and Mary who had moved into *Lashburn Cottage,* the name they gave to the newly built house in Salvington.[107] Frederick and his sister Florence were still living at the shop address in Newland Road.

Lashburn Cottage originally stood on a larger plot of land than it does today which had cost George and Frederick £482 to purchase in 1905. According to the details given in the Inland Revenue Valuation, it included a portion of land called *'back land'*, which is clearly shown on the map as a piece of land at the back of the house and running along the rear of some of the other properties.[108] It was run as a market garden.

The photograph right shows the house at some point during its construction between 1905 and

Photograph of *Lashburn Cottage* being built around 1906. Owned by Jane Dore

1907 when George Hill is first listed at the address in both the street directory and the electoral register. The cost of building the house was given as £200.

Photograph of the finished cottage in 1906/7 with Frederick, George and Mary standing in the garden. Owned by Jane Dore

Lashburn Cottage in 2015. Note the extension added on the right hand side. © Dave Pryce 2015

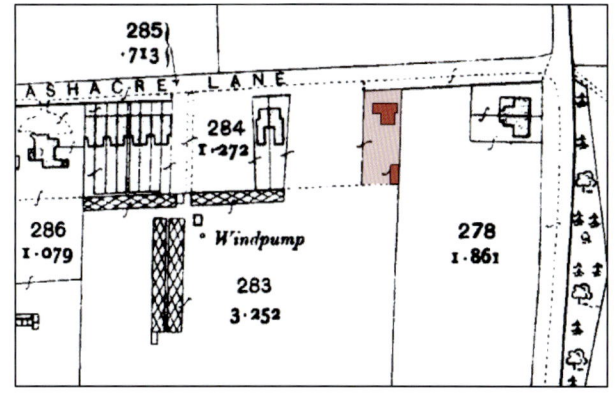

Excerpt taken from OS 25":1 mile Sheet LXIV: 10 3rd Edition 1912 (NTS)

77. Cutler's (Fuller's) Cottages, Ashacre Lane
(Now The Old House, No 54 Ashacre Lane)

This building stands on the north side of Ashacre Lane and dates in part from the fifteenth century. It is now a Grade II listed building which has undergone many changes in its lifetime. The house description given with its listing is as follows:

> 'House. Probable C15 open hall, ceiled over and chimney inserted in early C17 when a parlour wing was added to the east, extensively restored circa 1911. Timber framed building refronted in flint and render with roof mainly tiled but front slope of roof to original wing retaining Horsham stone slabs. Channelled brick stack to centre of original wing, external brick and flint stack to east of parlour wing and probable C18 brick stack to rear range. L-shaped plan. Two storeys, with attics to parlour wing; 5 windows. Front has former hall house of 3 bays to left. Three gabled dormers and three casement windows, all with early C20 leaded lights. Projecting parlour wing to right has gable hung with plain and fishscale tiles, 1;2;1 casements with leaded lights and early C20 porch on slender wooden columns and four panelled door. Rear elevation has circa 1911 gabled projection forming stair turret, two storey C17 or C18 service wing to right with one storey offices at end. Three leaded light casements. Interior has crownpost roof to original open hall with curved tiebeam, octagonal crown post with 4 headbraces, collar beam and rafters. The square crownpost to the smaller bedroom has a collar beam which is a reused beam from the top of a wallplate retaining the notches of the rafters. Ground floor has dining room with early C17 cross beams with 2 inch chamfers with lambstongue stops, c1911 stone fireplace and wooden panelling. Sitting room has open fireplace with moulded bressumer with crane marks and 2 salt recesses, but the seats and arched doorcases are early C20. Chamfered spine beam supported on wooden corbel. A series of plank doors probably assembled c1911 out of older floorboards. Parlour wing shows few visible signs of early C17 origin apart from a chamfered beam with lambs tongue stop on the first floor. The attic floor of this wing is boarded over. Old sales particulars indicate that this property was known as Cutler's House in 1795 and was later subdivided into three cottages. Later it became a farmhouse but was restored in 1911 and became a residence.'[109]

By 1795, it was already marked on maps as *Cutler's House,* named after the farmer living and working the farm at the time.

John Cutler was born around 1760, and by 1791 he had married **Elizabeth Penfold** in West Tarring. The couple made their home in the farmhouse and only a few years later the house had become synonymous with the family surname which stayed with the building for many years. John died in 1849.

The house had already been subdivided into three cottages by the time of the 1871 census as three families are listed at *Cutler's Farm.*[110] During the latter part of the 1890's and on the 1901 census, the cottages were known as *Fuller's Cottages.*[111] The only connection with this name appears to be a **C. H. Fuller**, listed as a dairyman in the street directories between 1891-1893 at the address, or a market gardener who was a lodger in the cottages for a short period. This does, however, seem a very slight connection.

The 1901 census lists three families living at *Fuller's Cottages*. The first of these was **Henry William Perham** (b.1873), his wife **Elizabeth Mary** (b.1876 nee Warr) and their children, **Robert Charles** (b.1897) and **Ethel Jane** (b.1898).[112] The Perhams moved next door around 1906, to the detached cottage called *Ivy Cottage*.

The second cottage was the home of a dairyman **James Stoner** (b.1874), his wife **Alice** (b.1878 nee Foster) and their young son **Barnard Alec James** (b.1899), whilst the third of the cottages was the home of **Catherine Steptoe** (b.1848).[113] She was a widow who was working at the time as a housekeeper, although the census does not tell us where she was employed. She also had an elderly lodger living with her, **John Hemmers (or Hemmings)** who had come originally from Hampshire. Both of them continued to live in the cottage until after the census in 1911, when all the occupants had to leave to allow the re-building work to begin which is described below.

Various other occupants are listed in street directories and electoral registers between the 1901 and 1911 censuses, with the cottages being variously called *Cutler's* or *Fuller's Cottages*. Among them were **John Joseph Tree** between 1903 and 1907, and one mention of a **Walter H. Goddard** in 1907. Not it would appear the same William Goddard who is listed elsewhere living in *Burt's Cottage* for most of this period.

Only one cottage had the same resident throughout the whole Edwardian period, and this was the one which housed **Catherine Steptoe**, who by 1911 was 64 years old and still working as a charwoman.[114] The same lodger, **John Hemmers/Hemmings,** was also living in the cottage.

By 1911, the residents of the other two cottages were a road labourer, **Francis William Richardson** (b.1875), his wife **Rosa Emma** (b.1887 nee Lewis) and two children, **Frances** and **Edward** (b.1910).[115] No birth is listed for Frances Richardson, but there is a possible birth registered for **Frances Louisa Lewis** in 1907. As **Francis Richardson** and **Rosa Lewis** were married in the last months of 1908, it is possible that Frances was born before the couple married. Rosa was the daughter of the farm bailiff **Edward Lewis,** who had previously lived with his family, including Rosa, at *Selden's Cottage* before moving to *East Villa* in Ashacre Lane. While the family were living in *Selden's Cottage* they had a lodger who was none other than Francis Richardson who Rosa went on to marry. The photograph of the three cottages, shown below, has a little girl peeking over the front wall. This may very well be Frances Richardson, as no other child in the right age range was living at the cottages during this period.

Cutlers' Cottages shortly before they became one house.
The little girl behind the wall may be Frances Richardson.
Worthing Library

The third of the cottages was the home the Peacock family in 1911, with **Luke Peacock** (b.1856) as the head.[116] Luke was already a widower by 1911 as his wife, **Mary Ann** (b.1861), had died in 1906 before the family moved to Salvington. Three of his youngest children were living with him: **(Ernest) George** (b.1893), **Violet Mabel** (b.1900) and **(James) William** (b.1904). His older daughter **Alice Harriett** (b.1885) was also living in the cottage with her husband **James William Madgwick** (b.1873) and their two children **Frederick William** (b.1906) and **Edwin James** (b.1910). James and Alice had married in 1906 and spent the first few years of their married life in Hove before coming to Salvington where they lived for a short while in *Beaconsfield Terrace,* before moving to this cottage where the widowed Luke would have needed help to raise his youngest children.

The Inland Revenue Valuation records that the three cottages were rented out on a sub-let basis. The cottages were owned by the Wisden estate who rented them as part of **Salvington Farm** to Edwin Lephard. He in turn rented them to '**Tyrrell',** whose actual identity has not been discovered, but we do know that he rented them to the numerous families listed above. Whatever the complexity of the renting procedures for these cottages the arrangement had come to an end by the time the valuation was recorded:

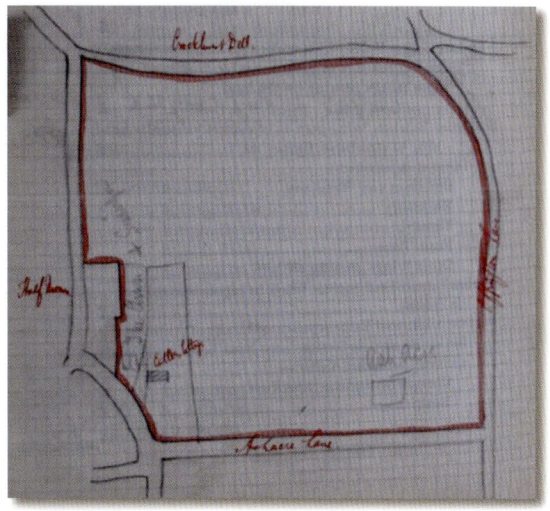

> *'Upon inspection this cottage together with 7878 & 7880 was found to be in the course of rebuilding. The three appear to be about to be thrown into one house.'[117]*

This is indeed what happened, although the terminology of being 'thrown' into one suggests something a little hurried and haphazard, the property was duly altered into one large dwelling. The house is still standing with many original features including the well in the back garden as the photographs below show.

Map of outline of area including *Cutler's Cottages* from Inland Revenue Valuation[118]

Modern photograph of The Old House. © Dave Pryce 2012

161

Original Roof trusses inside the cottage. © Dave Pryce 2012   The well still in the rear garden. © Dave Pryce 2012

Modern rear view of *The Old House (Cutler's Cottages)*. © Dave Pryce 2012

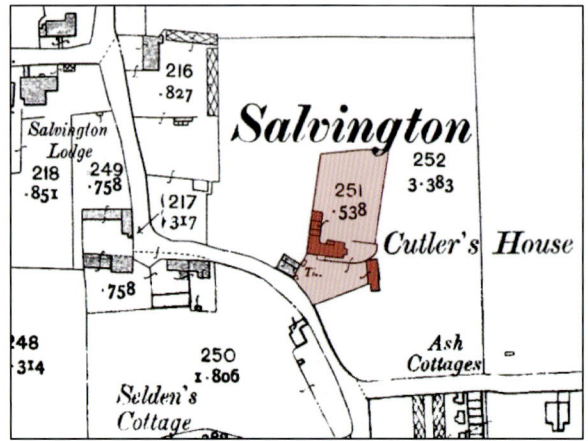

Excerpt taken from OS 25":1 mile Sheet LXIV: 10 3rd Edition 1912 (NTS)

78. Ivy Cottage, Ashacre Lane
(No longer standing)

This is another of the cottages owned by the **Wisden** family of Henfield and generally lived in by *Salvington Farm* workers. In 1901 it was the home of the Mears family although the cottage is not named.[119] **Thomas Mears** (b.1864 (Meers)) was the head of the house which he shared with his wife **Mary Ann** (b.1871 nee Mears) and their children: **Annie Ada** (b.1893), **Dora Christine** (b.1896), **Cecil George** (b.1899) and **Thomas** (b.1900). There are conflicting entries in street directories and electoral registers regarding their address and whether or not they moved to other addresses including a listing for *Yew Tree Cottages* which has not been confirmed. Thomas is last registered in 1905 so we do know that about this time they moved from the cottage.

In 1906 another cowman, named Henry Perham, made a move from *Cutler's Cottages* into this little cottage along with his growing family. **Henry William Perham** (b.1873) was originally from Somerset where, by the time he was 18, he was already working as a 'dairy lad' on a farm in Kington Magna. In 1896 he had married **Elizabeth (Eliza) Mary Warr** (b.1876) and they went on to have at least five children. The birth places of the children, as noted on the 1911 census form, reveal the journey the family took as their father moved from place to place to find work.[120] Their first son **Robert Charles** (b.1898) was born in Somerset, the second **Ethel Jane** (b.1898) in Henfield, Sussex and their third and fourth daughters **Elsie Winifred** (b.1904) and **Vera Gladys** (b.1905) both born in Salvington.

The 1911 census only lists these children but the school admissions register fills in other details and reveals that a few months after the census was taken Eliza had given birth to another son **Frank William** (b.1911). The two eldest of the Perham children had previously attended school in Goring and were among the first children to transfer to the newly opened Durrington Council School in June 1908. Robert left the school a few days before his 14th birthday in 1911 to work in the market gardens, whilst Ethel left in 1912 to work as an *'under nursemaid'*. By the time of the Inland Revenue Valuation in April 1913 the family were no longer listed as occupiers of the cottage.[121] It was now in the occupancy of a **Mr Holden,** his Christian name as yet unknown.

His shows the site of where Ivy Cottage once stood. © Dave Pryce 2014

79. Rose Cottage, Ashacre Lane
(Now Appleacre, No 62 Ashacre Lane)

This cottage is situated on the northern side of Ashacre Lane and owing to it being siting sideways onto the road, is in a beautifully secluded position. Originally, a tiny cottage built in the 1600's; it has been altered and added to throughout the years. Gordon Latham was the modern occupant of the cottage, now called *Appleacre*, from 1983 until 2014. He has outlined the architectural changes in the building in a written report added at the end of the book as an Appendix.

The occupants of the cottage had for many years been generations of the same family. The 1901 census records that **James Holden** (b.1833) was the present head of the house. James was the third son of the previous occupant of the cottage, **John Holden** (b.1806) and **Louisa** (b.1806 nee Hill), his wife. In 1906 the cottage was sold as part of the Wisden Estate. A photocopy of a portion of this sale catalogue is held in the archive of *High Salvington Windmill* and gives the following description of the cottage and gardens and reveals that James Holden was permitted to live in the cottage *'Rent Free'*:

Lot 6.
A VALUABLE
Freehold Detached Cottage,
AND GARDEN,

Situate in the Village of Salvington about 1 Mile from West Worthing Station

----

The COTTAGE is brick and flint-built and tile-healed and contains:- TWO BEDROOMS, LIVING ROOM with Brick Floor, Range and Cupboard, SCULLERY with Brick Floor and Copper, EARTH CLOSET.

There is a Large GARDEN well stocked with Apple and Plum Trees, and Ornamental Firs, and enclodsed on the Frontage by a good flint wall.

The Property has a Frontage of about 170ft to the Tarring Road.

It is in the occupation of MR. JAMES HOLDEN who has been allowed to live there Rent Free.

The vendors have no evidence of Land Tax being payable in respect of this Lot.

The Lot is subject to a small payment of Tithe.

Water can be laid on from the main immediately opposite the Garden. The hedge and oak fence on the east side and the flint wall on the north side are sold with this Lot.

By the time the 1901 census was taken, James was already a widower.[122] His wife Susannah (b.1834 nee Wood) had sadly died only a few weeks before. He was sharing the house with his daughter **Hannah Louise Warren** (b.1869). In 1902 Hannah had married **Robert Warren** (b.1871), and the 1911 census confirms that since their marriage they had had two children: **Arthur James** (b.1903) and **Louisa Clara** (b.1908). The census at this time also tells us that both men, even James at 76, were working in the nurseries. Arthur attended Durrington Council School but was removed, with special permission from the Education Committee, in 1915 when he was only 12 years old to work on the farm. Such was still the lot of poorer children during this time.

When the Inland Revenue Valuation was taken in 1913, it was clear that the cottage was not in a very good state of repair. The description reads:

'Old cottage, detached, bad structural & decorative repair ………….. good garden.'[123]

Obviously whatever the state of the house the garden was worthy of note, but we are not told if this was due to the soil condition or perhaps the beautiful plants and the care which the occupants had taken with its cultivation. The cottage building has been greatly improved in the years since this assessment was completed as the modern photographs show.

Modern photograph of Rose Cottage (now called Appleacre). © Dave Pryce 2016

---

[1] Town & Country Illustrated Supplement: 'Picture Review of the Business life of Worthing'. (1909) p.10 (WSL)
[2] www.britishlistedbuildings.co.uk No. 302217 (viewed 21.06.2012)
[3] IR58/94206 No.7855 (TNA)
[4] www.britishlistedbuildings.co.uk No. 302216 (viewed 21.06.2012)
[5] IR58/94206 No. 7870 (TNA)
[6] 1891 census RG12/837 ff.21 (TNA)
[7] 1911 census RG14/5342 sch 55 (TNA)
[8] 1901 census RG13/957 ff.60 (TNA)
[9] 1881 census RG11/1118 ff.32 (TNA)
[10] 1891 census RG12/837 ff.21 (TNA)
[11] 1911 census RG14/5342 sch 50 (TNA)
[12] Durrington Council School Admissions Register 1908- 1928 (Held at the school)
[13] IR58/94206 No.7894 (TNA)
[14] 1901 census RG13/957 ff.60 (TNA)
[15] 1911 census RG14/5342 sch 51 (TNA)
[16] 1901 census RG13/957 ff.60 (TNA)
[17] 1911 census RG14/5342 sch 52 (TNA)
[18] IR58/94206 No.7892 (TNA)
[19] IR58/94206 No.7869 (TNA)
[20] 1901 census RG13/957 ff.63 (TNA)
[21] 1861 census RG9/614 ff.203 (TNA)
[22] 1911 census RG14/5342 sch 53 (TNA)
[23] 1891 census RG12/836 ff.6 (TNA)
[24] 1901 census RG13/957 ff.63 (TNA)
[25] 1901 census RG13/957 ff.59 (TNA)
[26] 1881 census RG11/2098 ff.100 (TNA)
[27] 1911 census RG14/5342 sch 72 (TNA)
[28] 1911 census RG14/5342 sch 43 (TNA)
[29] 1901 census RG13/957 ff.60 (TNA)
[30] Linfield p.12
[31] Worthing Gazette 5th September 1906 p4
[32] Worthing Gazette 12th September 1906 p6
[33] 1901 census RG13/957 ff.59 (TNA)
[34] 1911 census RG14/5342 sch 45 (TNA)
[35] 1901 census RG13/957 ff.59 (TNA)
[36] 1911 census RG14/5342 sch 46 (TNA)
[37] IR58/94206 No. 7887 (TNA)
[38] GRO Index: Mar Q 1896 Vol 2b p.554 (Westbourne)
[39] 1901 census RG13/957 ff.59 (TNA)
[40] 1911 census RG14/5342 sch 47 (TNA)
[41] 1891 census RG12/1619 ff.78 (TNA)
[42] Durrington Council School Admissions Register 1908-1961 (Held at school)

[43] 1901 census RG13/957 ff.59 (TNA)
[44] Durrington Council School Log Book 1908-1928 p.33 (Held at the school)
[45] 1911 census RG14/5342 sch 48 (TNA)
[46] 1911 census RG14/5342 sch 42 (TNA)
[47] Military Campaign medal and Awards Roll 1793-1949. Held at PRO WO100/119 (viewed on Ancestrylibrary.com 01.11.2013)
[48] 1901 census RG13/957 ff.62 (TNA)
[49] 1911 census RG14/5342 sch 41 (TNA)
[50] Worthing Gazette 14th January 1914 p.8
[51] IR58/94206 No. 7843 (TNA)
[52] The Times (London, England), Saturday, 11th November 1848, p 6
[53] 1871 census RG10/3324 ff.47 (TNA)
[54] 1881 census RG11/3081 ff.17
[55] 1911 census RG14/5342 sch 40 (TNA)
[56] IR58/94206 No. 7842 (TNA)
[57] IR58/94206 No. 7834 – 7841 (TNA)
[58] 1911 census RG14/3303 sch 249 (TNA)
[59] EPRD Minutes 12th December 1905 p.209
[60] EPRD Minutes 17th April 1906 p.234
[61] EPRD Minutes 1st May 1906 p.237
[62] IR58/94206 No. 7834 (TNA)
[63] Worthing Gazette 12th September 1906 p4
[64] Durrington Council School Log Book 1908-1928 p.33 (Held at the school)
[65] 1911 census RG14/5342 sch 32 (TNA)
[66] Durrington Council School Admissions Register 1908- 1928 (Held at the school)
[67] 1901 census RG13/957 ff.61(TNA)
[68] 1891 census RG12/837 ff.120 (TNA)
[69] 1911 census RG14/5342 sch 33 (TNA)
[70] 1911 census RG14.5342 sch 34 (TNA)
[71] 1910 census RG13/957 ff.54 (TNA)
[72] Durrington Council School Log Book 1908-1928 p.5 (Held at the school)
[73] Durrington Council School Log Book 1908-1928 p.13 (Held at the school
[74] Durrington Council School Log Book 1908-1928 p.126 (Held at the school
[75] Durrington Council School Log Book 1908-1928 p.127 (Held at the school
[76] 1911 census RG14/5342 sch 35 (TNA)
[77] 1891 census RG12/835 ff.107 (TNA)
[78] 1891 census RG12/416 ff.143 (Ethel) & ff.145 (Edward) (TNA)
[79] 1901 census RG13/958 ff.134 (TNA)
[80] 1911 census RG14/5330 sch 259 (TNA)
[81] *Note: Administration was given to his widow, Clara but, for some reason, was not granted until 1925. The estate left was only £200. It is not known why there was a delay of twelve years for such a small estate. Arthur left the school in May 1914 and went to Watford Orphanage. When Clara herself died in 1962, in Lowdham Nottinghamshire, leaving £797 3s 4d, the administration of her estate was granted to her son, Arthur Stanley Dinsdale, Company Director. A full history of the Dinsdale family can be found in 'Blood's Thicker Than Water. The Story of the Search for our Dinsdales Past and Present' by Joan D. Dexter who is the daughter of Arthur Stanley.*
[82] 1911 census RG14/5342 sch 36 (TNA)
[83] 1911 census RG14/5343 sch145 (TNA)
[84] 1911 census RG14/5342 sch 37 (TNA)
[85] 1901 census RG13/957 ff.61 (TNA)
[86] 1901 census RG13/962 ff.83 (TNA)
[87] 1911 census RG14/5341 sch 32 (TNA)
[88] 1901 census RG13/961 ff.28 (TNA)
[89] 1911 census RG14/8793 sch 196 (TNA)
[90] 1911 census RG14/5342 sch 38 (TNA)
[91] IR58/94206 No. 7840 (TNA)
[92] 1901 census RG13/962 ff.83 (TNA)
[93] 1911 census RG14/5342 sch 39 (TNA)
[94] IR58/94206 No. 7841 (TNA)
[95] 1911 census RG14/5341 sch 232 (TNA)
[96] IR58/94218 No. 9064 (TNA)
[97] IR58/94218 No. 9010 (TNA)
[98] IR58/94206 No. 7831 (TNA)
[99] 1911 census RG14/5342 sch 31 (TNA)
[100] 1901 census RG13/938 ff.169 (TNA)
[101] 1911 census RG14/5342 sch 30 (TNA)
[102] The Times (London, England), 16th March 1897, p 10
[103] 1901 census RG13/1795 ff.38 (TNA)
[104] IR58/94206 No. 7830 (TNA)
[105] IR58/94206 No. 7829 (TNA)
[106] 1891 census RG12/835 ff.35 (TNA)
[107] 1911 census RG14/5342 sch 29 (TNA)
[108] IR58/94206 no. 7832 (TNA)
[109] www.britishlistedbuildings.co.uk No. 302215 (viewed 30.01.2016)

[110] 1871 census RG10/1107 ff.107 (TNA)
[111] 1901 census RG13/957 ff.60 (TNA)
[112] 1901 census RG13/957 ff.60 (TNA)
[113] 1901 census RG13/957 ff.60 (TNA)
[114] 1911 census RG14/5342 sch 57 (TNA)
[115] 1911 census RG14/5342 sch 56 (TNA)
[116] 1911 census RG14/5342 sch 58 (TNA)
[117] IR58/94206 No. 7879 (TNA)
[118] IR58/94206 No. 7857 (TNA)
[119] 1901 census RG13/957 ff.60 (TNA)
[120] 1911 census RG14/5342 sch 59 (TNA)
[121] IR58/94206 No. 7883 (TNA)
[122] 1901 census RG13/957 ff.60 (TNA)
[123] IR58/94206 No. 7883 (TNA)

Chapter 8
Half Moon Lane

Introduction

This road runs northwards from the junction where Salvington Road takes a gentle right turn and becomes Ashacre Lane. It is a very old road named after the inn that had stood in the road for many years. At its northern most point it reaches the main Arundel Road. The only two properties that stood in this road during Edwardian times were the *Half Moon Inn*, mentioned above and *Salvington Nurseries*. Opposite the *Half Moon Inn* there was a large pond which has long since disappeared.

Half Moon Lane around 1910, looking south. The buildings attached to the *Half Moon Inn* are on the right.
Worthing Library

View of Half Moon Lane looking north as it looks today. © Dave Pryce 2015

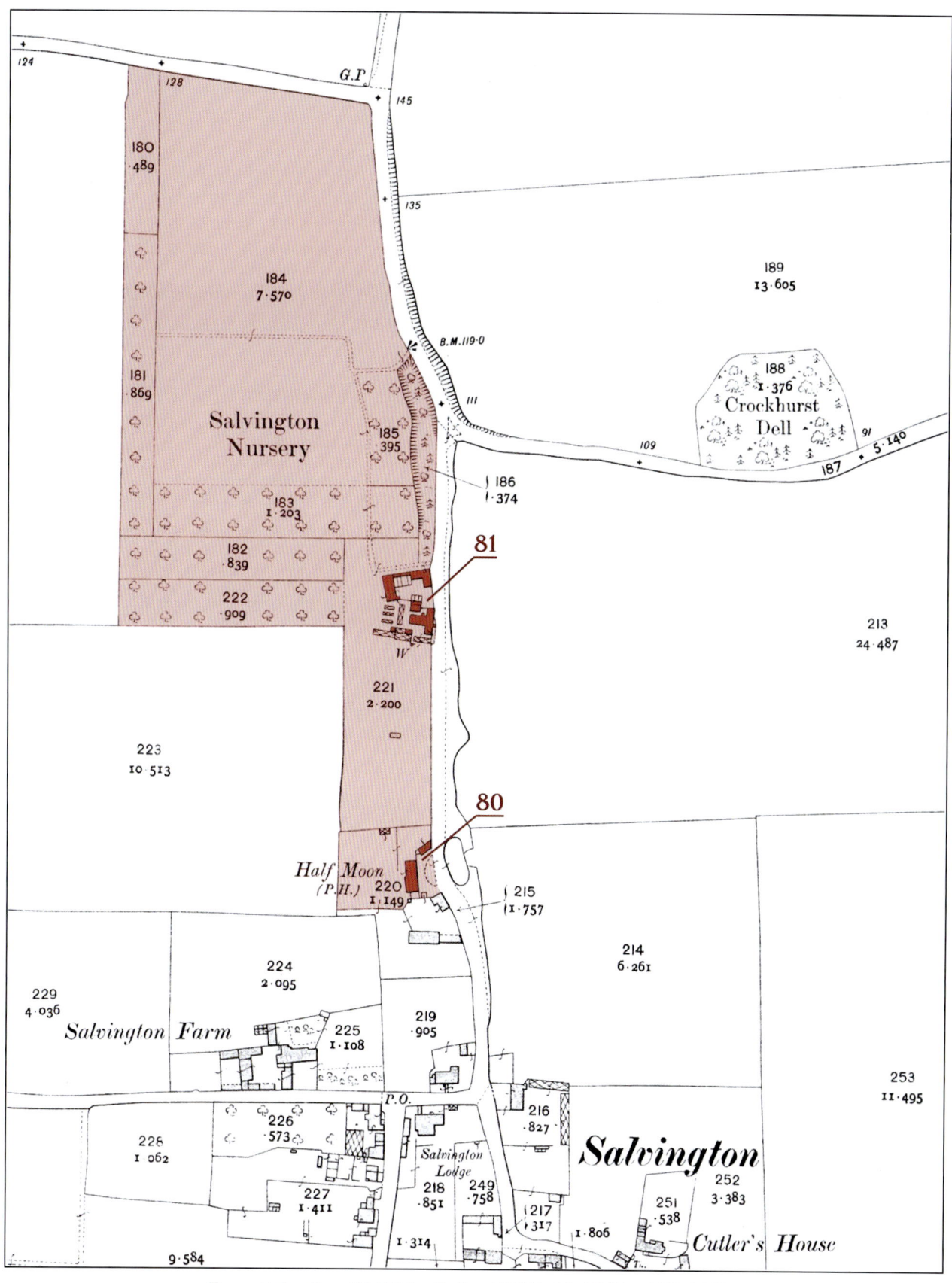

Excerpt taken from OS 25":1 mile Sheet LXIV: 6 3rd Edition 1912 (NTS)

80. Half Moon Inn, Half Moon Lane (Salvington Tea Rooms/Laundry)
(Now No 11 Half Moon Lane)

This property became a licensed public house and was named the *Half Moon Inn* around 1858 when the 18th century cottages on the site were amalgamated and the inn was opened. By the Edwardian period, it was a well-established hostelry in Salvington with **Leon Alexander Pierre** listed as the publican on the 1901 census.[1] He had already been working there for some time, as he was listed on the street directories before 1900. The inn was owned at the time by the brewers Lambert & Norris of Arundel.

There is some uncertainty as to where Leon Pierre was born, the 1881 census[2] lists Amsterdam, although later censuses give the place of birth as London. No record can be found on the birth indexes of any birth in England so it is probable that he was born abroad. In 1878, he married an Englishwoman named **Mary Walton** (b.1858) who was born in Lincolnshire and they went on to have eight children, five of whom were living at the *Half Moon Inn* with them in 1901: **Lena (Leonie)** (b.1882), **Reginald** (b.1891), **Harold** (b.1892), **Harry** (b.1896) and **Redvers** (b.1900).[3]

The public house regularly appears in the newspapers of the period, usually recording applications for extensions to licensing hours for the special events that were held there. However, in 1906 Mr Pierre's name was found in the newspaper for a different reason. He was summoned and fined for assaulting Thomas Tyrrell who lived in Stone Lane. The story seems to have revolved around Mr Tyrrell's son *'and others'* tormenting both a dog and some geese belonging to Mr Pierre.[4]

Worthing Gazette reports on the disagreement between Leon Pierre and Thomas Tyrrell in October 1906

This is a good example of some of the small altercations and events which would have been part of Edwardian life in a small Sussex hamlet.

The 1911 census returns reveal that by this date things had changed at the *Half Moon Inn*. The Pierre family had left and the new family who took up occupation in the property were the Wyatt family. The property itself had also undergone a change of use and was now called *Salvington Tea Gardens*. The photograph below shows the property at this time and a board attached to the outside wall confirms that the dwelling, as well as being a tea garden, was also functioning as a laundry.

Old photograph of Salvington Tea Gardens. Owned by John Green

For some years previous to this major change of use, the *Half Moon Inn* had worked alongside another drinking establishment which was situated just a few yards down the lane on the corner of Salvington Road, namely *The Spotted Cow*. This building had been demolished in 1909 and a new public house, which was to be named the *John Selden*, was completed towards the end of 1910. At this point the licence from the *Half Moon Inn* was transferred to the *John Selden* and the property in Half Moon Lane started its new life as a tea garden and a laundry.[5]

The 1911 census gives further details of the family who came to live in Half Moon Lane at the time.[6] The head of the house was **James Henry Wyatt** (b.1874) who gave his occupation as a domestic gardener, so it was probably his wife **Agnes Alice** (b.1884 nee Collard), whom he had married in 1901, who took on the major part of the work running the tea gardens and laundry. Living with them were their children: **William** (b.1903), **Albert** (b.1905) known as '**Tich**', **Percy** (b.1907) known as '**Pescoe**', **Reginald** (b.1909) and their daughter **Queenie** (b.1911). Also living with them was **James**' brother **Joseph Wyatt** (b.1876), a plasterer and his wife.

THE NEW LICENSED HOUSE AT SALVINGTON.

The Magistrates sanctioned the removal of the licence of the Half Moon Inn, Salvington, to the new premises, and allowed the application of Mr. E. B. Wannop (of Littlehampton) for the new premises to be called the John Selden Arms. There were historical reasons for the adoption of such a name, said Mr. Wannop. The Magistrates granted permission to Mr. Samuel Sandham to hold the licence.

Newspaper report in 1910 recording the change of licence from the *Half Moon* to the new *John Selden*

The family were to stay at the Half Moon for a few years before preparations to move again were underway. This is revealed in a message written on the back of a postcard by Agnes (Alice) herself. The postcard is a photograph of Alice and three of her children which she sent to her sister **Selina Bridger** (b.1879). The message on the postcard reveals that although the family were preparing to leave they, as yet, were not sure where they were going. The message reads:

'Dear Selina, Just a line to tell you we are leaving here in March but I don't know where we are going. We shall be very pleased to see you down. Love to all, Alice. What do you think of this photo?'

Alice and three of her children.
Worthing Library

This move was probably around 1914 and although Alice did not know it at the time of writing, their move was but a short distance down the road to live and work in the *John Selden Arms* where they were to remain for some years afterwards.

Alice Wyatt was one of four sisters originally from Devon, who all married local men. Three of the sisters were living in Salvington during the Edwardian period. Alice herself had married James Wyatt while of her two younger sisters, **Mildred Ethel**, (b.1886) had married **Frank White** and was living in Beaconsfield Terrace and **Sarah Jane** (b.1890) had married **Frederick Hayes** and was living next door to Mildred also in *Beaconsfield Terrace*. Their oldest sister **Selina Ellen** (b.1879) who is mentioned above as the recipient of the postcard, was living in Shoreham with **Percy Bridger**, her husband at the time of the 1911 census, although she later moved into Durrington as well.[7]

When the Inland Revenue Valuation describes the house in April 1913 it describes a large property with many of the features of a public house still in place.

'Gd floor. Shop & bar. 1 r(oom), 1 r(oom)
K(itchen) Sc(ullery).   large rooms
5 bed rooms
*   Coach house & stable'*[8]

The house in Half Moon Lane is still standing and is a Grade II listed building described as:

'Circa 1840. 2 storeys. 3 windows. Stuccoed. Slate roof. Doorway with Doric pilasters and emblature. Later addition of 1 window with higher façade to the north.[9]

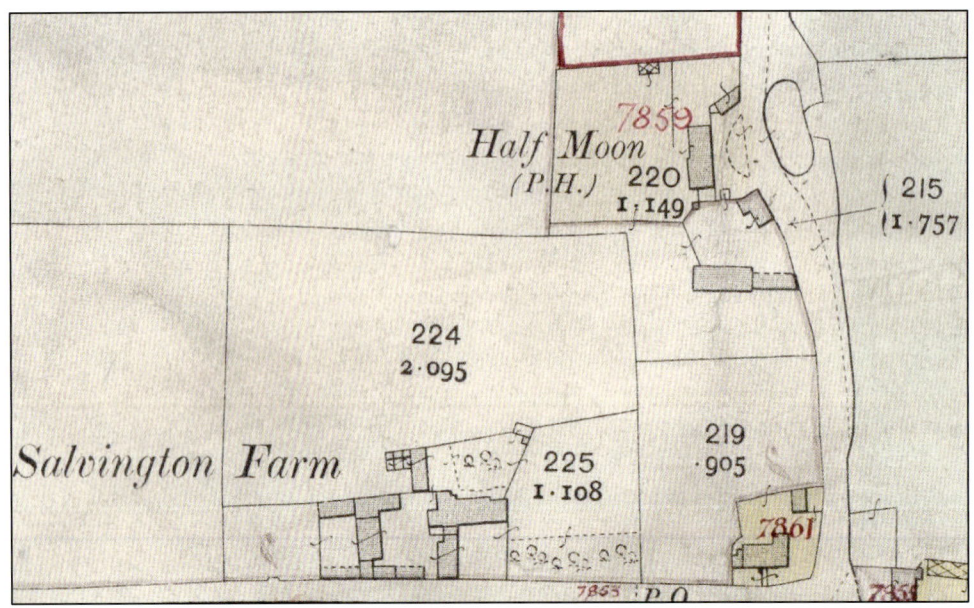

Excerpt taken from OS 25":1 mile Sheet LXIV: 6 3rd Edition 1912 (NTS)
Inland Revenue Valuation numbers added

81. Salvington Nursery, Half Moon Lane
(Now No 43 Half Moon Lane)

Photograph looking down Half Moon Lane with the cottage from *Salvington Nursery* on the right. © Dave Pryce 2015

This is one of the oldest nurseries in Salvington already being worked as a market garden in Victorian times by the same family who continued their occupancy through the Edwardian years. The land was owned by the

Wisden Estate and the family had taken out a new tenancy agreement of 14 years with the estate on September 29th 1903.

Malcolm Linfield describes the site:

> 'One of the largest market gardens was *Salvington Nurseries* in Half Moon Lane. It was managed by the Taylor family for several decades. According to the census returns, George Taylor was established in Salvington as a market gardener before 1881. Around 1890 he erected a number of small glasshouses which he probably used for some propagating and fruit growing...........Salvington Nurseries covered well over 14 acres, of which 4 acres were orchards. There was a group of various farm buildings, an old cottage with garden, packing shed and a large meadow.......... George senior died in 1892 at the age of 67, and his widow Fanny took over the business...................'[10]

The house itself dates back to the eighteenth century although later changes have been made. It is a Grade II listed building described as:

> 'Late C18. 2 storeys. 3 windows. Grey headers with red brick dressing. Mansarded roof of red tiles. Small cornice with modillions below eaves. Victorian porch added. Glazing bars missing.'[11]

The modern photograph shows how the front entrance to the house sits directly onto the road with no front garden or path area at all. This property and its garden is all that remains of *Salvington Nurseries*.

The occupants at the beginning of the twentieth century are recorded on the 1901 census.[12] The head of the household is **Fanny Taylor** (b.c1838) who as we know was already a widow. Also living in the property were three of her children: **Alic Basil** (b.1870), **William Samuel** (b.1875) and a daughter, **Florence (Kitty) Kithe** (b.1878). Two other females are listed as granddaughters: **Grace Taylor** aged 21 who was born in Ireland around 1878 and a little girl named **Lilly Ada Hedger** (b.1898).

During the next ten years much changed in the Taylor household. Fanny died in 1909 and the managing of the nursery was continued by her two sons.[13]

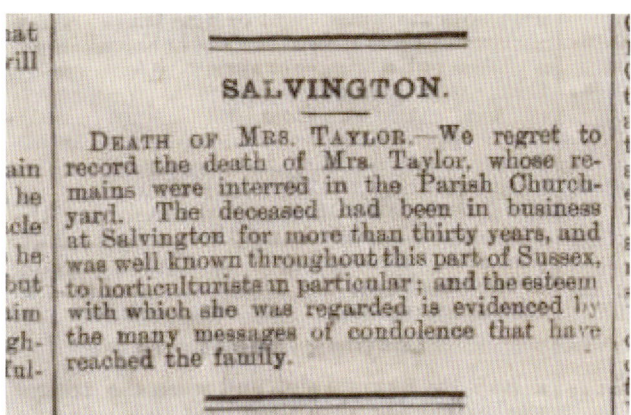

Death of Fanny Taylor in April 1909

Alic Taylor had married in 1910 and by the time of the 1911 census the household consisted of Alic, his wife Callista, who was the daughter of William and Callista Holden who ran the Post Office in Salvington, as well as his younger brother William and sister Florence.[14]

In October 1912 when the Inland Revenue Valuation was made the owners were listed as 'Taylor Bros' and the description was given as:

> 'Old Cottage. 4 bed(rooms). K(itchen). Shed
> Barn, Packing Sheds, Stable. 4 small glasshouses.
> Market garden, good deep loamy soil on south side poorer soil on north.'[15]

Although the nursery is no longer in existence the house still stands and until recently remained the home of members of the Taylor family.

Modern photograph of the *Old Cottage* at *Salvington Nursery*. © Dave Pryce 2015

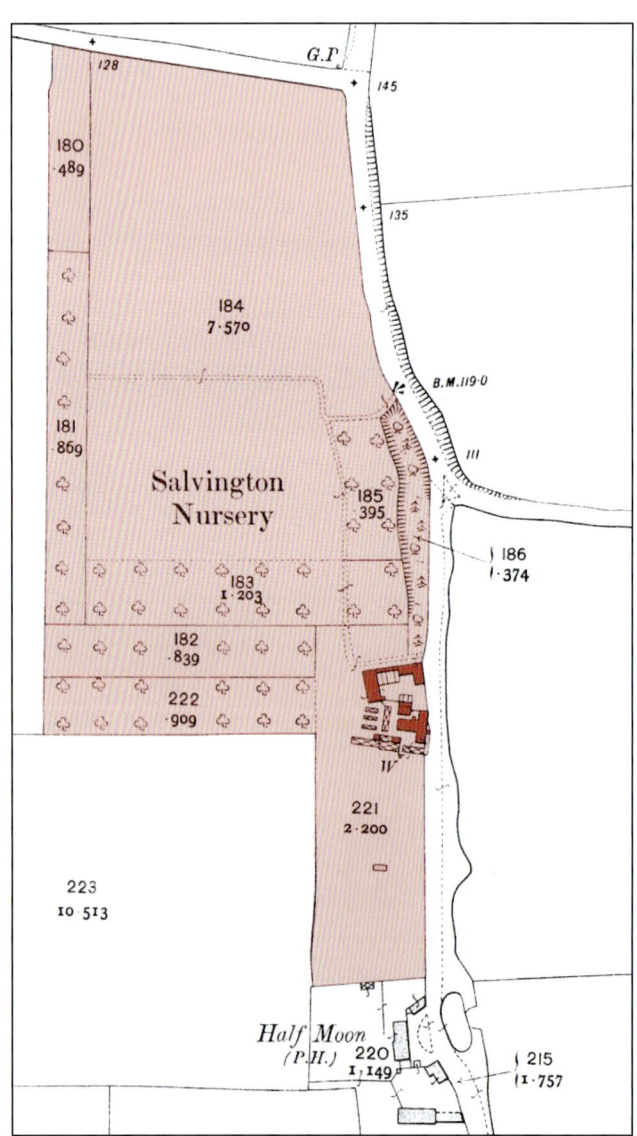

Excerpt taken from OS 25":1 mile Sheet LXIV: 10 3rd Edition (NTS)

[1] 1901 census RG13/957 ff.60 (TNA)
[2] 1881 census RG11/1088 ff.81 (TNA)
[3] 1901 census RG13/957 ff.60 (TNA)
[4] Worthing Gazette 3rd October 1906 p5
[5] Worthing Gazette 21st December 1910 p5
[6] 1911 census RG14/5342 sch 61 (TNA)
[7] 1911 census RG14/5215 sch 266 (TNA)
[8] IR58/94206 No. 7859 (TNA)
[9] www.britishlistedbuildings.co.uk viewed 16.01.2016 (No: 432522)
[10] Linfield p2-3
[11] www.britishlistedbuildings.co.uk viewed 21.06.2012 (No: 432523)
[12] 1901 census RG13/957 ff. 60 (TNA)
[13] Worthing Gazette 21st April 1909 p6
[14] 1911 census RG14/5342 sch 61(TNA)
[15] IR58/94206 No. 7864 (TNA)

Chapter 9
Arundel Road

Introduction

This is the main route between Worthing and Arundel and separates Durrington and Salvington to the south of the road from Coate Street and High Salvington to the north. Apart from Swandean and one other property there were no other inhabited properties on the road, but it was an important thoroughfare for coaches, ambulances, transportation of goods and general traffic travelling through this part of the county.

The crossroads on the Arundel Road showing High Salvington and Durrington Lane c1930.
Worthing Library

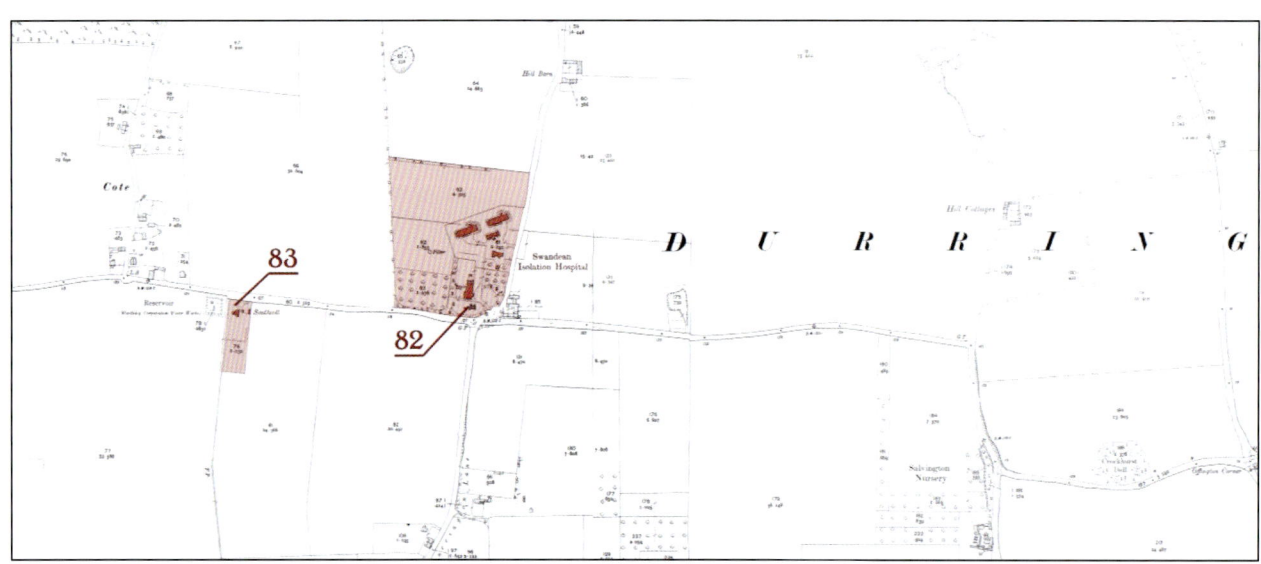

Excerpt taken from OS 25":1 mile Sheet LXIV: 5,6 3rd Edition 1912 (NTS)

82. Swandean Hospital, Arundel Road
(Now Swandean Hospital Site, Arundel Road)

During the Edwardian years this was an isolation hospital although it had not been built as a hospital. It was originally a private residence built in 1865[1] and owned jointly by J. E. Shelley and C. W. Dalbiac. It was sold in 1895 as part of the Durrington Estate sale of the same year and was purchased by Mr J. E. Fletcher.[2] In 1896 the house and over 6 acres of garden were leased by Mr Fletcher to Worthing Corporation enabling it to be used as a hospital. It was fairly soon afterwards that *Swandean*, being sited out of the town and in a fairly rural and isolated position at the foot of the downs, took on its Edwardian identity as an isolation hospital. Worthing Corporation finally purchased the house and its grounds in 1903 for a sum of £2,200.

The description of the house in 1895 is illustrated by the drawing found on the front of the sale catalogue:

The description inside the catalogue reads:

> *'It is of pleasing elevation, with Verandah along the South Front, and relieved by a Tower at one angle, the Walls being faced with Flints and prettily clad with creepers.'*[3]

A great deal of statistical and specific detail on the day to day issues of running *Swandean Hospital* can be discovered by reading the annual health reports produced for the county of West Sussex which are held in the local studies collection in Worthing Reference Library.[4] For the purpose of this book we will concentrate on the people who lived and worked at Swandean during the 1901 - 1913 period.

The 1901 census calls this simply *'Hospital'* and lists the head as Elizabeth Beck[5]. This lady's full name was **Elizabeth Fanny Beck** (b.1873), a Worthing lady employed for the task of running the hospital in 1897, even though she was not a professionally trained nurse.[6] With her were a married couple: **George Greenough** (b.1844) who worked as a gardener and his wife **Sarah Ann** (b.1845 nee Hoar) who was the housekeeper. This seems a very small staff for a working hospital but as they only had one patient listed on the 1901 census records, a young man named **Frederick Pitts** (b.1882) from Broadwater, they may not have needed more staff at the time. Other staff would probably have come in on a daily basis.

In 1905 Elizabeth Beck left to marry and *Swandean* employed its first qualified nurse, **Rose Agnes Hall** (b.1870), in the role of matron. As an isolation hospital in a single building, *Swandean* had its weaknesses as only one disease could be dealt with at any one time. This situation was greatly improved when in 1908 extra land was purchased and special buildings were erected north of the house. These buildings appear on the OS map below.

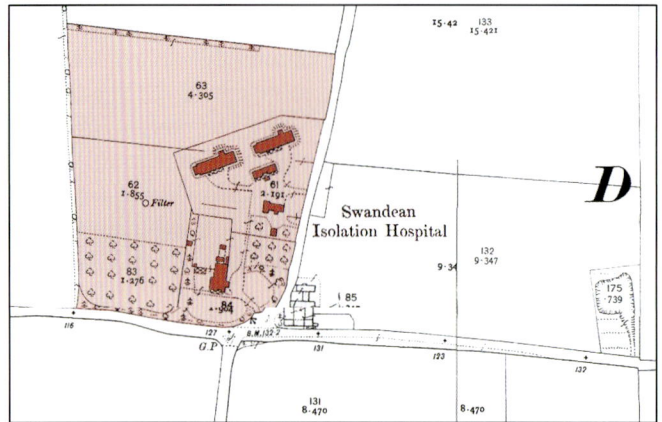

Excerpt taken from OS 25":1 mile Sheet LXIV: 5 3rd Edition 1912 (NTS)

The hospital was now able to house patients with different infections in different buildings while the main house was used for administration and staff accommodation.

By the 1911 census it is clear that the hospital is a larger establishment.[7] As well as the matron, Rose Hall, there are three qualified nurses: **Nellie Wace Hudson** (b.1886) born in Norfolk, **Margaret Ethel Deggar** (b.1885) born in Yorkshire and a lady originally from London named **Elsie Jane Saunders** (b.1890). There were a number of domestic staff consisting of a cook, **Laila Olseth Taylor** (b.1892), a laundress **Amelia Edith Fenson** (b.1881) and a wardmaid **Lily Burgin** (b.1884). There were four patients listed of which only one, **George Collins** (b.1896) came from Worthing or the surrounding area. The hospital clearly catered for those from further afield as well.

Modern photograph of *Swandean House* now used as offices for the hospital. © Dave Pryce 2016

83. Southcott, Arundel Road
(No longer standing)

The land on which this house was built was part of the portion of lane purchased by Mr Mills in 1895 when the Durrington Estate was auctioned for sale.[8] The Mills family had paid £7,000 for the complete parcel of land and then spent £900 building the property. The Inland Revenue Valuation describes the property as:

> 'Detached, modern, red brick house.
> Lounge, 1r(oom) k(itchen) Sc(ullery).
> 4 bed bath WC
> Stables & Coachhouse.'[9]

This was obviously a fairly large property on a good size piece of land. The valuation gives some interesting further details stating that included in the £900 cost of building was £43 5s spent on erecting fences around the boundary of the whole plot.

The first occupant, according to the electoral registers, was **Maurice Goodman.** Although he did not appear in street directories at the address until 1910 he was listed on the electoral registers as early as 1907 when he is listed at *South Cottage*, Furze Road, Coate, which is likely to have been an alternative name for *Southcott*. It is not clear exactly who this gentleman was but the 1911 census does list a solicitor, originally from Wiltshire, with the same name living in Worthing with his wife and daughter. This family could have made the move from *Southcott* to Worthing around 1910.[10]

The 1911 census lists the new householder, the head being an Australian *'French & Market Gardener'* named **James Christian Eisenhuth Lawson** (b.1855) born in Adelaide, Australia.[11] There is an interesting article in the Worthing Gazette in August 1910 which speaks of a connection between the previous occupant Maurice Goodman and James Lawson.[12] The article is reporting a request by letter to the Worthing Town Council made by Maurice Goodman for necessary piping to provide water for Mr Lawson's French gardening. One can only wonder if the previous occupant, a solicitor, was trying to help his replacement in the house to equip the property for the specialised gardening to be carried out at *Southcott*. Whatever the details of the story the occupancy of the house changed, Maurice Goodman moved on and James Lawson moved in.

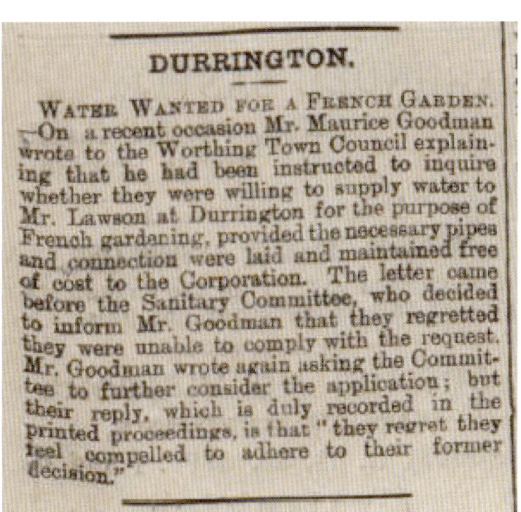

Request by Mr Goodman on behalf of Mr Lawson of *Southcott* in August 1910

In the house with him, according to the 1911 census, were his daughter **Sheila Eisenhuth** (b.1903), his aunt **Emily Lawson** (b.1843 nee Lewis) and a Spanish servant named **Adela Tarano.** (b.c1890). Both James Lawson and his aunt Emily claim on the census to be married although neither has their married partner in the house. Further investigation reveals that James had married a lady named **Mabel Emily** (b.1875 nee Lawson) in 1902 and it was her mother, Emily who was living at Southcott with James at the time. Emily Lawson had further stated on the census that she had been married for thirty eight years and with a little more investigation her husband can be traced to a house in Keymer, Sussex where he is living with James' wife Mabel and their young son Alistair C L W (b.1910).[13] It transpires that James had married his cousin, which explains the identical surnames, although the reason they were not with their partners remains unknown.

James does not appear on any other censuses suggesting he was not in England until after 1901 although the date of his marriage in 1902 and daughters birth in 1903 means that he must have arrived a short time after. The unusual Christian name of 'Eisenhuth' which both James and his daughter are registered with can be traced to James mother, as it was her maiden name.

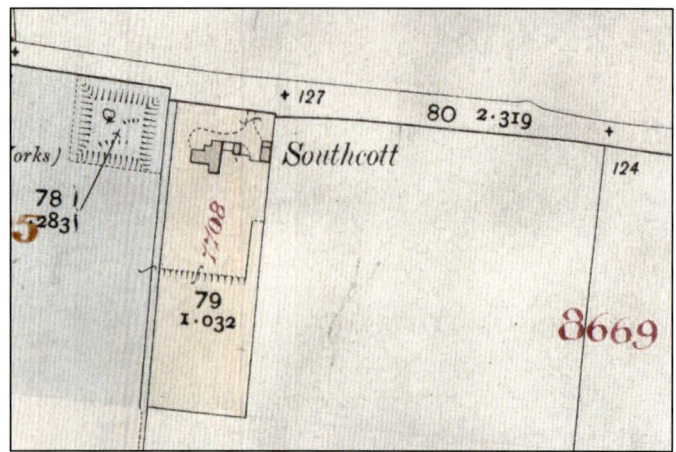

Excerpt taken from OS 25":1 mile Sheet LXIV: 5 3rd Edition 1912 (NTS)
Inland Revenue Valuation numbers added

---

[1] Elleray. p.83
[2] 'The Durrington Estate near Worthing' Sale Catalogue for auction held 4th July 1895 (Held at Worthing Reference Library. SC/WSL/000132a)
[3] 'The Durrington Estate near Worthing' Sale Catalogue for auction held 4th July 1895 (Held at Worthing Reference Library. SC/WSL/000132a)
[4] Annual Report on the Sanitary Condition of the Combined District of West Sussex… for the year (1900-1913 as well as other years are held at Worthing Reference Library.)
[5] 1901 census RG13/957 ff. 76 (TNA)
[6] Keech. p.75
[7] 1911 census RG14/5342 sch 95 (TNA)
[8] 'The Durrington Estate near Worthing' Sale Catalogue for auction held 4th July 1895 (Held at Worthing Reference Library. SC/WSL/000132a)
[9] IR58,94205 No. 7708 (TNA)
[10] 1911 census RG14/5338 sch 197 (TNA)
[11] 1911 census RG14/5342 sch 82 (TNA)
[12] Worthing Gazette 10th August 1910 p7
[13] 1911 census RG14/5025 sch 177 (TNA)

Chapter 10
Coate Street

Introduction

Coate Street is a single road leading from the Arundel Road northwards to an area called *Cote Bottom* and on into the farmland and fields of the South Downs. The hamlet of Coate, or Cote as it is sometimes written, nestles around the southernmost part of the road where numerous cottages and *Coate Farmhouse* stood in the Edwardian period. This chapter includes research and photography by Poppy Little (age 9).

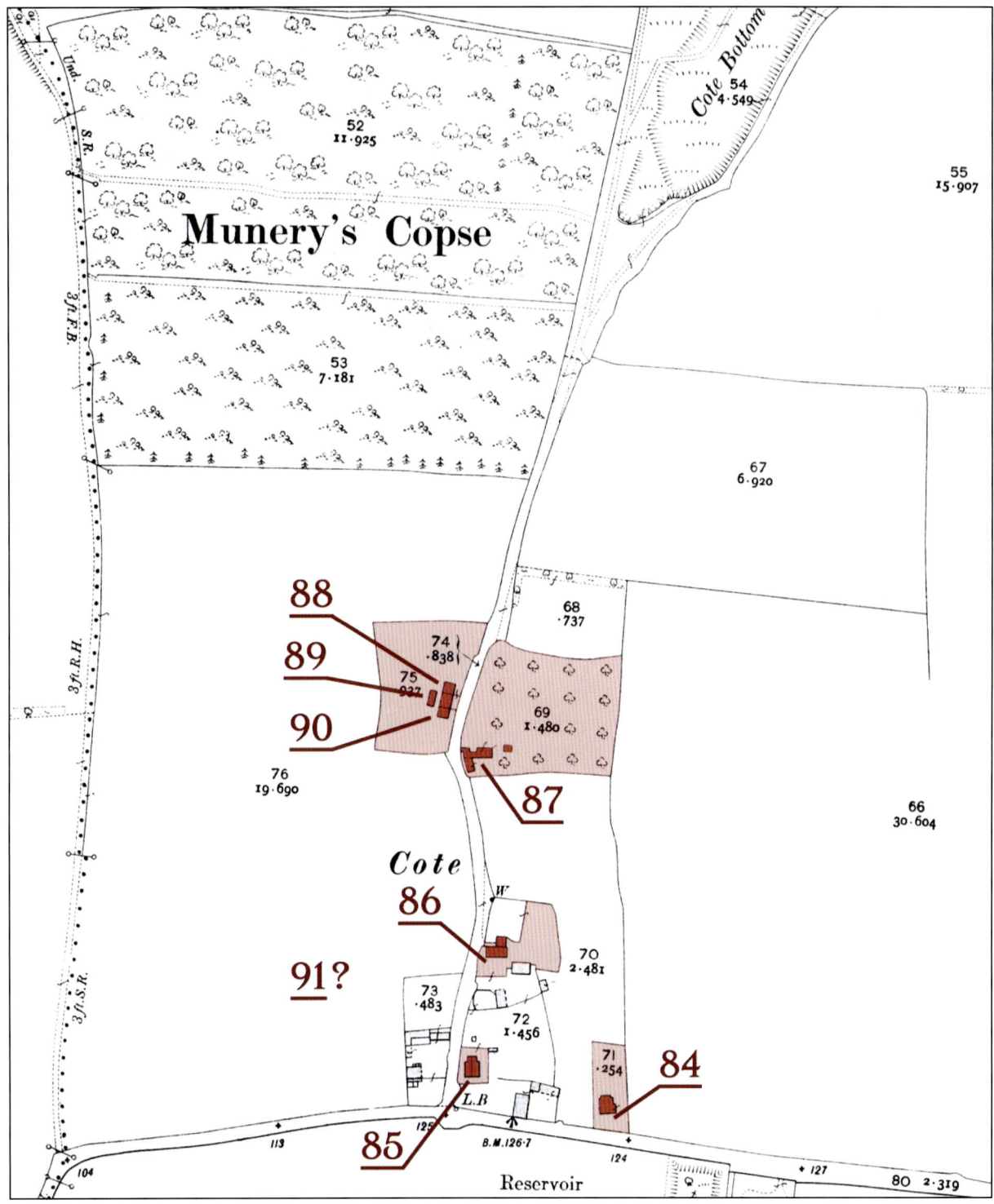

Excerpt taken from OS 25":1 mile Sheet LXIV:5 3rd Edition (NTS)

A Photograph of the north end of Coate Street. © Dave Pryce 2016

84. Coate Farm, Coate Street
(No longer standing)

This is a modern house built on the site of Coate Farm. © Poppy Little (age 9)

Coate Farm had been partially purchased in September 1892 by William Mills. The rest of the land he had continued to rent from Lady Somerset and in September 1902 he took out a 99 year lease on these rented areas securing his position on the farm. In January 1903 plans for the building of the farmhouse were passed by the East Preston Rural District Council.[1]

The farmhouse was described in the Inland Revenue Valuation as:

> *'Modern red brick house, rough cast, tile roof.*
> *1st floor. 3 bed W.C.*
> *Grd Floor. 2r(ooms) k(itchen) Sc(ullery) Dairy'*[2]

The house was entered from Arundel Road whilst all the farm buildings and fields spanned both sides of Coate Street. There was 66 acres of farmland, 11 acres of this were for pasture and the other 55 were arable. The farm also included a small carter's cottage although it has not been possible to trace who was living in this property.

The previous farmer, **Robert Holmes** (b.1825) had been resident at the farm before William Mills and as Poppy discovered he continued living at the farm, according to the 1911 census,[3] after the new farmer built the house and moved in:

> *'Robert Holmes, who was a retired farmer and landowner, was living as a lodger at Coate Farm. He was born in 1825 in Arundel and had run farms in other Sussex villages including a place called Littlehampton and another one called Bisham, near Yapton.'*

Robert had originally arrived at the farm in the mid-1800s, although as Poppy has stated, he had also worked farms elsewhere with his brother **Frederic** (b.1828). He was very involved in all aspects of village life and held office in the Durrington Parish Meeting, a forerunner of the Parish Council.

According to the 1901 census, **William Mills** (b.1845) lived at the farm with his wife **Elizabeth** (b.1855 nee Lord) whom he had married in 1886 and the previous farmer, Robert Holmes, who is often listed as *'retired'*.[4] William and Elizabeth only had one child who had died before the 1901 census was taken.

An event happened at the farm which was reported in the Worthing Gazette on the 3rd April 1901 (see below).[5] A fire which was begun by sparks from a chimney completely gutted three thatched cottages belonging to the farm. The article states that this fire occurred on a Wednesday meaning the probable date was 27th March, only a few days before the 1901 census was taken on the 31st March 1901.

The heart breaking story of loss is outlined in the newspaper article alongside the bravery and kindness of neighbours and the *'unaccountable delay'* of the fire brigade arriving from Worthing. The article is followed by a letter from Luke Leggett in his role as Chairman of the Durrington Parish Meeting, asking for donations to help the three families now left totally destitute.[6]

Two of the occupants of these cottages were **Mrs Jane Beaty** (b.c1822) and her grandson **(Walter) James Beaty** (b.1886), who were away at the time of the fire. James was employed by Edgar Overington at *The Forge* and was saving money from his wages. His savings of nearly £5 were destroyed in the fire which was quite a large sum for the time. The details for the Beaty family can be confirmed as they were living in the cottage at the time of the 1901 census.[7] Mr & Mrs Lambourne and child moved to *Hill Cottages* in High Salvington where they were living in 1911, but of Mr & Mrs Lillywhite we have discovered no further information.

The damage to the cottages was so severe that they were demolished and two new cottages, known as *Coate Cottages*, were erected using part of the site. The first listing of occupants occurred in directories and the census for 1911.

THE WORTHING GAZETTE.

DESTRUCTIVE FIRE at DURRINGTON.

Three Cottages Burnt Down.

Seven People Rendered Homeless.

THREE thatched cottages situated on Mr. Robert Holmes's farm at Coate, Durrington, were totally destroyed by fire on Wednesday afternoon. The outbreak is believed to be due to the circumstance that some sparks from one of the chimneys set fire to the thatched roof, which soon became ignited.

In the absence of any proper appliances it soon became evident that there was little chance of arresting the progress of the flames, and the neighbours and other willing helpers devoted their energies for the most part to saving the furniture, with the result that the greater part of the contents on the ground floors was saved from the flames.

AN UNACCOUNTABLE DELAY.

It was about two o'clock in the afternoon that the fire was discovered, but owing to some misunderstanding information of the outbreak did not reach Worthing till nearly five o'clock, with the result that by the time the Borough Fire Brigade, with their manual engine, arrived on the scene, the dwellings had been totally destroyed.

The greater portion of the furniture on the ground floors of the ill-fated houses was saved, but before the contents of the upper rooms could be removed to a place of safety the roof gave way, and consequently put a stop to the rescue work.

In the absence of Captain Crouch and the senior officers of the Brigade, Fireman G. H. Hunt was in charge of the firemen, the other members in attendance being Firemen H. E. Taylor, Longley, Hearsey, Burr, Burchell, Hide, Davidson and Stenning, and Messengers Bennett, Hews, and Peacock. Valuable assistance was rendered by Sergeant White, who turned out with the Fire Brigade on the engine.

THE INSURANCE.

The cottages, which were said to be valued at a total of £200, are understood to have been insured in the Royal Exchange Office, but the greater part of the furniture and contents was not insured.

Altogether seven people were rendered homeless, these being Mrs. Beaty and her grandson, James Beaty, Mr. and Mrs. Lambourne and child, and Mr. and Mrs. Lilywhite, but there was no lack of offers of temporary accommodation by the neighbours, who also assisted in no small degree in rescuing the furniture.

In the hurry and excitement of the moment the furniture and other belongings of Mrs. Beaty, who was away from home at the time, appear to have been overlooked until too late, and when the old lady, who is seventy-nine years of age, returned, she found her home completely destroyed, and herself and her orphan grandson left with practically nothing but the clothing which they stood up in. Mrs. Mills, one of the neighbours, kindly took Mrs. Beaty in; and Mr. Edgar Overington, in whose employment the grandson is, has taken charge of the boy. But in spite of this the fact still remains that they are

PRACTICALLY DESTITUTE,

and their case is certainly one that is deserving of public support.

The lad, who has evidently been taught the methods of thrift, had close on £5 in money carefully concealed in a chest of drawers in his grandmother's bedroom, but the flames unfortunately devoured this little hoarding.

Two or three people were more or less badly burnt, and one of them, Mr. Robert Searle, received such severe injuries that he had to be taken to the Infirmary, where he is, we are glad to state, making very satisfactory progress.

An Appeal to the Benevolent.

To the Editor of the GAZETTE.

DEAR SIR,—I should like to bring to the notice of your numerous readers the very sad cases of destitution resulting from the calamitous fire which occurred at Durrington on Wednesday last; and I think if the facts are known many will come forward and help.

As the result of the fire three farm cottages (the property of a neighbouring farmer) were burnt completely out. In all probability his loss is covered by insurance, but of the three families rendered homeless only one was insured.

An old lady nearly eighty years of age and her young grandson, an orphan, are, I believe the worst sufferers, for they have lost almost all, and the boy, who from his odd earnings had saved £5, has lost this, also in the flames. Another aged couple also had the greater part of their goods destroyed. The neighbours and friends in Durrington are at present housing and feeding the homeless until other arrangements can be made.

At the conclusion of the Parish Meeting held at Durrington on Friday evening last five of the ratepayers, including myself, formed ourselves into a working Committee for procuring help from the villagers; and I believe, Sir, if you will be good enough to publish this letter, many from the neighbourhood would be only too glad to render assistance.

Mr. Gay, of the Post Office, Durrington (a member of the Committee), has kindly consented to receive and acknowledge any donations that may be sent him.

Yours faithfully,
L. LEGGETT,
Chairman Durrington Parish Meeting.
Goring,
April 2nd, 1901.

Details of the fire and letter printed in the local newspaper asking for donations to help the families after the fire as reported in Worthing Gazette in April 1901

85. No's 1 & 2 Coate Cottages, Coate Street
(Now No's 1 & 2 Coate Cottages, Coate Street)

Poppy Little describes these two cottages:

> 'These are two old cottages built after the other cottages built near here burned down. The 1911 census says that **Mr. Jack Lock** (b.1885) lived in the house on the left, which is number 1 Coate Cottages, with his wife **Florence May** (b.1885) and their daughter **Alice Florence** (b.1909). Jack's job was a basket maker. The census also said that **Mr. Claude Field** (b.1887) lived in the house next door, which is

*number 2 Coate Cottages, with his wife **Fanny** (b.1883) and son **Victor** (b.1910). His job is to look after the horses in the racing stables probably at Findon.'*

The Inland Revenue Valuation gives further details about the cottages recording that they were *'....a pair of cottages, rendered. 3 bed.....'.*[8] By April 1913 when the valuation took place, the Lock family had left as their name was crossed through and the surname *'Heather'* was written in. A street directory entry for 1912-1913 tells us that this name was **G. Heather**, but no further detail has yet been discovered. The names of the other inhabitants are not found elsewhere except on the 1911 census.

No's *1 & 2 Coate Cottages* in 2014.   © Poppy Little (age 9)

86. Cottages, Coate Street
(Now Fig Tree, No 8 Coate Street)

These are two cottages that belonged to *Coate Farm*. The cottages would have been standing in 1901 but it has not proved possible to confirm who was resident at the time from the census. The Inland Revenue Valuation describes them as *'old boulder built cottages, walls badly bulged in places.'* The larger of the two cottages sits sideways onto the road; this is how Poppy has recorded the building:

> *'This is a very old cottage made of flint and brick. The 1911 census says that **Mark Saunders**, who was a French gardener, lived here with his wife **Ellen** and three sons, **Alfred**, **Horace** and **Mark**.[9] French gardening is a style of gardening using many shaped hedges and bushes made to look like architecture, with everything having a perfect shape. Mark Saunders had moved to this house in Coate in 1907 from Durrington Street.'*

Attached to the rear of the cottage is another small cottage shown in the photograph (below) and described by Poppy:

> *'You can see in the photograph on the next page that there is a tiny black cottage that is attached to the back of Mr. Saunders' cottage. In 1911 **Frederick Lucas** (b.1884) and his family lived here.[10] And he looked after the roads. Frederick had only been married for two years and lived in this cottage with his wife **Mabel Florence** (b.1890 nee Saunders) and their two children **Alice Ann** (b.1909) and **George Henry** (b.1910).'*

The tiny black cottage attached to the rear is clearly seen in this photograph. © Poppy Little (age 9)

Frederick did indeed look after the roads his occupation being given as *'Road Foreman'* working for West Sussex County Council in 1911.[11]

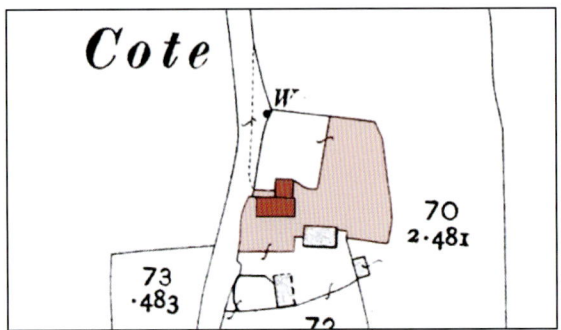

Excerpt taken from OS 25":1 mile Sheet LXIV: 5 3rd Edition 1912 (NTS)

Photograph of the beautiful cottage that sits sideways onto the road in Coate Street. © Poppy Little 2014 (age 9)

87. Castle View, Coate Street
(No longer standing)

This was a three-bedroomed house built of red brick which had a boulder built shop and small cottage attached to it. It is described on the Inland Revenue Valuation in some detail:

'Gd Floor, Shop. 2r K(itchen) Sc(ullery) built of red bricks. Shop boulder built fairly old.
3 bed
Cottage attached. 2r(ooms)
Large Orchard'

Unfortunately no date of building is mentioned.[12] The first date when documentary evidence has so far been discovered is in a newspaper advert from 1907 when *Castle View* was advertising furnished apartments for the winter months.[13] There is no name of occupant included with this advert but the Inland Revenue Valuation has a previous occupant crossed out which looks like *'Elgayder'*. This name is unknown in the area.

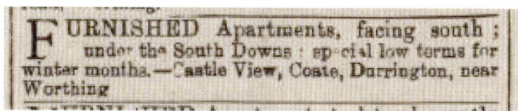

Advert for furnished apartments at *Castle View* in 1907

According to the 1911 census the head of the family in residence at the time was (**Ernest**) **Alfred Bish** (b.1872) who was listed as a poultry farmer.[14] He lived in the house with **Jessie Bertha** (b.1868 nee Rutherford) his wife and four children: **Ernest Alfred** (b.1895), **Gladys Bertha** (b.1897), **Doris Marjorie** (b.1903) and **Phyllis Mary** (b.1909). Alfred had previously lived in West Tarring where he was employed as an upholsterer but had moved to Coate at some time between the censuses. We know, from adverts regularly appearing in the newspapers, that at this time the property was continuing to rent rooms and was also working as a tea room.

Even with the various business opportunities the property offered the family it was not a financial success and a notice for bankruptcy appeared in the London Gazette on the 26th May 1911.[15]

In the notice the property address is given as *'Castle View Tea Rooms'* suggesting that this was the main occupation of the couple. It would appear that Mr Bish was prepared to turn his hand to various occupations; he was at times an upholsterer, poultry farmer and tea shop proprietor.

Alfred continued to be listed at this address in electoral registers through to the end of the period. Sadly in 1914 Jessie died although Alfred did later re-marry.

Modern house built on the old site of *Castle View*.
This property still uses the same house name. ©Poppy Little (age9)

Travelling up Coate Street there was a further row of three cottages sitting on the western side of the road at the top of the range of inhabited buildings. They were simply known as *1, 2 & 3 Coate Street,* all three being owned by *Holt Farm* in Clapham. We know the inhabitants of all three cottages in 1911 but certain identification from the earlier censuses has not proved so conclusive. Possible names of family residents include **Clement and Jane Searle** and **James and Edith Knight,** all listed on the 1901 census with their families but not yet identified to a specific property.[16]

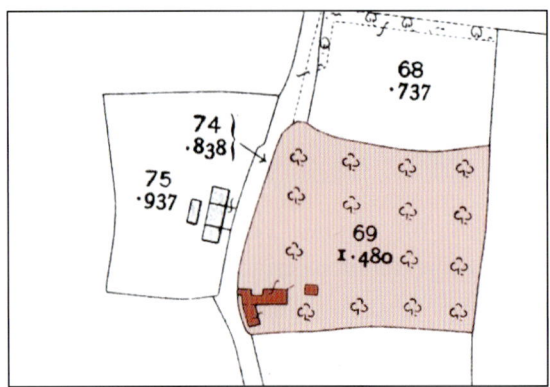

Excerpt taken from OS 25":1 mile Sheet LXIV: 5 3rd Edition 1912 (NTS)

The three cottages that are still there, 1 – 3 Coate Street. © Poppy Little (age 9)

88. No 1 Coate Street
(Now No 1 Coate Street)

There is no confirmation of the early occupants of this property but we do know that No 1 was the home of the Goatcher family in 1911.[17] The head of the family was a widower named **William Marner Goatcher** (b.1861) who may have been listed as a boarder on the 1901 census where a game keeper with the same name was living in Durrington Street.[18] Street directories begin to list him at *1 Coate Street* from as early as 1902. In 1901 William had married **Beatrice Parker** (b.c1860) on the 21st May 1901 in Findon where her family lived. The bride had been working in Worthing as a cook at the home of a local brewer and his family.[19] William and Beatrice were in their late thirties and forties when the marriage occurred and when their daughter was born the following year, unfortunately Beatrice did not survive the birth. She was buried in April 1902 whilst William's daughter **Beatrice Alice** (b.1902) was baptised in Durrington four months later. There was also a widowed lady named **Elizabeth Brown** (b.c1852) living in the house in 1911 as a housekeeper.

William Goatcher organising matches for Durrington cricket Club in 1904

William was working as a poultry keeper whilst they were living in Coate Street and was holding the post of Honorary Secretary of the very active Durrington Cricket Club in 1904 when he was recorded in the local paper seeking matches with other small clubs in the area.[20]

Modern photograph of *1 Coate Street*. © Dave Pryce 2016

89. No 2 Coate Street
(Now No 2 Coate Street)

This was the middle of the three cottages and was a substantially larger property than the cottages adjoining it at each end. It was described in the Inland Revenue Valuation as:

'One of a block of 3……..4 bed,
3 rooms 3/- a week
   This cottage probably belonged to Green Bros formerly, they have exchanged a cottage recently.'[21]

This reveals some useful information. The occupiers of *Holt Farm* were the Green brothers; which explains the note regarding the exchange of a cottage. It appears from the record that three rooms were being rented out for the sum of 5/- a week but to whom we are not told. The valuation record gives the occupier as Mr Woods which is confirmed on the 1911 census and the last interesting fact is that this cottage came with *'Shooting rights'*.

The 1911 census gives more detail on the family at the time.[22] The head was **Alfred James P Woods** (b.1866) who had moved to the address from Cootham, Storrington some years after the 1901 census was taken. He was working as a market gardener and living with his wife **Emily Jane** (b.1867 nee Parks) and eight children. Emily was Alfred's second wife so of the eight children mentioned on the 1911 census, Emily was the mother of the youngest **Lilian** (b.1898), **Allen** (b.1902), **Bertha** (b.1903), **Violet Emily** (b.1904), **Kathleen Dora** (b.1905) and **Alfred** (b.1908). The two older boys **Arthur** (b.1893) and **Edwin** (b.1896) being from his first marriage to **Sarah Merritt** from Storrington.

On October 22nd 1913 the Worthing Gazette had a report under the title *'Before the Bench'*.[23] A young man named **Luke Woods** was on leave from his regiment which was based in Woking, Surrey. He had obviously failed to return from leave on time and been found at Coate Street by a Sergeant Gilbert. Mr Woods' defence was that he had *'lost'* his train. One can only wonder what he meant by that phrase! He was, according to the report, due to be leaving England with his regiment in the next few days. He was probably a relative of the Woods family in No 2 although no connection has yet been traced.

There are some interesting facts found in this article. It is stated that Luke Woods was a soldier in the *'Second Sussex'* and that they were *'for the draft for India next Wednesday'*. This was absolutely true as the 2nd Battalion of the Royal Sussex Regiment did go to India where they spent the next few years in Peshawar, not returning to England until after the First World War.

The soldier, Luke Woods, before the bench for late return to his regiment in October 1913.

Modern photograph of No 2 *Coate Street*. © Dave Pryce 2016

90. No 3 Coate Street
(Now No 3 Coate Street)

Number 3 had been the home of members of the Clevitt (Clevett/Clevatt) family for many years. The first generation of the family to live in the property were **Reuben Clevett** (b.1867) and his wife **Emma (Emily) Jane** (b.1869 nee Long). Reuben had first been listed in Coate Street on the 1891 census,[24] having married Emma in 1888. They had most probably made this their first home and it was here their children were born: **Emily Ann** (b.1889), **Kate** (b.1891), **Alice Mary** (b.1893), **Reuben** (b. 1895/6) and **George Laban** (b.1901).

The cottage changed inhabitants around 1904 when Reuben and his family emigrated to Canada. Although the cottage changed householder it was Reuben's widowed aunt, **Jane Clevitt** (b.1855 nee Braby) from Angmering, who moved in with four of her children and two grandchildren. It is this family that is recorded on the 1911 census.[25] Jane was the second wife of **Charles Clevett** (b.1828) whom she had married in Angmering in 1876. Charles' first wife **Mary** (b.1852 nee Green) had died in 1874 and left Charles as a widower with six children to raise. He had married Jane two years later and they went on to have nine children of their own whom all survived. His children with Jane were **Charles** (b.1876), **William** (b.1878), **Harriet** (b.1880), **Mary** (b.1882), **Edith Emily** (b.1884), **Jane Elizabeth** (b.1887), **Herbert Daniel** (b.1888) who was blind, **Mabel Annie** (b.1891) and **Alfred Henry** (b.1894).

Jane had worked in domestic service when she was old enough and, while working in Storrington, had become pregnant and given birth to a little girl named **Florence Elizabeth** (b.1905). Florence's father, **Walter Medhurst**, had refused to accept the situation and Jane took him to court in an attempt to gain finance to raise the child. The case was reported in the local paper which reveals the whole story.[26] Jane won the case and for the next fourteen years was to receive 2s 6d a week from Walter Medhurst towards Florence's upbringing. All was not to run smoothly however as Walter, who was only seventeen at the time of the *'familiarity'*, did not pay her the maintenance money. His uncle had tried to buy Jane off with a lump sum and she, not accepting the money, proceeded to take him back to court for the sum of ten shillings which had so far not been paid.[27]

The court case report in May 1906

By the 1911 census Florence was still living with her grandparents in Coate Street and attending Durrington Council School. Her mother Jane was not in the house, she may have been working in service elsewhere.

In later years we find that another of the Clevitt children was mentioned in the newspaper but this time for a very different reason. One of their sons, Herbert, who had been listed on the 1911 census as *'blind'*, had trained as a shoe repairer and was the subject of an article in the Worthing Gazette in December 1925 highlighting the work of blind people in an exhibition held in the town.[28] The article refers to *'H. D. Clevitt of Coate'* which must surely have been the same person.

The Inland Revenue Valuation describes the building and confirms the occupant was *'Clevitt'*. It was *'The southern of a block of 3 cottages.......red brick & tile, good substantial repair.'* with two bedrooms on the first floor and two rooms

Continuing story of the dispute over maintenance for Jane Clevitt's daughter

and a scullery on the ground floor.²⁹ The family must have managed to all live in this small cottage but living conditions cannot have been very comfortable.

Modern photograph of 2 *Coate Street*. © Dave Pryce 2016

91. Oaks Barn, Coate Street
(Not identified)

This building is listed on the 1901 census giving **Richard Hunt** (b.c1858) as the head of the household.³⁰ Richard was listed as a labourer on the farm. This may give us a clue that it was one of the small cottages around *Coate Farm* or it may have been part of one of the farm barns standing in Coate Street. An exact identification has so far not been possible. Richard lived in the property with his wife **Lizzie** (b.c1866 nee Marden) who states she was born in Rutland and their nine year old son **John** (b.1891). Apart from entries for a Richard Hunt in street directories between 1911 and 1913 no other documentation for this family has been found.

The view from Coate Street looking west showing the Coach & Horses in the centre. © Poppy Little (age9)

[1] EDRP Minutes 31st January 1903 p.20
[2] IR58/94204 No. 7678 (TNA)
[3] 1911 census RG14,5342 sch 176 (TNA)
[4] 1901 census RG13/957 ff.80 (TNA)
[5] Worthing Gazette 3rd April 1901 p2
[6] Worthing Gazette 3rd April 1901 p2
[7] 1901 RG13/957 ff.80 (TNA)
[8] IR58/94204 No 7676 & 7677 (TNA)
[9] 1911 census RG14/5342 sch 88 (TNA)
[10] 1911 census RG14/5342 sch 89 (TNA)
[11] 1911 census RG14/5342 sch 89 (TNA)
[12] IRT58/94204 No. 7681 (TNA)
[13] Worthing Gazette 3rd July 1907
[14] 1911 census RG14/5342 sch 90 (TNA)
[15] The London Gazette 26th May 1911 p.4055
[16] 1901 census RG13/957 ff. 80 (TNA)
[17] 1911census RG14/5342 sch 94 (TNA)
[18] 1901 census RG13/957 ff.76 (TNA)
[19] 1901 census RG13/958 ff.60 (TNA)
[20] Worthing Gazette 1st June 1904 p2
[21] IR58/94205 No. 7671 & 7671a (TNA)
[22] 1911 census RG14/5342 sch 93 (TNA)
[23] Worthing Gazette October 22nd 1913 p5
[24] 1891 census RG12/837 ff.136 (TNA)
[25] 1911 census RG14/5342 sch 92 (TNA)
[26] Worthing Gazette 23rd May 1906, p5
[27] Worthing Gazette 4th July 1906 p7
[28] Worthing Gazette 9th December 1925 p3
[29] IR58/94205 No 7670 (TNA)
[30] 1901 census RG13/957 ff.80 (TNA)

Chapter 11
High Salvington

Introduction

High Salvington is the name given to the stretch of land lying to the north of the Arundel Road which encompasses the hamlet of Cote (Coate). At the turn of the century there were very few inhabited homes on this land which stretched northwards across the South Downs towards Findon. Cote was its own little hamlet nestled around Cote Farm and details can be found in the chapter dedicated to it. Swandean Hospital, by far the largest property in the area, had its main entrance in Arundel Road and is therefore included with the chapter on Arundel Road.

Postcard sent in September 1913 showing one of the typical views from High Salvington. Worthing Library

High Salvington was the site of the windmill which stood further north from Swandean and apart from a few farm cottages and the beginning of a few private houses the area was mostly downland and fields belonging to the farms of the area. As the Edwardian period unfolded the situation in High Salvington underwent changes. Much of the land had been purchased in 1887 by **Colonel F. T. Wisden** and when he died in October 1904 it had passed, as part of the inheritance, to his son, **Frederick Wisden.** In 1906 Frederick sold large parcels of the land in High Salvington and the building of houses and bungalows that followed this sale began to substantially change the landscape. By far the largest land purchaser in 1906 was Alfred Jackson from Worthing who not only bought the High Salvington Windmill site but obtained over twenty acres of other land which he proceeded to develop into housing.

Alfred Charles Jackson (b.1868) pictured right, came from a Quaker family originally from London, where his father **Thomas Jackson** had worked as a commercial traveller and tea dealer. The 1891 census lists Alfred living in London with his parents where his occupation is given as a 'Scientific Instrument Maker'.[1] Also in the house was a housekeeper named **Ida Edith Ablitt** (b.1866) who later, in 1894, became Alfred's wife and by 1901 the couple had moved to Worthing to live in their first house in Homefield Road.[2] They later moved to live in High Salvington in one of the properties owned by Alfred called *The Nest*.

Alfred was to make a great success of his life here in Worthing where he not only became an early property developer in High Salvington but also held political positions within the town. He died in 1943 and his obituary in the Worthing Gazette at the time of his death outlined the Durrington and Salvington connection very clearly. It states that he:

> '...bought a large amount of land in the Durrington district, including the Mill. He was responsible for the development of that part of the Borough, as he built many houses there, and also gave Durrington its original water supply by means of an artesian well on the hill.'[3]

His political career in the town began in 1907 when he was first elected to the town council. He continued in this role until he retired in 1921 when the family emigrated to Canada. In 1933 he returned to Worthing and moved back to High Salvington. He was again elected to the council, later becoming an alderman.

As the new homes were built and occupied the area became known as a fashionable place to visit, both for the views from Salvington Hill and for the delicacies of the tea-rooms which had begun to spring up. The countryside around the area was, and still is, very beautiful and its charms were well recognised; not to mention the superior black-berrying that was advertised at the appropriate time of the year.[4]

SALVINGTON.

BLACKBERRYING ON THE DOWNS.—The cosy tea room in the interior of the old windmill on Salvington Hill still remains open, and the proprietor declares, as a special reason for a visit, that the finest blackberries in Sussex are to be obtained on that section of the Downs.

Tea Rooms in The Mill being advertised at the time of the Blackberry harvest in September 1910

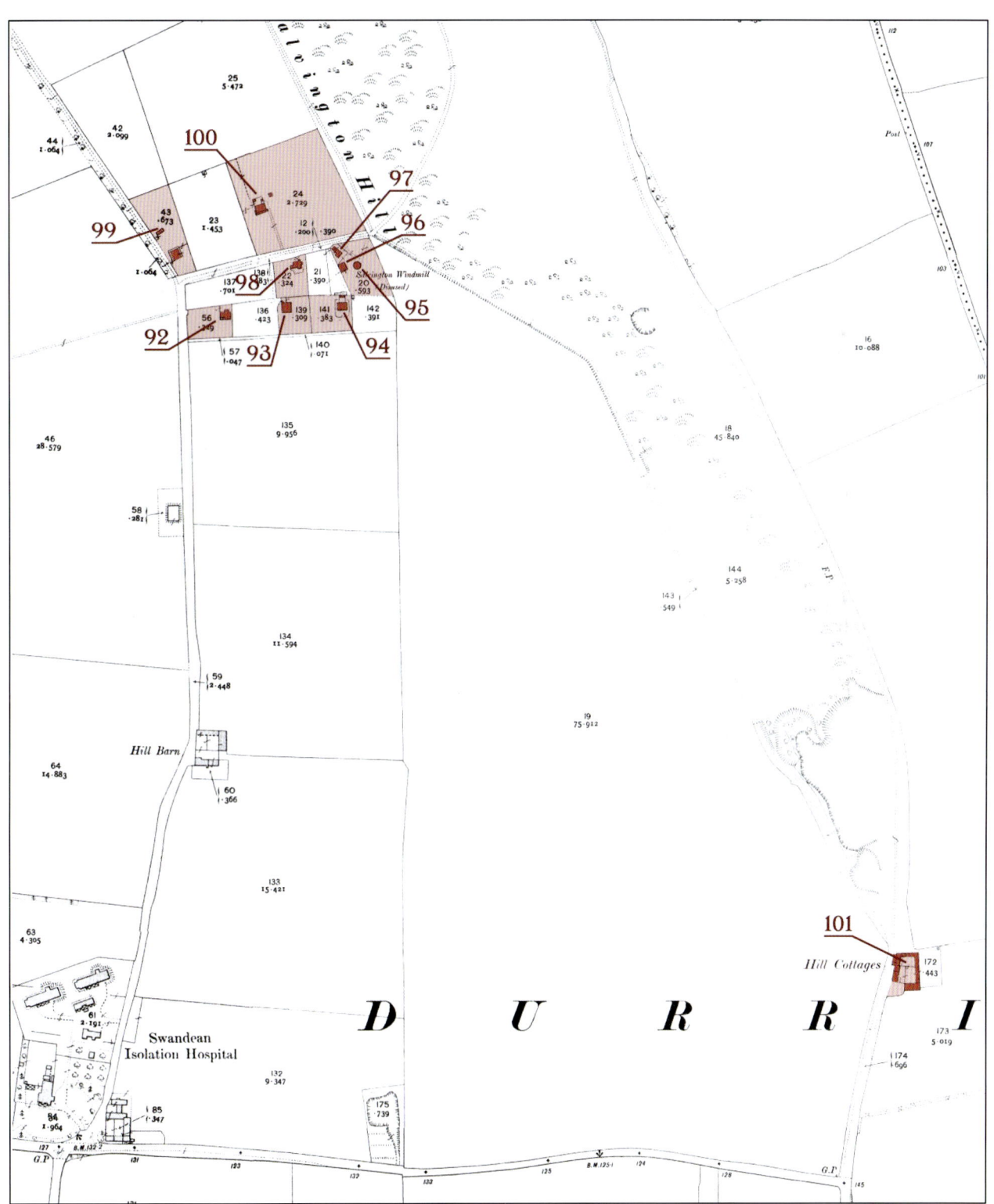

Excerpt taken from OS 25":1 mile Sheet LXIV: 1,2,5,6 3rd Edition 1912 (NTS)

92. Castle Bungalow, Salvington Hill
(Now No 96 Little Castle, Salvington Hill)

The date of the building of this property is not known but the land was part of that purchased, along with other land, by Alfred Jackson in 1906 for £185.

Castle Bungalow was a single storey bungalow which had been built at a cost of £343 7s 11d. Details of its occupants come from sources other than the 1911 census where, although it is listed in the summary books, it was recorded as *'Uninhabited'*.[5]

The Inland Revenue Valuation describes it as:

> *'Detached superior bungalow, b(ric)k & tile.*
> *4 r(ooms) K(itchen) Sc(ullery) verandah.'*[6]

The description is dated June 1913 and the valuation record lists **Dundeval, H** as the occupier at the time, nothing more is known of this person. The street directories between 1911 and 1913 list an occupier named Miss M Trapp and the address as *Little Castle.* The address and name appears only on the electoral register for 1913 and confirms that her name was **Miss Mary Trapp**. This name does not appear in any other source at the time.

Photograph of *Little Castle* the building that now stands on the site of *Castle Bungalow*. © Lyn Tiller 2016

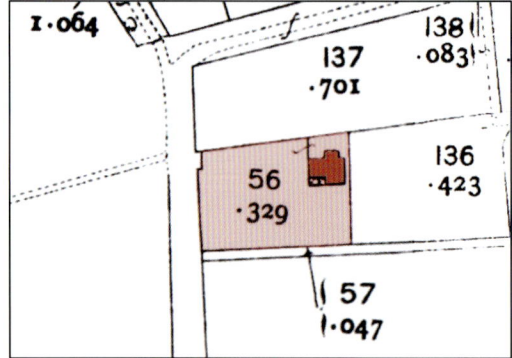

Excerpt taken from OS 25":1 mile Sheet LXIV: 5 3rd Edition 1912 (NTS)

93. Downlands, Salvington Hill
(Now a development of 7 houses called Downlands, Firsdown Close)

This was another property owned by Alfred Jackson listed on the 1911 census where the address is given as Salvington Hill. Other sources, including the street directories, were sometimes beginning to use the new name for this part of High Salvington and called it Furze Road.

The 1911 census gives the head of the household as **Francis Hamley Fawkes** (b.1879) originally from Buckinghamshire.[7] On 31st October 1908 he had married **Edith Mary** (b.c1878 nee Underwood) by special licence in London. This is an interesting marriage as the details recorded on the 1911 census records show. Edith had been born in India and the couple must have gone abroad fairly soon after their marriage as their young son, **Hamley Fawkes** (b.c1909) had his place of birth listed as *'Rhodesia'*. We do not know what Francis' occupation was, the census merely records that he was living on *'Private Means'*. His family were military, his father having been a Major in the British Army, which may explain the links with India and Rhodesia.

There is a wonderful little snippet in the Worthing Gazette revealing just a little about the life of the Fawkes family at *Downlands*. They were the owners of a Great Dane dog which had bitten a lady in High Salvington and Francis wrote an *'Explanatory'* in the newspaper assuring people that it was now safe to return to the area as the dog had been *'sent to London to live permanently,'*. There is no indication of how serious the bite was or if there had been any provocation which resulted in the action of the dog.[8]

Mr Fawkes and his Great Dane
Worthing Gazette March 1911

By May 1912 Francis Fawkes was advertising the bungalow for rent and we know from the Inland Revenue Valuation that they left around this period as their name does not appear on the valuation record either as present or previous occupiers.

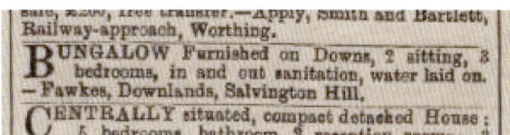

Downlands being offered for rent in May 1912

The Inland Revenue Valuation does not give any details of land purchase date or the price of building the bungalow but does give a description of the actual property:

> *'brick and rough cut Bungalow, good appearance.*
> *4 rooms. K(itchen) Sc(ullery) WC. Verandah'*[9]

The previous occupier listed at this time is **C. Home** which had been crossed through and the surname of **Ball** or **Bull** pencilled in. The name of C. Home is probably the proprietor of the *Windmill Tea Rooms* at the time, (as discussed below with the windmill) and the occupier of the house next door: *Dunkeld*. We know nothing of any other occupants.

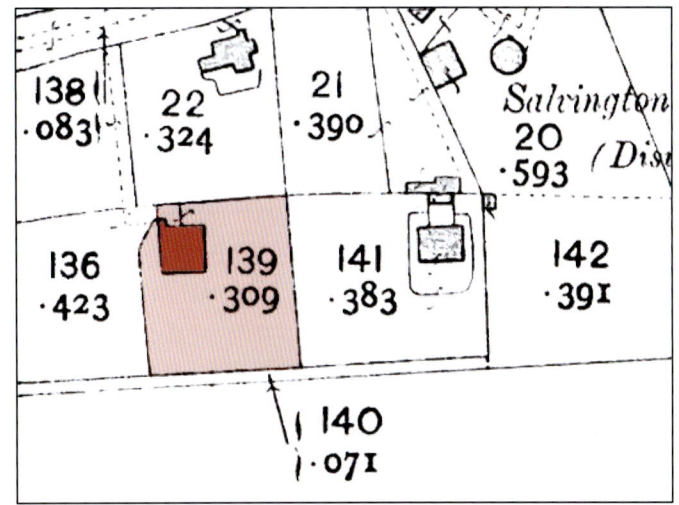

Excerpt taken from OS 25":1 mile Sheet LXIV: 6 3rd Edition 1912 (NTS)

New houses, retaining the name of *Downlands,* stand on the site of the original house. © Lyn Tiller 2016

94. The Nest, Salvington Hill
(Now Priory Cottage, Furze Road)

This was another of the properties owned by Alfred Jackson and was the house that he chose to make his family home around 1911. The census summary books record the property as another of the *'Uninhabited'* sites in High Salvington at the time when the census was taken although the family must have moved in soon afterwards as Alfred is listed at *The Nest* in both street directories and electoral registers from 1911 onwards.

Jackson had bought this land in 1906 along with other plots but we do not yet know in which order the properties were built on the land. The cost of development of this site is known in great detail as the Inland Revenue Valuation tells us that £413 11s 11d was spent on the property. Such detail may reflect Mr Jackson's book-keeping style or the need for accuracy on the valuation record, but it would be intriguing to know what resulted in the last 11d of expenditure.

The property as described shows that it was of a higher than average size and standard, a fitting building for Mr Jackson to make his home:

> *'Detached bungalow, superior appearance, rough cut & tiled*
> *One large sitting room. 3 bed, K(itchen) & Sc(ullery) combined*
> *outbuildings, WC. Coal shed*
> *Rainwater tank & cesspool'*[10]

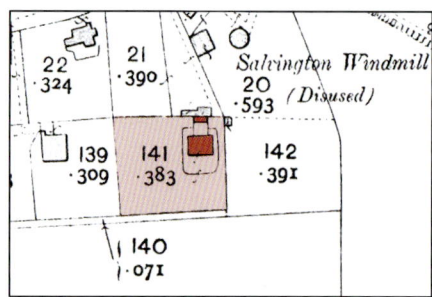

Excerpt taken from OS 25":1 mile Sheet LXIV: 6 3rd Edition 1912 (NTS)

The Nest has now been incorporated into this larger home called *Priory Cottage*. © Lyn Tiller 2016

95. High Salvington Windmill & Tea Rooms, Salvington Hill (including Salvington Mill Cottage and The Retreat)
(Only the Windmill is still standing, off Furze Road)

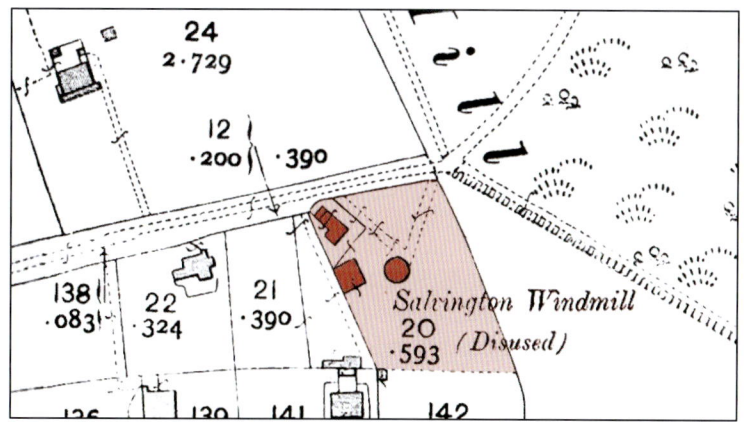

Excerpt taken from OS 25":1 mile Sheet LXIV: 2,6 3rd Edition 1912 (NTS)

Salvington Windmill as it is seen today © David Nicholls 2014

By September 1897 the windmill had ceased to work as a full-time mill, although it was still producing small amounts of animal feed. It was owned at the time by **Colonel F. T. Wisden** who had originally purchased it in 1887. When he died in October 1904 it had passed, as part of the inheritance, to his son, **Frederick Wisden.** When Frederick sold some of the land the windmill was included in the twenty acres or more purchased by Alfred Jackson, who later moved from Homefield Road, Worthing to live in *The Nest,* next door to the windmill site.

The windmill is still standing today and is a Grade II listed building. This listing was first registered as early as 1949 where it describes the windmill before all the restoration work was carried out by the High Salvington Mill Trust.[11] The description is a little out-of-date, as it mentions only three 'sweeps', the name given to the sails, and not the complete four sweeps of the restored building today:

> *'Originally Durrington Mill but now usually called Salvington Mill, as it is actually in High Salvington which did not exist when the mill was built. Post type with round house and fantail, (the round house modernised and windows inserted). Date 1700 over door. Timbers tarred. 3 sweeps intact, one missing. Machinery of the mill in working order.'*[12]

At the turn of the twentieth century the windmill included a wooden round house which had been functioning as a small tea room run by the last miller, Stephen Scutt and his wife in an effort, no doubt, to supplement their income.

When the Scutt family moved down into Salvington and the whole site was purchased by Alfred Jackson many changes took place. The East Preston Rural District minutes record the planning permission given to Mr Jackson for the alterations at the windmill to begin. On 16th April 1907 the following plans were passed:

> *'Alterations to Salvington Mill Durrington for Mr A. C. Jackson subject to drainage being carried out to the satisfaction of the Building Surveyor.'*[13]

Jackson had the old wooden round house demolished and a new concrete replacement built. The name of **Fletcher Cole** (b.1848) is first mentioned in connection with this re-building. In 1907 his name appears in a newspaper article discussing the excellent workmanship demonstrated in the newly built bungalows:

> *'....and if there should be any demand for them (the bungalows) it will probably be found that Mr F. Cole, who has carried out the structural part of the work, will find his services in this direction in further request.'*[14]

Fletcher Cole was a master carpenter who was only in the area for a short few years between two censuses. In 1901 he was listed on the census in Suffolk[15] whilst by 1911 the census records him living in Essex.[16] He was not only an important worker on this and other sites in High Salvington he must also have lived on or near the Windmill as he is listed at the *Windmill Tea Shop* in a street directory for 1909. There is another lady associated with the tea shop whose surname is Cole, she was possibly related in some way to Fletcher Cole, although her familial connection has not yet been discovered. A Miss Cole appears in adverts of the period as the *'proprietress'* of the tea shop.[17] [18]

The *Salvington Mill Tea Rooms* was a popular visiting place and often advertised and spoken of favourably in the local press.[19]

By 1910 the name of Cole has disappeared from the directories and the **Misses Darker** and **Homes** are listed as proprietors of the tea rooms. The two ladies are also listed as the occupants of the property next door called *Dunkeld.*

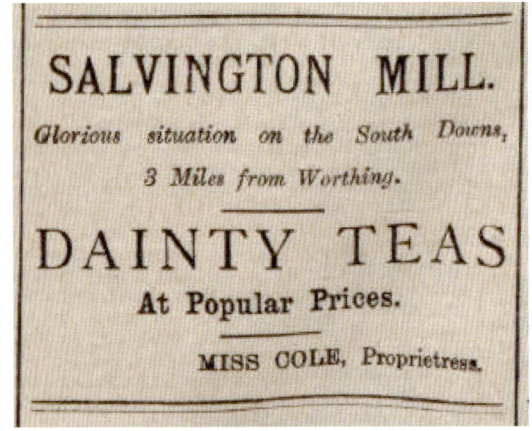

Miss Cole as proprietress of the tea rooms at *Salvington Mill Tea Rooms* in October 1907

The Inland Revenue Assessment for the complete windmill site is quite detailed:

'Property consists of an old Windmill, which has been repaired and there has been erected at foot a one storey circular building now used as a tea rooms. This building is well built and some underpinning was (unreadable word) and necessary before it could be built.

There is an old cottage, built of b(ric)k & partly of timber containing 3 roomsK(itchen). Sc(ullery). 2 ? C's. Water tank underground cost about £20. (PTO)

A newer building is a one storey cottage 'The Retreat' containing one room, small kitchen & large verandah in front. well built of brick.

There are altogether 3 tanks on the property & a cesspool.

Together with this property goes the right to use the road to the Mill from Salvington. (a valuable right according to Jackson's opinion)' [20]

The description given in the valuation records speaks of two other dwellings on the windmill site. The *'old cottage'* was called *Salvington Mill Cottage* and the other was called *The Retreat*. (Details of both of these properties is given below.)

A postcard showing *High Salvington Windmill* published by Studio Goring

96. Salvington Mill Cottage
(No longer standing)

The advert for the Wisden Estate sale catalogue in August 1906 listed Lot 3 for the Windmill plot and mentions a small freehold cottage standing on the site. This small cottage was *Salvington Mill Cottage*. A tenant already living in the cottage is named at the time of the sale as Walter Bailey, who paid a rent of £10 a year.[21]

The 1901 census gives more details of Mr Bailey naming him as a widower: **William Walter Bailey** (b.1841) who was living at *Mill House,* an alternative name for the property, with his daughter **Alice Maud** (b.1876).[22] William was a retired publican who had moved to High Salvington from London sometime before the 1901 census. He continues to be listed at the address on electoral registers until 1907 when, although he left this cottage, he must have stayed in the area as his death in 1910 was recorded as occurring in the East Preston registration district.[23]

Advert in 1906 showing Lot 3 for *Salvington Windmill* being offered for sale.

The next occupant was named **Louisa Elizabeth Field** (b.1840 nee Vernon). She was the widow of a master draper and furniture dealer named **James Buley Field** (b.1840) who had died in 1910. Louisa and her husband had originally come from London although they had been living in Worthing for over twenty years, firstly in Graham Road[24] and then in Warwick Street.[25] Louise's move to High Salvington took place soon after she was widowed as it was only a few months after James' death that the 1911 census lists her in *Salvington Mill Cottage*.[26] Also listed on the census schedule with her is her son **Cecil Oliver** (b.1877) who had continued with his father's business and is listed as a *'furniture dealer'*. The name of these occupants does not appear in any other records of the time.

97. The Retreat
(No longer standing)

The same advert in the Worthing Gazette which mentions the sale of the windmill shown above also speaks of *'a splendid site for the erection of a bungalow.'*[27] This was the ground used by Jackson to build another small bungalow. The East Preston Rural District minutes record permission being given to Alfred Jackson for the building of this bungalow in 1907.[28] When completed it was named *The Retreat* and is shown on the map extract sitting just behind *Salvington Mill Cottage,* to the left of the windmill. It has not been possible to confirm who the residents were during this period.

98. Olivet (Dunkeld), Salvington Hill
(Now Dunkeld, No 19 Furze Road)

This was another of the properties owned by Alfred Jackson, purchased in 1908 for £49. 15s 6d with a further £414 16s 6d spent on building the house. Its valuation record describes it as:

> '2 storey B(ric)k & slate house. Superior appearance. Modern 3 bed 2r(ooms) Sc(ullery) Covered in yard'[29]

The 1912 electoral register lists a lady named **Clara Home** at this address and we know from street directories between 1910 and 1913 that she was living in the house with another unmarried lady named **Miss Darker**. Together they were listed as poultry farmers and also ran the *Windmill Tea Rooms* for a period. It was during their occupancy that the house named changed from *Olivet* to *Dunkeld* and it is these two house names found in street directories and electoral registers up to 1913. When the Inland Revenue Assessment was taken in September 1913 not only was the house name change noted on the page but the new occupier was given as **Fraser M. D.** who is probably **Murray Douglas Fraser** listed on the 1911 electoral register for Durrington although no house name is given for him. Exactly where he was living in 1911 has not been confirmed but he was living in *Dunkeld* by 1913.

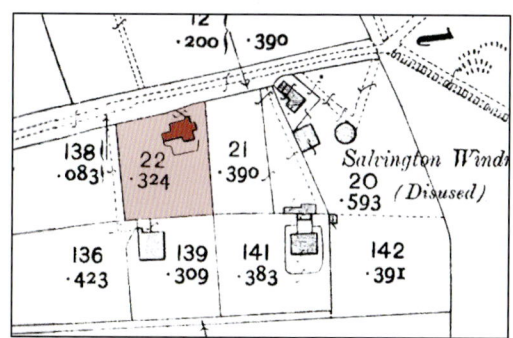

Excerpt taken from OS 25":1 mile Sheet LXIV: 2,6 3rd Edition 1912 (NTS)

How the house looks today, it is still called *Dunkeld*. © Lyn Tiller 2016

99. The Chalet, Salvington Hill
(No longer standing)

This property sits on the north side of the road being one of the few properties in the area that was not owned by Alfred Jackson. The Inland Revenue Valuation gives scarce detail on the pages, it does record the owner as **A Mitchell** but with no further details.

The first suggestion of a resident appears in an advert found in the local paper where a young lady was seeking employment. The advert clearly gives the address but only an initial of *'K'* gives any clue to who she was.[30]

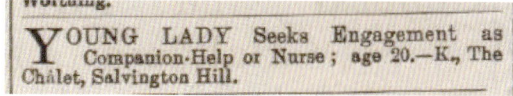

First mention of The Chalet in an advert August

The first fully identifiable occupant's name appears in street directories and electoral registers from 1909, until around 1912, when Richard Budd is listed. This is the name also appearing on the 1911 census where a retired miller **Richard Harry Budd** (b.1852) and his wife **Alice Mary** (b.1857 nee Close) are living in the house.[31]

Street directories for 1912 name a resident of *The Chalet* as **Alfred Mitchell.** This could be the full name of the owner and suggests he may have lived in the property at some point.

The Inland Revenue Valuation describes the two storey building in less than glowing terms:

> '*Timber Built Bungalow, covered ??? with galvanised
> iron. Roof is of gal iron. Poor appearance
> 3 r(ooms), K(itchen), 1st floor 2 rooms*'[32]

The valuation was dated January 1913 and lists the occupant as **Miss D Fisher.** Nothing else is known of this lady from documentation of the period except the suggestion from adverts in the Worthing Gazette around 1913 that she was renting rooms and also working as a poultry farmer.[33] No mention is made on the valuation records of poultry houses so they may have been added later.

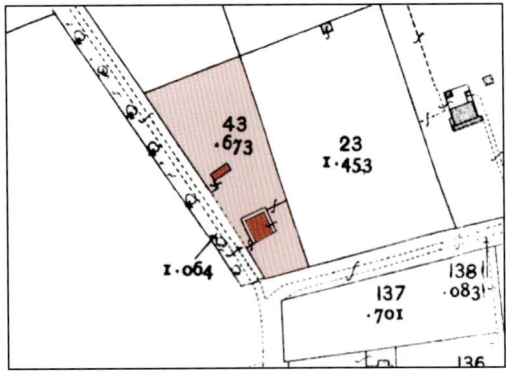

Excerpt taken from OS 25":1 mile Sheet LXIV: 1,2,5,6 3rd Edition 1912 (NTS)

The site of where *The Chalet* stood, now *Appletree Cottage*. © Lyn Tiller 2016

100. The Bungalow and Tea Rooms
(Now Furzeholme with a number of other properties built on the land)

The first resident identified is found in the 1901 census where a shepherd named **William Sharpe** (b.1839) and his wife **(Georgina Annie) Louisa** (b.1862 nee Gollop) appear. There is a suggestion on the 1901 census record that this gentleman was blind, although the word is in the occupation column alongside the word shepherd and not in the end column where disability is usually written.[34]

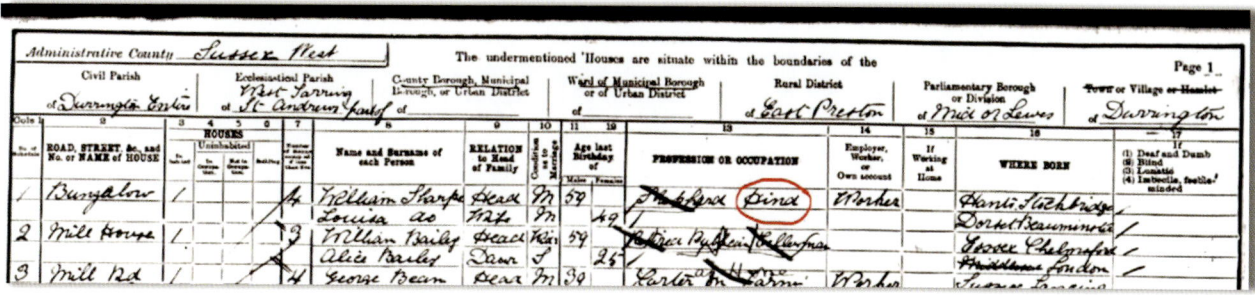

Blind marked in red from the 1901 census record.

This debility was not mentioned on the previous census when he is listed as a shepherd in Ferring so may not be correct or the deterioration of his eyesight in the ten years between censuses could have forced the change in occupation.[35] Whatever his circumstances were, by June 1908 he is advertising himself as the proprietor of a tea shop being run from *The Bungalow*. The newspaper advert confirms that this was an '*old-established Tea Grounds*' but we have no evidence when this enterprise began. [36]

Just a few months later, another newspaper announcement informs us that the Sharpe's have left the address and the new occupant is Frederick C. Worsley. The information was placed in the pages of the Worthing Gazette in November 1908 and gives a great deal of information on the expanding scope of work the tea room was now undertaking. Lunches were to be served and entertainment was also to be offered as a piano is mentioned.[37]

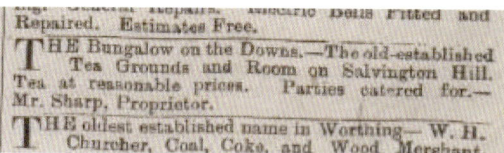

Mr Sharpe advertising the tea rooms in June 1908

Mr Worsley announcing the new management at *The Bungalow Tea Shop*

The 1911 census gives us further details of this family.[38] **Frederick Charles Worsley** (b.1874) was the head of the household living here with his wife **Elsie Grace** (b.1883 nee Pacy) and their daughter **Beatrice Rose** (b.1908). Elsie was a Worthing born lady who had met and married her husband in London in 1907, their daughter being born there some months later. The family had decided to make their home in Elsie's home town and as Frederick's occupation on the 1911 census was given as 'Caterer' the move to *The Bungalow Tea Rooms* was fitting for Frederick to work and provide for his family. Beatrice had been born in the summer of 1908 and they moved to High Salvington shortly after her birth.

The tea room flourished under Frederick's catering skills and we see various advertisements and notices of events being held there in local newspapers of the time. One such event was held in August 1912 when members of the Worthing branch of the National Amalgamated Union of Shop Assistants, Warehousemen and Clerks travelled by bus from Worthing to *The Bungalow* for an open air whist drive followed by a tea.[39]

Old photograph of *The Bungalow* at High Salvington. Worthing Libary

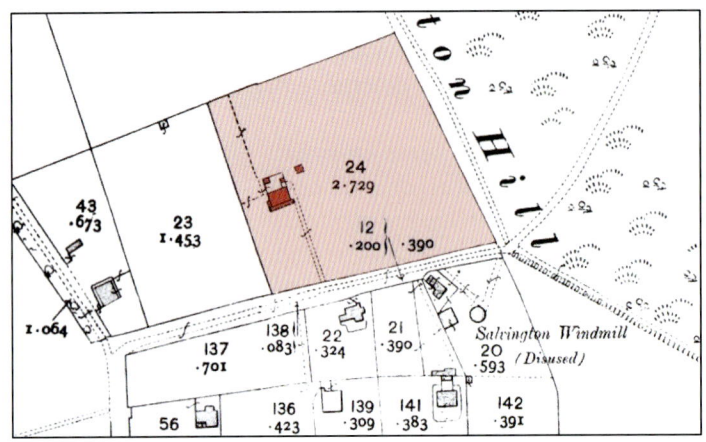
Excerpt taken from OS 25":1 mile Sheet LXIV: 2,6 3rd Edition 1912 (NTS)

101. No 8 Hill Cottages, Salvington Hill
(Now Mill Lane Mews, Mill Lane)

This is one of the names given to two small, four-roomed cottages forming part of a complex of farm buildings. They were sited at the very edge of the parish boundary and were the only inhabited buildings on the right hand side of the road, known at the time as Salvington Hill, running from the Arundel Road at the southern end, passed the windmill on the left when the road then becomes a farm track as it continues northwards onto the South Downs. The map extract shows the two cottages fronting on to the road with other buildings arranged behind them.

The cottages were known by various names during the Edwardian period including *Webb Cottages, Hill Cottages, Mill Cottages* and *Hill Farm*. They were part of *Salvington Farm* which was owned by the Wisden Estate and farmed by Allen Webb and then Edwin Lephard throughout the first years of the twentieth century. The occupants can be identified through the two censuses and the Inland Revenue Valuation information which all confirms the same details.

It is the Inland Revenue Valuation taken in October 1912 that names the four families who lived in the cottages both as previous and present occupiers. They are described on the pages of the Field Book which assess the value of the whole of *Salvington Farm,* the portion relating to the cottages records:

'Hill Cottages, tenants, Freeman & Lambourne (formerly Brace & Shepherd) 4 rooms each, Old. Cart Lodge, Barn. Stables 4' [40]

Modern photograph of the site, now *Mill Lane Mews*. © Lyn Tiller 2016

In the first of the cottages the 1901 census records the head of the household as **Thomas Brace** (b.1862), who was living here with his wife **Harriett** (b.1864 nee Hewlett) and their two daughters: **Harriett Ethel** (b.1891) and **Alice Eveline** (b.1892). A market gardener by the name of **Edward Greenfield** (b.1868) also lodged with them according to the census record.

There are some interesting stories connected with this family which are reported in the local and even national newspapers during the years they lived in *Hill Cottages*. They are the cuttings are reproduced on the next page.

The first concerns Thomas Brace himself whose name had appeared in the Daily Mail early in 1901 comparing him with another gentleman in Hungary, both men having a condition known as 'dextrocardia'.[41] This condition meant that their heart was positioned on the right hand side of the body and not the more normal left. Ever ready for a good and interesting story, the Worthing Gazette placed the snippet from the Daily Mail in the paper one week and then after further investigation the full story, including Thomas's address, was revealed the following week. [42]

Question of identification of Thomas Brace named in the Daily Mail in 1901

The second story regarding this family concerned Alice, the younger of their two daughters. In March 1906 Alice had been reading the sad story of a young girl who committed suicide and seems to have decided to emulate the girl's behaviour. It appears from reading the story from the report in the newspaper that everyone, including the Magistrate, was a little perplexed as to why Alice had behaved in this way and relates *'Curious Evidence at the Police Court'*.[43]

Worthing Gazette

SHOREHAM, LANCING, SOMPTING, BROADWATER, WEST TARRING, GORING, ANGMERING, FINDON, WASHINGTON, STORRINGTON, AND PULBOROUGH WEEKLY NEWS.

On the Right Side.

To speak of a man as having his heart in the right place is usually regarded as indicating an individual possessed of a very excellent quality; but this does not necessarily argue that one whose heart is in a physical sense in the wrong quarter is not an equally desirable member of society. The GAZETTE published last week a little on his right side. "Where is the Farm?" was the question that was asked, and Mr. S. Clark comes to the rescue with the necessary information, slyly adding that "if you want to know anything about Worthing district always come to Tarring for it!" But he tells us—and the statement is confirmed by an actual relative—that the subject of the paragraph is Mr. Thomas Brace, of Hill Cottage, Salvington, who is, and has been for some years past, in the service of Mr. A. E. Webb, of Salvington Farm. Mr. Brace was a former member of an Ambulance Class which Mr. Clark attended, "and," adds the latter, "you may guess that he made the Examiner look when he stated that his heart was on the right side!" Singularly enough, this misplaced organ is said to occasion no inconvenience whatever.

THE BOROUGH RECORDER.

Further revelations and details about Thomas Brace and his misplaced heart revealed in local papers in May 1901

SENSATIONAL INCIDENT AT EAST WORTHING.

A Schoolgirl's Attempted Suicide.

Curious Evidence at the Police Court.

"I Am Going to Heaven Now!"

AN incident of a startling character occurred at East Worthing on Saturday evening, and the sequel was seen at a special sitting of the Magistrates at the Town Hall on Monday morning, when a schoolgirl named Alice Brace, who lives with her parents at Salvington, was brought up in custody on a charge of attempting to take her life. Her father told the Court, in the course of his evidence, that his daughter had read the account in the GAZETTE of a recent distressing tragedy no fewer than three times during the course of one morning; and the girl herself told P.C. Slade that she had been reading in the papers about "the other girl who was found in the sea." The newspaper was found on the table by her father when he came indoors on Saturday afternoon, and there was no doubt that the girl had been reading it before she went out. She was found later in the day lying near the beach, opposite the Half Brick Inn, her clothes being wet; and she said as she was picked up that she wanted to drown herself. She is only thirteen years of age, but is well developed, and is of a bright and happy disposition.

The Magistrates by whom the case was heard were the Mayor, Councillor J. White, J.P. (in the Chair), and Mr. H. Hargood.

The Discovery.

The first witness called was William Francis, who deposed that he lived at Seamill Farm, East Worthing. He was coming down into the town on Saturday evening, along Brighton-road, and opposite the Half Brick a young man came out, and they saw the girl lying on the pathway on the south side side of the road, near the beach. They went to her and picked her up; and as they were doing so she said: "I wanted to drown myself;" and as they went across the road with her; "I am going to Heaven now!" They took her into the Half Brick Inn. Her clothes were wet at the bottom. When they found her, about ten minutes past seven, she was lying face downwards on the path. The tide was in.

Mr. Algernon Edward Rouse, surgeon, stated that he was called to the Half Brick Inn at about twenty minutes past seven. He saw the girl in the sitting room there. She was suffering from shock. Her hands, feet, and legs were very cold, and her pulse was rather feeble. He could not make her speak. Her stockings and boots were soaking wet, but her dress was only splashed. He had the former removed at once. Her dress was a short one. He tried to get her warm, and when she recovered somewhat and her pulse improved he had her

Taken To the Hospital.

She did not speak a word the whole time. Undoubtedly she was suffering from shock; but whether she was semi-conscious or semi-hysterical it was extremely difficult to say.

P.C. Pentecost stated that he received a call to the Half Brick Inn, in consequence of the girl being there. He saw her, and tried to get her to speak, but she would not do so. A piece of paper was pinned to her dress, and on it was written: "Miss Alice Brace, Salvington Hill, Salvington." The witness also produced the waistband of the girl's frock, which, he said, was wet through when it was taken off her. After her discharge from the Hospital on Sunday morning she was brought to the Police Station, and witness read the warrant to her. She did not say a word.

P.C. Slade deposed to fetching the girl from the Hospital on the preceding morning. She asked: "Where are you taking me to?" and witness told her, "To the Police Station." She said: "I don't care about that. I can't think why I did it; but I've been looking at the papers about the other girl who was found in the sea."

Always Bright and Happy.

Thomas Brace, the girl's father, said that he was a carter, and lived at Salvington Hill. Alice was his daughter, and she was thirteen years old last birthday. She left home at ten minutes to two on Saturday. He did not know where she was going. He found on the table a newspaper (the GAZETTE was here produced) containing an account of the inquest and burial of the girl who was drowned last week. His wife told him that the child read the account three times that day. She had always been very bright and happy, and had never said anything at all of that description, or that she would do herself harm. She attended Broadwater School, and he always had good reports of her. She was a good daughter. Finding that she did not return on Saturday he made inquiries.

On this evidence, after some little consultation with the Clerk (Mr. M. Goodman), the Magistrates adjourned the case until four o'clock in the afternoon, and when they resumed

The father informed the Bench that if they dismissed the case he could send the girl straight away that day for a holiday, to relations or friends, where she would be well cared for and properly looked after.

Kindly Advice from the Bench.

The Mayor then addressed the girl. He told her that she would be discharged, her father undertaking that she should be sent away some distance for a time, where she would be properly taken care of. If it was a fact that she had been incited by reading the account of the poor girl last week he thought it was a very great pity that those papers were brought before her notice, but he hoped, now that she saw how foolish she had been in doing what she had attempted, that no thought or word of such a kind would ever cross her mind again. Life was a very valuable thing, and she ought to treasure and take care of it. She ought to remember also what pain she gave her friends, her father and mother; and he hoped that they would hear no more of that, but that she would be a good girl.

The girl then left the Town Hall with her relatives and the Matron of the Shelter, Miss Higgs, who had been in attendance with her during the whole hearing of the case.

Worthing Gazette March 1906

Thomas Brace is only listed at this cottage until around 1907 when he disappeared from the address in the street directories. The 1911 census confirms that he had moved to *Swandean Cottage* in Arundel Road.[44]

The next residents at this cottage were another family with an interesting genealogy. **Charles Henry Freeman** (b.1882) was the head of the household. Charles was one of seven children of a blind organist from West Tarring Church, **Richard William Freeman,** who had mysteriously left Worthing in 1893, leaving behind his second wife and their small daughter, as well as most of his children from his first marriage. (This same Richard Freeman was the great grandfather of the actor Martin Freeman known for his roles in the TV programme 'The Office' and as Bilbo Baggins in the 'Lord of the Rings' films.)

On the 1911 census Charles claimed to have been married for three years to a lady named **Mary Jane Freeman.** They had a young son of a few months old, **Alfred Henry** (b.1910). A clue to help identify Mary Jane is the fact that three of her other children are living at the same address with her: **Gordon Searle** (b.1894), **John Stanley Searle** (b.1900) and **Elsie Searle** (b.1903). Mary Jane was actually the wife of Clement Searle who was still very much alive and living as a lodger in *Elder Tree Cottage* with another of their sons, **Thomas Edmund** (b.1892).

PRIVATE JOHN SEARLE.

The story of this family continues through to the First World War when John Searle became one of the youngest soldiers from Sussex to die, at the age of 15, when he fought at the Battle of Boar's Head on 30th June 1916. This five hour battle cost the lives of over 300 soldiers from the Royal Sussex Regiment.

The second cottage also had two families who lived there during the Edwardian years. The first was headed by a gentleman whose name was an aptronym, a name which perfectly suited his occupation. **Frederick Shepherd** (b.1844) was indeed a 'shepherd on farm' when he is listed on the 1901 census.[45] He was recorded on the census with his wife **Caroline** (b.1853 nee Collins) and three children: **Frederick James** (b.1885), **Fanny Dorothy** (b.1889) and **William James B.** (b.1894). The street directories include him at the address up until 1907 and electoral registers through to 1911 although the family must have moved before the early months of 1911 as they are not listed on the census for that year.

The 1911 census gives the details for the next family to occupy the cottage. The head of the house was **George Lambourne** (b.1862), his wife **Mary Ann** (b.1858 nee Strotten) and their only child **Kate** (b.1885) are also on the census page, as is a niece, staying with them at the time, named **Blanche Hughes** (b.1901). This family were one of the families who had lost their home and belongings in 1901 when the three cottages in Coate Street were burned to the ground.

High Salvington was considered a very favourable place to live with great benefits coming from its location and the properties that had already been built and were going to be built. The future for High Salvington was heralded throughout the period not least as illustrated by this gushing, enthusiastic and slightly tongue in cheek recommendation published in the Worthing Gazette in July 1912:

> *'Within the next few days an opportunity will be presented to those who possess the requisite means and inclination to secure a site for residential purposes on that charming section of the South Downs which is known as High Salvington; and it would not be at all surprising to find a real boom in the immediate future, and to witness the erection of the full number of bungalows provided for by the public disposal of the estate which Councillor Jackson acquired there, by the merest chance, a few years ago from the Executors of the late Colonel Wisden.*
> *In an illustrated booklet that has been in circulation during the past few weeks, in anticipation of the approaching auction, the compiler has made an effectual appeal to the sentimental side of those whom he desires to favourably influence in this matter, for the following prose poem, entitled "A Word to the Slaves of £ s d," makes its appearance in one of the earliest pages:*

"A day on the Downs is invigorating;
A week is a tonic to the nerves;
A bungalow there makes life worth living"
***

One envies the massive intellect that has evolved such a tribute to the charms of a particularly favoured section of those Sussex Downs which possess so sheer a delight for so many, native born and imported residents alike; but even if the prosiest of us are unable to rise to the poetical heights here indicated, we can presumably assess pretty accurately the hygienic value of permanent residence on the breezy summit of the everlasting hills.'
***

(From: 'The Trifler' Worthing Gazette 17th July 1912[46])

A modern view of the cottages inside the compound of *Mill Lane Mews*. © Dave Pryce 2016

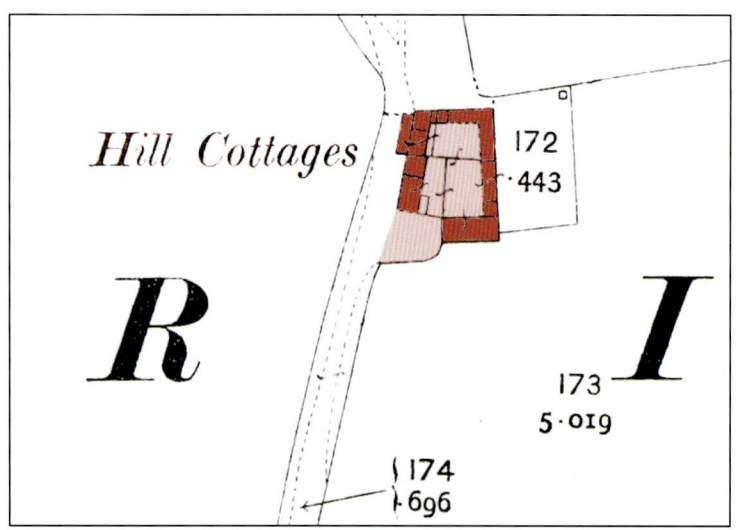

Excerpt taken from OS 25":1 mile Sheet LXIV: 6 3rd Edition 1912 (NTS)

---

[1] 1891 census RG12/186 ff.10 (TNA)
[2] 1901 census RG13/958 ff.26 (TNA)
[3] Worthing Gazette 29th September 1943 p6d
[4] Worthing Gazette 21-09-1910 p7
[5] Census of England and Wales 1911. Enumerators Summary Book: East Preston (84), Worthing (1), Durrington (District 3) (TNA)
[6] IR58/94204 No.7687 (TNA)

[7] 1911 census RG14/5342 (TNA)
[8] Worthing Gazette 15th March 1911 p5e
[9] IR58/94206 No.7805 (TNA)
[10] IR58/94204 No.7686 (TNA)
[11] http://www.highsalvingtonwindmill.co.uk
[12] www.britishlistedbuildings.co.uk   No. 432514 (viewed 21.6.2012)
[13] EPRD Minutes 16th April 1907 p.298 (WSRO)
[14] Worthing Gazette 22nd July 1907 p3
[15] 1901 census RG13/225 ff.114 (TNA)
[16] 1911 census RG14/9861 sch 121 (TNA)
[17] 'The Mill' Newsletter of the Friends of High Salvington Windmill. Issue 21: Spring 2015
[18] Worthing Gazette 2nd October 1907 p4
[19] Worthing Gazette 21st September 1910 p7
[20] IR58/94204 No.7684 (TNA)
[21] Worthing Gazette 22nd August 1906 p4
[22] 1901 census RG13/957 ff.76 (TNA)
[23] GRO Death Index Dec Q 1910 Vol 2b p.224
[24] 1891 census RG12/836 ff.96 (TNA)
[25] 1901 census RG13/958 ff.131 (TNA)
[26] 1911 census RG14/5342 sch 77 (TNA)
[27] Worthing Gazette 22nd August 1906 p4
[28] Worthing Gazette 22nd August 1906 p4
[29] IR58/94204 No. 7688 (TNA)
[30] Worthing Gazette 22nd August 1906 p8c
[31] 1911 census RG14/5342 sch 79 (TNA)
[32] IR58/94205 No.7712 (TNA)
[33] Worthing Gazette 15th January 1913 p8d
[34] 1901 census RG13/957 ff.76 (TNA)
[35] 1891 census RG12/838 ff.158 (TNA)
[36] Worthing Gazette 3rd June 1908 p8
[37] Worthing Gazette 4th November 1908 p4
[38] 1911 census RG14/5342 sch 78 (TNA)
[39] Worthing Gazette 21st August 1912 p4
[40] IR58/94206 No. 7855 (TNA)
[41] Worthing Gazette 24th April 1901 p5
[42] Worthing Gazette 1st May 1901 5
[43] Worthing Gazette 7th March 1906 p5
[44] 1911 census RG14/5342 sch 81
[45] 1901 census RG13/957 ff.61
[46] Worthing Gazette 17th July 1912 p6

Chapter 12
Littlehampton Road

Introduction

Littlehampton Road runs east to west along the southern boundary of the parish. It was and still is a major thoroughfare running from Worthing and continuing to other villages as you travel west until it reaches its namesake: Littlehampton.

The properties on the northern side of the road were in Durrington and Salvington whilst the few on the southern side were in Goring to the west and West Tarring to the east. As a major thoroughfare it was also the meeting point of various parish boundaries. During the Edwardian period it grew from being a roadway hedged only by farmland, with a local beer house and the occasional dwelling, to being another of the areas occupied by nurseries, houses and business properties.

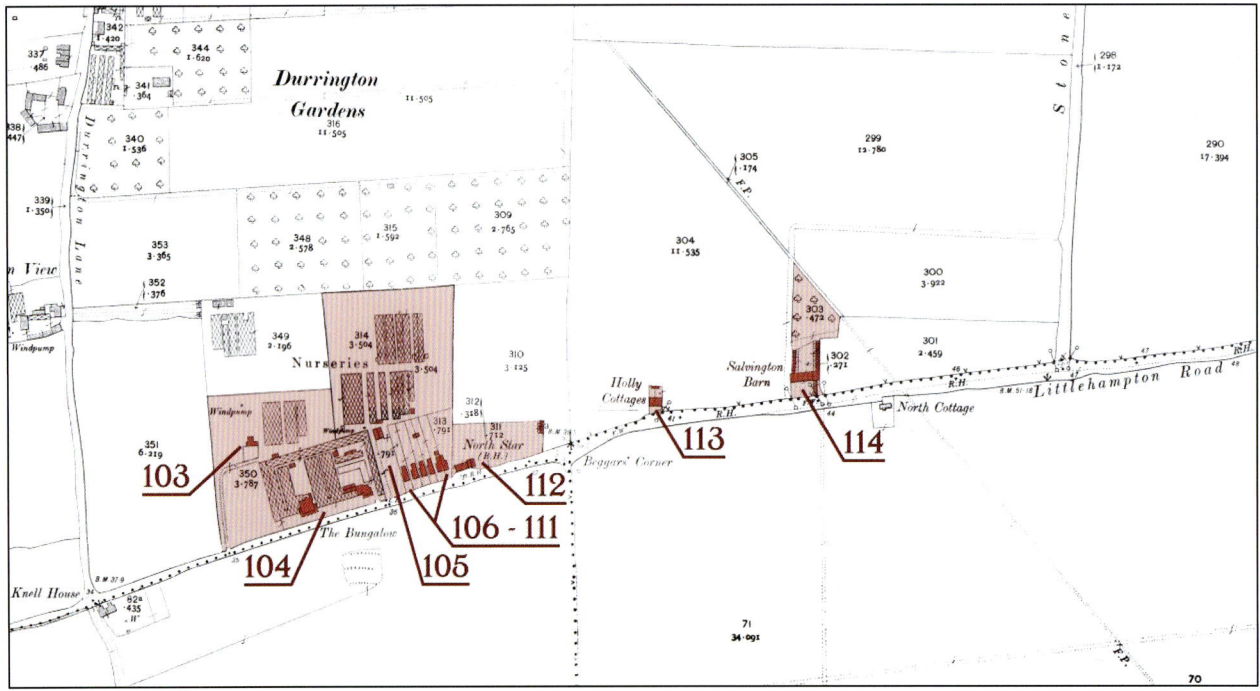

Excerpt taken from OS 25":1 mile Sheet LXIV: 9,10 3rd Edition 1912 (NTS)

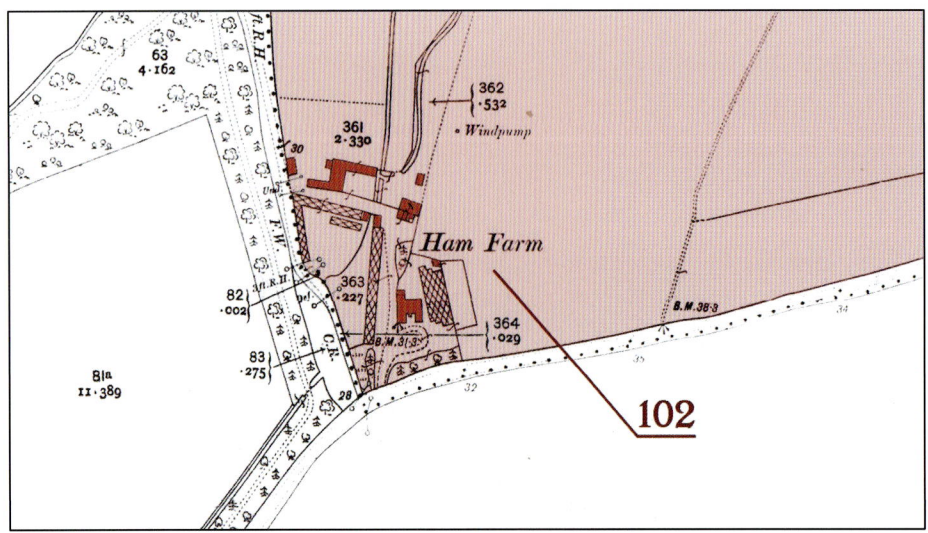

Excerpt taken from OS 25":1 mile Sheet LXIV: 9 3rd Edition 1912 (NTS)

102. Ham Farm (Inc. Hamleigh), Littlehampton Road
(Now the site of Northbrook College)

Photograph of the farmhouse at *Ham Farm*, known as *Hamleigh* taken around 1930. Worthing Library

This was a large farm with its farmhouse and main buildings situated on the farthest western edge of the parish on Littlehampton Road. The farmer, during the Edwardian period, was **Alfred Symons** who had been farming here for some years before the turn of the century.

Alfred was the son of a farmer; he had been born and raised in Brixham, Devon where the family farm was situated. He followed in his father's footsteps and at the young age of 25, according to the 1891 census records, he was already established as the farmer at *Ham Farm*.[1] The farm itself covered 168 acres of land which spanned Goring and Salvington as well as the land, main farm house and other buildings in Durrington. It was owned by **Arthur Henty** of Chestham Park, Henfield who was renting it to Alfred Symons for £235 a year at the time of the Inland Revenue Valuation.

Alfred Symons (b.1865) had married a lady from his home village named **Helen Burlace** at the end of 1890 just a short time before the census informs us that they were living at *Ham Farm*. It must have been quite a daunting task for the newly wedded couple to marry and take up the reigns of working a farm in a new county all within a few months.

By the time of the 1901 census Alfred and Helen had already been at the farm for a decade and were now calling the farmhouse where they lived *Hamleigh*.[2] They also had their own family of three children: **Thomas Stewart** (b.1892), **Helen Norah** (b.1893) and **Jeffrey (or Geoffrey) Burlace** (b.1897) all born in Durrington. During the next decade the couple went on to have two more children: **Mary** (b.1901) and **Philip Alexander** (b.1905).

The 1911 census records some interesting facts about the family. The eldest son was still living at home and had decided not to continue with the family tradition of farming as he was working as a *'junior in a bank'*.[3] The youngest daughter, Mary is listed as *'School part-time'* which seems a little different from the normal entry for school children. Mary is not listed in the school admissions for Durrington so we do not know why she only attended part-time.

The Symons family were also wealthy enough to have a servant living with them, a young woman from Goring named **Caroline E. Sopp** (b.1882). Caroline was listed as a domestic servant with the family in 1901 and was still single and working in the same capacity with the family in 1911.

The Inland Revenue Valuation is very informative in the listing of the buildings which made up the farm complex:

> *'2 Glasshouses……Very old. Cold*
> *1 Cucumber House…….4 rows*
> *Lean to*
> *4 Glasshouses*
> *Nags Stable - Piggeries - Loose Box*
> *Granary - Cart Lodge - Coach House*
> *Poultry House*
> *Cowshed. Good*
> *House. Thatched*
> *2 cottages. Coleman & Cousin'*[4]

The whereabouts of the two cottages mentioned above has not been confirmed but may refer to *Nell Cottages* on the southern side of Littlehampton Road just outside of the Durrington parish boundary or to have been part of the farm buildings around the main farmhouse. The Inland Revenue Valuation gives two occupiers' names, one being **Coleman,** which has not been traced elsewhere in the parish documents. The other is **Cousin,** which is probably an alternate spelling of **Cozens,** the name of a family living at these cottages in 1911.

There was also a separate set of buildings in Durrington which included ten cowsheds and two '*old thatched cottages*' occupied by **Ford** and **Swain**. These cottages belonged to the farm and possibly stood in the complex of farm buildings just south of the brickfields in Durrington Lane or across the road in what became known as the *'French Gardens'*. They have their own Inland Revenue Valuation numbers but no information has been entered onto the pages of the Field Book.

103. Raglan Nursery, Littlehampton Road
(No longer standing)

Malcolm Linfield has described this nursery:

> *'In 1900 **Robert Moore Cave** established a nursery (7792) on two acres of land immediately to the north of Thomas Blisset's nursery. Initially a partnership (Cave and Mead), the business was called 'Raglan Nurseries', where there were eventually 7 glasshouses with a total foot run of 900 feet. Robert was born in Weston-super-mare in 1873, and in 1907 he married into the Linfield family, well-known growers in East Worthing. His wife **Ethel Kate**, known as 'Sis', was a daughter of William Henry Linfield, relieving officer at Worthing in the service of the East Preston Guardians. He was also Registrar of Births and Deaths. Although he had a full time job, William also owned a small nursery attached to his house in Lyndhurst Road, where he grew grapes and tomatoes in the glasshouses. Ethel's uncle was **Arthur George Linfield,** one of the larger Worthing growers, with nurseries in Chesswood Road, Ham Road, Ladydell Road and on the seafront in Brighton Road. Robert died in 1935 at the age of 62: his widow outlived him by a further 40 years! Sometime after 1909, Robert built a house on the site…….. for himself and his new wife'.*[5]

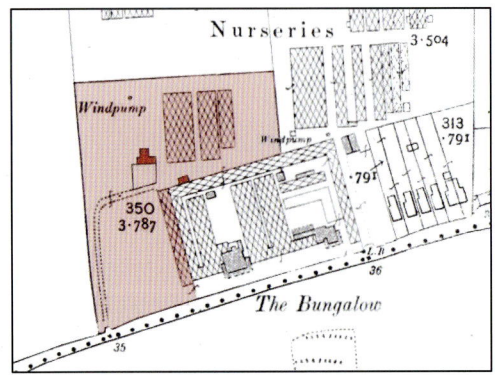

Excerpt taken from OS 25":1 mile Sheet LXIV: 9,10 3rd Edition 1912 (NTS)

104. The Bungalow and The Lodge, Littlehampton Road

These two properties are part of the plot of land outlined on the attached map, the whole site being run as a nursery by Thomas Blissett. Malcolm Linfield describes the beginning of this nursery:

> '***Thomas Blisset*** *was another glasshouse grower who set up during the Edwardian period. His nursery immediately faced the Littlehampton Road, putting him at the front of all the other nurseries in this vicinity. He bought the site in February 1900, and by 1914 had completely filled the one acre site with 12 glasshouses, amounting to 1300 ft in length. He had very little uncovered land, as he had also built two bungalows.'* [6]

Thomas Blissett must have built at least the first bungalow soon after he had taken possession of the land as he is recorded at the property on the 1901 census.[7] This strategically well sited piece of land had cost £450 and by 1914 he had spent a further £1800 on building the two bungalows and the glasshouses.

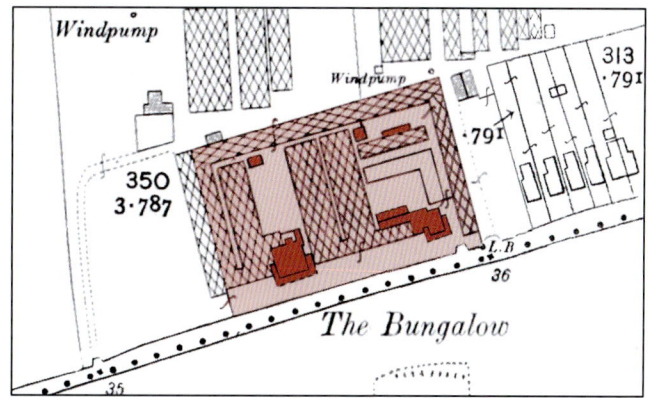

Excerpt taken from OS 25":1 mile Sheet LXIV: 9,10 3rd Edition 1912 (NTS)

The Bungalow
(Now No 212 Littlehampton Road)

This was the name usually given to the first and larger of the two properties built on the nursery land. They were fully described on the Inland Revenue Valuation page:

> '*Property consists of 2 well built modern bungalows*
> *& several well built glasshouses. There is a shortage of*
> *uncovered land for use with the glasshouses*
> *The bungalow well built of red brick tile roof & large verandah 7ft*
> *2 front rooms, 2r(ooms) K(itchen) Sc(ullery) Bath W C 1 attic*
> *The Lodge 4 rooms & K(itchen)*
> *Well dug 24ft wind pump* '[8]

The Bungalow was the home of the owner **Thomas Blissett** (b.1847) who had been born in Staffordshire. It would appear that he only came to this area when he purchased the land although it has proved difficult to track his movements using the censuses after 1861 when we know that he was a pupil at Townsend School in Kidderminster.[9]

In 1901 Thomas is listed on the census living in Littlehampton Road probably already in *The Bungalow* although the house name is not given. He records that he is single and living alone except for one visitor. This visitor was a 35 year old French lady by the name of **A de Polyach** who gives her occupation as a housekeeper. No other recording or details regarding this lady have been traced. Ten years later by the time of the 1911 census Thomas gives his status as *'widowed'*, although no marriage has been traced, and he states that he had no children. The mysterious French lady is still living in the house on this census where she is registered as **Miss de Polyach** and is now not only the *'housekeeper'* but a *'grower'* as well helping in the nursery.

He is listed in street directories all through the Edwardian period and also on the electoral registers where a second address at Lower Teddington Road, Hampton, is recorded as his residence in the 1907-1908 registers suggesting he may not have lived here continuously throughout the years. He was back living at *The Bungalow* from 1909 onwards however.

The Bungalow, Littlehampton Road in 1908. Worthing Library

Modern Photograph of *The Bungalow* as it looks today. © Dave Pryce 2016

The Lodge
(No longer standing)

The 1911 census gives us the first confirmation of a named occupant of this property. No earlier occupant has been traced which may mean that the bungalow was built a little later than the other property on the site namely *The Bungalow*. From the map it appears to have been built attached to and wrapped around the end of one of the glasshouses.

The head of the house as listed on the census was a doctor; **Alleyne Hayward Barker** (b.1860) who only stayed in the bungalow for a few years before moving on again to the Lindfield area where he spent the rest of his life. The 1911 census page gives us some very interesting information about this gentleman which has enabled further research into his early life.[10] He was born in Wantage, Berkshire, the son of an eminent surgeon. After his school years, some of which were spent at Lancing College where we have a record of him being part of their cricket team between 1877-1879,[11] he was to train as a surgeon like his father, going to Trinity College Cambridge where he was awarded his degree in May 1887.[12] In the same year he was also admitted to the Royal College of Surgeons and for the next twenty years he practised as a surgeon and physician in his birth town of Wantage.

The 1901 census confirms his position as surgeon in Wantage; he was by now 41 years of age and still single.[13] However between the 1901 and the 1911 census some changes happened in the life of Alleyne Barker and he made the move to Durrington where he is listed as having been married for one year to a lady much younger than he, **Florence Elizabeth Barker** (b.c1882). No marriage has been traced and therefore no more information can be discovered about Florence, as no death is recorded for anyone with that name either. What the status of their relationship may have been is unknown as is the reason for their short stay in Durrington. Dr Barker is only recorded in the electoral registers for Durrington for two years. He appears in the 1911 and the 1912 registers. There is an entry in the street directory for 1911 giving a *'Mr Barker'* living in Littlehampton Road and working as a fruitgrower which, if not an error, suggests he may have been helping in the nursery rather than practising as a surgeon for the short period of his occupation.

105. Vineyard Nursery, Littlehampton Road
(No longer standing)

Malcolm Linfield has described this nursery:

> *'A number of nurseries were also developed in the south of Durrington parish, on the northern side of Littlehampton Road. One of these (7802) was established by **Frederic Murrell Burt** during the 1890s, and was known as The Vineyard. The name implies that hothouse grapes were his main crop, and by 1913 he had 15 glasshouses amounting to 2060 ft in length on 3 acres of land. Burt was born in Gibraltar, and in 1891, when he was 25, he was an established fruit grower at Westhampnett. By 1913, although he is recorded in the relevant Field Book as owner and occupier of the nursery in Durrington, his address is given as Eastcheap in London. He died in 1926.'*[14]

The diagram on the right shows the outline of the plots of land that were sold during the Edwardian years to build a detached house and villas between the entrance to Vineyard Nurseries and the *North Star Inn*. The plan is taken from the Inland Revenue Valuation dated August 1912 and clearly shows that when the pages were prepared the first two properties had already been built.[15] These two properties were *The Hollies* and *The Cottage*. The later properties are named on the plan but no outline of the house was included although we know from the census returns that they were already being lived in.

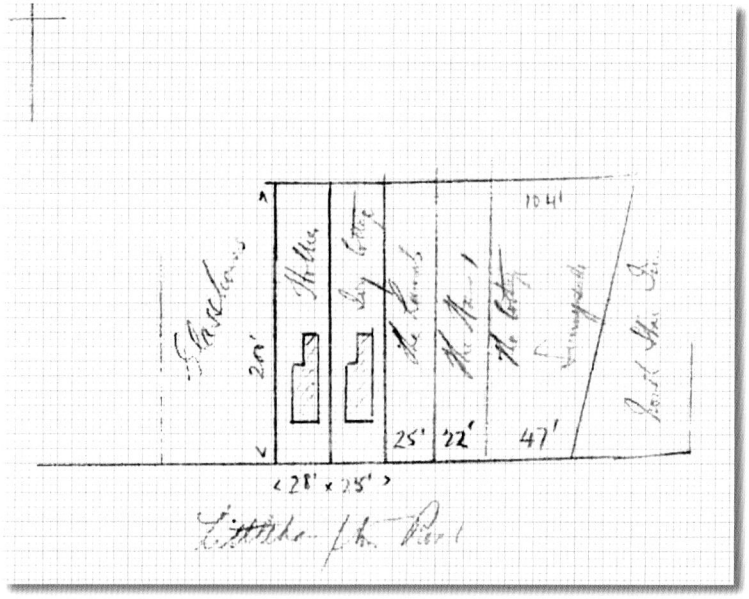

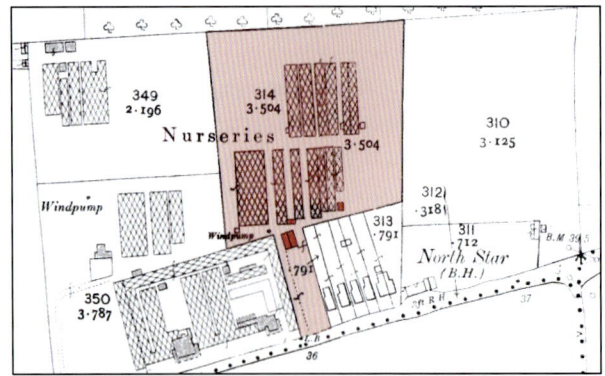

Excerpt taken from OS 25":1 mile Sheet LXIV: 9,10
3rd Edition 1912 (NTS)

106. The Hollies, Littlehampton Road
(Now a of Block of Flats No. 1-72 Carolyn House, Littlehampton Road)

On the 23rd August 1904 the East Preston Rural District Council minutes reported that permission had been granted to *'Mr Wood'* allowing him to build two cottages in Littlehampton Road.[16] The Inland Revenue Valuation confirms that these two properties were owned and built by **Mr Thomas Wood** of King Street, Broadwater. Throughout the Edwardian period Thomas Wood appears numerous times in the East Preston Rural District minutes either gaining planning permission for the building of other properties or obtaining permission to lay water pipes into those same properties both in Littlehampton Road and New Road. On 7th January 1908, when he was gaining permission for a Water Certificate for two houses in New Road, he is recorded as *'Mr Thomas Woods of Glebe Road'*, obviously this is where he was living at the time.[17] On the 1911 census he is lodging at 47 King Street, Broadwater, where his occupation is given as a *'bricklayer'*.[18]

Thomas had paid £42 for each of the two plots on which he built *The Hollies* and the next property called *Ivy Cottage* and spent a further £295 on the building costs of each of the cottages described in the Inland Revenue Valuation as *'Red brick, pretty villa'*.[19] The cottages each had three bedrooms and an upstairs toilet, plus a modern kitchen and scullery combined, although they did however have to share a well.

Henry Crofts (b.1848) was the first occupant of this new cottage. He was initially listed in the 1905 street directories and then appears in the 1909 electoral register at this address. Henry was a telegraphist in Dulwich where he appeared on the 1901 census working for the Post Office.[20] Henry duly retired around 1905 and like many other people through the years he chose to bring his wife **Elizabeth** (b.1848 nee Lennard) to their new retirement home in Durrington. They were accompanied by one of their six children **Elsie** (b.c1893) who gave her occupation as a *'Milliners Assistant'*.

This was, as previously mentioned, a three-bedroomed property and an advert in the local paper in January 1906 informs us that one of the rooms had obviously been rented and was being used by a lady named **Miss Jonas** who was offering her services as a typist.[21]

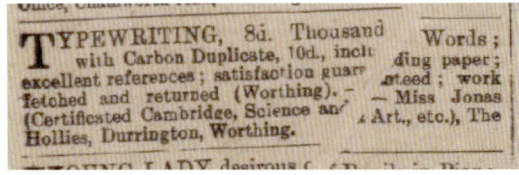

Typewriting skills being offered from *The Hollies* in 1906

In 1909 another advert appears in the Worthing Gazette, this time in Henry's name. He is advertising a three-bedroomed cottage, which sounds suspiciously like his own or the neighbouring cottage, for sale or to rent.[22]

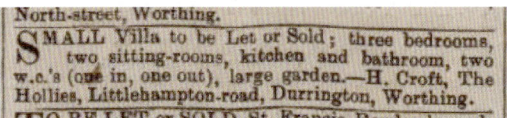

Advert for small villa which Henry was offering for sale or rent in February 1909

He was not, according to the Inland Revenue Valuation, the owner of the property at this time so he may have been acting as the agent for Thomas Wood for one of the properties in the road. Mr Crofts was still living in *The Hollies* being listed in both street directories and electoral registers up to and beyond 1913.

107. Ivy Cottage, Littlehampton Road
(Now a of Block of Flats No's 1-72 Carolyn House, Littlehampton Road)

Ivy Cottage was the name of the second of the properties built by Thomas Wood being another brick built detached villa.

The first occupant discovered for this property is not found until the electoral register of 1908 when **Henry Goble (Gobel)** appears. He is listed at the address until 1911, according to the electoral register, when he moved to 3 *Beaconsfield Terrace,* Ashacre Lane although he is not listed on the 1911 census.

The next householders are the Reed family who are listed as occupants on the 1911 census.[23] They comprised of **Charles Reed** (b.1868), his wife **Bessie** (b.c1869) and their only daughter **Mabel Emily** (b.1892). Charles was an *'upholsterer and house furnisher'* originally from Kent. Strangely it was the name of Bessie, his wife, that appears on the electoral register for 1913, there is no equivalent listing for Charles on any of the registers and the surname does not appear in any street directories for the period. The Inland Revenue Valuation of November 1912 lists the occupant as **Brightwell** which would confirm that the Reed family had already moved on by this period but does not throw any more light on the strange electoral listing for Bessie.[24]

108. The Laurels, Littlehampton Road
(Now a of Block of Flats No's 1-72 Carolyn House, Littlehampton Road)

This three bedroomed, detached property is described on the Inland Revenue Valuation as a *'Red brick pretty detached villa'*.[25] The Valuation also describes it as being identical to its neighbour, which was *Ivy Cottage,* owned and built by the builder **Thomas Wood** from King Street in Broadwater. It is most likely, therefore, that he also built this similar property.

According to the details in the valuation Mr Wood sold the property in April 1907 for £350 which would mean that he had made a small profit from the sale of the property. This sale passed ownership of *The Laurels* to **Mr. Raymond Goatcher** of Harry's Farm in West Chiltington.

The street directories give us no clues as to the early occupants as none are listed. However the electoral register does list **Charles Nettley** (b.1874) as householder from 1909 to 1911. The 1911 census only lists a widow of 70 named **Mary Nettley** (b.1841) born in Amberley.[26] Interestingly this lady claims on the census that she is living in four rooms although *The Laurels* was slightly larger than this having at least six rooms. It may mean that she rented out some rooms but no lodger is listed on the census records. Mary also records that she had no children alive which is strange as her son **Charles Nunn Nettley** (b.1874) is most probably the Charles mentioned above listed on the electoral register around the period. Maybe there had been a family issue which had caused the separation in some way.

The Inland Revenue Valuation has the name of '*Nettley'* crossed out and names the new occupant as *'Rockall'*. Nothing further is known of this occupant as the name does not appear in any street directories or electoral registers.

109. The Haven, Littlehampton Road
(Now a of Block of Flats No's 1-72 Carolyn House, Littlehampton Road)

The land for this property was purchased in March 1906 for £33 and the house was built for the sum of £295. It was owned by B. R. Ede of Newcastle House, South Farm Road in Worthing as was the next property along the road called *The Cottage*.

The Inland Revenue Valuation for *The Haven* refers back to the previous property for all other details and valuation as it is identical. The previous property is *The Laurels* which in turn was stated to be identical to *Ivy Cottage*. As previously stated the East Preston Rural District minutes had given permission for the building of "cottages" in Durrington to Mr Wood in 1904 and 1905. From these planning permissions it is highly probable that Mr Wood was the builder responsible for all of the detached cottages in this area of Littlehampton Road and that at some point after building he sold some of the cottages to new owners.

The first family we can identify and who may have been the first occupants are the Short family. They have been identified by an entry in the Durrington Council School log-book for April 4th 1910 which records:

'*Three children admitted, two coming from the house from which we lost the five Shorts.*'[27]

The '*five Shorts*' referred to above were: **Gladys Constance** (b.1898), **George Alfred** (b.1899), **Frederick Arthur** (b.1900), **Albert Edward** (b.1902) and **Winifred Gertrude** (b.1903). These details and the address are given in the school record books where we are informed the Short family were living at *The Haven*. Unusually, although we have the children's details, we know nothing of their parents from Durrington sources. However we can trace the family through the 1901 census when the children's names and father's occupation of '*fruit grower's labourer*' reveal the family were at that time living in Lancing.[28] The head of the household was **Alfred Frederick G Short** (b.1877) and his wife was named **Ellen Lucretia** (b.1877 nee Eve).

When the family left Durrington, which according to the date of the children's removal from school was in June 1910, we know they moved to Ham Road in East Worthing.[29] This was a strategic move, most probably again for work, as Ham Road was the home of a large number of working nurseries and market gardens at the time.

The next family to live in *The Haven* first appear in the street directories, electoral registers and the 1911 census all in the same year. The name registered is that of **James William Lambert** (b.1877), his wife **Maria Ann** (b.1878 nee Crayford) and their three children: **Joseph William James** (b.1902), **Elizabeth (Queenie) Annie** (b.1903) and **George Albert** (b. 1905).[30] The family must have moved to Durrington from Finchley in Middlesex as this is the place recorded on the census page as the children's birthplace. James was yet another of the migrant nursery workers who lived in and around Durrington for short periods of time. They did not stay for very long as by the time of the Inland Revenue Valuation in June 1913 their surname had been crossed out and the new name of '**Edney**' was written in.[31] Of this person we have no further information.

110. The Cottage, Littlehampton Road
(Now a of Block of Flats No. 1-72 Carolyn House, Littlehampton Road)

The 1901 census records occupants with the surname of '*Ruff*' living in Littlehampton Road, but the name of the house is not listed. The street directories also list the surname and they confirm that the address was *The Cottage*. This was an earlier cottage which must have been demolished at some point as the later building given the name was, according to the Inland Revenue Valuation, identical to its neighbour *Sunnyside* except that it had a smaller garden.[32]

This earlier family listed on the 1901 census, at *The Cottage* are: **Daniel Ruff** (b.1848), his wife **Sarah** (b.1849 nee Smart) and their children **William** (b.1877), **James** (b.1882), **Richard** (b.1886) and **Frances Eliza** (b.1888).[33] Daniel and his three sons are all listed as working with cattle or carting on the farm, probably in the fields that surrounded their home in 1901. They later moved to West Tarring and are recorded there in 1911.[34]

The Inland Revenue Valuation reveals that a plot of land on which the later home known as *The Cottage* was built was purchased in July 1904 for £32 10s by B. R. Ede of South Farm Road, Worthing.[35] The detail given on the valuation reveals that Mr Ede spent a further £252 having the house built.

The 1911 census gives us the names of the occupiers of the property at the time.[36] The head of the household was **James Stone** (b.1851) and he lived in the house with his wife **Amelia Anne** (nee Osborne). James and Amelia had married in 1873 and by the time of the 1891 census were running the Swan Inn in High Street,

Worthing.[37] This was a large establishment accommodating 28 lodgers on the night of the census. As well as fulfilling the role of publican James was working as a coal merchant and he continued this role even after leaving the inn and moving to Durrington.

111. Sunnyside, Littlehampton Road
(Now a of Block of Flats No's 1-72 Carolyn House, Littlehampton Road)

In 1911, according to the census, this three bedroomed property was the home of a cowman named **Charles Edward Mitchell Charman** (b.1874), his Irish born wife **Mary** (b.c1876) and Mary's daughter **Mary Robinson** (b.c1900) also born in Ireland.[38] According to details given in the census the couple had married around 1905 but no registration in England has yet been found for the event.

In 1901 Charles had been living with his father **Charles Mitchell Charman** (b.1852) and mother **Mary Jane** (b.1855 nee Sargent) in *Nell House* which stood on the south side of Littlehampton Road and was in the parish of West Tarring. At this time he was working as a domestic groom.[39]

According to the Inland Revenue Valuation the house had been purchased in June 1905 for £200.[40] The purchaser was Edward C. M. Charman, this is the man listed on the census as Charles as his birth registration is given as 'Edward Charles' rather than 'Charles Edward'. This confirms that the house was purchased around the time of the couple's marriage. The house has since been demolished.

Modern flats now stand on the site of these houses. © Dave Pryce 2016

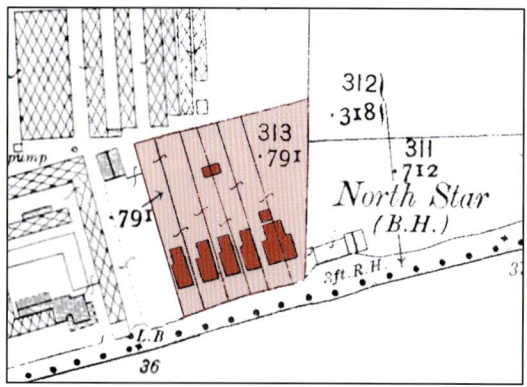

Excerpt taken from OS 25":1 mile Sheet LXIV: 9,10 3rd Edition 1912 (NTS)

112. North Star, Littlehampton Road
(Still standing but in a new building)

This is one of the four inns which were open for part or all of the Edwardian period in Durrington and Salvington. It was originally housed in a different building from that seen on the site today, the original being much smaller and standing on the far south western corner where today's entrance to the car park is situated.

The property was described in the Inland Revenue Valuation as *'Old premises'* which had a *'taproom, bar....cellar not underground & 3 bedrooms.'*[41]

The inn had its earliest listing in the 1861 census, where although it is mentioned in the description at the beginning of the portion of the census, it has not been traced in the actual schedules.[42] This may be due to the fact that the original pages are damaged with large pieces of the paper missing. It is also mentioned in 'The Worthing Annual List & Fashionable Weekly Journal' of 15th July 1869 where it is listed as a *'Beerhouse'*.[43]

The head of the household on the 1901 census was **Susan Elizabeth Curd** (b.1853 nee Willard), who was listed as a *'Beer-House Keeper'*.[44] Beer houses were licensed only for the sale of beer and ale; spirits could not be sold at these establishments. Susan Curd was running the *North Star* herself at the turn of the century as she had been widowed in 1898 when her husband, **Henry Curd** (b.1846) had died. His name does appear in some of the street directories right up until 1900 but this is an error. Henry and Susan had only one child, a son named **Charles Henry** (b.1885) who was listed on the 1901 census working as a carpenter's apprentice and living at the inn with his mother.

Henry and Susan had originally lived in Newhaven where Henry had worked on the railways but at some point after the 1891 census they had moved to Durrington to live and work at the *North Star*. Even after Henry's death in 1898 it was not until the September of 1907 that we have a report in the newspaper of the licence being transferred to a Mr George Willard and this is when Susan finally moved out of the inn to live in Worthing.[45]

TRANSFER OF LICENCES.
The licence of the White Hart Inn, Montague-street, was transferred from Mr. Wallace to Mr. Harcourt; that of the Victoria Arms, Montague-street, from Mr. Palmer to Mr. George Gilham; the Engineers' Arms, Broadwater, from Mr. W. J. Pullen to Mr. Alfred Lindup; and the North Star, Durrington, from Mrs. Curd to Mr. G. E. Willard.

Notice of the change of licensee for the North Star in 1907

The new landlord was a gentleman called **George Edwin Willard** (b.1867) who was Susan Curd's younger brother. He moved to the *North Star* with his wife **Ellen** (no birth or marriage traced) and four of their six children: **Edward Henry** (b.1895), **William John** (b.1900), **Lena Mabel** (b.1903) and **Frank Charles** (b.1910).

It was only a few years after the birth of Frank that Ellen was to die in rather sad circumstances. Her death was the subject of a Coroner's Inquiry in January 1913 when the details of her demise were reported in the local paper.[46]

Ellen had been walking to the train station with her older daughter **Daisy Eleanor** (b.1891) who had been visiting the family at the inn. Ellen was feeling very unwell and after encouraging her daughter to continue to the train station so that she did not miss her train, had seated herself on a chair near the church in West Tarring. She became even more unwell and her cries for help were heard by **Fanny Wareham** of 4 *Ashacre Cottages* who went to her aid and stayed with her until a doctor, summoned by a 'messenger' Fanny had engaged, arrived on the scene. All sadly to no avail and Ellen died a few minutes after the doctor arrived.

The outcome of the inquest was that Ellen had died of *'asphyxia, caused by the lungs becoming filled with fluid, the result of pleurisy'* and a verdict of *'Death from natural causes'* was returned.

George stayed at the *North Star* with the children for some years after Ellen's death. Of the children we know that William, who had originally gone to school in Goring, had been transferred to the new school in Durrington in June 1908 when it opened. He stayed there until October 1914 when he left to work as a *'Houseboy'*. Lena had joined the school when she was old enough eventually leaving during the war years to help her father at the inn.

As mentioned above the original inn was later demolished and replaced with the modern building standing on the site today.

DEATH BY THE ROADSIDE.

Woman's Sad End.

Coroner's Inquiry at Durrington.

THE West Sussex Coroner (Mr. F. W. Butler) conducted an inquiry at the North Star Inn, Durrington, on Monday afternoon, touching the death of Mrs. Ellen Willard, the wife of the landlord of the Inn, and which occurred suddenly while she was on her way to West Worthing Railway Station the previous Friday evening to see a daughter off by train.

Four witnesses were called, the first being GEORGE EDWIN WILLARD, landlord of the North Star, Durrington, who deposed that the deceased was his wife, and that she was forty years of age last birthday. Witness last saw her alive on Friday evening, about twenty minutes past six, when she left home to see a daughter off to Seaford by train. She then seemed to be in quite her usual health; she never complained, and had been out shopping the day before. Witness did not consider her to be in delicate health. She had rather a severe cold last October, but she got over that. She also complained at times of

A Little Shortness of Breath

when she went out into the open air, but that was all. She had never been ill a day in the sense of having to lay up. She ate rather a hearty dinner on Friday, but had nothing out of the ordinary for tea.

DAISY WILLARD, a daughter of the last witness, deposed that on Friday evening her mother was accompanying her to West Worthing Station, but when they got about half-way across the fields she stopped behind, as she was rather short of breath, and she was afraid they would not reach the Station in time. As a fact, they had plenty of time, for they had allowed themselves half-an-hour and five minutes. When they got half-way across the fields, and her mother decided to stay behind, witness

Bade Her Good-bye,

and she understood that she was going to come on till she got to the seat near Tarring Church, and wait there till witness's sister returned from the Station. Witness did not think her mother was ill at all, and she did not express any wish that one of them should stop with her. The wind was rather high on the Friday evening, and witness thought it was this that caused her mother to want to lag behind.

Mrs. FANNY WAREHAM, of 4, Ash Cottages, Salvington, deposed that she was going down into the town on Friday evening to do some shopping, and when she got to the corner of the wall near Tarring Church she heard someone shouting. On going a little further she noticed someone sitting on a seat. As witness was passing her the woman called out to her to come and help her. Witness unloosened her dress at the back to enable her to get her breath more easily, and then sent her little girl for a light. She also got a messenger to go for a doctor. The deceased was conscious, but she could hardly speak; she only asked her to help her. Witness remained with her till the doctor arrived.

The Medical Evidence.

Mr. JOHN SIDDONS CROOK a registered medical practitioner, residing at West Tarring, stated that deceased was sitting on the seat near the Church when he was called to see her on the Friday evening. She was almost insensible, and breathing very badly. There was a large quantity of white froth coming from her mouth and nose. Deceased died about five minutes after witness arrived. Witness had since made a post mortem examination. There were no marks of violence on the body, but he found that she had pleurisy on both sides with a considerable amount of fluid, which saturated the lungs. The heart was however perfectly healthy, and the other organs were normal. The cause of death had been asphyxia, caused by the lungs becoming filled with fluid, the result of pleurisy. The pleurisy might have been present for some time, but witness did not know that there would have been any pain.

The Jury returned a verdict of "Death from natural causes," in accordance with the medical evidence.

The Foreman also added an expression of the Jury's appreciation of the kindness of Mrs. Wareham.

Worthing Gazette 8th January 1913

The modern *North Star* building © David Nicholls 2014

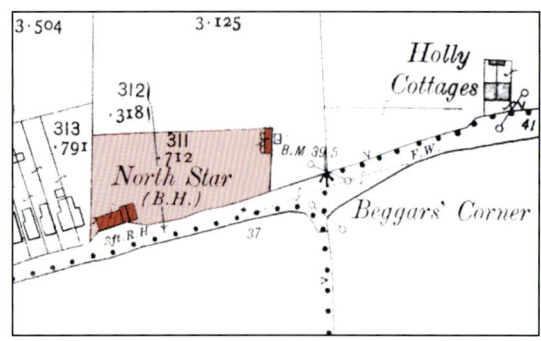

Excerpt taken from OS 25":1 mile Sheet LXIV: 9,10 3rd Edition 1912 (NTS)

113. Holly Cottages (No 1 & 2), Littlehampton Road
(Now No's 170 & 168 Littlehampton Road)

These were a pair of cottages that were owned by **Mr H. Gardiner** of Hove. Although the Inland Revenue Valuation states that they were occupied by the local farmer **Edwin Lephard** in November 1911, we know from the documentary evidence that he in turn had sub-let them to other families. The site of the two cottages was described at the time as: '*Old Gardens, Salvington*' and simply stating that it included two cottages. There are some interesting details on the pages of the Field Book for this site, one records that it is '*Subject to two years notice on either side expiring any Michaelmas*' while under the heading of '*Other Outgoings*' it has the remark:

'*Arbitrary fine on death or elimination*'[47]

These remarks, strange as they may seem, are concerned with the legal requirements of the holding of this land under 'copyhold' rather than 'freehold'. Copyhold is a form of land holding which originated in the medieval period where the land in question belonged to the manor, in this case the Manor of Durrington. Copyhold land could be bought and sold but technically it was always owned by the Lord of the Manor and as such had to be returned to him before any new owner or tenant could, for a fee, take up residence. The '*arbitrary fine*' referred to in the above quote refers to a 'heriot', which was the name of a payment made to the Lord of the Manor on the death of any tenant in copyhold premises. This form of land holding was finally abolished on 1st January 1926 when all copyhold land became freehold, although some existing rights did linger for a period.

Modern photograph of *Holly Cottages*. © Dave Pryce 2016

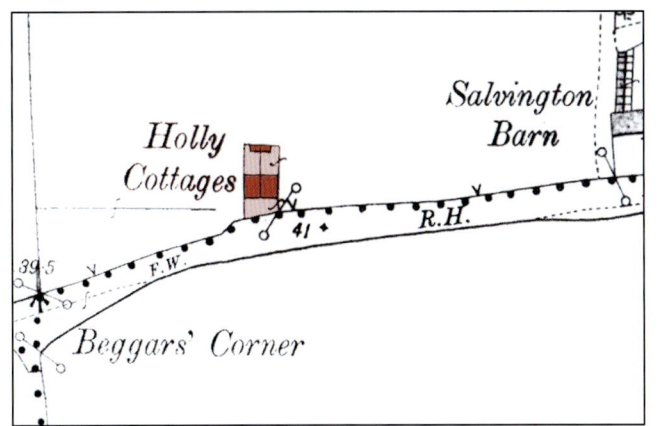

Excerpt taken from OS 25":1 mile Sheet LXIV: 9,10 3rd Edition 1912 (NTS)

No 1 Holly Cottages
(Now No 170 Littlehampton Road)

As stated above these cottages were ostensibly occupied by Edwin Lephard who in turn sub-let them, normally to farm workers. The first cottage was the home of two families during the years between the turn of the twentieth century and the outbreak of war in 1914. The first of these was **Charlie Knight** (b.1869) who is listed on the 1901 census and recorded in street directories through to 1903. Charlie had, according to the 1891 census records, previously been living in *2 Holly Cottages* with his parents William and Harriet Knight.[48] In 1894 Charlie had married **Harriett Austin** and a year later they had a son **Stanley Albert** (1895). By 1901 he was living with Harriett and Stanley in *1 Holly Cottages*, along with a boarder named **Edmund Boxall** (b.c1836).[49]

The second family lived in the house during the latter part of the Edwardian period. Street directories first list them in 1905 while the 1911 census gives us full details of the family.[50] The head of the house was a garden labourer by the name of **Richard Albert Stringer** (b.1855) who had come originally from Lewes but would have lived in the area for some while as he married a local lady by the name of **Elizabeth** (b.c1864 nee Goddard). They had moved to *Holly Cottages* from West Tarring where their son **Albert William** (b.1898) had been born. Richard was only listed on one electoral register which was for 1912 so the family probably moved on around that date.

No 2 Holly Cottages
(Now No 168 Littlehampton Road)

The second cottage was the home of **Henry Overington** (b.1856) and his wife **Annie Elizabeth** (b.1862 nee Collins). Henry was a member of the Overington family who were one of the more prominent families in the village working as blacksmiths from *The Forge* and holding leading roles within the parish. Henry had not chosen to work in the blacksmithing business alongside other males in the family, but had decided on the other Durrington speciality, that of a nurseryman. He and Annie had married in 1886 and had six children, five of whom were living with them in the cottage: **Arthur Cecil** (b.1888), **Dulcie** (b.1891), **Frank** (b.1892), **Wilfred Eustace** (b.1895) and **Maurice** (b.1897).[51]

We learn a little more about Henry through a letter he wrote to the Worthing Gazette in February 1904, where he was discussing the merits of Friendly Societies for the working man. This letter reveals that he was a member of one of these societies, the Ancient Order of Foresters. This society was established in 1834 for the purpose of *'assisting their fellow men who fell into need as they walked through the forests of life.'*[52] Henry, Annie and the children still living at home all moved around 1907 or 1908 to *1 Greenland Road* where their story continues.

The next occupants of *2 Holly Cottages* were members of another established Durrington and Salvington family of the period, namely the 'Mitchell Charmans'. Other members of this family were living on the south side of Littlehampton Road in *Nell House,* indeed it was this property that Herbert had grown up in with his parents. The parish boundary line runs through the middle of this road meaning that Herbert's relations may have been living in the same road but they were actually in the parish of Goring.

Herbert's full details and those of his family are recorded in the 1911 census where we are informed that the head of the household was **Herbert Edmund Mitchell Charman** (b.1881), alongside him was his wife **Robina Victoria** (b.1886 nee Lisher) and their children: **Maud Victoria** (b.1907), **Charles Alfred H** (b.1909) and **George Edward** (b.1911).[53] The family are first recorded at the address in a street directory for 1907 and we know from the census that he worked as a foreman in the market gardens, he may even have worked in one of the number of nurseries based in Littlehampton Road.

114. Sausage Skin Manufacturer
(No longer standing)

There is one other enterprise that was functioning in Littlehampton Road at this time which is of interest, although of a slightly unusual nature. It did not find its way onto a census and does not appear to have been listed in street directories as a business.

The clue to the existence of this enterprise is written within the Inland Revenue Valuation No. 7845 which refers to a secondary number within the description of the land and buildings. This second number included *Holly Cottages* described above and *Salvington Barn*. The description for this portion of buildings was:

> '*Land & buildings including Salvington Barn,*
> *1 large barn, boulder built tile roof*
> *Work Shop, 2 large sheds. 16 piggeries*
>   *Let to Mr Rank.*'[54]

The description holds some clues which, after further investigation, revealed an interesting story. There were 16 piggeries on the site which suggests the raising of pigs on a larger than average scale for the area. Quite a number of nurseries and private homes with enough land would raise a few pigs to help with the family income and table, but nothing on this scale was reflected anywhere else in the area. The sale of bacon, pork and ham might be the first presumption that comes to mind and although this may have been the destinations of many of the pigs there was another major cottage industry being carried out at these premises.

The clues begin to unravel when discovering who the *'Mr Rank'* was who was renting the property. The only gentleman with the correct surname living in the area was **Frederick Rank** (b.c1852) who lived in Highfield Road, West Tarring with his wife **Josephine** (b.c1865). From the 1901 and 1911 census returns we can only state presumed birth dates as both husband and wife, although British subjects, had originally been born in Bavaria and Austria respectively.

The interesting connection was Frederick's occupation which could have easily been that of the maker of the famous Bavarian Sausages but it was not. It was the specialised occupation of a *'sausage Skin Merchant'* in 1901,[55] and a *'sausage casing manufacturer'* in 1911.[56] The details of the art of creating sausage skins and the disposal and sale of the rest of the meat are not known but we do know that in some way the whole business was distasteful to the locals. A letter of complaint was duly sent by the Parish Council to East Preston Rural District Council in September 1911, as recorded in the minutes of the meeting:

> '*Nuisance*
> *Read a letter from the Parish Council forwarding complaints*
> *of nuisance at premises on the Littlehampton Road used for*
> *the preparation of sausage skins.*
>
> *Proposed by Mr Strong, seconded by Mr Overington and carried*
> *That the inspector be instructed to visit and report upon the same*'[57]

Nothing else is mentioned in the minutes so we may suppose that the inspector made his report. The issue did continue though and the story can be followed in the local newspapers. The East Preston District Council wanted the nuisance *'done away with,..'* whilst the local parish councillors were more sympathetic. Mr Overington commented that *'personally he had been passed the place several times since, and had not been able to detect anything wrong.'*[58]

This story obviously had some entertainment value as we find a satirical paragraph was inserted discussing *'the provision of overcoats for our sausages.'*[59] Nowhere in the text is the name of Mr Rank mentioned neither is the exact location given but it must surely be this business as no other of its kind appears anywhere in the area. There is no other mention of the business either in street directories or newspapers of the period. Whether Mr Rank ceased his operation or went on quietly creating sausage skins we have not so far discovered.

The barn, piggeries and other buildings have long since been demolished and replaced by modern housing.

An important branch of commercial industry concerns itself with the provision of overcoats for our sausages, which require to be comfortably clad before they are brought to the breakfast table; but it seems that this poetic occupation is not without its anxieties, for it has actually been suggested that a nuisance has been created at a neighbouring establishment where this fairly-like form of apparel is prepared.

Although the scene of the operations is not far distant from the borough boundary, the territory is actually within the parish of Durrington, and it is due to representations made by that authority that a suggested nuisance at the clothing factory has been suppressed, the occasion furnishing a member with the opportunity of pointing out how much better it is for parishioners to submit their grievances to the proper quarter, instead of grumbling amongst themselves.

Worthing Gazette 29th November 1911 discussing the manufacture of sausage skins in Littlehampton Road

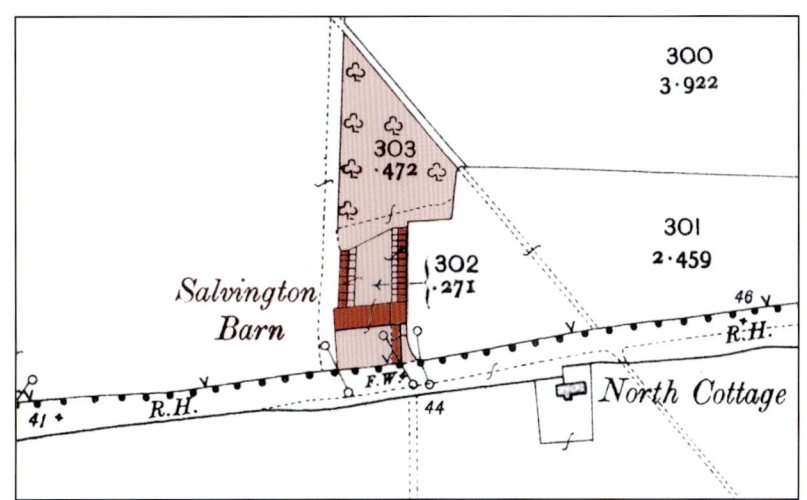

Excerpt taken from OS 25":1 mile Sheet LXIV: 9,10 3rd Edition 1912 (NTS)

---

[1] 1891 census RG12/837 ff. 134 (TNA)
[2] 1901 census RG13/957 ff. 87 (TNA)
[3] 1911 census RG14/5342 sch 189 (TNA)
[4] IR58/94203 No.7690 (TNA)
[5] Linfield, p 11-12
[6] Linfield p11
[7] 1901 census RG13/957 ff.78 (TNA)
[8] IR58/94205 No.7800 (TNA)
[9] 1861 census RG9/2080 ff.96 (TNA)
[10] 1911 census RG14/5342 sch 187 (TNA)
[11] www.cricketarchgive.com (viewed 4.1.2016)
[12] Alumni Cantabrigiensis Vol 2 Part 1 edited by John Venn 1940 p.150
[13] 1901 census RG13/1135 ff.64 (TNA)
[14] Linfield p11-12
[15] IR58/94205 No. 7795 (TNA)
[16] EPRD Minutes 23rd August 1904 p.115
[17] EPRD Minutes 7th January 1908 p.347
[18] 1911 census RG14/5321 sch 96 (TNA)
[19] IR58/94205 LT: 7795 (TNA)
[20] 1901 census RG13/492 ff. 104 (TNA)
[21] Worthing Gazette 3rd January 1906 p8
[22] Worthing Gazette 17th Feb 1909 p8d

[23] 1911 census RG14/5342 sch 184 (TNA)
[24] IR58/94205 sch 7796 (TNA)
[25] IR58/94205 No. 7797 (TNA)
[26] 1911 census RG14/5342 sch 183 (TNA)
[27] Durrington Council School Log Books 1908-1928 p 46
[28] 1901 census RG13/945 ff.49 (TNA)
[29] 1911 census RG14/5322 sch 146 (TNA)
[30] 1911 census RG14/5342 sch 184 (TNA)
[31] IR58/94205 No. 7798 (TNA)
[32] IR58/94205 No. 7794 (TNA)
[33] 1901 census RG13/957 ff. 62 (TNA)
[34] 1911 census RG14/5337 sch 291 (TNA)
[35] IR58/94205 No. 7793 (TNA)
[36] 1911 census RG14/5342 sch 181 (TNA)
[37] 1891 census RG12/836 ff.11 (TNA)
[38] 1911 census RG14/5342 sch 180 (TNA)
[39] 1901 census RG13/957 ff.63 (TNA)
[40] IR58/94205 No.7793 (TNA)
[41] IR58/94205 No 7660(TNA)
[42] 1861 census RG9/614 ff.200 (TNA)
[43] 'The Worthing Annual List & Fashionable Weekly Journal' 15th July 1869 (Worthing Library)
[44] 1901 census RG13/957 ff.78 (TNA)
[45] Worthing Gazette 18th September 1907 p5g
[46] Worthing Gazette 8th January 1913 p7b
[47] IR58/94206 No 7845 (TNA)
[48] 1891 census RG12/837 ff.119 (TNA)
[49] 1901 census RG13/957 ff. 62 (TNA)
[50] 1911 census RG14/5342 sch 75 (TNA)
[51] 1901 census RG13/957 ff.62 (TNA)
[52] www.foresterfriendlysociety.co.uk (viewed 4.8.2015)
[53] 1911 census RG14/5342 sch 76 (TNA)
[54] IR58/94206 No. 7846 (TNA)
[55] 1901 census RG13/997 ff.86 (TNA)
[56] 1911 census RG14/5337 sch 270 (TNA)
[57] EPRD Minutes 12th September 1911 p.191
[58] Worthing Gazette 29th November 1911 p7a
[59] Worthing Gazette 29th November 1911 p6b

Chapter 13
Offington Lane

Introduction

The properties in Offington Lane are all sited on the western side of the road on the land running from the southern corner of Ashacre Lane down to the Thomas a Becket crossroads. This line of properties lay on the eastern boundary line of the parish. The opposite side of the road was all part of the land belonging to the Offington Estate, the home of the Gaisford family. We have discovered very few early photographs of these properties.

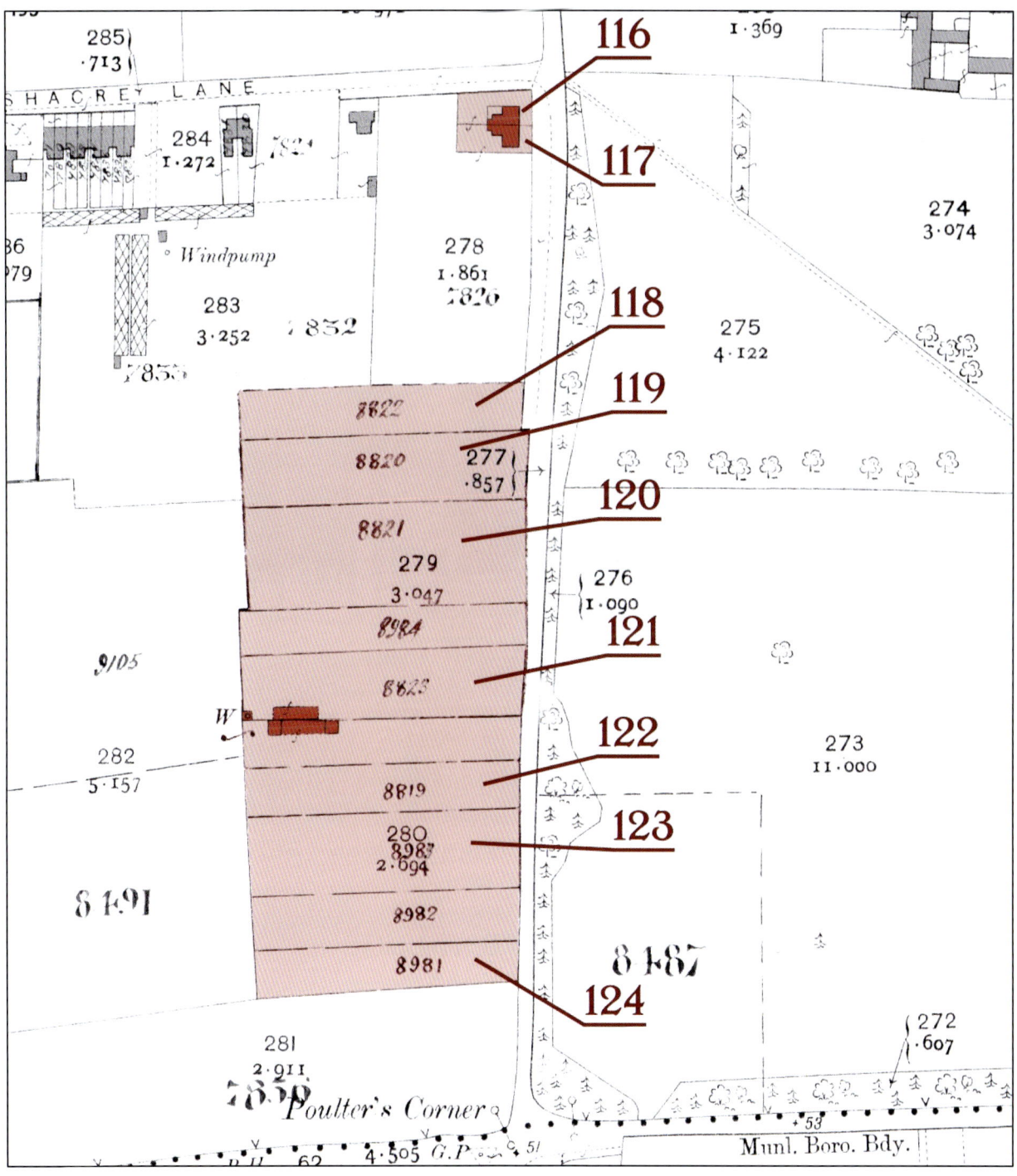

Excerpt taken from OS 25":1 mile Sheet LXIV:10 3rd Edition (NTS)
Inland Revenue Valuation numbers added

Edwardian view of *Offington Lodge* looking down Offington Lane on the right. Worthing Library

View looking north up Offington Lane with Rogate Road on the left. © Dave Pryce 2016

116. Offington Cottage, Offington Lane
(Now No 53 Offington Lane)

This property is one of a pair of semi-detached houses situated on the south west corner of the junction of Ashacre Lane with Offington Lane. Both this and the adjoining property, *Mimosa,* were owned and built by the Gaisford family of Howth Castle, Dublin. In the Edwardian period this cottage's address was given as Ashacre Lane, it is included at this point as it is attached to its neighbour and the present address is Offington Lane.

The Inland Revenue Valuation for *Offington Cottage* was taken in November 1911 and describes the property as:

> *'Modern attractive looking cottage, red brick tile hung*
> *1st floor 3 bedrooms*
> *Gd floor 1 r(oom). K(itchen). Sc(ullery) W.C.'*[1]

Modern Photograph of *Offington Cottage*. © Lyn Tiller 2016

The land for the two cottages was purchased in October 1905 as part of a larger piece of land stretching down the side of Offington Lane at a purchase price of £630 plus £5 commission. This property and its neighbour were the first two houses to be built on the site at a cost for both properties of £595.

The valuation records that the previous occupier was H. Boxall and the present O'Bierne. H. Boxall is likely to be **Henry Boxall** who is listed as living in Offington Park in various street directories from the period. He was probably working on the Offington Park estate. The 1911 electoral register lists Henry Boxall at *'House, Salvington'* which does not help to narrow down the address and other addresses during the period in Durrington and Salvington housed people with the Boxall surname.

The second name on the Inland Revenue Valuation is the family listed on the 1911 census. The head of the household was **Lewis Ormsby O'Bierne** (b.c1844) recorded at the address with his wife **Marian** (b.1855 nee Elms) and one of their three children, **Arthur Lloyd Stanley** (b.1889).[2]

Excerpt taken from OS 25":1 mile Sheet LXIV: 10 3rd Edition 1912 (NTS)

117. Mimosa, Offington Lane
(Now No 51 Offington Lane)

A modern photograph of *Mimosa*. © Lyn Tiller 2016

The earliest dated occupant discovered for *Mimosa* is given in electoral registers from 1910 where the name of Christian Seebold appears. This is confirmed by details on the 1911 census. The couple occupying the address were **Christian Ignas Martin Seebold** (b.c1864) and his wife **Annie Eliza** (b. 1869 nee Patrick).[3] Christian, who gave his occupation as that of a musician, was the older brother of **Karl Adolphus Seebold** (b.1873) also a musician and entrepreneur who was living in Worthing and is described by Elleray as a *'Cinema pioneer and leading promoter of entertainment in Worthing. A Swiss violinist, he became leader of his family's Swiss band.'*[4]

Karl had originally settled in Worthing around 1904 opening the New Theatre Royal in Bath Place. In 1909 he had built a roller skating rink in Marine Parade known as *The Kursaal,* which was later re-named *The Dome.* Other theatres were either built or run by Karl Seebold in Worthing and it would have been in these venues that Christian and other members of the Seebold family would have performed their music under Karl's leadership.

The Inland Revenue Valuation for this property gives very little extra detail to that already listed with its neighbour *Offington Cottage* except to point out that it was *'not a corner house and has not so large a garden.'*[5].

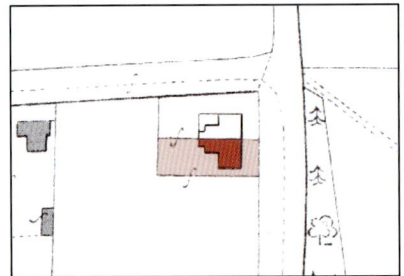

Excerpt taken from OS 25":1 mile Sheet LXIV: 10 3rd Edition 1912 (NTS)

118. Park Villa, Offington Lane
(Now No 39 Offington Lane)

Park Villa photographed in 2016. © Lyn Tiller

This property was not built in time to be recorded on the 1911 census but we know that permission to build was granted to Mr J Adams by the East Preston Rural District council on the 19th December 1911.[6] The name of this house is mentioned on the Inland Revenue Valuation where the address is *'Site of Park Villa, Offington Lane.'*[7] The owner of the property is given as **Mrs A Adams.** The electoral register for 1913 lists the occupant of this address as **John Adams** who had moved from *Sarum,* Heene Road to the newly built house in 1912 or 1913. The street directories confirm this name from 1912 onwards and add that he was a builder.

The 1911 census confirms that John Adams was indeed living in Heene Road, Worthing and furthermore it reveals that his wife's name was Ann.[8] We can suppose from this that she is the *'Mrs A. Adams'* who is listed as the owner of the house on the valuation.

The East Preston District Council minutes refer to Adams building properties and obtaining water certificates for properties on Offington Lane making it clear that he must have built two or three of the large houses including *White Hall* the property next door. The earliest plans appear in the minutes for 12th April 1910 when permission was passed for *'2 residences in Offington Lane for Mr J. Adams.'*[9] One of these was for *Park Villa* where four months later another permission to build was given, this time for stables to be added to the property.[10] The second permission for stables for Mr Adams was not passed until 28th March 1911 suggesting that the second house was built some time later.[11]

119. White Hall, Offington Lane
(Now No 37 Offington Lane)

This is another of the houses built and owned by the builder John Adams who was living next door in *Park Villa.*

The 1911 census lists a family living in the property and records the head of the household as **William Henry Dawes Jones** (b.1844).[12] William was age 66 at the time and gives his occupation as *'Lieut Col Indian Army Pensioner'*. With him were his wife **(Elizabeth) Emily Georgina** (b.1866) and four of their five children: **May Gordon** (b.c1893), **Gwladys** (b.c1895), **Dorothy Gordon** (b.c1896) and **Staveley Gordon Dawes** (b.1903). Their other son **Basil Gordon Dawes** (b.1897) was a student at a public school known as Haileybury College in Hertfordshire at the time of the census. It is interesting to note that the girls were all born in Bombay, India whilst their father was still serving in the Indian Army.

The family moved out of the house after the census and the next occupant is listed on a 1911 electoral register which gives the name of **Ella Mary Willicombe** and confirms that she had moved from Durrington into *White Hall* during the same year.

This house was not analysed at the time of the Inland Revenue Valuation although it was given an assessment number and listed as *'Site of White Hall, Offington Lane'* even though we know that the property was built and inhabited.[13] The valuation is not dated and records no occupant only giving the owner as *'A Willicombe, White Hall'*. This is confirmed by the surname given on the electoral register.

A modern view of *White Hall*. © Lyn Tiller 2016

120. Glengariff, Offington Lane
(Now No 35 Offington Lane)

The 1911 census lists a husband and wife living in this house whose names were **William Pering Paige** (b.1874) and his wife **Florence Annie** (b.1874 nee Hodson).[14] They were both recorded as living on private means and had a servant with them whose name was **Annie Ada Mears** (b.1893). The couple had married in 1906 in Brighton but had no children by the time of the census.

Once again this property, as the majority of Offington Lane was, is only partially recorded on the Inland Revenue Valuation where this house is listed as: *'Offington Lane, The site of Glengariff'* with Mrs F. A. Paige being given as the owner.[15] We do not know the date that the house was built, but William Paige was being given various planning permissions during the period. In April 1910 he had plans for *'an amended drainage plan of house in Offington Lane, Salvington for Mr Paige'* passed, although he owned more than one of the properties so it is difficult to know which house this was for.[16]

Interestingly, only Mrs Florence Paige is listed in street directories for this address between 1911 and 1913 and only her name appears on the electoral register for 1912 and 1913, although we know that her husband was with her in the house on the census. This is probably due to the fact that she is listed as the owner of the property.

Modern view of *Glengariff*. © Lyn Tiller 2016

121. The Faze, Offington Lane
(Now No 29 Offington House, Offington Lane)

The Faze photographed in 2016. © Lyn Tiller

There is very little information on this property that relates to the Edwardian period suggesting it was built quite late. There is, however, an uninhabited property listed in the summary books for the 1911 census that may be this property. The Inland Revenue Valuation has marked the plot with a number and the related book page for that number lists it as *'Land, Offington Lane…….Site of Faze The'*[17]

The only information we have connected with the early days of this house was that it was owned by **Aubrey A. Adams** of Llandoff, Heene Road, Worthing, who had agreed a five year tenancy with **C. Hobson** to run from the 25th March 1911 at £80. Aubrey Adams does not appear to be any relation to John Adams, the builder, who was living in *Park Villa* with his wife Annie and owned and probably built at least three properties in the road.

Aubrey Ashby Adams (b.1875) is listed on the 1911 census at the address mentioned above where his occupation is given as *'house builder and cartage contractor.'*[18]

122. Breinton, Offington Lane
(Now Cranleigh Lodge, No 21 Offington Lane)

The house originally called *Brienton*. © Lyn Tiller 2016

As with most of the properties on this part of Offington Lane the Inland Revenue Valuation's lack of detail suggests it was assessed in the early life of the property. The plot is described in a general format as *'Site of Breinton'* although it does confirm that the *'House now erected'*.[19] The owners name is given a Mrs A Adams of *Park Villa*, Offington Lane meaning that this was the third property to be built and owned by John and Ann (Annie) Adams along with *White Hall* and *Park Villa*. No occupant is given at the time of the valuation but there are residents recorded on the 1911 census.

In 1911 *Breinton* was the home of **Frederick Dutton** (b.1846), a retired accountant who had worked for the Inland Revenue and had decided to retire to Salvington, bringing his wife **Emily Sarah** (b.1843 nee Downing) and three of his daughters with him. His two oldest daughters were twins, **Emily Mary** (b.1874) and **Gertrude Jane** (b.1874) who had travelled to Worthing with their younger sister **Beatrice Maud** (b.1878). They are all listed as teachers in a private school with at least two of them teaching music.[20]

123. Ayston, Offington Lane
(Now No 19 Offington Lane)

Ayston is first recorded in the East Preston District Council minutes when permission was granted in October 1910 for the building of stables at the address.[21] The Inland Revenue Valuation uses the same format as the other Offington Lane houses when it lists the plot as *'Site of Ayston'* although it clarifies that there was a house and garden on the land. No date is given for the assessment which gives no further evidence for the building of the house. **Mrs B. McDonald** was listed as the owner and occupier at the time of the valuation.[22]

The property is included on the 1911 census returns but we only have the names of two servants who were in the house at the time. One was the cook **Mary Ann Caplin** (b.1879) and the other was a house maid **Martha Gosney** (b.1879).[23] The main occupants must have been away from home on the night of the census.

The street directories for 1911 list **Mrs B. McDonald** living at the address and also list another lady **Mrs Thomson** of whom nothing else has been found for the time. The only further information regarding these ladies is found in the electoral register for 1913 when we learn that Mrs McDonald's Christian name was *'Beatrice'*.

This modern view of *Ayston* was photographed in 2016. © Lyn Tiller 2016

124. The Homestead, Offington Lane
(No longer standing)

The Inland Revenue Valuation records this as *'Site of The Homestead, Offington Lane'* and gives the owner as E. O. Hanbury of Amatola, Shakespeare Road.[24] This was **Ernest Osgood Hanbury** who was a gentleman of private means living in Worthing at the time.[25]

The 1911 census lists a couple at the property who had only been married for a year. **Reginald William Bartleet** (b.1861) was the head of the household who gave his occupation as a *'retired Quantity Surveyors Clerk'*. He lived here with his wife **Eliza** (b.1870 nee Callaway) and a servant **Annie Elizabeth Stevens** (b.1892).[26]

Reginald is listed in street directories and the electoral registers from 1911 through to the end of the period. No photographs have been discovered for this property which has now been demolished.

[1] IR58/94206 No. 7827 (WSRO)
[2] 1911 census RG14/5342 sch 28 (TNA)
[3] 1911 census RG14/5342 sch 27 (TNA)
[4] Elleray p24
[5] IR58/94206 No 7828
[6] EPRD Mins 21st November 1911 p219 (WSRO)
[7] IR58/94216 No. 8822 (TNA)
[8] 1911 census RG14/959 sch 191 (TNA)
[9] EPRD Mins 12th April 1910 p83 (WSRO)
[10] EPRD Mins 30th August 1910 p113 (WSRO)
[11] EPRD Mins 28th March 1911 p155 (WSRO)
[12] 1911 census RG14/5342 sch 26 (TNA)
[13] IR58/94216 No. 8820 (TNA)
[14] 1911 census RG14/5342 sch 25 (TNA)
[15] IR58/94216 No. 8821 (TNA)
[16] EPRD Mins 12th April 1910 p83 (WSRO)
[17] IR58/94216 No. 8823 (TNA)
[18] 1911 census RG14/5338 sch 196 (TNA)
[19] IR58/ 94216 No. 8819 (TNA)
[20] 1911 census RG14/5342 sch 24 (TNA)
[21] EPRD Mins 11th October 1910 p124 (WSRO)
[22] IR58/94217 No. 8983 (TNA)
[23] 1911 census RG14/5342 sch 23 (TNA)
[24] IR58/94217 No. 8981 (TNA)
[25] 1911 census RG14/5339 sch 310 (TNA)
[26] 1911 census RG14/5342 sch 22 (TNA)

Appendix 1
'Appleacre', Salvington, West Sussex
Study by Gordon Latham

Postal Address: *'Appleacre', 62 Ashacre Lane, Worthing West Sussex, BN13 2DE*
Grid Reference: *TQ 129 051*

General
    The above dwelling was called 'Rose Cottage' until about 1920, then 'Corner Cottage' until 1930 when it became 'Appleacre'. It has been in the present ownership since 1983.
    Estate agent's particulars dated 1954 include the words '…part of which is reputed to date back 400 years…' Another agent's details (1983) state '…part of which is reputedly 16th century…'
    Large-scale Ordnance Survey maps of 1875-76, 1898 and 1914-1915 show only a very small building corresponding to the old part of the cottage. The 1932-33 map shows a building much extended towards the west.
    Solicitors' conveyances show the property changed hands in 1919 for £225, in 1920 for £475 and in 1925 for £1700. The price then remained relatively stable until WWII. The map changes and price increases suggest that the
Original building underwent major enlargement in 1920-25.
    Archives at Chichester show that a kitchen extension was built in 1945, and an application was made in 1954 for the garage and 'lobby' extension.
    The westwards extension of the west bedroom on the first floor for an 'en suite' shower room was built in 2004.

Outside
    The roof carries two types of tile. Those that appear to be older are at the eastern end, corresponding with that being the older part of the building.
    On the front, south-facing wall there is a slight vertical shrinkage crack just east of the oriel window, corresponding with other indications noted below of the demarcation between the old and new parts of the building.
    The north wall of the western part of the building encroaches on and appears to incorporate the flint garden wall that forms the north boundary.

Inside
    In the dining room most of the ceiling beams are longitudinal and evidently very old, contrasting with some newer transverse beams at the western end beyond the east side of the oriel window, suggesting perhaps a missing main west wall at this point. The pattern of the old longitudinal beams appears unusual with a short new transverse timber placed centrally across just three pitches of the old ones. By analogy with the beam pattern in the adjoining, newer lounge one wonders whether this could have been the position of a chimney-breast in the missing wall, about five foot or so east of the existing dining room fireplace.
    The south wall from here on shows a corresponding reduction of thickness of about three inches. A similar reduction of wall thickness might be expected in the north wall, but no such feature has been found.
    The dining room appears to have a solid floor whereas the adjacent lounge has a step up to a suspended floor. This has airbricks to the outside, which are not present in the older part.
    In the cupboard under the east staircase the short longitudinal beams are closed off by a transverse member that appears to be of similar age. Perhaps this suggests that the original stairs were in the same position as the existing (eastern) ones. The door of this cupboard is made out of three vertical boards and, together with two similar doors just above on the first floor, appears significantly older than the other internal doors that are all of five or more boards.
    In the kitchen, when the northernmost wall cabinet on the west wall of this room was replaced there were indications of an old window frame, suggesting that this may have been the outside wall at the east end of the building.
    A number of old timbers appear to have been used in 'erratic' locations, e.g. the two posts at the foot of the stairs with lap dovetail jointing at their upper ends. There are also several pieces around the dining room fireplace and mantelpiece, possibly some by the lounge mantelpiece and certainly the lintel above the lounge window.

Going upstairs there are various old timbers embedded in the walls, presumably wall plates, in the north, east and south walls. A chimneybreast in the east bedroom serves no fireplace in this room or the dining room below, and its purpose is not understood. Diagonal wall ties, perhaps of wrought iron, strengthen the NE and SE corners of the original building. The western ends of the wall plates in both the north and south main walls are shaped suggesting joints with adjacent timbers now missing, consistent with the idea of a missing west wall postulated above.

In the middle bedroom, now a study, there is a reduction of thickness in the south wall corresponding to that noticed downstairs. A vertical mark in this wall above the radiator in this room may be a witness of the inside of the suggested missing west wall.

The Loft

The loft can be viewed from the hatch in the main bedroom and shows old timbers of the original roof under those of a more modern one, considerably extended both east and west. The old rafters show that the roof was hipped at both ends, like the newer one, but with a very short ridge – almost a pyramid shape. The function of some of the timbers is not clear, the purlins being backed by some 10"x2" timbers directly inboard of them.

The east-sloping rafters explain the adjacent sloping ceiling (skeiling?) on the landing and in the adjoining bedroom. They presumably once extended as eaves into what is now the bathroom, having since been shortened and the wall extended upwards at reduced thickness, partially explaining the noticeable batter. (However in the final paragraph of these notes there is conjecture about these rafters extending over an outshot.) The bathroom doorway was presumably cut into this wall when the building was extended eastwards as previously there would have been very limited headroom for a doorway even to outside stairs. The stack from the chimneybreast already mentioned can be seen up close and is strongly corbelled across to the north. Perhaps this was done to avoid penetrating the ridge of the new roof at its junction with the hipped end. It is not clear whether there was originally a vertical stack that would have risen clear through the hipped end of the original roof.

The loft may also be viewed and accessed via the hatch in the middle bedroom, The position of the old west-sloping rafters accords with the assumed position of the missing west wall. A simple gauge has been made to illustrate this. There is a little discolouration on one of the rafters. If this is from smoke or soot it could be consistent with there having been a closely adjacent chimneystack from a fireplace in the dining room, as already suggested.

The old west-sloping rafters and also the north and south ones (old and new) are at 40 degrees to the horizontal, whereas the old eastern ones slope more nearly at 35 degrees.

Attached Drawing

The attached drawing shows the front (south) elevation of the present property at 1:100 scale marked up to show the outline of the original cottage based on the above assumptions. It maybe that the roof was extended either to the east or west over a single storey outshot, but no attempt has been made to show this.

The 1898 map, before the building was extended, shows the east end of the building hard against the boundary, whereas the accompanying marked up drawing, based on the old roof rafters, shows a space of around 10 feet clear of the boundary. If the map is accurate this could suggest an outshot at the east end. Better headroom here would have been provided by the reduced slope of the rafters at this end, mentioned above. No indications of such an outshot have yet been observed and these comments are merely conjectural and would not seem consistent with the precious remarks about a window frame in the existing kitchen wall.
G.L. 17.8.2007

Bibliography

This list does not include the original sources listed in the Introduction.

Ashton, Roger. *'Wind powered electrical generator at High Salvington.'* Sussex Industrial History (33) 2003 p.6-9

Dexter, Joan D. *Blood's Thicker than Water. The story of the Search for our Dinsdales Past and Present.* (Author, 2002)

Elleray, D Robert. *Millennium Encyclopaedia of Worthing History.* (Optimus, 1998)

Evans, Nat. *The Church and Parish of Durrington.* (Author, 1977)

Fruit, Flower and Vegetable Traders Journal. November 1909

The Gardeners Chronicle November 5th 1910 p.346 (www.forgottenbooks.com)

Godfrey, Sarah. *Beaconsfield Terrace, Ashacre Lane, Salvington and the story of the inhabitants during the Edwardian period.'* A case study written for the Edwardian Durrington project. Copies held at Worthing Library and West Sussex Record Office. (Unpublished, 2015)

Keech, Barry. *Doctors, Dentists and Death.* (West Sussex Heritage Booklet, No 2. 2011)

Levy, Angela. *A History of High Salvington. Book 1* (Author, 2014)

Levy, Angela. *A History of High Salvington. Book 2* (Author, 2015)

Linfield, Malcolm. *The Development of the Glasshouse Industry in Durrington.* A case study written for the Edwardian Durrington project. Copies held at Worthing Library and West Sussex Record Office. (Unpublished, 2014)

Picture Review of the Business Life of Worthing. (Supplement from 'Town and Country Illustrated' 6th February 1909)

The Mill. Newsletter of the Friends of High Salvington Windmill. Issue 21: Spring 2015

The Worthing Annual List & Fashionable Weekly Journal.' 15th July 1869

Walker, Derek. *The Worthing Mail Story. Vol 4. The Expansion of Post Offices from 1798. Including the names of sub-post masters & examples of labels'.* (Unpublished, 2003)

Worthing Golf Club 1905-1980, The Story of the First Seventy-Five Years. (Worthing Golf Club, 1980)

Index

Ablitt, Ida Edith 194
Adams, Ann(ie) 233, 236
   Aubrey Ashley 236
   John 233, 236
Allen, John 69
Alleyne Cottage 66-68
Alleyne Poultry Farm 67
Alpha Cottage 84-86
Amatola 237
Ansfield, Albert William 144
   Dorothy Kathleen 144
   Ella May 144-145
   Frances Ellen 87, 144
   Frederick 87, 144
   George Frederick 144
   Henry Gordon 144
   Louise Annie E 144
   sons 143
   Wilfred Clarence 144
Appleacre 163
Appletree Cottage 204
Apted, Henry 3
Archibald Road, Worthing 145
Armstrong, Fanny 116, 150
Arno, Carmen Wilson 64
   Henry (Harry) Fellowes 64
   Jack Jean 64
   Leonie Catherine 64
   Major Wilson 64
Arnold, George Sargeant 51
   Harold George 51
   Julia Alexandra 51
Arthur, Margaret Letitia 93
Arundel Road 28, 71, 168, 181, 183, 194, 206, 208
Ash Cottages 135-139, 151
Ash Grove 67
Ash Nurseries 151
(The) Ashacre 128
Ashacre Cottages 122, 133, 135-139, 150, 222
Ashacre Lane 32, 85, 89, 94, 110, 114, 115, 116, 117, 124, 150, 168, 219, 229, 230
Ashacre Nurseries 151
Ashington Water Mill 78
Austin, Harriet 225
Avoca 63-64
Avondale 65
Ayston 237
Bailey 202
   Alice Maud 202
   Rev. Canon 45
Baker, J 131
   Samuel 148
   Thomas Green 18
Bakers Court 78, 80
Ball, 197
Banks, Alfred 83
   Arthur 83
   Eda Georgiana 83
   Lionel 83
Barker, Alleyne Hayward 216-217
   Florence Elizabeth 217
Bartleet, Eliza 237
   Reginald William 237

Batchelor 86
Bateman, Ellen Douglas 35
   Hezekiah Linthicum 35
   Kate 35
   Sidney Frances 35
   Virginia 35
Bath Place, Worthing 232
Baynes, Emma 7
   Samuel 7
Beaconsfield Cottages 148
Beaconsfield Terrace 85, 87, 113, 115, 118, 128, 139, 142-150, 151, 170, 219
Bean, Charles 33
   Mary 33
   Thomas 33
Beaty, (Walter) James 183
   Jane 183
Beck, Elizabeth Fanny 177
Beckham, Emma 30
Beckton, Emily 30
Bedford Row, Broadwater 146
Beetle Alley 32
Bell, Elsie 39
   Fanny 39
   Henry Warland 39
Berry, Lucy 146
Beta House 84-86, 110, 111
Bethany 40-41, 72, 95
Betteridge, Edward 95
   Edward Charles 95
   Ellen Mary 95
Betts, Esther 41
Bicknell, Eliza (Elizabeth) Mary 149
Binstead, Edward Henry 18
Birklands 65, 105-106
Birklands Nursery 105-106
Bish, (Ernest) Alfred 187
   Doris Marjorie 187
   Ernest Alfred 187
   Gladys Bertha 187
   Jessie Bertha 187
   Phyllis Mary 187
Bisham 94
Blacksmith Cottage 53-54, 58, 105
Blaker, James 5
Blisset, Thomas 214, 215
Boje, Robert 71
Boniface, Elizabeth 150
   Kate 147
Boorer, Laban 81, 138, 144
Booth, Amy 30
   Caroline Amy 30
Borold, W 137
Bowers, George 7
   George (b.1889) 6
   Helen 7
   John Samuel 6-7
   Sarah 7
   Thomas 6
Boxall, Edmund Boxall 225
   Henry 231
Boxold, Edith Rosalind 116
   William Henry 33, 116
Braby, Jane 191

Brace, Alice Eveline 207
   Harriett 207
   Harriett Ethel 207
   Thomas 207-209
Bradford, Alfred 83
   Eda Georgiana 83
Brake, Mr A 96
   Mrs A 9
Bramble Lane 40
Breinton 236
(The) Briars 65-66, 105
Brickfield Cottages 5-7
Brickfields 5
Bridger, Percy 171
   Selina Ellen 171
Bridges, Supt. 19
Brightwell, 219
Bristow, Henrietta 137
Bromfield, Ellen Worth 48, 88, 140-141
   Emily 140
   George Henry 88, 140
   Helen (Ellen) 140
   Henry Jenkins 140
Brown, Edith Rosalind 116
   Elizabeth 189
   George (b.1878) 8
   George (b.1885) 139
Bruff, Florence (Frances) Daisey 35
Buckland, Dorothy 58
Budd, Albert 58
   Alice Mary 204
   Richard Harry 204
Bull, 197
(The) Bungalow Tea Rooms 205
(The) Bungalow, High Salvington 205-206
(The) Bungalow, Littlehampton Road 215-216
(The) Bungalow, Pond Lane 17
Burgin, Lily 178
Burlace, Helen 213
Burns, Edwin 81
Burridge, James 7
Bursell, Sarah Jane 30
Bursnall, Edward 55
   Nellie Floyd 55
   William Henry 55
Burt, Frederic Murrell 217
Burton, Ada Louisa Jane 138
   Ernest 138
Burt's Cottage 124-135, 60
Bush, George 59, 100
   Mary Ann 100
Bushby, Annie 8
   Thomas 5, 8
Bushby's Cottage 8-9
Bushby's Nursery 8
Butcher, Henry 22
Butchers Shop 56-67
Callaway, Eliza 237
Caplin, Mary Ann 237
Carey, John 55
Carolyn House 218
Castle, Elizabeth Fanny 116
Castle Bungalow 196

Castle View 187-188
Castle View Tea Rooms 187
Causton 89, 140-142, 150
Causton House, South Street, West Tarring 141
Cave, Robert Moore 214
(The) Chalet 203-204
Chalk, Emily 137
Charman, Albert 118, 119
  Annie 58
  Charles (b.1880) 134
  Charles Alfred H 226
  Charles Edward Mitchell 221
  Charles Mitchell 58
  Clara 133-134
  Edward Charles 221
  George Edward 226
  Herbert Edmund Mitchell 225-226
  James (b.1869/1870) 112, 118, 133-134
  Joseph 118
  Louisa Bessie M 112, 118
  Mary 221
  Mary Jane 221
  Mary Mitchell 58
  Maud Victoria 226
  Robina Victoria 226
  Thomas 58
Chesswood Road, Worthing 103
Cheviot Road 71
Chez Nory 116
Chez Nous (Laundry) 112, 116-119, 122, 124, 125, 134, 136, 150
Chipper, Alfred 5
Church, Eileen Carmen 57
  Lizzie 56
  Ruby Elizabeth 57
  William George Daniel (George) 56-57
Church Walk 102
Churcher, Mrs 112
Claremont Nursery 11-13
Clark, 102
Clarke, F W 67
Clevett, (Clevitt/Clevatt) 191
  Alice Mary 191
  Charles 191
  Emily Ann 191
  Emma (Emily) Jane 191
  George Laban 191
  Kate 191
  Mary 191
  Reuben (b.1867) 191
  Reuben (b.1895/6) 191
Clevitt, (Clevett/Clevatt) 191
  Alfred Henry 191
  Charles 191
  Edith Emily 191
  Elizabeth 134
  Florence Elizabeth 191
  Harriet 191
  Herbert Daniel 191
  Jane 191
  Jane Elizabeth 191
  Mabel Annie 191
  Mary 191
  William (b.1878) 191
  William (b.1879) 134
Clifford, Annie 8
Close, Alice Mary 204
Cloverly 156

(The) Coach and Horses 65
Coate (Cote) 179, 181, 194
Coate Cottages 183, 184-185
Coate (Cote) Farm 182-184, 192, 194
Coate Farmhouse 181
Coate (Cote) Street 5, 176, 209
Cobden Road, Worthing 146
Cole, Fletcher 200
  Mary 150
  Miss 200
  R 150
Coleman, 214
Collard, Agnes (b.1856) 149
  Agnes Alice 149, 171
  Mildred Ethel 148, 149, 171
  Robert 138
  Robert (b.1845) 148
  Sarah Jane 143, 148, 171
  Selina Ellen 149, 171
Collet, H N 115
Collins, Annie Elizabeth 225
  Caroline 209
  George 178
Columbia Drive 3
Cook, Ada 24
  Charles 24
  Hilda Alice 24
Cooper, Mary 116
Coote, Alfred 59, 78-79
  Alfred Samuel 78
  Alice (b.1881) 58
  Alice (b.1894) 78-79
  Bernard 58
  Cecil 78
  Charles 78-79
  Ganey 78
  John 78-79
  Muriel 59
  Rhoda 58, 59, 78-79
  Richard Henry 58, 78
  Samuel 78
  Sarah 59
Coote & Sons Bakery 78-80, 93, 97, 116
Cornwell, Kate 146
Cotching, Frank Irving 61, 105
  George Frederick 61, 105
Cote Bottom 181
Cottage 111
(The) Cottage, Littlehampton Road 217, 220-221
Cottages, Coate Street 185-186
Cottages, Franklin Road 97-98
Court, Ethel Charlotte Pigott 89
Cousin, 214
Cowell, Joseph 35
  Sidney Frances 35
Cox, Caroline Charlotte 16
  Harriet 16
Cozens, 214
Crane, A 81
Crayford, Maria Ann 220
Crofts, Elizabeth 218
  Elsie 218
  Henry 218
Crouch, C Douglas 102
Cuckney, Charles 145
  Doris 145
  Louisa 145
Cullen, Richard 152
Cunnell, James 58

Victoria Elizabeth 58
Curd, Charles Henry 222
  Henry 222
  Susan Elizabeth 222
Cureton, Thomas 140
Curtis, John 18
Cutler, Elizabeth 159
  John 159
Cutler's Cottages 32, 114, 115, 147, 159-162
Cutlers Farm 159
Cutler's House 159
Dalbiac, C W 177
  family 101
Dale, Alice Maud 138
  Eleanor 138
  Mabel Florence 138
  Percy Charles 138
Dalgleish, Emily Evelyn 153
  Lucy J M F 153
  Maude Lucy 153
  William Henry 153
Darker, Miss 200, 203
Davies, Amelia 68
  Edward Parry 68
de Polyach, A 215
Dean, 134
  Ada Louisa Jane 138
  Alfred Ernest 138
  Alfred Ernest (b.1896) 122, 136
  Amy (Emily) 122, 136
  Emily Louisa 134
  William Arthur (b.1874) 136, 137, 138
  William Arthur (b.1906) 138
  William John 122, 136
(The) Dean 94, 153-154
Dearlove, Alice 24
Deggar, Margaret Ethel 178
Denman, Sarah 59
Dennis, Benjamin John 10
  Euphemia Francis 10
  George 10
  Gladys 10
  William 10
  Winifred 10
Denyer, Maud 124
Dinnage, Alfred 155
Dinsdale, Arthur Stanley 146-147
  Clara 146-147
  Edward Arthur 143, 146-147
  Ethel Violette 146
  Lucy 146
  Stanley 147
Dockerill, Emily Evelyn 153
Doick, Fanny 37
  James 37
  Maud 37
  Walter Harold 37
  Winnifred 37
(The) Dome 232
Dorey, Charles 151
  James Reginald 139
  James Wares 139
  Jane 139
  Katherine 151
Douglas, Clare Henry 64, 105, 106
  Dorothy Christine 65, 106
  Edith Emily 65, 106
  Edwin 64
  Edwin James 64
  James Sholto 64, 105

Kenneth Gordon 65
Violet 64
Douglas Nurseries 64
(The) Dower House 37
Down View 145
Down View House 3
Down View Nursery 3
Downing, Emily Sarah 236
Downlands 197
Downsview House 73, 99, 101-103
Downsview Nursery 21, 73, 101-103
(The) Drive, Worthing 155
Drummer, George 22
Duffield Cottages 32, 115, 121-123
Dumbrell, Hannah Jane 137
Dundeval, H 196
Dunkeld 197, 200, 202-203
Dunlop, George 22
Duringmere 14, 15
Durrington (Council) School 15, 72, 81-82, 93, 106, 119, 137, 138, 145, 146, 147, 148, 150, 163, 164, 191
Durrington Brick Company 5-7
Durrington Church 1
(The) Durrington Cricket Club 52, 189
Durrington Estate 177, 179
Durrington Farm 42
Durrington Farmhouse 15-17, 69
Durrington First School 81-82
Durrington Free Church 41, 43, 71-77, 95, 102
Durrington Gardens 5
Durrington Hill 1, 28, 43, 72
Durrington House 16, 68-69, 79
Durrington Lane 98, 103, 176, 214
Durrington Mill 200
Durrington Mission Room 45
Durrington Police Cottage 10
(The) Durrington Slate Club 52
Durrington Station 32
Durrington Street 1, 28, 51, 95, 99, 100, 185, 189
Dutton, Beatrice Maud 236
Emily Mary 236
Emily Sarah 236
Frederick 236
Gertrude Jane 236
Dyer, Henry 64
East Preston Workhouse 79
East Villa 124, 139-140, 160
Ede, B R 219, 220
Edney, 220
Edser, Alfred (b.1872) 93
Alfred (b.1905) 93
Elder Tree Cottages 21, 22-23, 100, 209
Eldridge, 155
Elgayder, 187
Elliot(t), Alice Victoria 21
Ellen 21
Thomas (b.1852) 10, 21
Thomas (b.1885) 21
Elliott, Eliza 136
Ellison Court 67
Elm Bank 42
Elm Bank Cottages 32, 38-40, 51
Elm Bank House 42
Elm Croft 42
Elmcroft Cottage 42
Elms, Marian 231

Elmshurst 41, 95-96
Elmswood Terrace, Elm Grove, Worthing 148
Elsdale, Elizabeth 141
Evans, Elias (Ellis) 114
Ellen 114
Ellis (b.1893) 114
Kate 114
Percy 114
Eve, Ellen Lucretia 220
Evergreen Cottage 110, 112
Fairhead, Ada Elizabeth Broughton 155
(The) Farm 15
Farm Buildings 129-130
Farm Cottages 111
Faulkner, Douglas 145
Faull, Charles Edwin 17
Fawkes, Edith Mary 197
Francis Hamley 197
Hamley 197
(The) Faze 235-236
Fenson, Amelia Edith 178
Fernbank/villa 65
Field, Cecil Oliver 202
Claude 184-185
Fanny 185
James Buley 202
Louisa Elizabeth 202
Victor 185
Fig Tree 185
Fisher, D 204
Mrs 42
Fleck, Mr 87
Fletcher, J E 177
Flint Cottage 32
Ford, 214
(The) Forge 16, 22, 48, 53-54, 69, 80, 97, 225
Foster, Alice 160
Edwin Thomas 24
Ida Caroline 24
Katherine 24
Fowke, H N 106
Frankland Road 93
Franklin Road 8, 41, 58, 59, 152, 153
Fraser, Murray Douglas 203
Freeman, Alfred Henry 209
Charles Henry 22, 209
Mary Jane 209
Richard William 209
French Gardens 214
Fucher (Tucher), Ernest 139
Fuller, C H 159
Fuller's Cottages 159-162
Furze Road 179, 197, 202
Furzeholme 205
Gables Cottage 131
Gaisford, family 229, 230
Gardener's Cottage 42
Gardiner, Annie Elizabeth 43-44, 73
Ernest Freemantle 43
Frank Burrell 43
Gladys 43
Hubert James 43
John 43
Joyce 43
Mark 43
Mr 224
Walter James 43
William Raphael 43

Gay, Ada Elizabeth 55
Elizabeth 55
Ellen Margaret 55
Robert William Painter 55
Gilbert, Sergeant 190
Glebe Road, West Tarring 150, 218
Glencoe Nurseries 103-104, 105
Glengariff 234-235
Glenside 150
Goatcher, Beatrice 189
Beatrice Alice 189
Raymond 219
William Marner 189
Gobel (Goble), Henry 145, 219
Goble, H 10
Godard, Dorothy 12
Emily 11-12
George 12
Winifred 12
Goddard, Alfred 134
Charles 134
Charlotte 134
Edith 145
Edith Emily 134
Elizabeth 134, 225
Emily 134
Emily Louisa 134
Fanny 134
George 134
Mary Ann 134
Walter H 160
William 160
William Walter 134
William Walter George 134
Godwin, Alice 54
Charles 54
Ralph Jupp 54
Victor 54
William 54
Golds, Horace 139
Louisa Ellen 139
Golf Cottages, Broadwater 145
(The) Golf Links (Worthing Golf Club) 143, 145
Gollop, (Georgina Annie) Louisa 205
Goodman, Maurice 177, 179
Gosney, Martha 237
Gough, Alice 73, 95
Ernest F 73, 95
Graham Road, Worthing 202
Grant, Ann 94
George Thomas 94-95
Margaret 94
Norman Venn 94-95
Gray, Hubert Patrick 121
Green, brothers 190
Mary 191
Greenfield, Edward 207
Greenland Road 1, 10, 12, 21, 55, 58, 61, 65, 73, 74, 93, 225
Greenough, George 177
Sarah Ann 177
Greenstede (House) 30-31, 69
Greenyer, Eli 10, 24
Sarah 10
Greppo, Claude 35
Claudie 35
Ellen (b.1844) 35
Ellen (b.1873) 35
Francis 35-36
Irene 35

Robert 35
Theo 35
Greville, Francis 36
Greylingwell Hospital 58, 99, 144
Grover, Louisa 145
Gulliver, 142, 149
(The) Half Moon Inn 7, 16, 87, 144, 168, 170-172
Half Moon Lane 86, 87, 128, 149
Hall, Frances Ruth 112
    Rose Agnes 177-178
Ham Farm 121, 213-214
Ham Nurseries 3
Ham Road, East Worthing 220
Hamilton, Ernest 14
    Ethel 14
    Fanny 14
    Frederick (b.1873) 14
    Frederick (b.1900) 14
    Percy 14
Hamleigh 213
Hampshire, Annie 10
Hanbury, Ernest Osgood 237
Hardy, Louisa Bessie M 112, 118
Harness & Saddle Makers 55-56
Harrisons Farm 58
Harwood, Alexandre Irene 10
    Florence Daisy 10
    Sarah (b.1868) 22
    Sarah (b.1871) 10
    William (b.1871) 10
    William (b.1872) 22
Haslewood, Victoria Elizabeth 58
(The) Haven 219-220
Hayes, Arthur Thomas 149
    Frederick George 148, 149, 171
    Naomi Agnes 149
    Sarah Jane 143, 148, 171
Haywood, Captain J 115
Hazelgrove, Adelaide 147
    Adelaide Emily 147
    Henrietta 147
    Herbert William 147
    Jeremiah 147
    Lena Annie 147
    Mary 147
    William 143, 147
Hazell, Mary 66
    William George 105
Heather, Eleanor 32
    G 185
    Mary 32
(The) Heathers Nursing Home 63-64
Hedger, Lily Ada 172
Heene Road, Worthing 106, 236
Helsdon, Elizabeth 41, 72, 73
    Esther 41
    Jane 41, 72, 73
    Langley 41
    Mary Anne 41
    Ruth 41
    sisters 95
Hemmers, John 160
Hemmings, John 160
Henley, James 113, 115
    Mrs 115
Henty, Arthur 81, 213
    Helen 213
    Helen Norah 213
    Jeffrey (Geoffrey) Burlace 213
    Mary 213

Philip Alexander 213
    Thomas Stewart 213
Hermitage Cottages, Castle Goring 147
Hewlett, Harriett 207
Hide, George 71
    Thomas 7
High Down View Terrace 11
High Salvington Windmill 78, 116, 136, 150, 199-201
High Street, Worthing 220
Highdown View Terrace 9-11
Highdownview Terrace 24
Highfield Road, West Tarring 226
Hill, Florence 157
    Frederick George 157
    George 157
    Mary Ann 157
Hill Cottages 206-207
Hill Farm 206
Hillman, Rose Selina 98
Hillview 94, 153-155
Hoar, Sarah Ann 177
Hoare, Frederick J 19
    Susannah 19
Hobson, C 236
Hodson, Florence Annie 234
Holden, Albert 25
    Arthur Stanley (Stanley) 84
    Callista Augusta 84, 173
    Callista Augusta Godda Sophie May de Liancourt 84, 173
    Callistus Augustus de Liancourt 84
    Charlotte 25
    Dionysia (Dinina) 19
    Ellen 19
    Fanny 138
    Frances (Fanny) 84
    Frederick (b.1906) 25
    Frederick Charles 138
    Frederick Henry (b.1850) 19, 25
    Frederick William 138
    Grace 19
    Hannah Louise 164
    Harold 25
    Harvey 19
    James 164
    James Henry 19, 25
    John (b.1806) 164
    John (b.1886) 19
    John (b.1904) 25
    Levi 19
    Louisa 164
    Mary 19, 25
    Mr 163
    Susannah 164
    William 84, 115, 173
    William Alexander 85
Holder, Elizabeth 86
Holland, Mary Ann 131
(The) Hollies 217, 218-219
Holly Cottages 99, 224-226
Holly Grove 35, 38
Holmes, Frederic 183
    Robert 183
Holt Farm 188, 190
Home, Clara 197, 202
Homefield Road, Worthing 194, 200
Homes, Miss 200
(The) Homestead 237

Hooker 95
Hornsey, Constance Josephine G 30
Hudson, Nellie Wace 178
Hughes, Blanche 209
Hunt, John 192
    Lizzie 192
    Richard 192
Hyde, Alice 120
    Mary Ann 134
    Thomas 120
Ibeson, T 15
Ingram, Mary Ann 157
    Mary Elizabeth 93
Irene 94-95
Ivy Cottage, Ashacre Lane 160, 163
Ivy Cottage, Littlehampton Road 145, 218, 219, 220
Jackson, Alfred Charles 194-195, 196, 197, 198, 200, 202, 203, 209
    Ida Edith 194
    Thomas 194
Jay, Mr 57
Jays, Emily 10
    Ernest 9-10
    Ernest George H 10
Jenkins, Annie Elizabeth 43
(The) John Selden (Arms) 48, 71, 85, 128, 171
John Selden's Cottage 110
Jonas, Miss 218
Jones, Basil Gordon Dawes 234
    Clara 133
    Dorothy Gordon 234
    Edith 133
    (Elizabeth) Emily Georgina 234
    Gwladys 234
    John H 66
    May Gordon 234
    Mora 133-134
    Staveley Gordon Dawes 234
    William Henry Dawes 234
Kemp-Potter, Ethel K 42
Kent, Alice (b.1881) 58
    Alice (b.1882) 24
    Alice (b.1902) 24
    Frank 24
    Rose Mary 24
Kimberley 155-156
King, Charles 155
King Street, Broadwater 218, 219
Kingfisher House 106-107
Kinnard, Charles Albert 145
    Jane Louise 145
Knell House 58
Knight, Adeline Mary 32
    Alice Edith 32
    Charlie 225
    Edith 188
    Florence Winifred 32
    George Ernest 122
    Harriet 24, 225
    James 188
    John 122
    John (b.c.1836) 122
    Louis James (Jesse) 32, 122
    Stanley Albert 24, 225
    William 225
    Winifred Frances 32, 122
Knowles Bakery 80
(The) Kursaal 232
Lacies Cottage 124-127
Lagadere, Leonie Catherine 64

(The) Lamb (Inn)   18, 19, 22, 25, 36, 37, 48, 49, 50-52, 101
Lamb Pond   12
Lamb Pond Cottage   14
Lambert, Elizabeth (Queenie) Annie   220
   George Albert   220
   James William   220
   Joseph William James   220
   Maria Ann   220
   Mr   87
Lambourne, Albert   19
   Charles Daniel   19
   George   209
   Kate   209
   Mary Ann   209
   Millicent Emily   19
   Mr   183
   Mrs   183
   Susannah   19
   Thomas   19
Lampard, Annie Hall   55
Langham, G   33
Langrish, Ann Eliza   100
Lansdowne Road, Worthing   24, 60-62, 151
Lashburn Cottage   157-159
Laundry, Stone Lane   116-118
(The) Laurels   58-60, 219, 220
Lawrance, Emily   10
Lawson, Alistair C L W   179
   Emily   179
   James Christian Eisenhuth   179
   Mabel Emily   179
   Paul   107-108
   Shelia Eisenhuth   179
Leggett, Luke (b.1863)   3-4, 182
   Luke (b.1905)   3
   Mary Ann   124, 140
   Susan   3-4
Lennard, Elizabeth   218
Lephard, Edwin   83, 111, 113, 115, 125, 161, 206, 224
Lewis   124, 139
   Alice Mary   124, 140
   C   112
   Daisy Alma   124, 125
   Edward Henry (b.1864)   124, 139-140, 160
   Edward Henry C (b.1886)   124
   Emily   179
   Esther Louisa   112, 124
   family   139
   Frances   124
   Frances Eleanor   124, 140
   Frances Louisa   160
   Mary Ann   124, 140
   Ronald Silas   124
   Rosa Emma   124, 160
   Silas   112, 124
   Winifred Rosa   124
Liancourt, Augusta   84
   Callista Augusta de   84
   Count Callistus Augustus de Goddes   84
Lillywhite, Ellen Caroline   21
   George   33, 37
   Mary Ann   37
   Mr   183
   Mrs   183
Linberry,   10
   Albert   16, 42
   Barbara   16
   Ellen   16, 87, 144
   Frances Ellen   87, 144
   George   16, 87, 144
   George (b.1891)   16
   Leonard Charles   16
   Selina   16
Linfield, Arthur George   214
   Eric Sydney   116
   Ethel Kate (Sis)   214
   Henry (Harry)   116
   Henry Charles Vincent   116
   Mary   116
   William Henry   214
Lish, Albert Edwin   8, 97
   Albert Ernest   97
   Ethel Mary   8
   Ethel Nellie   8
   James   8, 97
   Rose Selina   97
Lisher, Charity   131
   Robina Victoria   226
Little Castle   196
Littlehampton Road   5, 58, 99, 110, 121
Llandoff   236
Lloyd, Esther Louisa   112, 124
   Fanny   7
Lock, Alice Florence   184
   Florence May   184
   Jack   184
(The) Lodge, Littlehampton Road   215-217
Long, Alice   148
   Doris (Dorothy) Mary   138, 148
   Edith Kate   138, 148
   Emma (Emily) Jane   191
   Frederick Arthur   148
   G   148
   George   138, 148
   Maurice (Morris) Lesley   148
   Mrs   138
   Thomas George   138, 148
Lord, Elizabeth   183
   Frances (Fanny)   136
   Henry James Maurice   133
   James William   116, 136-137
   Lena Mary   133
   Mary Ann   133
   Maurice (b.1875)   133
   Maurice (Morris) (b.1871)   136
   Sydney Herbert   133
Love, Frederick   22
   William   22
Lovell, Percy   36
Lovelock, Fanny   14
Lucas, Alice Ann   185
   Frederick   185-186
   George Henry   185
   Mabel Florence   185
Lyndhurst Nurseries   102
Lyndhurst Road, Worthing   102, 214
Madgwick   147
   Alice Harriett   147, 161
   Annie   58
   Edwin James   147, 161
   Frederick William   147, 161
   James William   139, 143, 147, 161
Maidment, Benjamin   147
   Kate   147
Manor Cotttage   35-37
(The) Manor House   1, 28, 30, 32, 35-36, 37, 38
(The) Manor House, West Worthing   83
Manor Nurseries   36
Manor of Durrington   224
Marden, Lizzie   192
Marshall, Daisy Alma   125
   Daisy May   125
   William Edward   125
   William James   125
Martin, Edward Rufus   105-106
   F   63
   Frank   106
   George   151
   Louisa   151
   Margaret Letitia   93
   Walter   93
Matthews, Harold   61, 105
   John Kenneth   24, 61, 105
   Thomas   61
Maun Cottage   35
Mayfield Lodge   146
McDonald, Beatrice   237
Mears (Meers), Annie Ada   163, 234
   Cecil George   163
   Dora Christine   163
   Mary Ann   163
   Thomas (b.1864)   163
   Thomas (b.1900)   163
Medhurst, Walter   191
Mendip Road   71
Merritt, Sarah   190
Mill Cottages, Lancing   116
Mill Cottages, Salvington Hill   206
Mill House   202
Mill Lane   206
Mill Lane Mews   206
Mill Road, Heene   66
Mills, Albert   7, 22
   Annie Hall   55
   Cephas Walter   7, 22
   Charles   55
   Edward   32, 35
   Edward H   100-101
   Elizabeth   183
   family   179
   George   5
   George Jonathan   18
   Harriet   100
   Henry   101
   Joseph Edward de Vere   77
   Mary Maud   77
   Mr   179
   Mrs   38
   Sarah   101
   W R   38
   William   183
Milner, Edith Selina   146
   Frank Thomas John   146
   Harry Ernest   146
   John   143, 146
   Kate   146
Mimosa   230, 232
(The) Mission Room   45, 71
Mitchell, Alfred   203-204
   Annie   58
Mitchell Charman   see Charman
Moore, Alfred   17
   Ann   17
   Arthur J   17
   Henry   17
   John George   64

Maria 17
  Robert Pyatt 64
Moores, Mary Maud 77
Moseley, Eliza 136
  Ellen 32
  Frederick 136
  George 136
Moulton, John 41
  Mary Anne 41, 73
Naldrett, George 106
  Mrs G E 106
Nash, Augusta Nepolia Goddes 84
  Harriet 84
Neal, Henrietta (Harriet) 66-67
  John 66-67
  John (b.1886) 66-67
  John (b.1906) 67
Nell Cottages 214
Nell House 58, 221, 225
(The) Nest 194, 198-199, 200
Netley, Alfred 19
  Charles 19
  Charles (b.1863) 19, 32
  Georgina 19
  Gertrude 19
  Jessie 19
  Matilda 19, 32
  Rhoda 19
Nettley, Charles Nunn 219
  Mary 219
New Cottages 10, 18-21, 25, 101
New Life Church 71
New Road 1, 22, 28, 30, 51, 69, 103, 218
New Theatre Royal 232
Newbury, 65
Newcastle House 219
Newhouse, Maurice 149
  May Harriet 149
Newland Road, Worthing 55, 157
Newnham, Ann 38
  Eliza 38
  James 38
  James (b.1849) 35, 38
  Lizzie 57
Nickolas, Norman 24
Norris, Alice Maud 122
  Ann 32
  Charles Richard 22
  Edith Mary 122
  George Arthur 22
  Heber William 22
  John (b.1832) 32
  John (b.1895) 22
  Lucy 22
  Lucy Lily 122
  Mary Louise 122
  Mr 87
  Sarah Jane 122
  Silas James 22
  William 115, 122
North Star (Inn) 217, 222-224
Northeast, Mary Jane 22
Nurseries 1
  (The) Nurseries 105
  Ash 151
  Ashacre 151
  Birklands 105-106
  Bushby 8
  Claremont 11, 12
  Cotching & Matthews 105
  Douglas 64

  Down View 3
  Downsview 21, 73, 102-103
  Glencoe 103-104, 105
  Ham 3
  Lyndhurst 102
  Manor 36
  Raglan 214
  Red Cedars 65, 106
  Rosslyn 102
  Salvington 5, 167, 172-174
  Saunders' 103
  Seaview, Lansdowne Road, Worthing 151
  Seaview, Salvington Road 24, 60-62, 105
  Star 3, 5
  Tirana 107-108
  Vineyard 217-218
(The) Nurseries 105
Oaks Barn 192
O'Bierne, Arthur Lloyd Stanley 231
  Lewis Ormsby 231
  Marian 231
Offington Cottage 230
Offington (Park) Estate 229, 231
Offington Lane 128
Offington Lodge 229
(The) Old Coach House 120
(The) Old Cottage 129-130
Old Gardens, Salvington 224
(The) Old House 159-162
Old Sussex Cottage 83
Older, Susan 1
Olivet 202-203
Onions, Rev. John 74
(The) Orchard 40
Orpington House 64
Osborne, Amelia Ann 220
Ottley, Ada Elizabeth Broughton 155
  John 154-155
  Kate Coppinger 154
Overington, Alfred 30, 53
  Amy 30, 53
  Annie Elizabeth 99, 225
  Arthur Cecil 99, 225
  Avis 53
  Benjamin 53
  Caroline Charlotte 15-16, 69
  Dulcie 225
  Edgar 16, 45, 53, 69, 183
  Edith 53
  Elizabeth (b.1865) 53
  Elizabeth (b.c.1826) 53
  family 48
  Fanny 53
  Frank 225
  Henry 53
  Henry 30
  Henry (b.1856) 99-100, 225
  Horace (b.1848) 15-16, 53, 69
  Ida 53
  Iza 53
  Janet 53
  Jessie/Luke 53
  Joan 53
  Laura 53
  Margaret 53
  Maurice 99, 225
  Minnie 53
  Mr 227
  Wilfred Eustace 99, 225

Pack, Annie 141
Pacy, Elsie Grace 205
Page, Albert 137
  Alice Alexandra 137
  Florence May 137
  Henrietta (b.1875) 137
  Henrietta (b.1904) 137
  Joe 137
  Thomas (Arthur) 137
Paige, Florence Annie 234
  William Pering 234
Palfrey, Agnes 149
Parick, Annie Eliza 232
Park, Augusta 84
Park Villa 233, 236
Parker, Beatrice 189
  Charity 131
  Edward 131
  Elizabeth 131
  Grace 131
  James 131
  John 131-132
  Mary Ann 131
Parks, Emily Jane 190
Patching, Jane 139
  Sarah Ann 139
Pavilion Road, Worthing 95
Payne, Sergeant 71
Peacock, Alice Harriett 147, 161
  (Ernest) George 147, 161
  (James) William 147, 161
  Luke 114, 115, 147, 161
  Mary Ann 161
  Violet Mabel 147, 161
Pear Tree Cottage 131
Pearless, Henry 69
  Kate 69
  Ronald 69
Peel, Thomas 152
Pelling, Edward Henry 39
Penfold, Elizabeth 159
  Frances Ruth 112
  George William 112
  James 112-113
  Percy 112
  William John 112
Perham, Elizabeth (Eliza) Mary 160, 163
  Elsie Winifred 163
  Ethel Jane 160, 163
  Frank William 163
  Henry William 160, 163
  Robert Charles 160, 163
  Vera Gladys 163
Pierre, Albert 116
  Harold 170
  Harry 170
  Lena (Leonie) 170
  Leon Alexander 116, 170
  Mary 170
  Redvers 170
  Reginald 170
Pigrome, Mary F 81
Piper, R 55
Pitts, Frederick 177
Pocock, Mary Ann 70
Pond Lane 1, 13, 57, 69
Pond Lane Cottage 10
Pond Lane Park 16, 22
Post Office, Durrington 49, 55
Post Office, Salvington 84, 173
Potten, Raymond 133

Pratt, Albert 143
  Frederick 143, 145
  Gladys M 145
  Hilda Lilian A 145
  Jane Louise 145
  Louisa 145
  Winifred C 145
Price, Emma 7
Princes Terrace, Tarring 150
Priory Cottage 198
Purley 42, 63-64
Putick, Mary 19
Pyke, Charles Barter 60, 61
Queen Street, Worthing 124
Raglan Nursery 214
Rank, Frederick 226, 227
  Josephine 226
Reading Rooms, West Tarring 146
Red Cedars House 70, 134
Red Cedars Nursery 65, 106
(The) Red House 141
Reed, Bessie 219
  Charles 219
  Edwin Alfred 6-7
  Mabel Emily 219
  Sarah 7
(The) Retreat 201, 202
Rice, Hannah 64
  William 64
Richards, Alfred 32
  Charles (Chad) 32
  Florence Annie 32
Richardson, 134
  Edward 160
  Emma 94
  Frances 160
  Francis William 160
  Rosa Emma 160
Richens, Mary Ann 133
Ridgley, Charles 125
Robinson, Mary (b.c1900) 221
  Mary (b.c1876) 221
  William L 35
Rock Cottages 58-60, 105
Rock Terrace 58
Rockall, 219
Rogate Road 229
Rogers, George 59
  Mary Ann 59
Rooke, Irene 35
(The) Rosary, Ashacre Lane 155-156
(The) Rosary, Mill Road 66
Rose Cottage, Ashacre Lane 163
Rose Cottage, Salvington Road 33, 53-54
Rose Cottage, Stone Lane 120
(The) Rosery 156
Rosslyn Nurseries 102
(The) Row 32-33, 35, 37, 116, 122
Royal, W 32
Rudd, Nellie Floyd 55
Ruff, Daniel (b.1848) 220
  Daniel (b.1879) 133
  Frances Eliza 220
  George 137
  Hannah Jane 137
  James 220
  Maria 133
  Muriel Maud 133
  Richard 220
  Sarah 220
  Sarah Gladys Hilda 133
  Stephen 137
  William 220
Rugby Road 42
Rutherford, Jessie Bertha 187
Sale, Mrs 42
Salvington 111
Salvington Cottages 111-116, 121-123, 125, 136
Salvington Farm 64, 83-84, 110, 113, 115, 124, 128, 129, 135, 137, 139, 161, 163, 206, 207
Salvington Farmhouse 48, 83-84
Salvington Hill 22, 194-198, 202, 203, 206
Salvington Laundry 170-172
Salvington Letts 83
Salvington Lodge 48, 83, 88-89, 110, 140
Salvington Mill Cottage 201, 202
Salvington Mill Tea Rooms 200
Salvington Nurseries 5, 167, 172-174
Salvington Road 1, 16, 24, 28, 32, 36, 41, 93, 96, 98, 102, 105, 106, 110, 122, 128, 134, 168, 170
Salvington Tea Gardens 149, 170
Salvington Tea Rooms 170-172
Salvington Windmill 78, 116, 136, 150, 199-201
Sandell, Frank 5
Sandham, Harriet Jane 87
  Samuel 87
Sargent, Mary Jane 221
Sarum 232
Saunders, Alfred 185
  Dorothy 118
  Edith 70
  Edith Emily 65, 106
  Ellen 185
  Elsie Jane 178
  Fanny 7
  Fanny (b.1848) 22, 100
  Florence 70
  Gosden William 7
  Harriet (b.1836) 32, 51
  Harriet (b.1875) 100
  Henry Capel 73, 74, 102
  Horace 185
  John 112, 118
  John Henry 112, 118, 119
  Lilian 112, 119
  Louisa Bessie M 112, 118, 134
  Mabel 73, 74, 103
  Mabel Florence 185
  Mark (jnr) 185
  Mark (snr) 185
  Mary Ann 70
  Percy Alfred T 112, 118, 119
  Sarah Jane 122
  Thomas 64
  Thomas (b.1846) 7, 22, 100
  William 22
  William 65
  William (b.1859) 32
  William Hoad 70
  William James 7
  William Nathaniel 70
  Winifred Elizabeth 112, 118, 119
Saunders' Nursery 103
Sausage Skin Manufacturer 226
Sayer, Frederick 55
Sayers, Ellen (Nellie) Mary 14
Schooley, E 87
Scott, Eliza 38
Scull, Edwin 141
Scutt, Arthur Allen 116, 118, 150
  Edwin (Edward) James 116
  Elizabeth Fanny 116
  Fanny 116-118, 136, 150
  Gladys Ada 116, 118, 150
  Mary Elizabeth 116
  Stephen 116-118, 136-137, 150, 200
Searle, Albert 21
  Clement 21, 22, 188, 209
  Ellen Caroline 21
  Elsie 209
  Fanny 21
  Gordon 209
  Mary 147
  Mary Jane (Jane) 22, 188, 208
  Noah 21, 101
  Thomas Edmund 22, 209
Seaview Nursery, Lansdowne Road, Worthing 151
Seaview Nursery, Salvington Road 24, 60-62, 105
Seebold, Annie Eliza 232
  Christian Ignas Martin 232
  Karl Adolphus 232
Selden, John 124
Selden/Selden's Cottage 112, 124-127, 160
Selden's Lane Cottage 123
Selden's Way 110, 112, 124-127, 134-135
Shakespeare Road, Worthing 237
Sharpe, (Georgina Annie) Louisa 205
  William 205
Shelley, J E 177
Shepherd, Fanny Dorothy 209
  Frederick 209
  Frederick James 209
  William James B 209
Sherwood 106
Shipp, Rebecca 66
Short, Albert Edward 220
  Alfred Frederick G 220
  Ellen Lucretia 220
  Frederick Arthur 220
  Gladys Constance 220
  Winifred Gertrude 220
Sivyer, Albert 100
  Ann Eliza 100
  James 100
  William (b.1864) 100
  William (b.1895) 100
Skinner, Albert 134
  C 155
Skinner/Charman, Albert 118
Smart, Sarah 220
Smith 103, 145
  Arthur 58
  Edward 58
  Emily 58
  Fanny 137
  Frederick 58, 105
  Henry 86
  Julia Alexandra 51
  M J 55
  R 58
  Robert 18, 21

Sarah 22
W 55
William (b.1869) 58
William Edmund Wenban 6
William Wenban 5-6
Somerset, Lady 183
Sopp, Caroline E 213
South Farm Road, Worthing 96, 219, 220
South View Terrace 1, 24-25, 51
Southcott 179-180
Southfield Road, Broadwater 147
Southview Terrace 10, 22
Sparkes, Katherine 151
Spillis, W 58
Spooner, Louisa Ellen (b.1882) 139
   Louisa Ellen (b.1898) 139
   Thomas 139
(The) Spotted Cow (Inn) 48, 71, 86-88, 112, 144, 171
Springett, Rev. 42, 46
St Symphorian Church 28, 45-46
Standin, Susannah Harriet 19
Standing, Albert James 22, 24
   Ernest Gordon 24
   Harriet 24
   Maurice Leslie 24
Stanley, Rev. William 45
Star Nursery 3, 5
Stenning, 58
Steptoe, Catherine 160
Stevens, Annie Elizabeth 237
Stone, Amelia Ann 220
   James 220
Stone Cottages 111-116, 125, 148
Stone(s) Lane 10, 32, 33, 49, 71, 81, 84, 134, 136, 139, 150, 170
Stoner, Alice 160
   Barnard Alec James 160
   James (b.1865) 6
   James (b.1874) 160
Stow, Selina 16
Street, Mr 142
Streeter, Henry Alfred 142
Stringer, Albert William 225
   Elizabeth 225
   Jessie Louisa 113
   Richard Albert 225
Strong, H 95
Strotten, Mary Ann 209
Stuart, Madelaine 141
Sunnyside 220, 221
Swain, 214
Swan, Mabel 102
Swan Inn 220-221
Swandean (House) 100-101, 176
Swandean Cottage 208
Swandean Hospital 52, 177-178, 194
Sydney Villa 63-64
Symonds, Arthur Henry 69
Symons, Alfred 213
Tarano, Adela 179
Tavenner, F K 55
Taylor, Alfred 17
   Alic William Basil 85, 173
   Callista Augusta Godda Sophie May de Liancourt 85, 173
   Claude Arthur 5
   Fanny 173
   Florence (Kitty) Kithe 173
   George 172

Grace 172
Henry 17
Laila Olseth 178
Maria 17
Maude 5
Philip 5
Thomas Otto 5
William Samuel 173
Tench, Edward 10
   Mary Ann 10
   Sarah 10
(The) Terrace 32
Terry, Alice Minnie 137
   Bertie James 137
   Emily 137
   Helen 7
   James 137
   May Blossm 137
   Violet Rose 137
   William 7
Thair, May Harriet 149
   Percy 148-149
Thatch Cottage 13-15
Thatched Cottage 13
Thomas, Elizabeth Ann 18, 50
   Sarah Ann 18, 39, 51
Thomas a Becket 229
Thompson, Edith 18
   Elizabeth 18
   Henry 18-19, 39, 51
   Henry (b.1910) 18
   John 18
   Nell 18
   Sarah Ann 18-19, 39, 51
   William 18
Thomson, Mrs 237
Thornberry 63-64, 83
Thorne, Kate Coppinger 154
Thorp, Harold W 103-105
Thorpe, Harriet Jane 87
(The) Timber Yard 69
Tirana Nursery 107-108
Titcombe, Esther Louisa 112, 124
Trapp, Mary 196
Treagus, Amy 53
Tree, Eleanor 32
   John Joseph 32, 160
Trim, Eleanor 94
   Emma 94
   Frederick 94
   George 59, 94, 152, 153-154
   Reginald James Douglas 94
Trollope, Howard 30
Tulett, Alfred 143, 149, 150
   Arthur Edward 150
   Dorothy 149
   Eliza (Elizabeth) Mary 149
   Elizabeth 150
   Frank 150
   Herbet William 150
   Horace Alfred (b.1881) 143, 149, 150
   Horace Alfred (b.1904) 149
   Leonard Victor 150
   Mr 150
   Percy 150
Tullett, 141
Tunstall, Caroline 73
   William Thomas 73
Tunstell, Hilda Grace 93
   Mary Elizabeth 93
   William 93

Turner, Clara 146
Tweed, Annie 65
   Charles 16
   Harriet 16
   Herbert 65
   Herbert Edgar 16, 65
Twyford 94, 152-153
Tyler, William George 143, 145
Tyrrell 161
Tyrrell (Tyrell), Frederick Thomas 113
   Jessie Louisa (b.1862) 113
   Jessie Louisa (b.1891) 113
   Thomas (Tom) 113, 144, 170
   Violet Mary 113, 144
Underwood, Edith Mary 197
Unwin, Elizabeth 53
Utley, Alice 148
   Maria 133
Van der Medon, Florence (Frances) Daisey 35
   Geoffrey 35
   Harold 35
   Louisa May 35
   Otto 35
   Reginald 35
Varley, George Herbert 21, 101-102
   Mary Louisa 101
Varndell, Arthur James 32
   Ellen 32
   Elsie May 32
   Ernest James 32
   George Charles 32
Venn, Ann 94
Vernon, Louisa Elizabeth 202
Victoria Bungalow 77-78
Victoria Road, Worthing 121
Vidal, Emilienne 77
Vineyard Nursery 217-218
Voak, Archibald 14
   Dorothy 14
   Ellen (Nellie) Mary 14
   Emily 14
   Emily (b.1899) 14
   George 14
   James (b.1874) 10, 14-15
   James (b.1903) 14
   Nora (Emily) 15
   Percy 14
   Sydney 14
Walder, Elizabeth 55
Walls, Frances (Fanny) 136
   Robert James 137
Walnut Tree Cottage 131-132
Walton, Mary 170
Wareham, Alfred 138
   Annie 137
   Edith 137-138
   Ellie 137-138
   Emily 137
   Fanny 138, 222
   Fanny (b.1907) 137
Warr, Elizabeth (Eliza) Mary 160, 163
Warren, Arthur James 164
   Hannah Louise 164
   Louisa Clara 164
   Robert 164
(The) Warren, Broadwater 48, 83, 88
Warrington, Fanny 138
Warwick Street, Worthing 202

Waterman, Soutton 86
Weatherell, John 42, 64, 73
   Sarah Annie 42, 64, 73
Webb, Alice 64, 83
   Allen 64, 83, 206
Webb Cottages 206
Wedge, Mary Ann 37
Wells, Andrew 113
   Fanny 113
   James 113
   Thomas 113
Wenban Road, Worthing 155
Wenban Smith see Smith
West Villa 139
White, Elizabeth Ann (Lizzie) 18-19, 25, 50-51
   Ethel Nellie 51
   Frank 113, 115, 148, 171
   Frederick Maurice 148
   Harriet 25, 51
   Jack 113, 148
   Mildred Ethel 143, 148, 149, 171
   Robert Walter 148
   Sarah Ann 113, 115, 148
   Sydney George 50
   Walter (b.1839) 113, 115, 148
   Walter (b.1891) 50
   Walter (m.1889) 18, 25, 50-51
White Hall 233-234, 236
(The) White House 43-44
White House Place 43-44
Whitehead, Sarah Caroline 94
Widge, Mary Ann 37
Wilburton 94, 152-153
Willard, Daisy Eleanor 222
   Edward Henry 222
   Ellen 138, 222
   Fanny 113
   Frank Charles 222
   George Edwin 222
   Lena Mabel 222
   Susan Elizabeth 222
   William John 222
Williams, Frank 97
   George Albert 97
   James 97
   Kitty 96-97
Willicombe, A 234
   Ella Mary 95, 234
Willow Cottage 32
Wilson, Mary Louisa 101
   Miss 41
Wilton, Frederick 11
   Zoe Irene 11-12
Windmill Tea Rooms 197, 199-201, 202
Windmill Tea Shop 200
Wingfield, Albert Henry J 7
   Edmund William 6
   John 6
Wisden 83, 89, 116
   Arthur (Patrick) 48, 83, 89
   Colonel F T 194, 200, 209
   Estate 111, 113, 117, 118, 121, 137, 161, 164, 173, 202, 206
   Ethel Charlotte Pigott 89
   family 88, 163
   Frederick (Frank) T 83, 89, 118, 194, 200
   Lieut. Col. Thomas Faulconer 83, 89, 116, 117
   Richard 89
   Thomas 89
Wood, P.C. 115
   Susannah 164
   Thomas 14, 22, 218, 219, 220
   Winifred Frances 32, 122
Woodbine Cottage 14
Woodlands 106
Woods, Alfred 190
   Alfred James P 190
   Allen 190
   Arthur 190
   Bertha 190
   Edwin 190
   Emily Jane 190
   Kathleen Dora 190
   Lilian 190
   Luke 190
   Sarah 190
   Violet Emily 190
Woolgar, Peter 32
World, Amy (Emily) 122, 136
Worsley, Beatrice Rose 205
   Elsie Grace 205
   Frederick Charles 205
Wratting, Agnes 10
   Albert 10
   Caroline 10
   Frederick 10
   Henry 10
Wyatt, Agnes Alice 149, 171
   Albert (Tich) 171
   H 86
   James Henry 149, 171
   Joseph 171
   Percy (Pescoe) 171
   Queenie 171
   Reginald 171
   William 171
Yew Tree Cottages 118, 132-134

Notes…

Notes…

Notes…

Notes…

Notes…

Notes…

Notes…

Notes…

Notes…

Notes…

Notes…

Notes…